Don Gleason Hill

An Alphabetical Abstract of the Record of Deaths, in the Town of

Dedham

Don Gleason Hill

An Alphabetical Abstract of the Record of Deaths, in the Town of Dedham

ISBN/EAN: 9783337403270

Printed in Europe, USA, Canada, Australia, Japan

Cover: Foto ©Suzi / pixelio.de

More available books at **www.hansebooks.com**

AN

ALPHABETICAL ABSTRACT

OF THE

RECORD OF DEATHS,

IN THE

TOWN OF DEDHAM,

MASSACHUSETTS,

1844—1890.

COMPILED BY

DON GLEASON HILL, Town Clerk.

DEDHAM, MASS.
OFFICE OF THE DEDHAM TRANSCRIPT.
1895.

Published Under the Vote of the Town,
Passed April 9, 1894.

INTRODUCTION.

In accordance with the vote passed by the Town at its last annual Town Meeting, I have compiled an Abstract of the Deaths recorded in Dedham from the middle of 1844 to the close of 1890, which is herewith submitted. The first seven entries in 1844 were made by Richard Ellis, the Town Clerk; then follows the record of his successor, Jonathan H. Cobb, which closes with 1874, except that Mr. Cobb records two deaths in January, 1875. Charles H. Farrington, the next Clerk, continues the record through 1879 and records ten deaths at the beginning of 1880. The rest of the records covered by this volume have been made by me, except fifteen deaths recorded by Mr. Farrington, from March to April 27, 1882, the time of his sudden death.

The same general plan has been adopted here as in the Abstract of Births, to give as much as possible in the most compact form. The figures at the left indicate the number of each death in the record of the year in which it appears; if a married woman, the maiden name is given in parenthesis immediately after the christian name, followed by the name of the husband; then comes the date of death, first the month in figures, then the day and year; following this are the cause of death, age, birthplace, names of parents with maiden name of mother in parenthesis, and finally the birthplaces of the parents. Of course many entries do not contain all these facts, and therefore not all could be given. Names which appear in brackets have been supplied by the

Editor from information outside the record. In a few instances we have discovered that the record did not correspond with the original returns on file. Words and figures printed from the files rather than the record have been marked with an asterisk.

All errors which are discovered in the printed record of births and deaths should be reported in writing to the Town Clerk, so that they may be properly corrected upon the record.

With the assistance of Dr. Francis L. Babcock of the Board of Health, a table has been constructed which shows the diseases from year to year, and the number who have died of each disease. We have also constructed a table showing the number of persons who have died at each age, from stillborn up to 102 years. It is believed that these two tables will be not only interesting, but valuable as statistics. In the table of diseases it did not seem necessary to take each year separately, and we have divided the first twenty years into five periods of four years each, and the balance of the time into periods of three years each, thus being able to show the whole number for each disease on one page. In most cases the diseases are called in this table by the names as they appear on the record, in order to show the changes in nomenclature, from time to time. At the end of the book is given an index of the cities and towns in the United States, also an index of the names which appear as maiden names, together with a list of the men who are recorded as soldiers.

The copy for the printer has been made by Miss Martha A. Smith, who has also assisted the Editor in proof reading and making indexes.

Don Eleazer Hill

Town Clerk.

Dedham, January 1, 1895.

TABLE SHOWING NUMBER OF DEATHS OF EACH DISEASE.

	1844-'47.	1848-'51.	1852-'55.	1856-'59.	1860-'63.	1864-'66.	1867-'69.	1870-'72.	1873-'75.	1876-'78.	1879-'81.	1882-'84.	1885-'87.	1888-'90.	Total
Abscess								1		1		1	1	1	5
Accident	6	5	8	5	18	20	9	11	3	8	8	9	12	15	137
Albuminuria										2		1			3
Alcoholism			3	2	9	3					3	1		2	23
Anaemia					1						2	2	1		6
Anasarca												1			1
Aneurism, aortic												1			1
Angina maligna							3								3
Angina pectoris													2		2
Apoplexy		3	3	6	5	3		3	3	1	1	4	11	10	53
Artery, rupture of								1							1
Ascites													2		2
Asphyxia								1							1
Asthma				1	1						2	.	1	1	6
Bowel complaint	4	9	3	2	1		2	1	2			1		1	26
Bowels, consumption of							2								2
hemorrhage of ...										1			1		2
inflam. of		3	5		9	2		4	1						24
intersusception of										1		1		2	4
malignant dis. of										1					1
mortification of ..		1		1											2
Brain, concussion of ...						1									1
congestion of	1	2	4	3	14	11	8	4	1	3	2				53
consumption on ..				2											2
contraction of ...			1												1
disease		2	10	5	6		6		2			3	4	6	44
enlargement of ..				1											1
inflam. of	2		3	1	4				2	1		1			14
paralysis of											1				1
softening of							1	3	1	1	1			2	9
tumor of										1		1	1	1	4
water on	1		2	1	1	3	3								11
Bright's disease							2	1	1	3	7	5	2	10	31
Bronchitis					1		2			4	1	4		5	17
Cancer	3	6	3	8	4	9	7	1	7	7	4	9	15	10	93
Canker			4	4	5		3	3	1	4	1	1			26
Canker rash				2						1					3
Carbuncle										1					1
Catarrh												1			1
Chest, dropsy of										1					1
Childbirth			1	1	3	4	1	3	2	1	3	2		1	22
Cholera		1													1
infantum	5	9	21	23	22	9	9	16	11	15	11	18	8	3	180
morbus	1			1	2	2	1	3	1		1	1	1		14
Chronic disease			1												1
Cirrhosis													1		1
Colic	1	1		1	1	1									5
bilious							1								1
Congenital					1										1
Consumption	47	65	111	74	89	85	75	48	46	55	46	46	50	10	877
of blood	1		1					1	3	3					9
Convulsions					3		5	4	8	10	17	12	9	8	76
puerperal											1	2			3
Cramp						1			1						2
Croup	2	2	6	21	16	6	6	7	3	2		1		2	74

	1844-'47	1848-'51	1852-'55	1856-'59	1860-'63	1864-'66	1867-'69	1870-'72	1873-'75	1876-'78	1879-'81	1882-'84	1885-'87	1888-'90	Total
Croup, membranous...					2	2					4	3	3		14
Cyanosis					1					2	4	1	3		11
Cystitis					1				2	1	1	3	1		9
Debility					3	1	3		1	1	1			1	11
infantile					1	1									2
Diabetes				1	1			1		1	1		1		6
Diarrhoea					5	3		1	1	1		3	2	1	17
chronic		1		2	1	9			1		1		1		16
Diphtheria					10	5	3	5		7	34	20	8	14	106
Dropsy	4	7	5	9	10	9	7	8	6	7	1	2	3	1	79
Dysentery	13	30	24	9	9	10	6	12	4	5	3	4	3	2	134
Dyspepsia													1		1
Embolism												1			1
Emphysema									1						1
Empyaemia									1	1			2		4
Enteritis			3			3	4	1	2	5	1	2	3	3	27
Enterocolitis												1			1
Epilepsy	1			1				1		1	1	1			6
Epistaxis											1				1
Erysipelas	2	1	6	2	2	2	1	3		2		1	2		24
Exhaustion								1				2	2	7	12
Fever	25	12	7	3			3	2							52
billous		1		1	1				1			2			6
brain		3		2	4	2		2	3						16
intermittent					1										1
lung	4	12	16	18	23	12	11								96
nervous			1												1
pleurisy		1													1
puerperal	1	2	3	2											8
rheumatic		1		1					1				1		4
scarlet	3	3	7	9	31	16	17	3	6	1	3	2	4	3	108
ship		1													1
slow				2				1	2						5
typhoid	1	1	8	15	25	14	6	11	8	4	12	8	5	6	124
typhus	2	3		1	2										8
Fistula				1											1
Fits	5	8	15	5	6	8	3	2							52
Found dead				2		1				1					4
Gangrene	1		1	1			1	1		1				1	7
senile														1	1
Gastritis					1	1	1	1	1			2	1	1	9
Gastro enteritis											1		1	2	4
Gland, enlargement of													1		1
Gravel		1					2	1	1						5
Hanged					1				1						2
Heart cramp		1													1
disease	4	5	13	16	8	17	11	17	14	12	29	25	26	53	250
enlargement of											1				1
failure														4	4
fatty deg. of													2		2
rheumatism of					1				1	1					3
rupture of														1	1
Hemorrhage		1			2		2	1	1		1	1		5	14
umbilical											1				1
Hemorrhagica purpurea								1			1				2

	1844-'47.	1848-'51.	1852-'55.	1856-'59.	1860-'63.	1864-'66.	1867-'69.	1870-'72.	1873-'75.	1876-'78.	1879-'81.	1882-'84.	1885-'87.	1888-'90.	Total.
Hepatitis............			1								1	2			4
Hip complaint........				1								1			2
Humor...............					1			1							2
Hydrocephaloid......				1							1	1			3
Hydrocephalus.......				1		1	1			1		1	3		8
Hydrophobia.........			1											1	2
Hydrothorax.........											2	1		1	4
Inanition............						1	1					3	5	2	12
Infantile disease.....		3	5	3	3	4						2			20
inflammation........	1														1
influenza............				1											1
Insanity.............				1	3								1		5
Jaundice............			1												1
Kidney disease.......			2	1		1	1						1	1	7
Killed in battle......				1											1
Liver, abscess of.....											1			1	2
complaint.......		4	7	5	2	5	4	1		1	1	2	1	3	36
congestion of....								4	1						5
enlargement of..								1						2	3
Leucocythaemia.......										1				2	3
Lung disease........						1		2							3
Lungs, abscess of.....											1				1
congestion of....				4	6	6	1	7	2	1	1			3	31
hemorrhage of...			1	1				1	2	3			1		9
inflammation of.				2	2										4
oedema of.......												2			2
Malnutrition.........											1				1
Marasmus............							1	2	6	3	5	3	6	8	34
Measles.............			2	2	1			1				1	1		8
Melancholia..........														1	1
Meningitis...........					1	2			5	4	13	7	14	16	62
cerebro spinal...				1			1				1	7		1	11
tubercular.......												1			1
Metritis.............					1	1		1							3
Mouth, sore..........						1									1
Murder..............						3						1	1		5
Myalitis, acute.......													1		1
Nephritis............					1			1		1		1			4
Neuralgia............							1			1					2
Neuritis, multiple.....														1	1
Old age.............	17	34	27	37	18	18	25	31	26	15	19	25	19	15	326
Palsy................	1	2	2	4			4								13
Paralysis............	2		4	5	12	14	9	9	19	13	25	18	18	13	161
progressive......					1						1	4		2	8
Pericarditis....;....													1		1
Peritonitis...........	1	1						1		3		6	7	5	24
Placenta praevia......										1					1
Pleurisy.............			1	2	5	3	1	2	1	4	1	1		1	22
Pneumonia...........					27	27	13	12	14	6	18	18	29	29	193
pleuro...........											4		1	1	6
Poison..............			1			1		1							3
Premature birth.......										4	3	8	8	11	34
Prostate gland,hyp'y of.													1		1
Pyaemia.............														1	1
Pyrexia.............											1				1

	1844-'47.	1848-'51.	1852-'55.	1856-'59.	1860-'63.	1864-'66.	1867-'69.	1870-'72.	1873-'75.	1876-'78.	1879-'81.	1882-'84.	1885-'87.	1888-'90.	Total.
Rachitis...............											1		1		2
Rash, scarlet.........					2			1							3
Rheumatism...........	1		2	3		3	1	3							13
Rupture...............				1	1		1				1	1			5
Sclerosis, cerebro spinal												1			1
Scrofula..............	1	2			3	2	1	1		3	2	1			16
Septicaemia...........													2	1	3
Shock.................														1	1
Small pox.............		2				1	8	2	1						14
Spina bifida..........										1					1
Spinal caries.........												1	1		2
disease...........	1	1	1	1	2	1	2	1							10
Stillborn.............					4	2	6	2	8	9	16	11	13	7	78
Stomach, degenerat'n of												1			1
disease of.......			1												1
hemorrhage of...								1						1	2
inflammation of..					1										1
ulcer of.........				1		2						1		2	6
Stoppage..............		1	1	2				1	1		2	1	1	1	11
Suffocation...........				2							1				3
Suicide...............		1		2	2	1	2	2			5	3	1	3	22
Sunstroke.............					2										2
Syphilis..............					1						1				2
hereditary.......													1		1
Tabes mesenterica.....														1	1
Teething..............				2	4	12	5	3	3		5	6	1	1	42
Tetanus...............			1	1				1			1			1	5
Throat distemper......	3														3
imperfect........				1											1
putrid sore......							1								1
sore.............		1	2			2									5
ulcerated........											1				1
Tuberculosis.....											1				1
Tumor.................	1	1	2	4		1		2		5	1	1	1	2	21
Typhlitis.............													1		1
Uraemia...............										1					1
Urinary disease.......					1										1
Varioloid.............				1											1
Whooping cough.......		7	5	2	7	2	5	3	5	1				3	40
Worms.................			1									1			2
Total........	169	261	367	353	480	414	317	301	255	282	342	343	338	374	4595

Imperfect record, 320, making in all 4915.

TABLE SHOWING THE NUMBER OF DEATHS AT EACH AGE FROM 0 TO 102.

Age.	No.	Age.	No.	Age.	No.	Age.	No.
0–1,	[1]860	26–27,	48	52–53,	34	78–79,	40
1–2,	273	27–28,	48	53–54,	31	79–80,	49
2–3,	147	28–29,	57	54–55,	29	80–81,	60
3–4,	109	29–30,	46	55–56,	37	81–82,	44
4–5,	80	30–31,	38	56–57,	33	82–83,	49
5–6,	61	31–32,	35	57–58,	24	83–84,	32
6–7,	47	32–33,	59	58–59,	24	84–85,	38
7–8,	38	33–34,	34	59–60,	36	85–86,	32
8–9,	33	34–35,	40	60–61,	37	86–87,	30
9–10,	28	35–36,	53	61–62,	36	87–88,	30
10–11,	30	36–37,	43	62–63,	48	88–89,	23
11–12,	27	37–38,	26	63–64,	43	89–90,	20
12–13,	16	38–39,	46	64–65,	33	90–91,	15
13–14,	19	39–40,	16	65–66,	59	91–92,	8
14–15,	18	40–41,	48	66–67,	48	92–93,	8
15–16,	31	41–42,	26	67–68,	44	93–94,	10
16–17,	24	42–43,	34	68–69,	53	94–95,	8
17–18,	34	43–44,	36	69–70,	58	95–96,	7
18–19,	38	44–45,	21	70–71,	63	96–97,	4
19–20,	41	45–46,	43	71–72,	40	97–98,	2
20–21,	49	46–47,	22	72–73,	67	98–99,	3
21–22,	50	47–48,	21	73–74,	43	99–100,	1
22–23,	61	48–49,	26	74–75,	50	100–101,	1
23–24,	47	49–50,	24	75–76,	66	101–102,	0
24–25,	54	50–51,	47	76–77,	43	102–103,	1
25–26,	58	51–52,	26	77–78,	33	Age not given,	52

Total, 4915

Average age for whole table except 78 stillborn, 35.22.
    "   " omitting all under one year,   42.
    "   " omitting all under five years,   49.09.

[1] Includes 78 stillborn.

RECORD OF DEATHS IN DEDHAM,

1844—1890.

ABBOTT.

40 Katie V. (Hogan), 5: 10: 85, peritonitis, æ. 27-0-0, b. Ded., of John & Catharine, N. B., Ire.

ACKER.

51 Theresa (Ross), 5: 1: 68, consumption, æ. 36-0-0, b. Germ., of Barney & ——, Germ.. do.

ACORN.

54 (D. at Sharon) Lucy G. (Partridge), w. of A. G., 1: 23: 56, lung fever, æ. 28-0-0, b. Rockland Me.

ADAMS.

42 ——, 12: 25: 45, ——, æ. 18-0-0, b. Ded.

11 Amos, 2: 6: 64, pneumonia, æ. 35-0-0, b. Brookfield, of Jos & Phebe. [soldier.]

42 Ann M., 12: 4: 51, liver comp., æ. 40-0-0, b. Portsmouth N. H., of Ephraim & Temperance.

90 Benj. H., 3: 31: 76, consumption, æ. 63-11-16, b. Portsmouth N. H., of Benj. & Eliz'h T., Portsmouth N. H., do.

54 Chas. L., 9: 28: 74, typhoid fever, æ. 32-4-28, b. Boston, of Wm. J. & Deborah F., Ellsworth Me., Ded.

29 Deborah F. (Chickering), 5: 1: 79, Bright's disease, æ. 65-5-21, b. Ded., of Jabez & Deborah L. F., Ded., Quincy.

51 Elijah H., 6: 28: 84, aortic aneurism, æ. 47-1-21, b Ded., of Chas. & Mary J., Medfield, Goshen N. H.

71 Eliza F., 12: 12: 57, consumption, æ. 18-2-5, b. Ded., of Horret & Eliza.

19 Emily A. (Debbins), 3: 5: 86, phthisis, æ. 25-0-5, b. P. E. I., of Samuel & Eliz'h, P. E. I, Eng.

104 Hiram A., 9: 11: 61, inflam. of lungs, æ. 25-3-16, b. Ded., of Horret & Eliza. Marlboro Vt., Ded.

34 Horatio C., 9: 25: 50, consumption, æ. 14-1-27, b. Boston, of Wm. J. & Deborah F.

1 John, 1: 2: 87, paralysis, æ. 89-11-18, b. Boston, of Thos. & Mercy, Kingston, Carver.

50 John G., 8: 18: 57, typhoid fever, æ. 8-8-14, b. Ded., of Benj. H. & Eliz'h.

33 Laura, 1: 28: 65, scarlet fever, æ. 1-5-0, b. Ded., of Elias W. & Eliz'h M.

19 Mary J. (Lewis), 3: 10: 77, uterine tumor, æ. 65-10-0, b. Goshen N. H., of
Seth & ——.

19 Nancy (Pratt), 3: 25: 60, dis. of spine, æ. 64-7-8, b. Plymouth, of Eben'r &
Hannah.

49 Robert, 4: 12: 46, neck broke by fall, æ. 30-0-0, b. Eng.

30 Sarah J., 3: 3: 66, dropsy, æ. 20-4-15, b. Ded., of Chas. &. Mary J.

28 Sophronia B. (Kimball), 3: 10: 73, consumption, æ. 34-0-16, b. Ded., of Theodore T. & Abby S., Kennebunk Me., Ded.

50 Wm. F., 3: 31: 45, epilepsy, æ. 1-6-0.

AECHTLER.

106 Catherine C. (Jacobs), 11: 25: 82, embolism, æ. 24-7-18, b. Buffalo N. Y., of
Henry & Catherine, Bavaria, do.

73 Wm., 8: 23: 79, teething, æ. 0-9-0, b. Boston, of Wm. & Catherine, Rox.,
Buffalo N. Y.

AHLBORN.

44 Sarah J., 7: 24: 60, dysentery, æ. 0-3-24, b. Ded., of Henry & Rebecca, Germ.,
New Brunswick N. J.

AINSWORTH.

116 Jos. F., 10: 20: 88, marasmus, æ. 64-1-20, b. Bethel Vt., of Artemas & Catherine F., Dudley, Walpole N. H.

AKERMAN.

35 Mary A. (Saunders), 4: 8: 73, heart dis., æ. 67-2-14, b. Eng., of Samuel &
Mary, Eng., do.

ALBERT.

95 ——, 9: 2: 65, ——, æ. 0-0-1, b. Ded., d. of Jacob & Mary.

97 ——, 9: 6: 65, ——, æ. 0-0-4, b. Ded., s. of Jacob & Mary.

61 Emma E., 7: 16: 68, bowel comp., æ. 0-1-3, b. Ded., of Jacob & Mary,
Germ., do.

ALCORN.

63 Eliz'h, 8: 28: 86, old age, æ. 69-0-0, b. Scot., of Wm. & Margaret, Scot., do.

ALDEN.

29 ——, 4: 19: 77, ——, æ. 0 0-2, b. Ded., d. of Elisha C. & S. Jennie, Ded., do.

7 ——, 1: 25: 78, stillborn, b. Ded., d. of Wm. H. & Amanda, Ded., Harpswell Me.

37 Abigail, 1: 24: 67, old age, æ. 95-0-0, b. Needham, of Samuel & Susanna,
Needham, do.

70 Amasa, 12: 7: 57, old age, æ. 86-0-0, b. Need., of Silas & Margaret.

26 Francis, 3: 17: 75, old age, æ. 82-1-27, b. Needham, of Amasa & Patty D.,
Needham, Milton.

76 George, 8: 25: 62, paralysis, æ. 57-11-25, b. Nelson N. H., of Amasa & Martha.

19 Hannah (Eaton), 3: 6: 78, consumption, æ. 74-5-0, b. Ded., of John & Hannah, Ded., Canton.

63 Leonard, 10: 27: 74, old age, æ. 78-9-25, b. Roxbury N. H., of Amasa & Patty,
Needham, Milton.

25 Maria A. (Fenderson), 3: 17: 76, ——, æ. 55-0-0, b. Saco Me.

14 [Patty], w. of Amasa, 9: 8: 46, palsy, æ. 70-0 0.

4 Rebecca N. (Newell), 1: 14: 56, lung fever, æ. 82-10-26, b. Need., of Eben'r & Eliz. A.

63 (D. at Newton) Roxanna, 6: 2: 63, consumption, æ. 63-1-3, b. Newton, of Paul & Rebecca, Newton, Needham.

13 Sarah E., w. of Francis Jr., 4: 23: 52, consumption, æ. 23-1-25, b. Bolton.

112 Sarah J., 11: 30: 61, consumption, æ. 28-8-16, b. Ded., of Francis & Sarah S.

61 Sarah S. (Crehore), 9: 6: 66, consumption, æ. 68-4-16, b. Ded., of Elisha & Sarah.

ALDRICH.

52 Edith M., 5: 28: 81, diphtheria, æ. 7-0-12, b. Ded., of Edgar E. & Georgianna E., Millville, Northbridge.

ALEXANDER.

15 Arthur V., 3: 2: 78, congestion of lungs, æ. 0-9-16, b. Ded., of Henry R. & Selina, Eng., do.

70 John, 7: 2: 63, pneumonia, æ. 30-0-0. [soldier.]

140 Perry C., 10: 15: 64, chronic diarrhœa, æ. 24-11-0, b. Upton. [soldier.]

ALGER.

53 Mary A., 10: 22: 54, canker, æ. 0-2-0, b. Ded., of David & Hannah S.

ALLEN.

48 Mrs., 9: 3: 46, ——, æ. 66-0-0, b. Ded.

115 Addie, 3: 10: 67, hemorrhage, æ. 0-0-4, b. Ded., of Augustus M. & Lydia E., Mansfield, Stark Me.

52 Amelia, 4: 8: 67, consumption, æ. 65-0-0, b. Medford.

114 Anna, 3: 10: 67, hemorrhage, æ. 0-0-4, b. Ded., of Augustus M. & Lydia E., Mansfield, Stark Me.

31 Chas. A., 2: 5: 64, typhoid fever, æ. ——. [soldier.]

108 Edmund F. A., 9: 8: 72, cholera infantum, æ. 0-5-4, b. Stoneham, of Timothy & Sarah, Brookline, Ded.

57 Frances D. (Clapp), w. of Wm., 5: 17: 52, fit, æ. 22-0-0, b. Walpole, of Nathan & ——.

86 James, 4: 11: 64, consumption, æ. ——. [soldier.]

61 Jennie, 6: 4: 89, marasmus, æ. 0-4-12, b. Boston, of —— & Annie, ——, Scot.

58 Lucretia (Barber), 7: 29: 80, paralysis, æ. 49-0-0, b. Va., of Isaac & Ann, Va., do.

48 Lucy M., 12: 12: 52, consumption, æ. 28-6-6, b. Ded., of Nathan & Catherine.

3 Mary, 1: 27: 48, lung fever, æ. 57-0-0.

99 Mary G., 9: 10: 65, dysentery, æ. 0-7-15, b. Ded., of Nathan B. & Emma L.

21 Nathan, 7: 23: 50, accident, æ. 66-1-10, b. Medfield, of Nathan & Miriam.

26 Sarah, 11: 12: 46, consumption, æ. 48-0-0.

18 Sarah (Chickering), 10: 28: 65, cancer, æ. 71-6-0, b. Medfield, of David & Sarah.

92 Timothy, 4: 3: 69, accident, æ. 87-0-0, b. Dover, of Timothy & ——, Dover, do.

145 Walter F., 12: 13: 63, typhoid fever, æ. 24-6-17, b. Monmouth Me., of Daniel & A. E., Monmouth Me., Bath Me.

ALLENSPACKER.

32 Henry, 4: 11: 76, croup, æ. 2-7-0, b. Ded., of Nepomuk & Sophia, Germ., do.

60 Jos. T., 7: 3: 82, bronchitis, æ. 0-0-5 wks., b. Ded., of John N. & Sophia, Germany, do.

65 Marie, 8: 12: 76, cholera infantum, æ. 0-9-0, b. Ded., of N. & S., Germ., do.

50 Wm., 6: 17: 73, inflam. of brain, æ. 1-10-22, b. Boston, of Nepomuck & Sophia, Germ., do.

ALLWRIGHT.

20 ——, 1: 6: 46, ——, æ. 0-5-0, b. Ded., of Alfred A. & ——.

77 Alfred, 11: 14: 73, consumption, æ. 58-6-1, b. Eng., of —— & Maria, Eng., do.

91 Edw. W., 9: 13: 49, cholera infantum, æ. 0-6-20, b. Ded., of Alfred & ——.

18 Samuel A., 2: 28: 45, ——, æ. 1-0-0.

ALSTON.

50 Wm., 5: 26: 63, inflam. of stomach, æ. 41-0-0. [soldier]

AMES.

9 Ida J., 1: 16: 89, peritonitis, æ. 9: 11: 25, b. W. Bridgewater, of Wm. B. & Annie C. (Chase), W. Bridgewater, New Bedford.

17 Lewis P., 2: 21: 84, spinal meningitis, æ. 0-7-2, b. Ded., of Theron B. & Mary L., Dorch., Mattapoisett.

12 Susan (Lewis), 2: 13: 80, paralysis of brain, æ. 65-9-18, b. Ded., of Samuel & Ann, Ded., do.

117 Theron B., 12: 7: 90, erysipelas & pneumonia, æ. 39-9-25, b. Dorch., of Wm. & Susan (Lewis), Groton, Ded.

108 (D. at Springfield), Wm., 5: 19: 80, heart dis., æ. 79-7-16, b. Ded., of Fisher & Frances (Worthington), Ded., Springfield.

ANDERSON.

34 Peter, 4: 12: 82, consumption, æ. 45-0-18, b. Sweden, of Andrew & Ann, Sweden, do.

83 Robert, 4: 1: 64, ——, æ. ——. [soldier.]

ANDREWS.

100 Caroline, 9: 30: 53, dis. of liver, æ. 50-9-0, b. Ded., of David & Susan E.

100 (D. at N.Y. City) David, 12: 14: 58, old age, æ. 85-0-0, b. Ded., of Jas. & ——.

9 John, 3: 1: 66, heart dis., æ. 62-11-0, b. Ded., of Joel & Lavina.

7 Newell, 1: 26: 64, lung fever, æ. 20-0-0, b. Ills., of Jerome & ——. [soldier.]

58 Permelia H. (Harding), 10: 14: 53, consumption, æ. 25-1-4, b. Baldwin Me., of John & Temperance.

ARNOLD.

82 Adeline, 10: 9: 57, consumption, æ. 1-0-0, b. Ded., of Chas. & Adeline.

7 Arthur H., 1: 20: 86, membranous croup, æ. 0-9-1, b. Ded., of Arthur H. & Ada M., New Orleans, Warwick Neck R. I.

88 Chas. A., 6: 30: 58, consumption on brain, æ. 0-6-0, b. Ded., of Charles & Adeline.

34 Ellen J. (O'Bryan), 5: 4: 79, heart disease, æ. 23-1-22, b. Ire., of James & ——, Ire., do.

72 Minnie, 9: 14: 72, dysentery, æ. 0-9-9, b. Ded., of Chas. A. & Emma, Valley Falls R. I., Prov. R. I.

89 Minnie M., 10: 27: 76, accident, æ. 1-5-23, b. Ded., of Geo. & Nellie, Prov. R. I., Ded.

106 Roger, 12: 17: 49, ——, æ. 40-0-0.

ARRIS.
11 James, 5: 18: 60, heart dis., æ. 74-0-0, b. Danville Me., of Jas. & ——.
35 (D. at Dorch.) John, 7: 6: 62, cancer, æ. 50-1-21, b. Lisbon Me., of Jas. & Mary (Harrington), Danville Me., ——.

ASHCROFT.
38 ——, 4: 20: 45, ——, æ. 0-0-7, b. Ded., of Edw. & ——.

ASTIN.
13 John, 3: 22: 62, consumption, æ. 28-0-0, b. Ire., of Jas. & Isabella.

ATCHKINSON.
45 John, 3: 25: 63, lung fever, æ. 35-0-0, b. Norfolk Va., of Jesse & Hannah, Va., do. [soldier.]

ATEN.
42 Helen F. (Morgan), 2: 26: 63, consumption, æ. 28-8-12, b. Meredith N. H., of Chas. & Sarah H., Kingston N. H., Meredith N. H.

ATHERTON.
44 Abner, 12: 24: 47, flt, æ. 72-0-0.
32 Benj. F., 4: 26: 57, consumption, æ. 22-8-13, b. Boston, of Jonathan & Eliza.
46 Betsy, w. of Abner, 8: 16: 49, sore throat, æ. 66-0-0.
20 Frances M., 6: 23: 50, consumption, æ. 24-10-23, b. Boston, of Jonathan & Eliza.

ATKINSON.
19 Maria F., 4: 5: 53, scarlet fever, æ. 4-1-14, b. Grafton, of Kinsman & Dorothy M.

ATWOOD.
97 Martin C. S., 10: 24: 79, typhoid pneumonia, æ. 15-5-12, b. Prov. R. I., of Henry A. & Hattie C., Prov. R. I., Pawtucket R. I.

AUSTIN.
27 Adelbert M., 8: 17: 52, cholera infantum, æ. 1-6-6, b. Ded., of James & Caroline.
23 Edgar V., 2: 11: 90, heart failure, æ. 27-0-0, b. Stow, of Gilman & Eliza, Marlboro, Me.

AYER, AYERS.
50 Catherine (Morse), 5: 27: 80, pleuro pneumonia, æ. 69-10-0, b. Medfield, of Nathan & Elenor (Lawrence.)
131 Mary (Trull), 12: 7: 67, old age, æ. 90-1-7, b. Natick, of —— & Jemima, ——, Natick.
49 Wm., 8: 25: 60, drowned, æ. 62-4-17, b. Portsmouth N. H., of John & Mercy, Portsmouth, do.

BABCOCK.
83 E. Francena, 11: 16: 77, cancer, æ. 42-8-0, b. Boston, of Wm. & Rebecca, Milton, Westford.
6 Emmeline (Foxcroft), 1: 26: 83, paralysis, æ. 71 7 15, b. Boston, of Francis A. & Betsey, Brookfield, Boston.
89 (D. at Boston) Samuel B., 10: 25: 73, apoplexy, æ. 65 0-9, b. Boston, of Samuel H. & Eliza (Brazer), Milton, Boston.

71 Wm. R., 8: 19: 70, consumption, æ. 42-6-16, b. Milton, of Wm. & Rebecca, Milton, Westford.

BABSON.

6 Sarah A. (Bradford), 4: 15: 72, inflam. of bowels, æ. 40-9-4, b. Canterbury Ct., of Thos. & Sophronia.

BACH.

52 Jakob, 6: 29: 84, consumption, æ. 38-0-0, b. Germ.

BACON.

2 ——, 1: 12: 82, stillborn, b. Ded., s. of Silas E. & Sarah L., Newton, Boston.

65 Geo. M., 7: 20: 75, empyema, æ. 53-0-0, b. N. Y. City, of Bela & Lucy M., ——, Needham.

72 Lucy (Mills), 10: 19: 86, old age, æ. 89-0-0, b. Needham, of Paul & Ada, Needham, Dedham.

65 Lydia J. (Smith), 7: 30: 70, congestion of lungs, æ. 40-0-0, b. Ded., of Humphrey & Wealthy, Vt.. Halifax Mass.

81 Wm. M., 6: 12: 88, apoplexy, æ. 55-4-8, b. Prov. R. I., of Wm. & Mary A. (Cole), Prov. R. I., do.

BAGLEY, BEGLEY.

57 Bridget (O'Hare), w. of Martin, 5: 22: 89, enteritis, æ. 58-0-0, b. Ire., of John & ——. (Donahoe), Ire., do.

9 Harriet J., 8: 12: 45, ——, æ. 11-6-0, b. Ded.

52 Margaret L., 5: 13: 80, intussusception of bowels, æ. 31-1-14, b. Ded., of Martin & Bridget (O'Hare), Ire., do.

37 Mary, 5: 18: 79, anaemia, æ. 9-1-8, b. Ded., of Martin & Bridget, Ire., do.

7 Mary A., 1: 29: 59, scarlet fever, æ. 2-3-0, b. Ded., of Martin & Bridget.

79 Thomas J., 5: 1: 55. lung fever, æ. 50-0-0, b. Candia N. H., of Nathan & Rhoda.

BAILEY.

31 Abby A. (Larkins), 12: 28: 63, dis. of kidneys, æ. 32-5-0, b. Dorch., of John S. & Harriet T. B.

100 Caroline A. (Draper), 6: 5: 70, consumption, æ. 19-6-0, b. Ded., of George & Cordelia, Ded., Me.

41 Joseph, 3: 25: 90, senile gangrene, æ. 77-3-3, b. Medfield, of Martin & Asenath (Kingsbury), Vt., Foxboro.

33 Julia A. (Ayers), 10: 20: 71, lockjaw, æ. 47-0-0, b. Lisbon Me., of Jas. & ——.

BAIN.

78 Mehitable S. (Sweetser), 11: 15: 73, dropsy, æ. 88-9-27, b. Charlestown, of Benj. & Martha M., Charlestown, Cambridge.

37 William, 10: 21: 45, old age, æ. 68-0-0, b. Eng.

BAKER.

73 ——, 7: 12: 67, stillborn, b. Ded., d. of Geo. & Ellen, Ded., Walpole.

74 Aaron, 6: 25: 56, dis. of chest, æ. 78-0-0, b. Ded., of Timothy & Cynthia.

55 Abigail P., w. of Jere, 10: 31: 48, consumption, æ. 57-0-0, b. Medfield.

33 A'mer W., 6: 29: 60, struck by lightning, æ. 19-0-0, b. Ded., of Timothy & Hannah, Ded., do.

23 Alford, 5: 16: 71, suicide, æ. 61-2-0, b. Ded., of Sabin & Abigail, Ded., ——.

11 Alford E., 2:27:80, consumption, æ. 47-4-10, b. Ded., of Alford & Julia A. G., Ded., do.

77 Al'ston, 8:31:85, premature birth, æ. 0-0-5, b. Ded., of Fred'k A. & Mary E., Kingston. Canton.

72 Amy (Williams), 11:11:66, old age, æ. 87-9-18, b. Rox., of John & Mary.

60 Anne E. (Eaton). 10:30:53, apoplexy, æ. 84-9-5, b. Ded., of John & Desire.

25 Arthur C., 3:8:81, acute bronchitis, æ. 0-3-12, b. Ded., of Willie W. & Viola L. (White), Ded., Munson.

42 Becca (Fisher), w. of John, 3:7:50, old age, æ. 82-0-0, b. Ded., of Asa & ——.

133 Betsy (Metcalf), 2:24:67, bilious colic, æ. 80-11-0, b. Prov. R. I., of Joel & Lucy, Prov. R. I., Attleboro.

71 Charlotte, 8:1:54, old age, æ. 79-9-9.

56 Christopher II., 8:10:73, cholera infantum, æ. 0-3-0, b. Boston, of Geo. L. & Margaret II., Boston, Baltimore.

61 Cynthia, 10:3:52, fever, æ. 71-0-9, b. Ded., of Timothy & Cynthia.

49 Dene (Holmes), 7:15:50, ——, æ. 63-0-9, b. Sharon, of John & ——.

105 Eliz'h P. (Sanford). 11:25:70, typhoid fever, æ. 57-5-0, b. Tiverton R. I., of —— & Ann, Tiverton, do.

136 Eveline (Blake), 8:9:63, consumption, æ. 57-11-1, b. Walpole, of Eben'r & Ede, ——, Franklin.

77 Fanny E. 8:28:81, dysentery, æ. 77-1-15, b. Ded., of Aaron & Hannah (Gay), Ded., do.

140 (D. at Danvers), Frank D., 4:4:87, ——, æ. 16-8-13, b. ——, of Chas. D. & Rachel R.

29 Fred E., 4:10:61, scarlet fever, æ. 5-9-13, b. Danvers, of Robert E. & Mary E., Ded., Danvers.

16 Hannah G. (Baker), 2:20:82, exhaustion, æ. 68-2-14, b. Ded., of Aaron & Roxy (Whiting), Ded., do.

16 Harriet, [no date, Rec. 6:24:46], ——, æ. 29-0-0.

58 Horace, 6:26:51, fever, æ. 53-9-9, b. Ded., of John & Becca.

62 Horace, 9:19:51, fever, æ. 5-9-0, b. Boston, of Horace & ——.

6 Jane A. (Grover), 1:21:81, paralysis, æ. 71-7-9, b. Foxboro, of Calvin & Ruth, Foxboro, do.

40 Jennie B., 4:21:83, inflam. of brain, æ. 1-11-11, b. Ded., of Wm. & Jennie G., Ded., Montville Ct.

98 Jeremiah, 9:12:55, old age, æ. 94-0-9, b. Ded.

45 John, 7:21:46, consumption, æ. 83-0-0, b. Ded.

96 Laurinda A. (Woodward), w. of Eustis, 10:3:90, heart failure, æ. 70-9-23, b. Plainfield N. H., of David & Hannah (Putnam), Brooklyn Ct., N. H.

83 Mary M. (Sawin). 9:24:76, dropsy of chest, æ. 63-4-7, b. Dover, of Joel & Polly B., Natick, Dover.

44 Nelson, 4:20:89, marasmus, æ. 1-0-7, b. Salem, of Milton & Eliza J., N. S., Ire.

11 Obed, 3:24:68, old age, æ. 84-9-9, b. Ded., of Timothy & Cynthia, Ded., do

15 Patty E. (Ellis), 2:14:76, old age, æ. 85-3-3, b. Medfield, of Geo. & Martha C., Medfield, ——.

64 Robert II., 5:25:52, consumption, æ. 51-9-0, b. Prov. R. I., of Hinsdale & Jemima.

52 Roxa (Whiting), w. of Aaron, 2: 29: 52, fever, æ. 63-0-0, b. Ded., of Abner & Loacada.

29 Samuel W., 2: 23: 90, softening of brain, æ. 72-10-27, b. Ded., of Aaron & Roxy (Whiting), Ded., do.

47 Sarah, 6: 5: 50, old age, æ. 74-0-0, b. Ded., of Eliph't & ——.

88 Sarah A., 12: 21: 77, neuralgia, æ. 62-4-0, b. Ded., of Aaron & Roxy W., Ded., do.

18 Susan C. (Colburn), 9: 21: 68, cancer, æ. 58-9-15, b. Ded., of Abijah & Susanna, Ded., Medfield.

98 Timothy, 10: 9: 90, brain dis., æ. 76-10-15, b. Ded., of Obed & Betsey (Metcalf), Ded., Prov. R. I.

85 Walter G., 7: 31: 83, cerebro spinal meningitis, æ. 11-0-0, b. Ded., of Jas. B. & Martha G., Ded., do.

85 Willie E., 2: 23: 71, asphyxia, æ. 0-0-1, b. Ded., of Eben & Mattie J., Ded., Long Island N. Y.

BALCH.

6 Sarah (Eaton), w. of Wm., 2: 21: 50, lung fever, æ. 67-9-2, b. Ded., of Isaac & Sarah.

BALKHAM.

10 Edith, 2: 3: 81, meningitis, æ. 0-12-0, b. Ded., of Wm. & Sarah (Morang), Eastport Me., Lubec Me.

BALL.

23 Carrie L., 4: 3: 61, croup, æ. 5-5-11, b. Marlboro, of Lyman E. & Jane P.

5 John B., 2: 17: 50, consumption, æ. 29-11-15, b. Orange Vt., of Rufus & Rebecca.

44 Theodore F., 3: 26: 68, consumption, æ. 19-4-9, b. Ded., of John B. & Sarah D., Orange Vt., Milton.

BALLOU.

96 Mary E., 10: 23: 79, consumption, æ. 33-2-25, b. Ded., of Sylvanus & Tryphena, Burrilville R. I., Ded.

89 Sylvanus, 10: 13: 85, diabetes, æ. 69-3-26, b. R. I., of Daniel & Mercy, R.I., do.

BAMBAUER.

48 Catharine (Schutz), 6: 13: 73, paralysis, æ. 57-7-0, b. Germ., of Philip & Catharine, Germ., do.

50 Catharine, 7: 10: 78, consumption, æ. 31-2-22, b. Boston, of Jacob & Catharine, Germ., do.

BARNARD.

56 Samuel G., 5: 19: 89, phthisis pulmonalis, æ. 26-2-14, b. Marblehead, of Geo. B. & Abbie S. (Morse), Bradford N. H., Marblehead.

BARNETT.

96 (D. at Walpole) Winthrop B., 4: 23: 53, consumption, æ. 26-0-0, b. Derry N. H., of Robert & Sarah N.

BARRETT.

67 Annie M. (Dolan), w. of Martin J., 6: 16: 89, peritonitis, æ. 25-1-24, b. Ded., of Thomas F. & Margaret (Moore), Ire., do.

58 Bridget L. (Darcy), 8:5:86, typhoid fever, æ. 31 10-13, b. Waterford, of Edw. & Bridget, Ire., do.

31 Catharine, 10:18:56, summer comp., æ. 0-9-0, b. Ded., of Thos. & Margaret.

12 James, 8:22:66, diarrhoea, æ. 0-0-19, b. Ded., of Thos. & Margaret.

61 Wm. J., 8:20:86, cholera infantum, æ. 0-11-4, b. Ded., of Michael J. & Bridget L., Ded., Waterford.

BARROWS.

69 Eliz'h (Bosworth), 8:6:60, paralysis, æ. 66-6-0, b. Halifax Mass., of Asaph & Eliz'h, Halifax, do.

17 Henry H., 9:1:68, suicide, æ. 24-0-0.

94 (D. at Hartford Ct.) Thos., 10:29:63, R. R. accident, æ. 38-0-0, b. Halifax, of Thos. & Eliz'h, Halifax, do.

40 Thos., 5:7:80, old age, æ. 84-9-1, b. Middleboro, of Abner & Hannah, Middleboro, do.

BARRY.

84 (D. at Munson) Abbie T., 10:4:84, paralysis, æ. 12-0-0, b. Boston, of Paul & Abbie, Ire., do.

144 Paul P., 12:30:88,——, æ. 41-6-13, b. Ire., of Dennis & Kate (Leary), Ire., do.

BARTHOLOMEW.

49 Stephen, 3:16:64, pneumonia, æ. ——. [soldier.]

BARTLETT.

107 Ann C. (Lyon), 5:19:64, lung fever, æ. 55-4-0, b. W. Rox., of Benj. & Eliz'h, Rox., do.

51 Frances P. (Whittemore), 10:3:50, fever, æ. 46-0-0, b. Rox., of J. & ——.

BARTOL.

26 Joseph, 6:9:58, lung fever, æ. 57-0-0, b. France.

BARTON.

47 Janet (Chisholm), w. of Anson F., 11:23:52, consumption, æ. 26-9 25, b. Southbridge, of Wm. & Isabel.

BASSETT.

49 Martha R. (Raymond), 2:26:70, dropsy, æ. 79-3-20, b. Westford, of John & Phebe, Westford, do.

BATCHELDER.

20 Francis, 4:16:53, drowned, æ. 6:0:13, b. Easton, of Jos. & Maria.

37 Joseph R., 9:30:52, consumption, æ. 31-0-0, b. Salem.

BATEMAN.

44 Lilla F., 3:7:64, diphtheria, æ.——, b. Sharon, of Wm. & Harriet, N. Y.,do.

BATES.

90 Abner L., 9:22:81, paralysis, æ. 66-9-0, b. Dighton, of Asa & Ruth, Abington, do.

72 Betsey (Kenney), 9:17:77, paralysis, æ. 80-4-3, b. Yarmouth Me., of Samuel & Hannah.

94 Charlotte W. (Wood), 12:20:70, paralysis, æ. 82-11-25, b. Boxford, of Lemuel & Frances, Eng., Boxford.

26 Emma F. (Weed), 4:22:79, drowned, æ. 26-3-30, b. Malden, of Otis H. & Susan, N. Brookfield, Boston.

60 Martin, 12: 8: 69, old age, æ. 81-9-20, b. Ded., of Samuel & Mary.

50 Mary F. (Sisson), 6: 17: 85, old age, æ. 81-8-23, b. Charlestown, of Edw. & Susannah, Milton, Ded.

BAUER.

36 Edw. F., 3: 13: 90, consumption, æ. 40-9-0, b. Germ., of Gottlieb P. & Christiana (Bickman), Germ., do.

49 Paul, 9: 10: 74, cholera infantum, æ. 1-1-21, b. Ded., of Frank & Maria, Germ., do.

BAYER, BYER. (*See also Bier.*)

87 Casper, 6: 7: 59, croup, æ. 8-0-0, b. Germ., of Casper & Mary.

133 Henry, 4: 30: 65, consumption, æ. 19-4-1, b. Germ., of Christian & Anna M.

44 John, 5: 25: 79, diphtheria, æ. 1-10-16, b. Ded., of Michael & Mary, Germ., Ire.

42 Lizzie, 5: 25: 79, diphtheria, æ. 3-7-0, b. Ded., of Michael & Mary, Germ., Ire.

38 Louisa, 5: 19: 79, diphtheria, æ. 6-6-0, b. Ded., of Michael & Mary, Germ., Ire.

70 Maggie, 7: 25: 87, marasmus, æ. 0-2-23, b. Ded., of —— & Mary, ——, Ire.

49 Mary, 3: 31: 67, heart dis., æ. 48-1-2, b. Germ., of Casper & Mary, Germ., do.

43 Mary, 5: 25: 79, diphtheria, æ. 9-6-16, b. Ded., of Michael & Mary, Germ., Ire.

18 Michael, 2: 25: 86, consumption, æ. 40-9-22, b. Germ., of Casher & Mary, Germ., do.

BEACH.

51 ——, 5: 29: 76, stillborn, b. Ded., s. of Seth C. & Frances H., Marion N. J., Augusta Me.

89 ——, 9: 14: 82, premature birth, b. Ded., d. of Edw. & Cora, Springfield, Hanover.

BEAL, BEALS.

122 Edw. F., 12: 19: 90, heart dis., æ. 67-9-0, b. Boston, of Samuel & Ruth (Loring), Hingham, Boston.

109 Henry, 10: 2: 88, apoplexy, æ. 80-3-8, b. Milton, of John & Ruth, U. S., do.

21 Ruth, 10: 18: 46, consumption, æ. 75-0-0.

BEAN.

18 Albion, 3: 5: 60, lung fever, æ. 36-8-22, b. Naples Me., of Jacob & Sarah.

96 Geo. E., 10: 1: 49, cholera infantum, æ. 0-11-8, b. Ded., of Albion & Mary E.

71 Mary E., 9: 15: 77, consumption, æ. 21-11-3, b. Ded., of Albion & Mary E., Alfred Me., Milton.

104 Mary E. (Holmes), 12: 2: 85, tumor, æ. 63-10-2, b. Milton, of Philip & Margaret. Milton, Robinstown Me.

BEARSE.

96 Artemas, 1: 30: 61, small pox, æ. 36-2-4, b. Barnstable, of Moses H. & Rebecca, Barnstable. do.

BECKER.

27 Barbara (Kuhn), 5: 31: 62, consumption, æ. 30-6-9, b. Germ., of George & Grence.

31 Barbara (Schmerer), 4: 19: 87, paralysis, æ. 64-3-0, b. Germ., of —— & ——, Germ., do.

33 Florian, 3: 10: 90, ulceration of stomach, æ. 66-1-0. b. Germ., of Frank C. & Catharine (Martin), Germ., do.

19 Ludwig, 2: 23: 81, pleuro pneumonia, æ. 38-0-0, b. Germ., of Jos. & Genoye, Germ, do.

6 Teresia, 5: 11: 74, lung fever, æ. 0-7-0, b. Ded., of John & Mary, Boston, Phila.

BECKETT.

56 Paul, 7: 28: 78, cyanosis, æ. 0-0-4, b. Ded., of Bartlett G. & Ella M., Jefferson Tex., Dayton Me.

BEERS.

53 Jos. W., 5: 8: 68, heart dis., æ. 50-0-0, b. Woburn, of Jos. & Jerusha, Woburn, Wellington.

BELENGER.

87 Admonto, 11: 19: 70, croup, æ. 1-4-0, b. Canada, of Peter & Caroline, Canada, do.

74 Albert F., 9: 15: 72, bowel comp., æ. 0-2-28, b. Ded., of Peter & Caroline, Canada, do.

86 Joseph, 11: 17: 70, croup, æ. 4-0-0, b. Canada, of Peter & Caroline, Canada, do

BELKNAP.

25 Daniel F., 9: 3: 50, suicide, æ. 44-0-0, b. Ded.

BELL.

98 Susan (Cox), w. of John, 10: 5: 89, old age, æ. 78-0-0, b. Ire., of Hugh & Margaret (Cox), Ire., do.

33 Wm., 4: 10: 69, consumption, æ. 26-0-0, b. W. Indies, of Wm. & Rosanna, W. Indies, do.

BELUMBY.

36 John O'B., 9: 20: 52, dysentery, æ. 1-9-0, b. Ded., of David & Catherine.

BENJAMIN.

72 Marcia H. (Savage), 8: 22: 76, hypertrophy of heart, æ. 45-0-0, b. N. Anson Me., of John G. & Fannie, N. Anson Me., do.

BENT.

85 Hannah (Jordan), 9: 13: 63, dropsy, æ. 73-5-16, b. Needham, of Jesse & Hannah.

25 John, 1: 17: 72, old age, æ. 93-2-25, b. Milton.

BENTLEY.

45 Wm. H., 2: 15: 70, erysipelas, æ. 0-2-14, b. Ded., of——& Mary J. (Guild), Eng., Ded.

BERGDELL.

25 John, 3: 19: 57, consumption, æ. 23-0-0, b. Germany.

BESOM.

79 Richard, 6: 20: 49, old age, æ. 76-0-0, b. Marblehead, of John & Sarah.

BESTWICK.

80 Albert G., 10: 7: 62, diphtheria, æ. 7-4-22, b. Ded., of Fred L. & Mary, Medway, Me.

5 Cordelia P. (Young), 1: 8: 57, consumption, æ. 27-6-18, b. Chatham, of Elisha & Esther.

77 Isabel A., 9: 9: 62, membranous croup, æ. 3-4-2, b. Ded., of [Alfred] A. & Abigail, Ded., Wiscasset Me.

8 Isabella M., 9: 2: 48, dysentery, æ. 2-0-0, b. Ded., of Fred L. & ——

32 John, 5: 29: 74, paralysis, æ. 84-8-27, b. Eng., of —— & ——, Eng., do.

41 Mary L. (Litchfield), 3: 3: 68, heart dis., æ. 74-7-8, b. Eng., of Thos. & Mary, Eng., do.

20 Mary S. (Thompson), 3: 2: 57, consumption, æ. 35-0-18, b. Wiscasset Me., of Wm. & Abigail.

BETTERSHOUS.

112 Otto, 2: 18: 63, croup, æ. 1-11-13, b. Ded., of Jacob & Sibila, Germ., do.

BICKNER.

17 Alexander R., 6: 4: 50, erysipelas, æ. 0-1-0, b. Ded., of Wm. & Mary.

25 Betsy, 3: 10: 49, old age, æ. 85-0-0.

35 Charles, 5: 5: 49, old age, æ. 83-0-0.

16 Chas. F., 6: 1: 50, fit, æ. 7-5-20, b. Ded., of Wm. & Mary.

17 Eliza, 5: 10: 59, paralysis, æ. 64-0-0, b. Boston, of Chas. & Eliz'h.

82 Florence C., 8: 30: 49, cholera infantum, æ. 0-11-0, b. Ded., of Samuel R. & Lucretia P.

67 Lucretia P. (Eastman), 12: 4: 57, consumption, æ. 44-6-10, b. Hollis N. H., of Chas. & Rebecca.

10 Samuel R., 2: 10: 87, fatty degeneration of heart, æ. 79-9-0, b. Boston, of Chas. & Eliz'h, Boston, do.

BIER. (*See also Bayer.*)

43 Christopher, 7: 14: 63, scrofula, æ. 42-0-0, b. Germ., of Geo. & Eliz'h, Germ., do.

—— D. at W. Rox.) Louisa, 6: 4: 75, convulsions, æ. 0-0-14, b. W. Rox., of Christian & Mary, Germ., do.

BIGELOW.

94 ——, 12: 15: 72, ——, æ. 0-0-2, b. Ded., s. of Chas. H. & Christine, Keene N. H., Winsor Locks Ct.

122 John, 8: 30: 64, congestion of lungs, æ. 35-0-0, b. Ire. [soldier.]

BILLINGS.

122 David, 4: 29: 63, lung fever, æ. 64-6-0, b. Sedgwick Me., of Isaac & Sarah Sedgwick Me., do.

BILLS.

65 Betsy, 11: 21: 51, fever, æ. 48-0-0.

151 Fanny F. (Abbot), 11: 14: 63, consumption, æ. 38-4-2,, b. Hanover, of Hazen, K. & Louisa P.

76 Geo. L., 8: 1: 56, typhoid fever, æ. 5-0-0, b. Ded., of Lewis & Fanny.

75 Henry B., 6: 25: 61, dropsy on brain, æ. 0-4-0, b. Ded., of Lewis & Sarah, Ded., Medway.

156 Mary L., 5: 7: 64, lung fever, æ. 10-0-10, b. Ded., of Lewis A. & Fanny L.H., Ded., Hanover N. H.

BINGHAM.

49 Bertha L., 5: 23: 76, canker, æ. 0-0-22, b. Ded., of Thomas A. H. & Louisa M., Spencer, Ded.

92 Daniel, 9: 14: 49, consumption, æ. 46-0-0, b. Ded., of Pliny & Jerusha.

10 Eva M., 1: 30: 78, premature birth, æ. 0-0-2, b. Ded., of Thos. A. H. & Louisa M., Spencer, Ded.

14 Jerusha (Avery), 12: 1: 74. old age, æ. 94-2-18, b. Ded., of Jonathan & Jerusha N., Ded., Boston.

BIRD.

42 Catharine (Gay), 5: 13: 73, old age, æ. 85-2-22, b. Sharon, of David & Catharine, Sharon, Ded.

49 Lyman E., 10: 15: 54, dysentery, æ. 0-5-0, b. Ded., of Francis & Emily M.

75 Martha (Newell), 9: 24: 52, dysentery, æ. 81-0-0, b. Need., of Josiah & ——.

18 Samuel, 1: 12: 66, dropsy, æ. 80-1-6, b. Dorch., of Samuel & Susanna.

58 Sarah M., 7: 6: 75, heart dis., æ. 16-1-28, b. Boston, of Geo. M. & Sarah F., Ded., Addison Me.

31 Walter F., 9: 2: 52, dysentery, æ. 0-4-0, b. Ded., of Francis & Emily.

BISHOP.

69 Benj., 11: 29: 52, consumption, æ. 84-0-0, b. Attleboro, of Simeon & ——.

91 Hannah (Everett), 4: 15: 68, old age, æ. 87-9-9, b. Ded., of Abel & Mary, Ded., Stoughton.

67 Maria R. (Ricker), 9: 6: 72, dropsy, æ. 43-9-3, b. Green Me., of Henry & Margaret, Sanford Me., Henniker N. H.

50 Robert, 7: 10: 61, congestion of brain, æ. 28-0-0, b. Eng., of Jos. & Charlotte, Ire., do.

BIXBY.

69 Rosilie (Rouviere), w. of Eben F,. 7: 2: 87, acute myelitis of spinal cord, æ. 43-10-22, b. Hartford Ct., of Louis C. & Harriet. Hebron Ct., Litchfield Ct.

BLACKMORE.

70 Mary, 9: 9: 68, inflam. of bowels, æ. 22-7-15, b. Eng., of John & Frances, Eng., do.

BLAIR.

62 George, 12: 11: 69, typhoid fever, æ. 43-1-16, b. Ire., of Wm. & Jane., Ire., do.

3 Jefferson, 1: 18: 76, hemorrhage of bowels, æ. 34-0-0, b. Richmond Va., of Jefferson & Mary A.

BLAKE.

42 Chas. L., 5: 12: 82, old age, æ. 85-6-19, b. Boston, of Jas & ——. Boston, do.

96 Ellen J., 8: 1: 71, angina maligna, æ. 38-0-23, b. Wrentham, of Asa & Harriet, Wrentham, Franklin.

22 James, 4: 12: 60, old age, æ. 80-0-0, b. Boston.

146 John, 11: 19: 64, pleurisy, æ. 32-0-0, b. Ire. [soldier.]

BLANCHARD.

53 Rachel (Hawes), 5: 29: 81, progressive paralysis, æ. 82-11-9, b. Weymouth, of Jos. & Sarah, Weymouth, do.

BLANK.

2 Joseph, 1: 4: 60, lung fever, æ. 43-0-0. b. Germ., of Nepomook & ——.

BLENUS.

155 Albert H., 12: 23: 65, inflam. of brain, æ. 1-7-23, b. Ded., of Chas. W. & Vesta G.

37 Fred., 11: 3: 51, dis. of brain, æ. 0-8-0, b. Ded., of Isaac & Polly.

92 Geo. B., 7: 9: 61, scarlet fever, æ. 3-0-4, b. Ded., of Isaac & Olivia B., N. S., Albion Me.

103 Isaac W., 9: 7: 61, typhoid fever, æ. 43-3-2, b. ——, of Thos. & Phebe.

17 John D., 5: 25: 51, consumption, æ. 28-3-15, b. N. S., of Thos. & Phebe.

33 Willet C., 9: 21: 50, consumption, æ. 25-7-8, b. N. S., of Thos. & Phebe.

BLOOD.

108 Fanny (Haskell), 10: 23: 67, fever, æ. 72-7-0, b. Cape Ann, of Nath'l & Sally, Cape Ann, Canaan N. Y.

22 Moody, 3: 24: 78, old age, æ 74-10-0, b. Nashua N. H., of Wm. & Abigail S., Dunstable N. H., Woburn.

94 Wm., 12: 6: 69, debility, æ. 72-10-0, b. Nashua N. H., of Wm. & ——.

BLUITE.

63 Thos., 8: 10: 80, cholera infantum, æ. 0-8-0, b. Prov. R. I., of Wm. & Kate, Ire., do.

BOARDMAN.

90 Chas. F., 9: 13: 49, dysentery, æ. 2-9-18, b. Charlestown, of Richard & Sarah E.

49 Pamelia H., 1: 20: 45, pul. consumption, æ. 22-0-0.

BOCK.

133 Alfred T., 7: 11: 63, cholera infantum, æ. 1-11-6, b. Ded., of Theodore & Miriam, Germ., Eng.

BODENSCHATZ.

99 John, 10: 11: 90, ——, æ. 64-4-27, b. Germ., of John & Zillman, Germ., do.

BOLAND.

51 Wm., 7: 20: 61, diarrhoea, æ. 0-4-0, b. Ded., of Thos. & Bridget.

BONNEMORT.

11 ——, 8: 29: 46, dysentery, æ. 4-0-0, b. Ded.

14 Mary (Gill), 5: 4: 56, falling down stairs, æ. 46-5-0, b. Canton, of John & Mary.

96 Nicholas, 11: 3: 85, old age, æ. 85-3-7, b. Boston, of Nicholas M. & Eunice, France, Attleboro.

BONNEY.

78 Cordelia C. E. (Coney), 12: 1: 66, accidental, æ. 54-7-0, b. Eastport Me., of Wm. & Abigail.

90 Florence (Bridge), w. of Henry C., 7: 19: 88, consumption, æ. 40-10-15, b. New Orleans La., of Isaac & —— (Berry), Boston, Bath Me.

76 Grace, 9: 10: 76, erysipelas, æ. 0-1-3, b. Ded., of Henry C. & Florence B., Ded., New Orleans La.

6 John, 3: 31: 52, congestion of brain, æ. 0 7-2, b. Ded., of Daniel & Cordelia C.

BOOCOCK.

85 Wm., 11: 16: 70, consumption, æ 29-11-3, b. Eng., of John & Ann, Eng., do.

BOOTH.

28 Margaret S., 6: 11: 62, canker, æ. 0 10-8, b. Ded., of John & Mary.

BOSSETT.

22 Josie, 2: 19: 74, pneumonia, æ. 0-5-20, b. Lawrence, of —— & Agnes Powers.

BOSTWICK.
24 Catharine (Whiting), 11: 4: 46, fever, æ. 68-0-0, of Moses & ——.
BOURNE.
109 Silas. 1: 13: 49, pleurisy fever, æ. 43-0-0, b. Sandwich.
BOWDWITCH.
36 Grenville, 10: 11: 45, fever, æ. 11-0-0, b. Boston, of Jona & ——.
BOWE.
1 Edward, 1: 1: 75, diarrhoea, æ. 23-9-0, b. Ire., of Philip & Mary, Ire., do.
BOWERS.
92 Jane, 7: 20: 58, consumption, æ. 0-0-30, b. Ded., of Henry & Margaret.
66 Lewis, 11: 16: 53, accidental shooting, æ. 15-10-23, b. Boston, of John & Catharine.
91 Sarah, 7: 10: 58, consumption, æ. 0-0-20, b. Ded., of Henry & Margaret.
BOYD.
39 David, 1: 28: 71, old age, æ. 92-9-19, b. Ded., of —— & ——. Ded., do.
92 David, 10: 5: 79, consumption, æ. 73-11-28, b. Ded., of David & Polly, Ded., do.
34 David H., 4: 26: 69, kidney dis., æ. 20-4-26, b. Boston, of David & Eliz'h, Ded., Damariscotta Me.
73 Eliz'h S. (Dorety), 10: 21: 86, obstruction of mitral valve, æ. 66-9-20, b. Damariscotta Me., of John & Mary, Damariscotta, do.
111 Henry W., 10: 30: 61, typhoid fever, æ. 15-11-17, b. Ded., of Moses & Olive, Ded., do.
44 Milton T., 3: 22: 63, lung fever, æ. 33-0-0, b. Chester Co. Pa. [soldier].
2 Olive (Guild), 1: 10: 84, heart dis., æ. 63-10-15, b. Ded., of Reuben & Olive, Ded., do.
74 Polly (French). 7: 22: 65, dysentery, æ. 86-5-8, b. Ded., of Samuel & Mary.
35 Wesley W., 3: 12: 88, inflam. of lungs and brain, æ. 1-10-18, b. Ded., of Moses G. & Harriet T. (Wolcott), Ded., Rox.
BOYDEN.
30 Almon E., 8: 16: 70, cholera infantum, æ. 0-7-8, b. Ded., of Ellis & Eliza M., Walpole, Medfield.
120 Annie M., 9: 6: 61, dis. of brain, æ. 3-8-6, b. Ded., of Ellis & Eliza, Walpole, Medfield.
84 Benj., 6: 20: 88, paralysis, æ. 81-4-18, b. Ded., of Benj. & Roxa.
77 Benj. L., 11: 5: 61, scarlet fever, æ. 3-10-26, b. Ded., of Hartshorn & Ursula A., Ded., Dover.
118 Charlie E., 11: 26: 62. trouble on brain, æ. 9-2-26, b. Walpole, of Ellis & Eliza, Walpole, Medfield.
59 Eliz'h A. (Alexander), 12: 7: 69. typhoid fever, æ. 62-5-16, b. Worcester, of Wm. & Anna.
2 Francis W., 1: 22: 61. lung fever, æ. 23-9-26, b. Medfield, of Silas & Caroline, Medfield, do.
68 Hartshorn, 5: 16: 59, rupture, æ. 47-0-0, b. Ded., of Benj. & ——.
30 John E., 4: 13: 61, heart dis., æ. 52-8-2, b. Ded., of Spencer & Rebecca, Walpole, Ded.
72 Josephine A., 9: 1: 48, dysentery, æ. 2-0-11, of Lewis & Permelia.

136 Mary R. H. (Holmes), 8: 15: 65, cancer, æ. 52-5-24, b. Ded., of Jere'h & Priscilla.
 80 Sally (Fuller), 9: 12: 57, consumption, æ. 66-0-0, b. Ded., of Jona. & Anna.
 78 Susan V., 11: 6: 61, scarlet fever, æ. 8-1-23, b. Ded., of Hartshorn & Ursula A., Ded., Dover.

BOYNTON.

 1 ——, w. of Luther, 5: 16: 46, old age, æ. 75-0-0.
 42 Luther, 7: 24: 49, fits, æ. 79-0-0.

BOSWORTH.

 23 Albert, 7: 18: 56, inflam. of brain, æ. 6-9-19, b. Ded., of Isaac & Susan.
 34 Edw. H., 11: 21: 56, cholera infantum, æ. 1: 1: 15, b. Ded., of Francis & Betsey G.
 52 Herbert, 9: 17: 58, dysentery, æ. 1-9-4, b. Ded., of Isaac & Susan H.
 39 Isaac C., 3: 24: 66, inflam. of heart, æ. 59-1-10, b. Halifax Mass., of Asa & Eliz'h.

BRACKETT.

 65 Arabella S. (Whitney), 7: 24: 68, consumption, æ. 25-10-18, b. Newton, of Geo. & Eliz'h, Watertown, Portsmouth N. H.
 34 Betsey (Galucia), 2: 25: 72, consumption, æ. 51-2-0, b. Danvers, of Isaac & Betsey, Danvers, do.
  8 Gilbert O., 1: 31: 83, consumption, æ. 43-5-18, b. Swampscott, of Elijah & Abbie, Eastham, Danvers.
 24 Isabel, 1: 23: 64, consumption, æ. 17-6-12, b. Boston, of Elijah C. & Betsey, Eastham, Lynn.
 20 Mary A. (Richardson), 3: 16: 77, consumption, æ. 28-3-8, b. ——, of T. B. & M. J.
 24 Mary W. (Hill), 4: 24: 60, consumption, 32-10-21, b. Ded., of Geo. & Lenda.
 79 Warren U., 12: 13: 66, consumption, æ. 24-3-3, b. Boston, of Elijah C. and Betsy.

BRACKIN.

 29 Bridgett, 4: 11: 85, pleuro pneumonia, æ. 63-10-19, b. Ire., of—— & ——, Ire., do.

BRADLEE, BRADLEY.

 42 ——, 5: 8: 80, stillborn, b. Ded., d. of Geo. E. & Annie, Boston, Ded.
 41 Annie (Coyne), 5: 8: 80, puerperal convulsions, æ. 25 1-21, b. Ded., of Patrick & Mary, Ire., do.
 24 Lemuel, 11: 1: 63, ——, æ. 67-0-0, b. Rox.

BRADY.

101 Wm. J., 11: 7: 81, marasmus, æ. 0-4-2, b. Ded., of James & Margaret, Ire., do.

BRANDON.

 51 John R., 4: 17: 63, dropsy, æ. 27-0-0, b. St. Jose Cal. [soldier.]

BRANIGAN.

105 Ann (Kelley), 4: 7: 86, phthisis, æ. 37-0-0, b. Ire., of Robert & Mary, Ire., do.

BRAUAR.

 29 Ernest, 3: 30: 82, marasmus, æ. 0-7-0, b. Ded., of Anton & Amelia, Germ. do.

BRAYDON.
  10 Lucy C. (Finn), 12: 13: 73, paralysis, æ. 60-0-0, b. Ire., of Wm. & Mary, Ire., do.
BREEN.
  48 Mary E., 7: 2: 86, heart dis., æ. 5-11-0, b. Ded., of David & Mary. Ire., do.
  3 Nora E., 1: 5: 87, rheumatic fever, æ. 20-7-0, b. Wales, of David & Mary, Ire., do.
BRENNAN, BRANNAN.
  3 Ellen, 1: 5: 59, croup, æ. 3-0-0, b. Ded., of Patrick & Mary.
  30 Francis, 3: 28: 84, old age, æ. 83-3-0, b. Ire., of Patrick & Belle, Ire., do.
  88 Harriet (Randall), 9: 2: 59, mortification of bowels, æ. 33-0-0, b. Johnston R. I., of Jas. & Amand.
  26 Harriet E., 5: 13: 62, lung fever, æ. 2-8-16, b. Ded., of Dennis & Harriet.
  105 Owen, 11: 16: 84, hypertrophy of heart, æ. 70-0-0, b. Ire., of —— & ——, Ire., do.
  35 Patrick, 4: 10: 84, cancer, æ. 70-0-0, b. Ire., of John & Ellen, Ire., do.
  64 Walter, 7: 7: 87, meningitis, æ. 5-10-7, b. Ded., of John J. & Bridget M., Ded., Ire.
BREWER.
  22 Daniel, 5: 6: 70, heart dis., æ. 68-2-0, b. Brewer Me., of Josiah & Anna, Worcester, Orrington Me.
BRICK.
  123 Julia A., 8: 31: 64, dysentery, æ. 1-0-18, b. Amesbury, of John & Ann, Ire., do.
  149 Margaret, 12: 7: 64, lung fever, æ. 22-0-0, b. Ire., of Daniel & Ellen, Ire., do.
BRIDGE.
  48 Caroline F., 9: 6: 53, cholera infantum, æ. 0-8-26, b. Boston, of Jere'h E. & Caroline A.
  51 Martha K., 7: 5: 73, ——, æ. 35-8-11, b. New Orleans, of Isaac & Mary B., Boston, Me.
BRIGGS.
  46 ——, 2: 20: 46, fever, æ. 3-0-0, b. Ded., s. of Joseph & ——.
  54 Caroline (Morton), w. of Robert, 5: 15: 90, old age, æ. 93-11-15, b. Hanover, of Silas & Eliz'h (Foster), Plymouth, Kingston.
  18 Chloe (Tucker), 5: 31: 50, cancer, æ. 73-0-0, b. Walp., of Jos. & Abigail.
  55 Maria (Swinburn), 4: 29: 70, ——, æ. 70-0-0.
  72 Robert, 7: 24: 82, spindle cell sarcoma of brain, æ. 60-2-6, b. Boston, of Robert & Caroline (Morton), Pembroke, Hanover.
  27 Solomon, 5: 23: 45, fever. æ. 70-0-0, b. Easton.
  25 Wm., 4: 29: 60, dropsy, æ. 50-9-24, b. Ded., of Solomon & Chloe.
BRIGHAM.
  31 Chas. W., 4: 21: 61, scarlatina, æ. 2-9-17, b. Ded., of Geo. M. & Olivia, Cambridge, Derby Vt.
BROAD.
  33 Ada A., 7: 17: 58, canker, æ. 2-4-9, b. Ded., of Salisbury & Mary J.
  90 Annette E., 11: 25: 72, consumption, æ. 20-2-11, b. Ded., of Horace & Maria, Albion Me., do.
  17 Francis S., 3: 21: 55, lung fever, æ. 0-4-0, b. Ded., of Salisbury & Mary J.

75 Francis S., 7: 13: 63, whooping cough, æ. 4-8-5, b. Ded., of Salisbury & Mary J., ——, Limington Me.

23 Herbert W., 1: 17: 64, scarlatina, æ. 5-6-6, b. Ded., of Nath'l W. & Mary E., Rox., Camden Me.

59 Horace, 11: 4: 58, inflam. of lungs, æ. 51-9-0, b. Albion Me., of Wilder & Hannah.

58 Mary J. (Kelly), 5: 26: 63, chronic diarrhœa, æ. 31-4-15, b. Limington Me., of —— & Hannah, ——, Limington Me.

BROADBENT.
103 Wm., 11: 4: 49, consumption, æ. 40-0-0.

BRODBECK.
73 Bertha (Meyer), 8: 25: 76, consumption, æ. 45-6-0, b. Wurtemburg, of Wm. & Caroline, Wurtemburg, do.

18 Ernst, 1: 25: 77, accident, æ. 5-0-0, b. Ded., of Fred'k & Bertha. Germ., do.

BRODERICK.
21 Catharine (Mullen), 3: 5: 83, consumption, æ. 36-0-0, b. Ire., of Wm. & Catharine, Ire., do.

BROMILY.
71 Ann (Hulmes), 1: 13: 52, dis. of stomach, æ. 56-0-0, b. Eng., of Jas. & Ellis.

BRONSON.
23 Alfred A., 8: 15: 50, cholera infantum, æ. 1-8-22, b. Ded., of Alfred R. & Sarah A.

9 Laura E., 3: 3: 53, scarlet fever, æ. 7-2-23, b. Ded., of Alfred R. & Sarah A.

21 Wm., 4: 18: 53, scarlet fever, æ. 0-5-0, b. Ded., of Alfred R. & Sarah A.

BROOKS.
49 Edith H., 7: 6: 78, peritonitis, æ. 12-1-21, b. Rox., of Chas. D. & Dorcas S., Eastport Me., Boston.

34 Fred'k W., 3: 21: 75, consumption, æ. 20-11-0, b. Ded., of Lemuel A. & Eliza, Boston, Conway N. H.

11 Henry, 2: 14: 87, dis. of brain, æ. 0-16-9, b. Milton, of Newman C. & Sally, Va., do.

54 Lemuel, 9: 5: 57, dis. of brain, æ. 48-10-20, b. Boston, of Wm. & Abigail.

49 Mary A. (Fullerton), 6: 15: 73, consumption, æ. 17-6-0, b. New Market N. H., of Chas. & Eliz'h, New Market N. H., Barrington N. H.

48 Mary E., 8: 25: 55, cholera infantum, æ. 1-0-22, b. Scot., of Mark & Jane.

109 Sarah (Thomas), w. of Fred'k, 10: 14: 87, phthisis pulmonalis, æ. 40-0-0, b. Orange Co. Va., of —— & Jane, Va., do.

73 Wm., 10: 6: 64, membranous croup, æ. 2-10-0, b. Ded., of Wm. & Catharine.

BROSNON.
45 ——, 5: 4: 75, stillborn, b. Ded., s. of Daniel & ——.

BROUGHTON.
41 Cornelius, 2: 2: 71, old age, æ. 93-0-0, b. Ire., of John & Catharine, Ire., do.

2 Mary, 1: 4: 59, dis. of heart, æ. 65-0-0, b. Ire.

17 Peter, 1: 16: 69, consumption, æ. 1-0-0, b. Ded., of John & Ann, Ire., do.

BROWN, BROWNE.

121 Miss, 5: 12: 48, old age, æ. ——.

63 Ann H., 6: 26: 65, typhoid fever, æ. 9-2-4, b. Newburyport, of Chas. H. & Ellen F.

83 Chas. H., 10: 17: 62, diphtheria, æ. 6-3-4, b. Ded., of Henry G. & Olive A., Rumford Me., Buckfield Me.

29 Eliza A., 9: 22: 44, typhus fever, æ 43-0-0.

63 Emma F. (Chatfield), 7: 19: 75, phthisis, æ. 24-8-0, b. Boston, of Wm. & Elizabeth, Eng., Boston.

130 Goodwin B., 11: 8: 67, consumption, æ. 32-6-6, b. Newbern N. C., of John & Jane B., Newbern N. C., do.

20 Hattie A., 3: 9: 85, cyanosis, æ. 0-0-4, b. Ded., of Willie H. & Louiza S. (Meyers), Me., Rox.

71 Jas. E., 10: 13: 86, cholera infantum, æ. 0-2-7, b. Ded., of Jas. E. & Ella E., N. S., Ded.

68 Josephine A. (Dunlap), 8: 12: 84, tuberculosis pulmonalis, æ. 36-2-0, b. Ded., of Robert H. & Mary A., Boston, Dorch.

50 Juliette (Childs), w. of Edwin N., 4: 26: 90, hemorrhage, æ. 52-0-0, b. Rox., of Jas. B. & Julia A. (Pearson), Weston, Rox.

110 Mabel F., 12: 9: 82, diphtheria, æ. 10-11-7, b. Ded., of Geo. E. & Emma F., Sudbury, Walpole.

19 Martha E. (Alden), 2: 24: 76, cancer, æ. 44-7-23, b. Ded., of Geo. & Hannah, Francestown N. H., Ded.

25 Mary W. (Weatherbee), 3: 14: 75, old age, æ. 81-7-28, b. Ded., of Comfort & Reney, Ded., do.

105 Nancy (Wellington), 12: 27: 76, obstruction of bowels, æ. 92-3-27, b. Charlestown, of Jona. & Anna, Watertown, Waltham.

55 Samuel, 2: 7: 46, ——, æ. 56-0-9.

86 Theodore F., 8: 6: 83, hydrocephaloid, æ. 0-3-18, b. Ded. of John C. & Mary L., Milton, Dorch.

107 Theodore L., 9: 4: 88, rupture of heart, æ. 66-0-14, b. Sudbury, of Israel H. & Lucy (Adams), Sudbury, Hubbardston.

119 Walter E., 8: 27: 61, pneumonia, æ. 3-5-13, b. Walpole, of Erastus & Eliza A., Mansfield, Walpole.

110 Wm. D., 11: 17: 90, R.R. accident, æ. 25-7-17, b. Sharon, of Wm. D. & Annie M. (Holmes), S. America, Sharon.

BROWNIN.

62 Arline A., 10: 9: 55, cholera infantum, æ. 1-4-0, b. Johnston R. I., of Dennis & Harriet.

BRYANT.

19 Austin, 6: 23: 51, tumor, æ. 48-0-0, b. Pembroke.

23 Luther A., 7: 19: 44, inflam. of peritoneum, æ. 11-0-0, b. Ded., of Austin & Miranda.

3 Maranda (Richards), w. of Austin, 2: 2: 50, consumption, æ. 46-6-0, b. Ded., of Luther & Polly.

22 Samuel, 7: 9: 52, old age, æ. 69-4-5, b. Petersham, of Thos. & Zuba.

BRYSON.
54 Henry L., 3: 25: 64, pneumonia, æ. ——. [soldier.]
BUCHANAN.
28 Mary B., 4: 4: 87, acute phthisis, æ. 19–6–0, b. P. E. I., of Alex'r B. & Flora
   (McDonald), Eng., P. E. I.
BUCKLEY.
110 Margaret, 12: 30: 72, small pox, æ. 40-0-9, b. Ire., of —— & ——, Ire., do.
BUDLONG.
77 Sarah E., 5: 29: 58, fits, æ. 0–0–21, b. Ded., of Albert & Sarah.
BULLARD.
130 (D. at sea) Alfred R., 5: 5: 67, phthisis, æ. 32–11–15, b. Framingham, of Geo.
    & Mary C., Framingham, Wayland.
 67 Chas., 7: 29: 71, heart comp., æ. 76–11–15, b. Ded., of Wm. & Lydia W.,
    Ded., do.
  4 Clara M., 3: 8: 51, consumption. æ. 32-0-0, b. Ded., of Elijah & Olive.
 93 (D. at Sutton), Elijah, 9: 1: 58, cholera morbus, æ. 72–0–0, b. Sutton.
 69 Eliz'h (Paul), w. of Chas., 5: 21: 88, heart dis., æ. 91–9–2, b. Dorch., of Wm.
    & Anna Damon, Ded., Attleboro.
 52 Geo. H., 7: 19: 73, consumption, æ. 24–10-1, b. Ded., of B. O. A. & Lucy A.,
    Ded., N. Y. City.
  2 John, 2: 25: 52, affection of heart, æ. 79–1–16, b. Ded., of Isaac & Patience.
 94 Lucy (Richards), 12: 30: 60, peripneumonia, æ. 80–5–12, b. Ded., of Solomon
    & Sarah, Dover, Rox.
 75 Lucy A. (Bacon), 11: 15: 71, typhoid fever, æ. 47–7–22, b. N. Y. City, of Bela
    & Lucy, Dover, do.
 56 Lydia (Whiting), 11: 24: 59, old age, æ. 87–11–0, b. Ded., of Wm. & Lydia.
 69 Lydia M., 8: 5: 71, consumption, æ. 47–9–16, b. Ded., of Wm. & Rebecca,
    Ded., do.
 13 Martha C. (Alden), 2: 19: 87, cancer, æ. 54–2–3, b. Ded., of Leonard & Ada-
    line (Swan), Roxbury N. H., Ded.
 46 Mary R. (Henderson), 6: 13: 84, fatty degeneration of heart, æ. 62–8–10, b.
    Thomaston Me., of Wm. & Lucy, Thomaston, do.
 48 Susan (Thurston), 3: 2: 71, congestion of brain, æ. 82–2–0, b. Franklin, of ——
    & Bethsheba.
 33 Willard, 8: 12: 59, chronic diarrhœa, æ. 72–5–12, b. Ded., of John & Abby.
 86 Wm., 9: 28: 79, ossification & rupture of left subclavian artery, æ. 63–5–8, b.
    Ded., of John & Lucy R., Ded., do.
BUNKER.
 38 Stephen J., 8: 30: 58, typhoid fever, æ. 21–5–0, b. Cambridge, of Stephen &
    Sarah E.
BURBANK.
 71 Isabella (Roberts), 8: 22: 80, inflam. of bowels, æ. 76–8–2, b. Eng., of Jas.
    & ——.
BURGESS.
 29 Abby P., 4: 24: 55, dis. of brain, æ. 0–7–29, b. Springfield, of Eben'r P. &
    Carrie F.

53 Abigail B. (Phillips), 7: 1: 72, old age, æ. 82-4-24, b. Bos., of Wm. & Miriam M., Boston, do.

96 Anne, 2: 2: 70, old age, æ. 81-10-0, b. Great Britain.

1 Carrie F. (Guild), 1: 3: 59, ulcer on stomach, æ. 29-0-0, b. Ded., of Francis & Caroline E.

89 Eben'r, 12: 5: 70, inflam. of kidneys, æ. 80-8-5, b. Wareham, of Eben'r & Martha (Swift), Wareham, Mass.

89 D. in Paris, France Eben'r G., 5: 14: 77, tumor on brain, æ. 50 10-0, b. Ded., of Eben'r & Abigail B., Wareham, Boston.

108 Lucy (Baker), w. of Isaac J., 11: 3: 90, heart dis., æ. 74-6-14, b. Ded., of David & Dene (Holmes), Ded., Sharon.

BURKE.

60 Bridget, 4: 19: 64, scarlatina, æ. 1-4-0, b. Ded., of Thos. & Mary.

95 Frances, 11: 25: 63, consumption, æ. 10-5-0, b. W. Rox., of John & Winifred, Ire., do.

42 John, 9: 21: 62, teething, æ. 1-1-27, b. Ded., of Thos. & Mary. Ire., do.

BURLINGAME.

108 Ada M., 11: 18: 83, dis. of heart, æ. 16-9-7, b. Medway, of Adin B. & Eliz'h.

BURNAM.

40 ——, 11: 1: 47, cholera infantum, æ. 8-0-0.

BURNETT.

44 Warren W., 5: 6: 72, accidental, æ. 72-3-17, b. Oxford, of Warren & Emeline.

BURNS, BYRNES.

44 Bridget, 10: 7: 62, fits, æ. 7-6-7, b. Ded., of Michael & Mary.

46 Esther (Quigg), 3: 13: 67, old age, æ. 88-2-3, b. Litchfield N. H., of David & Mary, Litchfield N. H., do.

78 Frank, 9: 4: 85, convulsions, æ. 0-0-8, b. Ded., of Thos. J. & Maria, Ire., do.

70 Henry, 11: 8: 66, consumption, æ. 20-0-0, b. Ire., of Michael & Mary.

7 John, 2: 1: 79, pneumonia, æ. 65-0-0, b. Ire., of David & Johanna, Ire., do.

27 John J., 3: 19: 83, membraneous croup, æ. 5-6-15, b. Ded., of Jos. & Catharine, Ire., do.

22 Jos. A., 3: 14: 87, premature birth, æ. 0-0-1, b. Ded., of Jos. F. & Catharine, Ire., do.

35 Julia, 2: 6: 68, burnt, æ. 9-11-0, b. Ded., of Michael & Mary, Ire., do.

95 Laura, 10: 22: 79, consumption, æ. 15-3-0, b. N. C., of Jas. & Susan.

1 Mary (Lynch), 1: 3: 86, heart dis., æ. 56-0-0, b. Ire., of Jas. & Mary. Ire., do.

27 Mary A., 8: 9: 51, fit, æ. 2-10-0, b. Ire., of Michael & Mary.

5 Mary A., 2: 8: 54, fits, æ 0-0-19, b. Ded., Michael & Mary.

110 Michael, 10: 22: 89, hemorrhage of stomach, æ. 53-0-0, b. Ire., of Daniel & Bridget (Darcey), Ire., do.

45 Thomas, 7: 9: 61, consumption, æ. 32-0-0, b. Ire.

2 Wm. E., 1: 8: 64, teething, 0-10-0, b. Woonsocket R. I., of Edw. & Margaret.

BURR.

81 Ann S. (Smith), 12: 3: 73, slow fever, æ. 64: 11: 20, b. Walpole, of John & Mariam, Walpole, do.

10 Chas. F., 7: 20: 76, cholera infantum, æ. 0-0-14, b. Ded., of Sanford S. & E.
     J., Foxboro, Suncook N. H.

19 Chas. T., 8: 28: 67, marasmus, æ. 0-2-9, b. Ded., of Lafayette & Abby S.,
     Prov. R. I., Amherst.

73 Freddie W., 12: 30: 74, inflam. of lungs, æ. 0-4-10, b. Ded., of Sanford S. &
     Eliza J., Foxboro, Suncook N. H.

BUSSEY.

17 ——, 1: 26: 88, stillborn, b. Ded., d. of Horace G. & Henrietta L., Medfield,
     Dorch.

107 ——, 10: 27: 90, stillborn, b. Ded., d. of Horace G. & Henrietta L. (Clapp),
     Medfield, Dorch.

BUTLER.

24 Edward, 3: 19: 57, stagnat'n of blood, æ. 36-0-0, b. Ire., of Rich'd & Bridget.

65 Hannah, 6: 11: 89, heart dis., æ. 59-4-0, b. Ire., of John & Mary (Coney),
     Ire., do.

65 Mary A., 12: 14: 58, canker, æ. 0-2-3, b. Ded., of Wm. & Winneford.

BUTNAM.

42 Edward, 4: 6: 77, old age, æ. 77-3-0, b. Tyngsboro, of Thos. & Sarah P., Mar-
     blehead, Newburyport.

107 Thos. P., 8: 31: 72, pulmonary consumption, æ. 32-1-10, b. Boston, of Edw.
     & Nancy, Tyngsboro, Boston.

BUTTERFIELD.

73 D. at Boston) Sarah K., 6: 9: 89, peritonitis, æ. 42-0-0, b. Wilton Me., of
     Geo. & ——.

CAGEN.

51 Wm., 11: 7: 59, cancer, æ. 70-0-0, b. Ire., of Patrick & Rose.

CAHILL.

93 Annie A., 10: 31: 80, dis. of heart, æ. 17-6-0, b. Ded., of John & Annie,
     Ire., do.

121 Bridget, 8: 30: 64, cholera morbus, æ. 0-9-28, b. Ded., of John & Honora,
     Ire., do.

112 Honora (Flanagan), w. of John, 10: 24: 87, pneumonia, æ. 55-0-0, b. Ire., of
     Dennis & ——, Ire., do.

69 Julia A., 10: 2: 86, heart dis., æ. 29- 6-0, b. Lawrence, of John & Honora,
     Ire., do.

39 Mary (Flaharty), 5: 15: 69, lung fever, æ. 66-0-0, b. Ire., of Patrick & Honora.

29 Michael, 12: 27: 67, inflam. of lungs, æ. 0-5-0, b. Ded., of John & Honora,
     Ire., do.

CAIN.

26 Eliz'h (Wright), 3: 19: 57, paralysis, æ. 73-0-0, b. Dunbarton N. H., of John
     & Abigail.

CALDER.

24 David B., 7: 3: 59, accidental shooting, æ. 13-7-22, b. Ded., of Jas. & Anna H.

97 Lucy A., 9: 10: 87, oedema pulmonum, æ. 52-4-4, b. Ded., of Jas. & Anna H.
     (Baker), Prov. R. I., Ded.

CALDWELL.
23 ——, 5: 14: 45, inflam. of bowels, æ. 17-0-0, b. ——, d. of —— &

CALLAHAN (see also O'Callaghan.)
117 Cornelius, 2: 6: 67, dis. of brain, æ. 1-5-13, b. Ded., of Morty & Catharine, Ire., do.
126 Dennis, 12: 31: 62, brain fever, æ. 1-2-10, b. Ded., of Morty & Catharine. Ire., do.
47 Maggie, 5: 12: 83, meningitis, æ. 3-4-0, b. Ded., of Daniel & Mary, Ire., do.
102 Wm., 11: 16: 84, catarrhal pneumonia, æ. 0-3-0, b. Ded., of Daniel & Mary, Ire., do.

CALLAN.
70 Barnard, 3: 24: 69, croup, æ. 2-11-2, b. Sharon, of Edw. & Johanna, Ire, do.

CALLEHN.
14 John, 2: 5: 57, lung fever, æ. 0-3-4, b. Ded., of Cornelius & Hannah.

CAMERON.
68 Walter J., 7: 18: 87, cholera morbus, æ. 6-10-1, b. Ded., of Jas. B. & Eliz'h H., N. S., do.

CAMPBELL.
58 Annie (Erons), 7: 1: 85, cerebral meningitis, æ. 61-11-13, b. N. B., of John & Eliz'h.
82 Caroline E. (Hayden), 9: 30: 77, childbirth, æ. 28-8-20, b. Framingham, of Chas. & Mary D., Framingham, Waltham.
101 Laura, 9: 14: 65, dysentery, æ. 0-5-25, b. Ded., of Robert & Mary A.
69 Mary, 9: 28: 73, teething, æ. 1-3-21, b. Bridgewater, of —— & Mary, ——, N. B.

CANING.
78 Thos., 12: 11: 64, consumption, æ. 34-0-0, b. Ire., of Thos. & Bridget.

CANNON.
120 Bridget, 12: 4: 65, croup, æ. 1-3-0, b. Ded., of Michael & Bridget.
68 Bridget (Gilroy), 6: 22: 67, congestion of brain, æ. 38-0-0, b. Ire., of Michael & Dorothy, Ire., do.
74 Michael, 7: 19: 62, scarlet fever, æ. 1-6-0, b. Canton, of Patrick & Bridget, Ire., do.
11 Thos., 8: 12: 66, infantile dis., æ. 0-0-7, b. Ded., of John & Margaret.

CAPEN.
23 Betsey J. (Johnson), 9: 2: 47, cholera morbus, æ. 58-0-0, b. Sharon, of Caleb & ——.
115 Lucy R. (Seaver), 12: 17: 81, pneumonia, æ. 64-6-20, b. Easton, of Calvin & Dolly (Austin), Bridgewater, Easton.
110 Oliver, 10: 23: 65, tumor in throat, æ. 61-0-9, b. Ded., of Nath'l & Submit.
42 Sarah A. (Whiting), w. of Oliver, 3: 27: 88, broncho pneumonia, æ. 79-3-17. b. Ded., of Calvin & Eliz'h (Fuller), Ded., do.

CARBERRY.
78 ——, 9: 1: 79, stillborn, b. Ded., s. of John & Minnie, Ire., Eng.
55 Clifton G., 6: 4: 76, albuminuria, æ. 4-5-26, b. Ded., of Wm. & Eliz'h, Scot., Eng.

34 Lizzie A., 4:6:81, meningitis. æ. 0-9-0, b. Ded.,of Andrew & Anna M. (Rich),
　　Ire., Bos.
80 Minnie (Sullivan), 9: 7: 79, childbirth. æ. 23-0-0, b. Eng., of Timothy & Nora,
　　Ire., Eng.

CARDEN.
15 ——, 7: 10: 47, ——, æ. ——.

CARLETON.
5 Dana F., 1:6:90, pneumonia. æ. 1-11-27, b. Ded., of John E. & Mary T.
　　(Smith), Me., do.

CARLON.
7 ——, 2: 13:62, stillborn, b. Ded., of Lawrence & Ann.
56 Ann (Fagan), 7: 29: 86, cancer, æ. 61-0-0, b. Ire., of Thos. & Ellen, Ire., do.
93 James, 4: 19: 64, consumption, æ. 6-8-14, b. Ded., of Michael & Ann, Ire.,do.
4 Margaret, 1: 30: 53, convulsion fits, æ. 0-4-22, b. Ded., of Michael & Ann.
81 Michael, 9: 14: 79, consumption, æ. 63-0-0, b. Ire., of Thos. & Rose, Ire., do.
8 Rose (Denner) 6: 2: 72, old age, æ. 77-0-0, b. Ire., of Patrick & Mary.
31 Thos., 6: 13: 60, scarlatina, æ. 3-3-13, b. Ded., of Lawrence & Anna, Ire., do.
67 Thos. H., 11: 23: 53, typhoid fever, æ. 6-10-11, b. Taunton, of Michael & Ann.

CARNS.
81 John, 2: 12: 59, dis. of brain, æ. 4-0-0, b. Medway, of Stephen & Catherine.

CARPENTER.
50 ——, 7:3: 77, stillborn, b. Ded., s. of Chas. & Rosa, Canada, do.
32 Timothy, 6: 15: 69, drowning, æ. 55-3-10, b. S. Kingston, of Timothy &
　　Mary, S, Kingston, Charlestown R. I.

CARR.
60 Sarah (Higgins), 8: 4: 72, consumption of blood, æ. 77-5-11, b. Bath Me., of
　　Benj. & Hannah, Bath Me., do.

CARRIGAN.
16 Eugene, 3: 31: 54, fits, æ. 3-4-0, b. Ded., of James & Mary.
27 Honora, 7: 18: 54, consumption, æ. 29-0-0, b. Ire., of Eugene & Catharine.
67 James, 11: 2: 55, consumption. æ. 1-9-0, b. Ded., of Jas. & Mary.
21 Mary, 6: 26: 51, bowel comp., æ. 25-0-0, b. Ire.

CARROLL.
27 Catharine (Daily), 7: 10: 59, scarlet fever, æ. 33-0-0, b. Ire., of Thomas &
　　Catharine.
3 Catharine A. (Welch), 1: 3: 79, liver comp., æ. 31-3-3, b. W. Rox., of Patrick
　　& Bridget, Ire., do.
[D. at Bull Run, Va., Chas. W., 9: 2: 62, killed in battle, æ. 26-3-2, b. Ded.,
　　of Sanford & Harriet (Whiting), Walpole, Ded.]
54 Clara M., 10: 30: 51, croup, æ. 6-7-9, b. Ded., of Sanford & Clarissa.
100 Clarissa (Alden), w. of Sanford, 10: 13: 99, heart dis., æ. 67-10-25, b. Ded., of
　　Francis & Sarah (Crehore), Needham, Ded.
39 Emily F., 4: 29: 45, ——, æ. 0-5-0, b. Ded., d. of Sanford & Clarissa.
16 Emma J., 3: 30: 53, consumption, æ. 3-1-20, b. Ded., of Sanford & Clarissa.
107 Grace M., 12: 13: 85, typhilitis, æ. 11-2-23, b. Ded., of Wm. F. & Grace, Ire.,do.

35 Gracie M., 5:13: 87, membranous croup, æ. 1-5-0, b. Ded., of Wm. F. & Grace M., Ire., do.

73 Hannah E. (Curran), 8:23: 85, consumption, æ. 24-7-2, b. Boston, of Daniel & Eliz'h, Ire., do.

1 Henry G., 1: 11: 74, consumption, æ. 28-0-6, b. Ire., of Henry & Isabella, Ire., do.

60 Isabella, 8: 22: 73, cholera infantum, æ. 0-7-4, b. Rox., of Henry G. & Catherine, Ire., Rox.

3 Jas., 1: 15: 81, pyrexia, æ. 0-10-16, b. Ded., of Jas. & Mary, Ire., do.

97 Katie, 11: 21: 80, diphtheria, æ. 3-0-0, b. Ded., of Wm. F. & Grace, Ire., do.

32 Kittie, 5:3: 87, diphtheria, æ. 5-10-24, b. Ded., of Wm. F. & Grace M., Ire., do.

13 Mary, 11: 3: 70, enlargement of liver, æ. 0-6-0, b. Ded., of Wm. F. & Grace, Ire., W. Rox.

7 Sally, 8: 21 : 46, fever, æ. 35-0-0.

96 Wm., 11: 20: 80, diphtheria, æ. 4-6-0, b. Ded., of Wm. F. & Grace, Ire., do.

103 Wm. T., 4: 3: 86, pneumonia, æ. 2-9-25, b. Ded., of Wm. F. & Grace, Ire., do.

CARSON.

75 Mary G., 8: 25: 80, cholera infantum, æ. 0-4-29, b. Boston, of —— & Fannie, ——, N. F.

CARTER.

19 Chas., 4: 21: 58, typhoid fever, æ. 10-7-24, b. Pottsville Pa., of Joshua E. & Susan.

56 Ellen (Holt), 10: 8: 58, consumption, æ. 50-0-0, b. Eng., of Chris'r & Eliz'h.

57 Eva I., 3: 31: 64, water on brain, æ. 0-8-10, b. Ded., of Henry J. & Louisa, Hudson N. Y., Pittsfield.

89 Harriet (Tyler), 10: 24: 78, old age, æ. 89-10-0, b. Boston.

89 Joshua E., 6: 13: 61, apoplectic fit, æ. 48-4-8, b. Warner N. H., of Thos. & Susan, Warner N. H., do.

66 Susan (Reed), 6: 12: 63, consumption, æ. 50-0-0, b. Freeport Me., of Reuben & Mary, Freeport, do.

44 Theresa P., 12: 17: 51, croup, æ. 1-8-13, b. Ded., of John D. & Eliz.

48 Wm., 5: 13: 83, bilious fever, æ. 70-7-0, b. Boston, of Thos. & Mary.

CARTWRIGHT.

47——, 5: 28: 75, stillborn, b. Ded., of John W. & ——.

CARVERHILL.

124 David, 11: 7: 88, R. R. accident, æ. 40-0-0, b. Eng.

CARY, CAREY.

41 Catherine, 7: 14: 55, consumption, æ. 12-0-0, b. Ire., of Thos. & Bridget.

45 Ellen, 8: 15: 55, cholera infantum, æ. 0-0-11, b. Ded., of Thos. & Bridget.

71 John, 7: 2: 63, congestion of lungs, æ. 45-0-0, b. Ire., of Michael & Ellen, Ire., do.

2 Margaret B. (Everett), w. of A., 1: 12: 55, consumption, æ. 38-7-1, b. Ded., of Willard & Sarah.

CASEY.

115 ——, 3: 13: 63, ——, æ. 0-0-1, b. Ded., d. of Thos. & Mary M. N., Ire., do.

148 Edward, 12: 28: 63, ——, æ. 0-0-1, b. Ded., of Thos. & Mary.

204 John, 12: 9: 64, ——, æ. 0-0-10, b. Ded., of Thos. & Mary, Ire., do.

CASHMAN.

52 Katherine (Sullivan), 6: 19: 85, pneumonia, æ. 50-0-9, b. Ire., of Timothy & Ellen, Ire., do.

CASSEDY.

49 Andrew, 3: 8: 71, drowned, æ. 45-0-0, b. Ire.

CASSELL.

95 Edmund D., 8: 6: 88, cirrhosis, æ. 86-4-6, b. Boston, of James and Abigail (Dolbeare), Eng., Boston.

107 Sophia P. (Parker), 11: 29: 79, paralysis, æ. 73-7-19, b. ——, of Jonas & Esther L.

CASSIER.

3 Anthony, 4: 12: 69, Bright's dis., æ. 2-11-27, b. Ded., of Leon & Josephine, Holland, Austria.

2 Katie, 3: 26: 69, scarlet fever, æ. 3-6-0, b. Ded., of Leon & Josephine, Holland, Austria.

CAWLEY.

38 Ellen (Gleason), 5: 27: 86, pneumonia, æ. 57-9-0, b. Ire., of Michael & Johanna, Ire., do.

10 James, 2: 13: 83, cancer, æ. 61-10-0, b. Ire., of Hugh & Margaret, Ire., do.

8 Joanna, 11: 29: 73, inflam. of bowels, æ. 21-10-0, b. Ded., of John & Ellen, Ire., do.

80 Margaret M., 11: 10: 86, phthisis, æ. 33-9-10, b. Ded., of John & Ellen, Ire., do.

42 Winnifred, 7: 13: 60, scarlatina, æ. 3-4-0, b. Ded., of John & Ellen, Ire., do.

CHAMBERLAIN.

41 Alfred E., 7: 23: 74, dysentery, æ. 1-11-4, b. Ded., of Curtis & Anna H., W. Rox., Brighton.

46 Arthur D., 3: 27: 68, lung fever, æ. 0-1-18, b. Ded., of Geo. & Mary L., W. Rox., Boston.

45 Geo. J., 5: 7: 66, drowned, æ. 1-8-26, b. Cal., of Geo. W. & Louisa.

80 Harriet E., 8: 10: 90, cancer, æ. 21-2-7, b. W. Rox., of Warren R. & Mary E. (Onion), W. Rox., do.

92 Isaac E., 5: 9: 71, phthisis, æ. 73-1-0, b. Rox., of Isaac & Sarah, ——, Ded.

33 Mary A., 5: 3: 75, croup, æ. 0-1-0, b. Ded., of Geo. W. & Mary L., Boston, do.

61 Mary F., 6: 12: 90, tabes mesenterica, æ. 31-9-16, b. Lawrence, of Chas. T. & Harriet (Fales), Westboro, Ded.

32 Mary L. (Gray), 4: 20: 75, pneumonia, æ. 37-9-6, b. Boston, of Samuel W. & Mary A., N. H., Boston.

67 Nancy, w. of Isaac, 6: 5: 48, mortification in bowels, æ. 33-0-0, b. Canton.

2 Sarah, 1: 7: 51, old age, æ. 77-0-0.

47 Wm., 3: 1: 71, ——, æ. 0-0-12, b. Ded., of Geo. W. & Mary L., W. Rox., Bost.

CHANDLER.

35 —— (White), 10: 2: 45, consumption, æ. 24-0-0, b. Ded., of Joseph & Lois.

22 Eliza J. (Wentworth), 7: 11: 56, consumption, æ. 34-11-11, b. Dorch., of Jason & Bethiah.

CHAPMAN.
26 Daniel, 4: 4: 78, tumor, æ. 66–10–24, b. Salem.
 1 Geo. A., 2: 11: 65, disease of liver, æ. 18–9–0, b. Haverhill, of Andrew J. & Ann D. [soldier].

CHARRON.
 5 Henry, 4: 13: 72, typhoid fever, æ. 19–6–0, b. Canada, of Wm. & Mary.

CHASE.
33 Bertha F., 4: 1: 83, convulsions, æ. 0–10–3, b. Ded., of Albert S. & Mary E., Ded., do.
74 Betsey J. (Bolton), 1: 13: 74, old age, æ. 82–0–0, b. Taunton, of —— & ——, ——, Taunton.
21 Caroline (Colburn), 4: 7: 60, consumption, æ. 23–8–25, b. Ded., of James & Charlotte.
61 David, 12: 27: 54, liver complaint, æ. 72–6–13, b. Pomfret Ct., of Seth & Mary.
21 David N., 2: 9: 90, paralysis, æ. 74–0–19, b. Ded., of David & Betsey J., Ded., do.
18 Frankie, 2: 22: 76, scrofula, æ. 2–0–0, b. Ded., of Wm. & Lucy, Pa., Va.
10 George H., 2: 19: 55, fit, æ. 24–0–10, b. Boston, of John & Achsah.
26 Grace L., 3: 24: 80, membranous laryngitis, æ. 0–8–6, b. Ded., of John W. & Harriett E., Epping N. H., Freeport Me.
27 Harriet (Rice), 5: 24: 53, consumption, æ. 29–0–0, b. Charlestown, of Phineas & Sally.
42 Henry A., 9: 23: 54, dysentery, æ. 2–11–14, b. Ded., of David N. & Anna E.
86 Jas. M., 10: 18: 60, liver comp., æ. 42–7–6, b. Ded., of David & Betsey, Pomfret Ct., Taunton.
47 Lizzie J., 4: 7: 88, diphtheria, æ. 23–2–4, b. Ded., of David N. & Anna E., Ded., do.
70 Willie E., 8: 6: 75, scrofula, æ. 3–4–9, b. Windsor Ct., of Wm. H. & Lucy, Harrisburg Pa., Culpepper Va.

CHATER.
15 ——, w. of Wm., 9: 17: 46, fever, æ. 55–0–0.

CHENEY.
58 ——, 4: 30: 45, ——, æ. 0–1–0, —— of L. & E.
171 (D. at Weston, Vt.) Adeline F., 2: 1: 64, inflam. of bowels, æ. 14–5–9, b. Boston, of Oramel F. & Mary A., Thetford Vt., Londonderry Vt.
144 Alfred S., 12: 7: 63, inflam. of bowels, æ. 5–7–6, b. Ded., of Simon & Eliza A., ——, Ded.
80 Amanda, 10: 16: 56, fits, æ. 44–0–0, b. Dover, of Simon & ——.
75 Chas. E., 3: 18: 57, consumption, æ. 0–4–9, b. Ded., of Simon & Eliza A.
79 (D. at Walpole) Fred. A., 8: 24: 79, convulsions, æ. 1–11–22, b. Ded., of Martin L. & Harriet A., Ded., Andover.
48 Harriet A. (Smith), 6: 10: 79, epilepsy, æ. 34–6–22, b. Andover, of Thos. & Harriet P., Andover, N. S.
34 Henry C., 4: 25: 61, debility, æ. 0–0–14, b. Ded., of O. F. & Mary A., Thetford Vt., Londonderry Vt.

24 Henry H., 12: 7: 68, liver comp., æ. 11-0-0, b. Ded., of Samuel & Sarah.

141 (D. at N. Y. City) Lucy E. (Chickering), w. of Wm. F., 4: 20: 87, apoplexy, æ. 37-1-2, b. St. Louis Mo., of Wm. & Abigail F. (Monroe), Ded., Boston.

92 Luther, 3: 21: 73, dropsy, æ. 65-8-0, b. Dover, of Simon & ——.

33 Mary A. (Warner), 4: 18: 61, puerperal fever, æ. 34-0-0, b. Londonderry Vt., of Daniel & Huldah (Howe).

59 Olive, 10: 16: 57, tumor, æ. 64-5-28, b. Dover, of John & Hannah.

119 Oramel F., 12: 2: 62, accidental burning, æ. 36-0-20, b. Thetford Vt., of Elias E. & Lucy. Campton N. H., Dunstable.

14 Sarah D. (Dascomb), 2: 7: 77, cancer, æ. 63-0-0, b. W. Rox., of —— & Hannah J., Eng., W. Rox.

CHESTER.

115 John, 12: 31: 82, old age, æ. 86-4-18, b. Boston, of Christopher & Lucy.

33 Rebecca (Ralston), 10: 28: 56, paralysis, æ. 65-0-0, b. Philadelphia, of Robert & Sarah.

54 Sarah (Wellington), w. of John, 5: 15: 89, old age, æ. 88-5-3, b. Boston, of Jonathan & Annie (Garfield), Boston, do.

CHICKERING.

44 Abigail F. (Munroe), 5: 16: 80, paralysis, æ. 57-3-17, b. Northboro, of Wm. & Rebecca, Northboro, do.

22 (D. at Medfield) David, 12: 3: 68, lung fever, æ. ——, b. Medfield.

78 Dean, 12: 20: 52, dis. of heart, æ. 65-0-0, b. Andover, of Dean & Mary.

64 Gertrude E., 12: 26: 60, scarlet fever, æ. 11-4-22, b. Ded., of Wm. & Abby F., Ded., Northboro.

53 Hannah B., 7: 3: 79, paralysis, æ. 61-11-3, b. Ded., of Jabez & Deborah D. F., Ded., Quincy.

5 Horatio, 4: 8: 75, apoplexy, æ. 65-0-0, b. Ded., of Jabez & Dorothy D., Ded., Milton.

28 Horatio L., 9: 20: 56, dis. of brain, æ. 0-5-0, b. Ded., of Wm. & Abby R.

53 Lucy E., 7: 12: 84, progressive paralysis, æ. 78-3-3, b. Ded., of Jabez & Dorothy D. F. A., Ded., Milton.

76 William H., 14: 73, apoplexy, æ. 58-0-0, b. Ded., of Jabez & Deborah D., Ded., ——.

CHILD.

71 Lewis F., 9: 13: 68, teething, æ. 0-10-4, b. Ded., of Lewis & Sarah F., Fairlee Vt., Prov. R. I.

CHIPMAN.

79 Hubert, 8: 25: 82, cholera infantum, æ. 0-11-27, b. Boston, of —— & Annie A., ——, Germ.

53 Rosanna (Waver), 6: 21: 85, cardiac paralysis, æ. 69-0-0, b. Germ., of —— & ——, Germ., do.

CHISHOLM.

56 Isabel (Graham), 6: 30: 68, old age, æ. 74-4-23, b. Scot., of John & Janet, Scot., do.

26 Wm., 1: 3: 68, heart dis., æ. 73-11-14, b. Scot., of Geo. & Mary, Scot., do.

CHOATE.

1 Lucy P. (Roberts), w. of Albert F., 1: 1: 88, tumor of brain, æ. 41-11-7. b. Biddeford, Me., of Daniel & Sarah G., Lyman Me., Guilford Me.

CHURCH.

31 Eliza, 7: 29: 59, dis. of heart, æ. 0-5-0, b. Ded., of John & Abby.

43 Ellen, 8: 15: 53, cholera infantum, æ. 1-4-16, b. Ded., of John & Mary.

42 Wm., 8: 25: 58, cholera infantum, æ. 0-8-0, b. Ded., of John & Abby.

CHURCHILL.

6 Caroline A., 2: 18: 53, croup, æ. 3-4-17, b. Ded., of Chauncey C. & Permelia.

39 Chauncey C., 4: 18: 80, chronic dis. of digestive organs, æ. 73 6-23, b. W. Fairlee Vt., of Wm. L. & Eliza (Lamphear).

CIRIACK.

104 Chas. L., 10: 30: 82, phthisis, æ. 56-0-0, b. Germ., of John G. & Christiana E., Germ., do.

64 Frank, 6: 9: 67, lung fever, æ. 4-5-6, b. Ded., of Lewis & Honora, Germ., Ireland.

CLAFLIN.

50 Rebecca G. (Starkweather), 4: 5: 64, congestion of lungs, æ. 61-11-26, b. Pawtucket R. I., of Oliver & Miriam.

CLAP, CLAPP.

46 ——, 5: 21: 66, ——, æ. 0-0-0, b. Ded., s. of John & Sarah A.

56 ——, 4: 30: 70, convulsions, æ. 0-0-3, b. Ded., s. of John & Sarah A., Walpole, do.

41 Betsy (Doggett), 12: 20: 50, lung fever, æ. 72-5-26, b. Ded., of Samuel & Eliz.

43 Chas. W., 5: 17: 76, heart dis., æ. 31-11-10, b Ded., of Nath'n'l & Eliz'h D., Walpole, Ded.

9 Eliz., 6: 13: 44, consumption, æ. 75-0-0.

29 Ellen F., 4: 2: 49, consumption, æ. 23-0-0, b.Ded., of Supply & Priscilla.

55 Henry F., 1: 2: 62, consumption, æ. 27-10-27, b. Ded., of Nath'l & Eliz'h D., Walpole, Ded.

73 Jane D., 10: 22: 73, consumption, æ. 19-4-14, b. Ded., of Nath'l & Elizabeth D., Walpole, Ded.

71 Mary B., 9: 13: 72, consumption, æ. 24-6-4, b. Ded., of Nath'l & Eliz'h D., Walpole, Ded.

75 Nath'l, 7: 27: 80, pneumonia, æ. 85-10-14, b. Walpole, of Levi & Eliz'h (Wallace), Walpole, Mass.

18 Priscilla, 11: 22: 48, consumption, æ. 57-0-0.

77 Sarah A. (Bullard), 9: 28: 72, prostration, æ. 34-5-2, b. Walpole, of Horace & Ann, Walpole, Taunton.

56 Supply, 8: 5: 65, paralysis, æ. 82-0-22, b. Walpole, of Seth & Eliz'h.

58 Susanna, 9: 26: 57, cholera infantum, æ. 0-10-21, b. Ded., of Albert S. & Susanna.

CLARK, CLARKE.

100 —— (Jordan), w. of David, 12: 17: 57, old age, æ. 78-0-0, b. Stoughton, of Abraham & ——.

2 Bridget, 2: 25: 68, whooping cough, æ. 0-3-0, b. Ded., of John & Ann, Ire.,do.

97 Catharine, 8: 26: 57, old age, æ. 80-0-0.
79 Chas. H., 9: 25: 78, enteritis, æ. 1-8-16, b. Ded., of Edw. F. & Evelyn A., Friendship Me., Sudbury.
100 Elvira R. (Richards), 11: 4: 81, obstruction of bowels, æ. 67-10-18, b. Ded., of Joel & Susan, Ded., Stoughton.
58 Horatio, 8: 16: 73, consumption, æ. 63-5-8, b. Ded., of Jacob & Prudence, Medfield, Ded.
93 Katy, 11: 11: 76, puerperal convulsions, æ. 16-7-4, b. Ded., of John & Ann, Ire., do.
94 Katy, 11: 12: 76, convulsions, æ. 0-0-2, b. Ded., of —— & Katy, ——, Ded.
54 Pitt, 4: 27: 70, pneumonia, æ. 62-11-13, b. Ded., of Jacob & Prudence, Medfield, Ded.
5 Randolph M., 9: 11: 73, rheumatism of heart, æ. 38-1-5, b. Boston, of Jos. W. & Eleanor, East Hampton, Prov. R. I.
45 Sophia (Warren) 8: 30: 74, old age, æ. 80-9-9, b. Royalston, of Alvan & Mary.
132 Wm. A., 9: 25: 64, membranous croup, æ. 3-5-25, b Rox., of Franklin & Ann, Amherst N. H., Friendship Me.

CLARKIN.
30 Mary (McGinn), 4: 11: 80, consumption, æ. 76-0-0, b. Ire., of Hugh & Mary, Ire., do.

CLAYTON.
27 Lucy A. (Wilson), 3: 18: 75, consumption, æ. 46-0-0, b. Enfield Ct., of Eli & Lucy.

CLEARY. CLARY.
14 Francis, 1: 20: 90, pleuro pneumonia, æ. 26-0-0, b. Ire., of Philip & Margaret Ire., do.
64 John, 8: 29: 86. convulsions, æ. 0-9-15, b. Ded., of Edw. F. & Mary V., Boston, Millville R. I.
75 Mary (Watson), 11: 12: 64, consumption, æ. 65-0-0, b. Ire., of Patrick &——.
7 Michael, 1: 27: 76, convulsions, æ. 0-0-7, b. Ded., of John & Bridget, Ire.,do.
47 Wm., 9: 4: 58, congestion of lungs, æ. 0-4-18, b. Ded., of Thos. & Eliza.

CLEMENT.
76 Jas. W., 7: 22: 83, summer comp., æ. 0-9-0, b. Ded.. of Wm. & Mary M., Boston, do.

CLEVELAND.
122 Ira, 12: 21: 89, congestion of lungs, æ. 87-10-20, b. Hopkinton, of Ira & Mehitable (Battelle), Dover, do.

CLIFFORD.
28 Ella J., 5: 31: 53, inflam. of bowels, æ. 0-0-25, b. Ded., of John W. & Ellen E.
38 Samuel N., 6: 16: 49, drowned, æ. 25-7-0.

CLIFTON.
40 Maria F. (Cobb), 5: 5: 84, acute pneumonia, æ. 74-0-5, b. Sharon, of Jonathan & Sibbel, Taunton, Sharon.

CLISBY.

41 Florence M., 5: 22: 79, consumption, æ. 0–10–0, b. Ded., of Alphonso E. & Lizzie J., Me., Ct.

61 Mary A. (Withington), 6: 23: 70, consumption of blood, æ. 26–8–10, b. Rox., of Warren & Watey, Canton, Chatham.

106 Medora I. (Withington), 11: 12: 83, consumption, æ. 29–11–22, b. Ded., of Warren & Watey, Canton, Chatham.

CLOSE.

83 ——, 12: 8: 73, stillborn, b. Ded., d. of John & Mary, Eng., do.

12 ——, 1: 22: 75, stillborn, b. Ded., s. of John & Mary, Eng., Ire.

CLYNE.

66 Angelina, 8: 13: 76, teething, æ. 0–3–0, b. Ded., of Christian & Amelia, Germ., do.

COAKLEY.

90 John, 4: 25: 57, consumption, æ. 29–1–21, b. Hallowell Me., of Jas. & Ellen.

119 John E., 12: 31: 81, consumption, æ. 24–5–23, b. Ded., of John & Henrietta L. (Robinson), Rox., Richmond Me.

COAN.

62 John, 2: 22: 49, consumption, æ. 25–0–0, b. Ire.

COBB.

15 Daniel, 3: 12: 55, hemorrhage of lungs, æ. 63–10–23, b. Ded., of Daniel & Deliverance.

33 Henry W., 6: 8: 74, congestion of lungs, æ. 1–6–17, b. Ded., of Jonathan & Martha S., Ded., Boston.

11 Jennie E., 2: 14: 83, ——, æ. 3–6–10, b. Ded., of Samuel D. & Mary T., Ded., do.

22 Jonathan H., 3: 12: 82, progressive paralysis, æ. 82–8–4, b. Sharon, of Jonathan & Sibbel (Holmes), Attleboro, Sharon.

92 Joseph H., 11: 16: 76, strangulated hernia, æ. 20–0–0, b. Chicago Ill., of Henry L. & Sophia S., ——, Rox.

47 Martha S. (Wales) 6: 29: 77, diabetes, æ. 45–3–5, b. Boston, of Samuel Jr., & Martha A., Stoughton, Boston.

15 Mary G. (Gay), 1: 7: 74, paralysis, æ. 74–11–0, b. Ded., of Thaddeus & Charlotte, Ded., do.

5 Sophia D. (Doggett), 1: 13: 78, tumor, æ. 72–7–20, b. Rox., of John & Eliz'h M., Ded., Milton.

COBBETT.

14 Francis L., [no date, Rec. 6: 24: 46], ——, æ. 5–7–0.

52 Lovina, 10: 21: 54, liver comp., æ. 48–0–2, b. Ded., of Thos. & Peggy.

13 Peggy (Cobb), w. of Thos., 4: 2: 51, fit, æ. 69–0–1, b. Walpole, of Daniel & Deliverance.

COBURN.

39 ——, 10: 27: 45, croup, æ. 4–0–0, b. Ded., ——, of Chas. & ——.

43 ——, 2: 10: 46, croup, æ. 8–0–0, b. Ded., d. of Chas. & ——.

6 Alvan, 1: 27: 56, asthma, æ. 62–0–0, b. Dracut, of Nath'l & Mercy.

60 Augustus R., 11: 7: 58, erysipelas, æ. 54–0–4, b. Boxf'd, of Justus & Hannah.

28 Chas., 2: 27: 66, paralysis, æ. 65–4–2, b. Dracut, of Nath'l & Mercy.

25 Hannah (Allen), 2:20:66, inflam. of bowels, æ. 61-1-4, b. Bridgewater, of Byram & Betsey.

29 Merida (Churchill), 9:14:50, consumption, æ. 21-0-0, b. Buckfield Me., of Amos & Rouhma.

17 Wm. A., 5:23:52, consumption of blood, æ. 26-10-0, b. Halifax Mass., of Chas. & Hannah.

COCHRANE.

61 Margaret (Hyland), 6:5:83, cancer, æ. 82-2-9, b. Ire., of —— & ——, Eng.,do.

COCKING.

29 Leonard, 2:3:72, consumption, æ. 17-4-0, b. Woodstock Ct., of Walter & Mary A., Eng., Pomfret Ct.

CODY.

96 Bridget E. (Finn), 10:18:81, consumption, æ. 25-1-20, b. Ded., of James & Mary J., Ire., do.

90 Jas. J., 8:11:83, cholera infantum, æ. 0-1-21, b. Ded., of John & Kate, Ire., N. F.

85 Jas. W., 9:9:81, cholera infantum, æ. 0-0-19, b. Ded., of Wm. H. & Bridget E., Norfolk, Ded.

105 Margaret A., 12:2:85, meningitis, æ. 1-2-14, b. Ded., of John P. & Katie, Ire., N. F.

COFFEY.

33 Wm., 3:29, 73, convulsions, æ. 0-6-3, b. Ded., of Patrick & Catherine, Ire.,do.

COFFIN.

67 Emma, 8:2:70, brain fever, æ. 6-6-0, b. Boston, of Chas. H. & Charlotte, Nantucket, do.

COGAN.

44 Wm., 2:21:71, congestion of liver, æ. 45-0-0, b. Ire., of Edmund & Mary, Ire., do.

COHN.

20 Isaac, 12:3:72, phthisis, æ. 68-4-10, b. Germania, of Jos. & Sarah.

COLBERT.

88 Eliza (Ford), 11:5:75, consumption, æ. 43-4-25, b. Ire., of Patrick & Mary, Ire., do.

74 Mary A., 8:6:82, meningitis, æ. 2-3-7, b. Ded., of John and Margaret, Ire., do.

COLBURN.

20 ——, 10:17:46, bowel comp., æ. 5-0-0, b. Ded., of James & ——.

118 ——, 8:—:49, dysentery, æ. 6-0-0, b. Ded., d. of Amos & ——.

116 ——, 10:—:49, infantile dis., æ. 6-0-0, b. Ded., d. of Walter and Sally.

38 ——, 2:15:64, stillborn, b. Ded., s. of Wm. & Louisa.

98 Abigail (Cushman), 8:31:57, old age, æ. 81-0-0, b. Ded., of Samuel & ——.

74 Abijah, 12:25:54, old age, æ. 75-0-0, b. Ded., of Samuel & ——.

91 Adeline F., 2:5:55, dropsy on brain, æ. 2-5-0, b. Ded., of Frank & Emeline.

95 Amasa, 6:20:73, old age, æ. 76-0-0, b. Ded., of Eliph't & Cynthia, Ded.,——.

123 Amos, 12:26:83, old age, æ. 78-1-15, b. Ded., of Geo. & Olive (Clark), Ded., Sherborn.

57 Ann, 5: 28: 90, paralysis, æ. 75-9-20, b. Ded., of Abijah & Susan Clark, Ded., Medfield.

106 Anna (Jones), 5: 1: 67, heart dis., æ. 68-10-24, b. Weston, of Jas. & Eliz'h, Weston, Waltham.

56 Benj., 11: 29: 49, dropsy, æ. 74-0-0, b. Ded.

62 (D. at Waltham), Celia (Baker), 1: 8: 54, tumor, æ. 67-0-0, b. Ded., of Joseph & ——.

78 Charles, 3: 15: 53, consumption, æ. 57-0-0, b. Ded., of Thos. & ——.

26 Chas. C., 6: 5: 65, lung fever, æ. 55-5-0, b. Sherborn, of Danforth & Clarissa.

88 Charles E., 11: 5: 60, concussion of brain, æ. 21-11-22, b. Ded., of Thomas & Sophia G., Ded., Boston.

71 Chas. E., 11: 9: 66, brain fever, æ. 0-0-31, b. Boston, adopted son of Wm. W. & Mary L..

9 Charlotte (Allen), 1: 23: 87, schirrous of stomach, æ. 78-6-19, b. Medway, of Moses & Betsey (Freeman), Medway. Cumberland R. I.

137 Clarissa (Coolidge), 12: 28: 67, paralysis, æ. 84-8-0, b. Sherborn, of Daniel & Beulah, Sherborn, ——.

39 Clarissa (Sawin), 4: 15: 83, pneumonia, æ. 78-1-26, b. Dover, of Levi & Lurana (Morse), Natick, do.

30 Creighton S., 4: 12: 87, asthma, æ. 0-9-2, b. Ded., of A. Burkley & Isabel S., Ded., do.

12 Cynthia, 3: 30: 68, old age, æ. 94-0-10.

76 Daford, 9: 21: 61, old age, æ. 90-0-16, b. Ded., of Samuel & Mehitable.

97 (D. at Bristol, R. I.) Dana F., 12: 15: 59, accident, æ. 36-2-16, b. Ded., of Isaac & Mary.

107 David C., 12: 14: 70, diphtheria, æ. 0-10-0, b. Ded., of Creighton & Jennie, Ded., do.

119 Edson M., 3: 14: 67, consumption, æ. 35-8-14, b. Hopkinton, of David G. & Calista, Holliston, do.

57 Eliph't, 1: 16: 49, consumption, æ. 34-0-0, b. Ded., of Eliph't & Cynthia.

25 Eliza B. (Parker), 4: 21: 86, carcinoma of bowels, æ. 65-9-0, b. Ded., of Abijah & Sarah, Sterling. Pepperell.

63 Eliz'h (Chandler), 11: 17: 52, bowel comp., æ. 68-0-0, b. Ashford Ct., of Peter & ——.

80 Granville W., 7: 26: 83, cerebro spinal meningitis, æ. 9-9-22, b. Ded., of Creighton & Jane E., Ded., Prov. R. I.

73 (D. at Waltham) Hannah E., 11: 23: 54, consumption, æ. 26-0-0, b. Ded., of Ellis & Celia.

67 Hitty (Cleveland), 7: 26: 81, paralysis, æ. 86-7-0, b. Dover, of David & Rachel (Allen), ——, Dover.

59 Ichabod E., 1: 21: 48, fever, æ. 19-0-0.

12 Isaac, [no date, Rec. 6: 24: 46], ——, æ. 79-0-0, b. Ded.

1 Isaacus, 1: 5: 79, old age, æ. 85-10-0, b. Ded., of Isaac & Eliz'h, Ded., Marlboro.

26 James, 9: 22: 47, drowned, æ. 32-0-0, b. Ded.

16 James, 8: 16: 68, consumption, æ. 61-5-0, b. Ded., of Geo. & Olive.

52 Jas., 5: 19: 83, apoplexy, æ. 69-2-4, b. Ded., of Thos. & Eliz'h (Chandler), Ded., Pomfret Ct.

63 Jas. P., 4: 21: 88, paralysis, æ. 76-7-1, b. Ded., of Ellis & Celia (Baker), Ded., do.

55 Jason, 3: 6: 45, consumption, æ. 64-0-0, b. Ded.

117 Jeremiah, 12: 20: 81, suicide, æ. 73-2-0, b. Ded., of Geo. & Olive (Clark), Ded., Sherborn.

83 (D. at Worcester) Joanna, 5: 13: 53, old age, æ. 80-0-0, b. Ded. [Mother of Warren Colburn, the mathematician.]

97 Lizzie J., 9: 18: 83, diphtheritic croup, æ. 9-8-12, b. Ded., of Wm. & Martha J. (Atkins), Ded., Orrington Me.

91 Lorenza H. (Howes), 10: 25: 80, chronic pleurisy, æ. 71-3-0, b. Dennis, of Elisha & Deborah, Ashfield, Dennis.

46 Louisa (Fisher), 5: 17: 82, enlarg't of heart, æ. 80-9-16, b. Wendell, of Jesse & Mary (Skinner).

54 Lucy, 5: 10: 51, old age, æ. 90-0-0, b. Ded.

118 Lucy (Deane), w. of Jere'h, 12: 8: 90, paralysis, æ. 71-6-26, b. Ded., of Richard & Cally (Herring), Dover, Ded.

128 Maria A. (Reed), 11: 8: 61, consumption, æ. 36-4-3, b. Fairfield Vt., of David & Judith M., Benson, Bakersfield Vt.

51 Martha, 3: 6: 51, consumption, æ. 31-0-0, b. Ded., of Isaac & ——.

95 Mary (Harris), 1: 12: 62, old age, æ. 82-0-0, b. Needham, of Michael & Mary.

49 Mary E. (Gay), w. of Waldo, 10: 22: 59, consumption, æ. 29-0-18, b. Ded., of Bunker & Mille.

106 Mary E., 12: 8: 70, diphtheria, æ. 5-2-0, b. Ded., of Creighton & Jennie, Ded., do.

62 Morrissey, 11: 28: 58, liver comp., æ 40-0-0, b. Ire.

99 Nancy (Colburn), 9: 28: 57, childbirth, æ. 22-0-0, b. Ded., of Walter & Sally.

29 Nathan, 7: 28: 45, consumption, æ. 75-0-0, b. Ded.

86 Nathaniel, 7: 22: 53, dis. of heart, æ. 54-0-0, b. Ded., of Benj. & ——.

53 Olive, 4: 28: 51, old age, æ. 78-0-0, b. Ded.

85 Patty (Richardson), 10: 7: 84, diarrhoea, æ. 79-3-16, b. Medfield, of Moses & Patty Wight, Medway, do.

62 Perez, 10: 22: 52, consumption, æ. 22-0-0, b. Ded., of Nath'l & ——.

19 Phineas, 1: 20: 71, heart dis., æ. 49-10-0, b. Ded., of Ellis & Celia, Ded., do.

60 Sally, wife of Walter, 1: 28: 49, puerperal fever, æ. 38-0-0, b. Ded.

65 Seth, 7: —: 49, consumption, æ. 37-0-0, b. Ded., of Eliph't & ——.

46 Susannah (Clark), 2: 16: 61, congestion of brain, æ. 78-0-0, b. Medfield, of Elias & Anna.

91 Thacher, 12: 26: 66, palsy, æ. 79-10-0, b. Ded., of Ichabod & Anna.

84 Waldo, 9: 26: 85, atheroma of brain, æ. 60-10-13, b. Ded., of Thatcher & Hitty, Ded., Dover.

69 Waldo C., 9: 9: 72, dysentery, æ. 1-7-5, b. Ded., of Waldo & Eliz'h C., Ded., Braintree.

64 Warren, 1: 22: 59, dropsy, æ. 56-0-0, b. Ded., of Benj. & ——.

COLE.

57 Abigail (Gay), 12: 4: 59, bilious fever, æ. 59-11-1, b. Walp., of Joel & Priscilla.

62 (D. at Boston), Benj. G., 4: 18: 88, typhoid fever, æ. 25–2–0, b. Haverhill, of
Chas. C. & Anna Goodrich. Norway Me., Haverhill. (*See Favor.*)

20 Chas. G., 5: 19: 59, consumption. æ. 27–0–3, b. Ded., of Francis & Abigail.

71 Clara L., 7: 14: 65, dysentery, æ. 7–3–22, b. Ded., of Lemuel & Mary A. P.

42 Eliza (Fletcher), 4: 26: 83, Bright's dis., æ. 79–5–7, b. Acton, of John & Lucy,
Acton, do.

11 Ellen (Ruth), 9: 7: 70, consumption, æ. 53–0–0, b. Ire., of Daniel & Margaret,
Ire., do.

14 Francis, 1: 10: 60, consumption, æ. 56–6–16, b. Medfield, of Asa & Sarah.

7 Francis H., 2: 23: 53, consumption, æ. 23–9–14, b. Ded., of Francis & Abigail.

62 Freeman, 11: 25: 44, fever, æ. 20 0–0, b. Ded., of Noah & [Sally].

69 Noah, 4: 30: 58, suicide, æ. 59–0–0, b. Ded., of Geo. & Irene.

6 Peter, 1: 19: 64, inflam. of brain, æ. 22–0–0, b. Woburn. [soldier.]

COLEMAN.

52 Henry, 6:—: 47, ——, æ. 30–0–0, b. Ire.

84 Mary (Coleman), 8: 3: 65, dysentery, æ. 81–0–0, b. Ire., of Daniel & Mary.

103 Morris E., 8: 26: 88, inanition, æ. 0–1–0, b. Ded., of Thos. & Julia P., Ire.,do.

48 Wm. H., 4: 17: 90, tubercular consumption, æ. 29–0–0, b. Ire., of Gerrett &
Mary (Mansville), Ire., do.

COLLARD.

16 Frances, 12: 10: 66, heart dis., æ. 0–3–14, b. Ded., of Nelson & Ellen.

COLLINS.

103 Catharine V., 10: 8: 89, hemorrhage of lungs, æ. 21–5–7, b. Ded., of John &
Catharine (Kelly), Ire., do.

27 Chas., 3: 24: 84, paralysis, æ. 48–9–0, b. Eng., of Patrick & Ellen, Ire., Eng.

109 Daniel J., 10: 21: 89, dis. of heart, æ. 31–7 15, b. Ded., of John & Catharine
(Kelly), Ire., do.

99 Eliz'h, 3: 29: 86, hemorrhage of lungs, æ. 16 4–18, b. Ded., of John & Catharine. Ire., do.

6 Ellen (Cahill), 9: 11: 73, dropsy, æ. 75–0 0, b. Ire., of John & Mary, Ire., do.

88 Ellen E., 8: 20: 65, dysentery, æ. 21–11–6, b. Ire., or Eng.

86 Isabella, 12: 22: 77, cerebral meningitis, æ. 0 11–0, b. Ded., of Dennis P. &
Mary, Ire., do.

45 Mary A., 5: 24: 87, meningitis, æ. 28–2–8, b. Ded., of John & Catharine,
Ire., do.

93 (D. at Walpole) Thos., 2: 20: 66, congestion of brain, æ. 0–9–10, b. Walpole, of
Thos. & Julia.

11 Timothy, 3: 16: 62, whooping cough, æ. 1–2–12, b. Ded., of John & Catharine.

COMER.

86 Robert B., 11: 8: 72, consumption, æ. 34 0–0, b. N. F., of Wm. & Jane,
Eng., do.

COMEY.

127 Louise G., 9: 1: 67, dysentery, æ. 5–5–0, b. Ded., of C. H. & Sarah D. R., Foxboro, Provincetown.

CONANT.

66 (D. at Walpole) Abby M., 4:4:59, consumption, æ. 18-0-0, b. Walpole, of Geo. & ——.

156 Artemas, 8:16:65, old age, æ. 86-6-0, b. Concord, of Levi & ——.

105 George, 1:19:67, consumption, æ. 66-5-0, b. Framingham, of —— & Relief, ——, Framingham.

52 Geo. II., 4:13:51, fever, æ. 7-6-0, b. Walpole, of Geo. & ——.

85 (D. at Walpole) Lucy, 11:27:60, consumption, æ. 23-0-0, b. Walpole, of Geo. & Mary, Framingham, Walpole.

152 (D. at Walpole) Mary M., 11:24:63, consumption, æ. 34-0-0, b. Walpole, of Geo. & Mary M., Framingham, Walpole.

CONCANNON.

100 Bridget, 5:7:64, scarlet fever, æ. 0-9-0, b. Quincy, of Patrick & Bridget, Ire., do.

34 John, 7:24:62, scarlatina, æ. 3-0-9, b. Ded., of Patrick & Bridget (Burk), Ire., do.

31 Michael, 7:19:62, scarlatina, æ. 1-6-0, b. Canton, of Patrick & Bridget (Burk), Ire., do.

CONDON.

36 Bridget, 12:4:56, suffocation, æ. 35-0-0, b. Ire.

48 Bridget, 8:3:57, consumption, æ. 28-0-0, b. Ire., of Thos. & Catherine.

37 John, 12:4:56, suffocation, æ. 3-8-0, b. Ded., of Patrick & Bridget.

22 Michael, 5:1:45, ——, æ. 0-21-0, b. Ded., of Michael & ——.

3 Patrick, 1:24:55, lung fever, æ. 28-0-0, b. Ire., of John & Fanny B.

CONEY.

80 Caty (Baker), 2:24:64, ——, æ. 84-0-0, b. Ded., of Eliph't & Catharine C., Ded., do.

67 Luke, 11:16:51, brain fever, æ. 72-0-0, b. Ded., of Wm. &. Rebecca.

37 Margaret E., 4:11:83, diphtheria, æ. 12-2-0, b. Boston, of Patrick & Mary, Ire., do.

22 Mary A., 3:6:81, typhoid fever, æ. 71-6-28, b. Ded., of Lewis & Mary (Fales), Ded., New London N. H.

CONLAN, CONLON.

65 Chas. A., 11:14:57, inflam. of lungs, æ. 1-3-16, b. Ded., of Peter S. & Marg't M.

17 Chas. E., 2:20:76, ulcerated sore throat, æ. 2-10-0, b. Ded., of Dennis & Mary A., Ded., Boston.

62 Daniel J., 8:24:77, enteritis, æ. 0-5-0, b. Ded., of Peter J. & Julia E., Ded., Boston.

42 Ellen M., 3:29:90, pneumonia, æ. 1-11-18, b. Ded., of Dennis & Mary (McCarma), Ded., Boston.

102 Francis E., 10:21:83, cholera infantum, æ. 0-3-7, b. Ded., of Peter J. & Julia E., Boston, Ded.

76 James, 7:24:65, dysentery, æ. 59-0-0, b. Ire., of Peter & Bridget.

51 James, 7:3:77, convulsions, æ. 0-0-10, b. Ded., of Dennis & Mary, Ded., Boston.

2 Jas. T., 8: 11: 73, cholera infantum, æ. 0-7-18, b. Ded., of Peter J. & Julia E., Ded., Boston.
44 Lawrence, 2: 27: 67, consumption, æ. 47-0-0, b. Ire., of —— & ——, Ire., do.
7 Mary (Kensilla), 1: 13: 87, old age, æ. 86-0-0, b. Ire., of Edw. & Catherine, Ire., do.
32 Mary A., 8: 9: 54, fits, æ. 0-0-21, b. Ded., of Michael & Catharine.
22 Mary A., 4: 13: 86, heart disease, æ. 39-0-0, b. N. Y. State, of Michael & Ellen, Ire., do.
51 Michael, 3: 4: 70, paralysis, æ. 63-0-0, b. Ire., of Peter & Bridget, Ire., do.
111 Michael J., 10: 20: 87, typhoid fever, æ. 16-4-14, b. Ded., of Dennis & Mary A. T., Ded., Boston.
40 Susan, 3: 12: 72, diphtheria, æ. 2-6-13, b. Ded., of Dennis & Mary, Ded., Boston.
20 Thos., 4: 15: 62, scalded, æ. 2-6-7, b. Ded., of Daniel & Maria E.
10 Wm. P., 2: 4: 80, marasmus, æ. 0-0-19, b. Ded., of Peter J. & Julia E., Ded., Boston.

CONNELLY, CONOLLY, CONLEY.
131 Bridget, 6: 28: 63, measles, æ. 0-6-24, b. Ded., of Michael & Bridget.
192 John, 6: 7: 64, scarlet fever, æ. 3-5-21, b. Ded., of Michael & Bridget, Ire., do.
28 Joseph, 4: 24: 55, croup, æ. 3-0-3, b. Framingham, of Owen & Ann C.
38 Mary (Katon), 12: 17: 70, old age, æ. 70-0-0, b. Ire., of Patrick & Mary, Ire., do.
129 Michael, 6: 13: 63, dropsy, æ. 27-0-0, b. Ire., of John & Pligil.

CONNERY.
67 Michael, 5: 4: 54, ship fever, æ. 22-0-0, b. Ireland.

CONNOR, CONNORS, CONNER.
15 Catherine, 9: 24: 66, palsy, æ. 33-0-0, b. Ire.
6 John, 10: 4: 68, rupture, æ. 55-0-0, b. Ire., of —— & ——, Ire., do.
24 Julia, 4: 19: 79, typhoid fever, æ. 7-5-9, b. Ded., of Wm. & Margaret, Ire., do.
23 (D. at N. Y. City.) Martin, 3: 17: 87, fatty degeneration of heart, æ. 41-0-0, b. Ded., of John & Margaret, Ire., do.
27 Michael, 4: 6: 74, softening of brain, æ. 53-0-0, b. Ire., of —— & Eliza.
7 Patrick, 8: 8: 69, fever, æ. 50-0-0, b. Ire., of Edw. & Mary, Ire., do.
58 Patrick, 10: 12: 74, killed by cars, æ. 30-0-0, b. Ire., of Patrick & Catharine, Ire., do.
22 Sarah E. (Kennard), 2: 12: 66, consumption, æ. 28-1-14, b. Weston Ct., of Jas. B. & Catharine B.
99 Wm., 12: 31: 72, spinal comp., æ. 74-0-0, b. Ire., of Thos. & ——, Ire., do.

CONRICK.
1 Ellen, 1: 4: 71, croup, æ. 1-7-0, b. Cambridge, of Edw. & Margaret, Ire., do.
7 John, 2: 26: 61, membranous croup, æ. 1-8-12, b. Ded., of Edw. & Margaret (Ryan).
57 Margaret (Conway), w. of Wm., 4: 23: 88, ——, æ. 84-0-0, b. Ire., of —— & ——, Ire., do.
1 Wm., 1: 20: 62, congestion of brain, æ. 1-2-6, b. W. Rox., of Richard & Catharine.

CONSTANTINE.

22 David, 12: 25: 72, heart dis., æ. 55-1-11, b. Bangor Me., of Jesse & Susan.

COOK, COOKE.

57 Chas. H., 2: 18: 56, croup, æ. 1-3-0, b. Dorch., of John & Catherine M.

92 Edgar, 9: 16: 90, cholera infantum, æ. 0-8-12, b. Ded., of Edgar & Annie, Nantucket, Ire.

81 Hannah, 8: 15: 75, teething, æ. 0-3-15, b. Ded., of Lewis & Lena, Germany, Boston.

60 Mabel L., 6: 4: 83, diphtheria, æ. 9-4-23, b. Sharon Wis., of Geo. W. & Lucy N., Comstock Mich., Mukwanago Wis.

67 Minnie, 8: 13: 76. convulsions, æ. 0-0-16, b. Ded., of Lewis & Lena, Germ., Cambridge.

COOLIDGE.

101 (D. at Taunton) Curtis, 10: 16: 68, dis. of brain, æ. 53-10-23, b. Chester, of Calvin & Patty, Sherborn, Newton.

37 Geo., 3: 14: 88, Bright's disease, æ. 70-7-7, b. Boston, of Samuel & Mary Bates, Natick, Ded.

191 Lucy J., 6: 1: 64, consumption, æ. 14-5-10, b. Ded., of Curtis & Lydia, Fitzwilliam N. H., Portland Me.

65 Mary L., 2: 12: 69, phthisis, æ. 26-1-27, b. Ded., of Curtis & Lydia L., Fitzwilliam N. H., Portland Me.

12 Samuel H., 2: 2: 57, croup, æ. 4-5-4, b. Ded., of Geo. & Hepza A.

COOPER.

61 Henry, 5: 30: 63, pneumonia, æ. 20-0-0. [soldier.]

COPP.

78 Jas. S., 8: 28: 81, acute meningitis, æ. 72-7-0, b. Killingly Ct., of Simon & Mary (Torrey), Killingly Ct., do.

15 M. Henrietta (Cole), 2: 18: 85, heart dis., æ. 52-0-17, b. Germantown N.Y., of John H. & Esther P., Hudson N. Y., Ct.

CORBETT.

30 ——, 9: 26: 47, dysentery, æ. 2-0-0.

23 Bridget (McDonald), w. of John, 2: 14: 88, pneumonia, æ. 72-0-0, b. Ire., of Edw. & Kate, Ire., do.

40 Eliz'h, 5: 22: 79. diphtheria, æ. 1-8-19, b. Ded., of Patrick F. & Mary, Ire.,do.

59 Harriet F., 12: 19: 50, dis. of head, æ. 7-6-0, b. Rox., of Timothy & ——.

68 Harriet R. (Thompson), 11: 26: 51, consumption, æ. 35-0-0, b. Ded., of Rob't R. & Sally.

88 Herbert A., 2: 18: 68, fits, æ. 1-7-0, b. Ded., of David H. & Sarah P., N. S., Stoughton.

32 John F., 5: 3: 79, diphtheria, æ. 3-6-21, b. Ded., of Patrick F. & Mary, Ire., do.

CORTHELL.

56 Mehitable, 4: 17: 71, heart dis., æ. 69-2-14, b. Hingham, of Robert & Eliz'h, Hingham, do.

COREY.

12 Hannah M., 7: 26: 67, dysentery, æ. 35-0-0, b. Andover.

CORMERAIS.

36 Fred'k A., 4: 8: 89, heart dis., æ. 26–11–18, b. Ded., of Henry & Mary O. (Sampson), Boston, Braintree.

75 Henry, 9: 3: 76, paralysis, æ. 56–4–10, b. Boston, of John & Sarah, Boston, Westboro.

12 Maria E. (Cobb), w. of Henry, 2: 23: 55, consumption, æ. 28–3 10, b. Pe l., of Jonathan H. & Sophia D.

75 Maria E., 9: 5: 55, dropsy on brain, æ. 1–7–19, b. Ded., of Henry & Maria E.

COSTLY.

55 James H., 6: 25: 75, executed, æ. 33–0–0, b. N. S.

COSTELLO.

142 (D. at Colorado Springs, Col.) Mary C., 11: 26: 87, consumption, æ. 24–3–0, b. Rox., of John & Mary A. (Dervan), Ire., do.

COTTER.

102 Margaret, 11: 23: 71, typhoid fever, æ. 70–0–0, b. Ire., of Patrick & Margaret, Ire., do.

56 Mary (Farrell), 2: 1: 56, bleeding at lungs, æ. 30–0–0, b. Ire., of Michael & Mary.

COVELL.

56 Catherine E., w. of Warren, 2: 8: 47, consumption, æ. 28–0 0, b. Ded.

17 Daniel, [no date, Rec. 6: 24: 46], ——, æ. 67–0–0.

COX.

142 Edward G., 10: 22: 64, consumption, æ. 25–0–0, b. Quincy, of Wm. H. & Louisa D., Quincy, Ded. [soldier].

119 Eloisa (Lamb), 12: 14: 83, Bright's disease, æ. 81–9–20, b. N. B., of Jas. & Harriet Woods, Scot., Eng.

100 (D. at Walpole) Henrietta C., 5: 4: 62, consumption, æ. 23–10 18, b. Walpole, of Geo. & Hannah C., Dorch., Yarmouth Me.

42 James, 7: 15: 57, consumption, æ. 1–9–0, b. Ded, of John & Mary.

95 John, 11: 17: 78, old age, æ. 87–0–0, b. Dorch., of Samuel & Mary.

7 John H., 4: 6: 67, convulsion fit, æ. 0–0–8, b. Ded., of Patrick & Margaret, Ire., N. Y.

17 Lucretia D. (Damon), 1: 17: 73, heart comp., æ. 76 0 0, b. Ded., of John & ——, Quincy, do.

17 Nancy, 3: 31: 53, consumption, æ. 18–3–0, b. Ded., of John & Lucretia.

COY.

2 Sylvanus B., 1: 2: 78, chronic pleurisy, æ. 67 1 -20, b. Charlestown Me., of John & Olive W., ——, Bridgewater.

COYNE.

2 Eliz'h M., 1: 5: 86, phthisis, æ. 34–0–0, b. Boston, of Patrick & Mary, Ire., do.

32 John H., 3: 9: 66, heart dis., æ. 9–9 0, b. Ded., of Patrick & Mary.

115 Patrick, 11: 14: 87, heart dis., æ. 69 7 25, b. Ire., of Edw. & Fannie, Ire., do.

CRAIG.

11 Sarah, 7: 19: 71, cholera morbus, æ. 70 9 0, b. Va.

CRANE.
119 ——, w. of Nathan, 12: 25: 49, bowel comp., æ. 34-0-0, b. Canton.
31 Edw. H., 4: 28: 75, typhoid fever, æ. 8-11-0, b. Willimantic Ct., of Eben B. & Rosella S., Seekonk, Mansfield Ct.
49 Hannah, 5: 5: 48, old age, æ. 81-0-0.
31 Joseph, 3: 27: 83, bilious fever, æ. 72-7-20, b. Canton, of Silas & Eliz'h (Wentworth), Canton, do.
48 Lorenzo C., 1: 15: 45, lung fever, æ. 1-6-0.
116 Sarah S. (Clarke), 12: 20: 81, paralysis of heart, æ. 69-8-23, b. Ded., of Jacob & Prudence (Stowe), Medfield, Ded.
70 Susan (Boyden), 8: 15: 84, paralysis, æ. 77-0-23, b. Ded., of Jason & Hannah M., Walpole, do.

CRATTY.
87 Agneth, 6: 28: 66, typhoid fever, æ. 2-8-0, b. Ded., of Peter & Mary.
107 John, 6: 3: 67, congestion of brain, æ. 1-2-0, b. Ded., of Peter & Mary, Pa., Scot.

CRAWFORD.
41 Mary A. (Dighton), 5: 6: 73, heart disease, æ. 68-4-17, b. Paris, of Wm. & Eliz'h, Paris, do.
30 Wm. K., 4: 20: 74, spina bifida, æ. 0-5-5, b. Ded., of John & Jennett, Scot., do.

CRAWLEY.
108 Mary (Sullivan), 11: 23: 76, dropsy of blood, æ. 68-0-0, b. Ire.

CREEDEN.
26 Wm., 3: 31: 87, apoplexy, æ. 80-0-0, b. Ire., of —— & ——, Ire., do.

CREHORE.
15 Hannah (Lyon), 5: 7: 51, old age, æ. 86-1-2, b. Spencer, of Elkanah & Rebecca.
48 Jeremiah, 5: 23: 76, old age, æ. 80-5-4, b. Dorch., of John S. & Hannah L., Dorch., Canton.
62 Joan (Dunbar), 7: 30: 84, old age, æ. 87-1-16, b. Charleton, of Samuel & Sarah (Davenport), Canton, do.
86 Sarah, w. of Elisha, 9: 4: 49, dysentery, æ. 79-0-0, b. Canton.

CRITTENDEN.
43 J. R., 3: 7: 64, lung fever, æ. 20-0-0. [Soldier.]

CROCKER.
162 D. at Hanson Amos H., 7: 8: 64, consumption, æ. 53-3-0, b. Hanson.
96 Irene (Morse), 8: 15: 57, dropsy, æ. 49-0-0, b. Ded., of Geo. & Irene.

CROCKETT.
50 Geo., 9: 15: 53, tetanus, æ. 43-0-0, b. Portland.
31 Margaret B. (Symond), 6: 26: 58, dis. of heart, æ. 35-6-0, b. Boston, of —— & Catharine.

CRONAN.
21 Mary J., 5: 5: 70, whooping cough, æ. 0-3-14, b. Ded., of James & Nancy, Ire., do.

CROOKER.
108 Evanette O., 9: 27: 66, dysentery, æ. 1-0-23, b. Ded., of Jas. T. & Martha G.

CROSBY.

4 ——, w. of Heman, 7: 27: 46, consumption, æ. 60-0-0.

13 Chas. S., 9: 19: 48, dysentery, æ. 0-8-0, b. Ded., of Wm. S. & ——.

23 Edmund, 3: 3: 75, heart dis., æ. 70-2 1, b. Woburn, of Edmund M. & Ann, ——, Boston.

35 Franklin S., 10: 15: 51, congestion of brain, æ. 2-6-20, b. Ded., of Wm. S. & Clementine,

23 Heman, 6: 18: 59, dis. of heart, æ. 79-0-20, b. Brewster, of Heman & ——.

25 Rachael A. (Newell), 7: 9: 59, typhoid fever, æ. 51-1 0, b. Need., of Calvin & Dorcas.

15 Wm. H., 9: 27: 48, dysentery, æ. 2-5-0, b. Ded., of Wm. S. & ——.

CROSSMAN.

43 Chas. L., 3: 31: 90, membraneous laryngitis, æ. 6-3-22, b. Needham, of Thos. J. & Eliza A. (Sutton), N. B., Rox.

CROWE.

50 Bridget M. (Tyne), w. of Thomas, 4: 7: 88, ——, æ. 82-0-0, b. Ire., of —— & ——, Ire., do.

3 Catharine (O'Brien), 3: 4: 75, consumption, æ. 50 0-0, b. Ire., of Derby & Ellen, Ire., do.

CROWELL.

10 Geo. W., 8: 3: 65, R.R. accident, æ. 23-0-0, b. Pawtucket, of Henry & Eliza. [soldier.]

CROWLEY.

47 Florence, 5: 25: 72, Bright's dis., æ. 23-0-13, b. Ire., of Florence & Margaret, Ire., do.

32 Joanna (Wade), 1: 25: 68, paralysis, æ. 25-0-0, b. Ire., of Wm. & Catharine.

40 John, 4: 13: 81, tuberculosis, æ. 34-0-0, b. Ire., of John & Mary, Ire., do.

27 Mary H., 12: 17: 63, consumption, æ. 15-11-13, b. Rochester N. H., of Michael & ——.

CROUISE.

72 Margaret J. (Crouise), 8: 19: 70, consumption, æ. 22-0-19, b. Weymouth, of Thos. & Catharine, Ire., do.

CRUSE.

60 Thos., 5: 29: 63, small pox, æ. 20-11-0, b. Rox., of Thos. & Catharine, Ire., do. [Soldier.]

CUFF.

33 Catharine, 9: 26: 70, typhoid fever, æ. 10-6-27, b. Ded., of Wm. & Margaret, Ire., do.

75 Margaret (Welch), 6: 25: 69, phthisis, æ. 40-0-0, b. Ire., of Patrick & Mary, Ire., do.

55 Mary (Mansfield), 5: 27: 83, consumption, æ. 70-0-0, b. Ire., af Jas. & Mary, Ire., do.

12 Patrick, 3: 19: 62, croup, æ. 0-10-0, b. Ded., of Wm. & Margaret.

200 Richard, 9: 18: 64, *congestion of brain, æ. 1-5-23, b. Ded., of Wm. & Margaret, Ire., do.

CULL.

10 David. 2: 2: 58, consumption, æ. 58-0-0, b. Ire., of Wm. & Ellen, Ire., do.

40 Ellen Barnich, 6: 1: 56, fatty degeneration of heart, æ. 95-0-0, b. Ire., of John & Ellen, Ire., do.

40 Grace Quigley, 7: 9: 60, consumption, æ. 30-0-0, b. Ire., of Owen & Margaret, Ire., do.

20 James, 3: 16: 75, consumption, æ. 44-0-0, b. Ire., of Wm. & Ellen, Ire., do.

85 John, 9: 28: 79, consumption, æ. 63-0-0, b. Ire., of Wm. & Ellen, Ire., do.

89 Margaret, 9: 5: 59, cholera infantum, æ. 0-3-0, b. Ded., of Jas & Grace.

47 Wm., 3: 10: 64, consumption, æ. 30-0-0, b. Ire., of Wm. & Ellen, Ire., do.

40 Wm., 2: 29: 68, old age, æ. 90-0-0, b. Ire., of John & Mary, Ire, do.

CUMMINGS, CUMMINS.

28 Arthur E., 3: 24: 61, congestion of brain, æ. 4-4-15, b. Ded., of George S. & Sarah A., Plymouth N. H., Moultonboro N. H.

96 Eliz'h A. Davis, 11: 23: 78, consumption, æ. 36-10-15, b. Castleton Vt., of Isaac & Aurila.

113 Lizzie L., 11: 21: 87, meningitis, æ. 0-13-1, b. Ded., of Frank P. & Emma P., Winthrop Me., Augusta Me.

37 Mary, 2: 6: 63, lung fever, æ. 0-4-0, b. N. Y. City, of Edw. & Mary.

45 Moses, 5: 21: 80, paralysis, æ. 74-2-11, b. Lyman N. H., of Cyrus & Abigail, Merrimac N. H., Minot Me.

100 Polly Gould, 12: 18: 63, lung fever, æ. 83-3-2, b. Greenfield N. H., of Daniel & Mary, Wilton N. H., do.

CUNNINGHAM.

31 John, 3: 5: 66, consumption, æ. 27-0-0, b. Hartford Ct. [soldier.

CURLEY.

53 Edward, 8: 23: 54, delirium tremens, æ. 30-0-0, b. Ireland.

CURRAN.

194 Ann, 6: 23: 64, scarlet fever, æ. 2-0-13, b. Ded., of Stephen & Catherine, Ire., do.

28 Chas., 8: 13: 79, diarrhoea, æ. 1-10-0, b. Ded., of Stephen & Catharine, Ire., do.

8 Elizabeth, 8: 19: 69, cancer, æ. 80-0-0, b. Ire.

96 Mary E., 2: 8: 68, scarlet fever, æ. 2-9-3, b. Blackstone, of Martin & Eliz'h, Ire., do.

146 Steven, 12: 17: 63, consumption, æ. 3-7-0, b. Del., of Steven & Catharine, Ire., do.

CURRIER.

24 Mary, 10: 30: 71, old age, æ. 81-0-0, b. Scotland.

CURTIS.

129 D. at Boston, Albert F., 11: 24: 87, consumption, æ. 19-11-10, b. Ded., of Geo. H. & Catherine C., Me., N. S.

8 Bartholomew, 5: 22: 74, convulsion, æ. 0-0-6, b. Del., of Patrick & Frances, Ire., do.

25 Catherine C. Hogan, 5: 15: 84, consumption, æ. 51-11-21, b. N. S., of Patrick & Annstacia, Ire., do.

109 Charlotte A. Edwards, 10: 15: 65, dysentery, æ. 54–4–5, b. Bost·n, t Chas. & Eliza.

8 Ellen, 2: 2: 79, cyanosis, æ. 0–0–6, b. Ded., of Patrick & Frances, Ire., do.

92 Ellen A., 12: 22: 86, icterus neonatorum, æ. 0–0–11, b. Ded., of Patrick & Frances, Ire., do.

78 Geo. H., 8: 22: 82, scrofulous tumor, æ. 51–0–1, b. Boston, of Geo. & Susan. Bath Me., do.

69 Hannah C. Noyes, 8: 9: 70, consumption of blood, æ. 46–5–22, b. Ded., of Otis & Nancy, Ded., Francestown N. H.

69 Jeremiah, 8: 4: 75, ——, æ. 0–0–3, b. Ded., of Patrick & Frances, Ire., de.

5 John, 9: 19: 68, consumption, æ. 65–0–0, b. Ire., of —— & ——, Ire., do.

15 Margaret, 10: 14: 65, cholera infantum, æ. 1–8–9, b. Rox., of Patrick & Frances.

67 Mary Tray, w. of John, 6: 29: 90, fatty degeneration of heart, æ. 84–0–0, b. Ire., of —— & Mary Linnihan, Ire., do.

39 Patrick, 6: 9: 77, convulsions, æ. 0–1–3, b. Ded., of Patrick & Frances, Ire., do.

104 Patrick, 8: 31: 88, cancer, æ. 51–0–0, b. Ire., of John & Mary Tray, Ire., do.

62 Wm., 8: 5: 80, cholera infantum, æ. 0–1–18, b. Ded., of Patrick & Frances, Ire., do.

CUSACK.

87 Lizzie F., 11: 11: 72, consumption, æ 19–5–29, b. Ded., of Peter & Mary A., Ire., do.

62 Wm. H., 9: 1: 73, consumption, æ. 21–5–25, b. Ded., of Peter & Mary, Ire., do.

CUSHMAN.

81 Ann, 9: 8: 85, paralysis, æ. 85–0–0.

9 Cyrus, 2: 3: 85, old age, æ. 82–7–0, b. Hebron Me., of Hosea & Lydia Barrows, Hebron, Me.

86 Gideon, 6: 15: 66, consumption, æ. 55–0–0, b. Minot Me., of Hosea & Lydia.

DAGGETT.

41 Lydia, 7: 16: 49, old age, æ. 88–0–0.

DAHLMAN.

130 Frederic, 11: 15: 61, inflam. of bowels, æ. 62–0–0.

DAIX.

98 ——, 12: 26: 72, ——, æ. 0–0–1, b. Ded., s. of —— & Eliz'h. ——, Ded.

DAKIN.

41 Sarah, 11: 28: 51, palsy, æ. 80–9–13, b. Boston, of Jos. & Mary.

DALEY, DAILEY.

66 Charles, 9: 8: 48, fever, æ. 21–0–0.

37 Ella, 4: 29: 69, scarlet fever, æ. 10–0–0, b. Ded., of Phi'ip & Mary, Ire., do.

65 John J., 7: 17: 71, dysentery, æ. 2–0–15, b. W. Rox., of Patrick & Ann, Ire., do.

35 Mary, 4: 14: 82, old age, æ. 83–0–0, b. Ire., of Christopher & Ann, Ire., do.

63 Mary Heef, 6: 9: 83, tumor, æ. 64–0–0, b. Ire., of —— & —— Ire., do.

51 Michael D., 3: 22: 64, lung fever, 32–0–0, b. Ire., of Wm. & Mary, Ire., do. soldier.

58 Morris, 6: 17: 81, stillborn, b. Ded., of Daniel & Hannah, Ire., do.

14 Patrick J., 2: 7: 86, rachitis, æ. 2–7–9, b. Ded., of Daniel & Hannah, Ire., do.

33 (D. at W. Rox.) Philip, 1 : 27 : 68, found dead, æ. 50-0-0, b. Ire., of —— & ——, Ire., do.

17 Thos. V., 8 : 12 : 72, teething, æ. 0-9-14, b. Ded., of Patrick & Ann, Ire., do.

DALTON.

11 Wm., 1 : 19 : 88, marasmus, æ. 0-6-18, b. Ded., of John E. & Mary E., Gardner Me., Charlestown.

DAMM.

131 ——, 12 : 1 : 61, stillborn, b. Ded., s. of John & Isabel, Germ., Scot.

DAMON.

53 Anna, 11 : 1 : 50, old age, æ. 78-0-0.

51 David, 4 : 18 : 45, fever, æ. 73-0-0.

16 Mary, 4 : 28 : 59, old age, æ. 79-0-0, b. Ded., of Jonathan & Mary.

30 Nancy, 7 : 29 : 59, drowning, æ. 69-7-0, b. Ded., of Jonathan & Mary.

DAMRELL·

93 Augusta, 9 : 15 : 49, dysentery, æ. 18-0-0, of Wm. S. & [Adeline].

36 Catharine (Shapley), 9 : 4 : 54, old age, æ. 71-2-3, b. Portsmouth N.H., of John & Catharine.

103 Lucius M. S., 5 : 15 : 72, inflam. of bowels, æ. 38-8-0, b. Boston, of Wm. S. & Adeline, Portsmouth N. H., Newcastle N. H.

1 Wm. S., 1 : 1 : 78, diphtheria, æ. 6-2-15, b. Ded., of Lucius S. & Mary M., Boston, Ded.

DANA.

56 Daniel, 6 : 9 : 81, cirrhosis of liver, æ. 45-0-0, b. Ohio, of Jos. & Anna, Newburyport, Ohio.

23 Hannah (Eames), 1 : 1 : 72, dropsy, æ. 79-7-0, b. Haverhill, of Daniel & Joanna, Haverhill, do.

106 Kate, 11 : 22 : 79, convulsions, æ. 0-8-22, b. Ded., of Daniel & Mary, Ohio, Ire.

70 Lemuel, 12 : 19 : 74, old age, æ. 85-0-0, b. Ded., of David & Rebecca, Ded., Dover.

41 Mary E., 12 : 20 : 56, croup, æ. 4-11-15, b. Ded., of Wm. & Harriet.

29 Mary E., 3 : 9 : 89, premature birth, æ. 0-0-11, b. Ded., of Wm. H. & Sarah, E. (O'Neil), Ded., do.

29 Rebecca (Richards), 8 : 27 : 52, old age, æ. 85-11-23, b. Ded., of Lemuel & Rebecca.

75 Wm. C., 7 : 27 : 67, consumption, æ. 60-7-22, b. Ded., of David & Rebecca, Ded., do.

DANIELL, DANIELS.

90 (D. in Fla.) Ellery C., 12 : 6 : 84, drowning, æ. 23-3-21, b. Ded., of Ellery C. & Olive C., Ded., do.

88 Emma A. (Broad), 12 : 3 : 70, inflammation, æ. 26-8-0, b. Houlton Me., of Horace & Maria, Albion Me., do.

73 Fred T., 8 : 29 : 71, consumption, æ. 0-9-7, b. Ded., of Frank J. & Emma A., N. H., Houlton Me.

38 Hannah R. (Whitney), 1 : 29 : 67, paralysis, æ. 65-0-0, b. Natick, of George & Esther, Natick, do.

116 Mary (Fisher), 11 : 19 : 65, insanity, æ. 77-8-15, b. Princeton.

57 Mary C. (Richards), 10: 11: 58, old age, æ. 77-6-24, b. Ded., of Tim'y & Sarah.
78 Mary E. (Hoyt), 7: 24: 83, consumption, æ. 38-6-4, b. Troy N. Y., of John & Mary E., ——, Troy N. Y.

DANNER, DONNER.
26 ——, 3: 5: 73, stillborn, b. Ded., of August & ——, Germ., do.
54 August, 8: 6: 73, marasmus, æ. 0-5-0, b. Ded., of August & Catharine, Germ., do.
83 James H., 8: 14: 90. meningitis, æ. 0-6-0, b. Ded., of Henry F. & Fannie A. (Paterson), Ded., Boston.
80 Rowey, 10: 19: 72, scarlet rash, æ. 4-4-19, b. Ded., of August & Catharine, Germ., do.

DARBEY.
39 Mary, 3: 18: 90, cancer, æ. 53-0-0, b. Ire.

DARCY.
14 Bridget (Bugey), 2: 7: 83. chronic bronchitis, æ. 69-0-0, b. Ire., of Edw. & Margaret, Ire., do.
2 Jas. F., 2: 5: 74. consumption, æ. 40-8-0, b. Ire., of Edw. & Bridget, Ire., do.

DARLING.
71 Chas. B., 6: 29: 82, paralysis, æ. 76-11-16, b. Leominster, of Jos. & Mary, Leominster, Bath Me.
71 Fred'k P., 10: 12: 73, marasmus, æ. 0-2-12, b. Southampton, of Horace E. & D. Jennie, Boston, Southampton.
92 Horace B., 9: 6: 87, exhaustion, æ. 76-1-1, b. Amherst, of Benj. & Selina Cook, ——, Wrentham.

DASCOMB.
14 William, 3: 6: 55, intemperance, æ. 50-0-9. b. Rox.

DAVENPORT.
45 Geo., 5: 10: 72, accidental, 67-3-7, b. Milton, of Nath'l & Nancy, Milton, Canton.
9 Harriet C. (Davenport), 6: 24: 72, erysipelas, æ. 66-5-14. b. Boston, of Elijah & Susan W.
39 Joanna, 12: 6: 56, rheumatism, æ. 75-3-9, b. Canton, of Lemuel & Patience.
105 Sarah B. (Pratt), 12: 22: 80, Bright's dis., æ. 74-5-17, b. Plymouth Vt., of Wm. & Sally (Bond), Vt., N. H.

DAVIS.
73 Ada M., 7: 14: 83, cholera morbus, æ. 19-6-10, b. Rox., of Enoch P. & Susan S. (Page), Washington N. H., Sutton N. H.
38 Almira W. (Cook), 3: 24: 66, lung fever, æ. 67-11-9, b. Cumberland R. I., of Annanias & Sarah.
42 Ann (Grafton), 4: 27: 75, pneumonia, æ. 75-6-0, b. Friendship Me., of Benj. & Eliz'h, Waldoboro Me., ——.
55 Caroline (Colburn), 5: 14: 51, small pox, æ. 25-0-0, b. Ded., of Ellis & Lucy.
59 Catharine, 9: 24: 55, erysipelas, æ. 65-0-9, b. Rox.
21 Joel, 3: 8: 89, paralysis, æ. 89-1-21, b. W. Rox., of Ezra & Sarah Mayo, Rox., do.
42 John F., 7: 14: 55, cholera infantum, æ. 0-2-0, b. Ded., of Orin & Catharine.

26 Maggie, 4: 6: 77, scrofulosis, æ. 6-4-10, b. Manchester N. H., of John & Jane, Scot., do.

56 Nellie F., 9: 29: 74, cholera infantum, æ. 1-0-1, b. Ded., of Thos. C. & Mary E., N. Y.. Bellows Falls N. H.

104 Sophia R. (Abbott), 4: 7: 86, pneumonia, æ. 88-8-20, b. W. Rox., of —— & ——, Boston, Me.

15 Ward, 5: 10: 63, dropsy, æ. 83-0-0, b. Oxford.

DAWES.

6 Ethelind, 1: 9: 89, heart failure, æ. 0-1-23, b. Ded., of Wm. H. & Hattie P. (Bates), Malden, Cohasset.

DAWSON.

59 Emily, 8: 19: 73, marasmus, æ. 0-6-12, b. W. Bridgewater, of Geo. & Hannah, Eng., do.

DAY.

52 H. Faustina, 12: 22: 56, ——, æ. 23-5-0, b. Ded., of Jos. & Hannah.

126 Hannah E. (Rhoades), 6: 2: 63, lung fever, æ. 54-8-22, b. Ded., of Lewis & Hannah, ——, Ded.

101 Lucinda L., 11: 16: 84, typhoid fever, æ. 12-5-2, b. Monmouth Me., of W. H. & Victoria, Farmington Me., Augusta Me.

DEAN, DEANE, DEANS.

64 ——, 9: 8: 47, dysentery, æ. 2-0-0, b. Ded., d. of Ebenezer & Mary.

51 Annie L. W., 8: 19: 57, brain fever, æ. 1-6-2, b. Ded., of Geo. W. & Annie S.

101 Balch S., 5: 22: 62, ——, æ. 0-0-2, b. Ded., of Balch & Susan S., Ded., Gloucester.

47 Betsey (Dean), 2: 22: 70, lung fever, æ. 82-3-20, b. Francestown N. H., of Phineas & Jerusha, Ded., do.

135 Cally (Herring), 3: 20: 62, old age, æ. 87-0-0, b. Ded., of David & Miriam.

100 Chas., 12: 24: 73, heart dis., æ. 71-8-0, b. Ded.. of Richard & ——, Ded., ——.

43 Deborah, 3: 29: 47, apoplexy, æ. 80-0-0, b. Walpole.

72 Dexter, 2: 13: 52, palsy, æ. 51-0-0, b. Ded., of Sam'l H. & Deborah.

86 Ebenezer, 10: 23: 54, old age, æ. 82-0-0, b. Ded.

99 Eben'r, 9: 11: 71, suicide, æ. 60-5-11, b. Ded., of Eben'r & Lois, Ded., Canton.

23 Eleanor R.. 3: 15: 85, cerebro meningitis, æ. 1-5-5, b. Ded., of Geo. & Laura T., Rox., Ded.

17 Eliz'h B., 2: 22: 77, phthisis, æ. 69-6-8, b. Ded., of Josiah & Mary, Ded., do.

27 Emily E. (Crosby), 3: 8: 73, consumption, æ. 37-5-16, b. Ded., of Edmund & Rachael, ——, Needham.

99 Emma L., 9: 24: 68, typhoid fever, æ. 21-8-25, b. Ded., of Thos. B. & Catherine S., Ded., do.

117 Fannie M., 8: 20: 64, scarlet fever, æ. 5-0-0, b. Ded., of Geo. V. & Mary E., Ded., Nashua N. H.

94 George, 4: 21: 64, smallpox, æ. ——, b. Ded., of Jas. & Cynthia, Ded., Ded.

41 Geo. B., 4: 28: 76, softening of brain, æ. 58-0-0, b. Ded., of Richard & Cally H., Dover, Ded.

13 Hannah B. (Walker), 2: 16: 83, obstruction of mitral valve, æ. 54-4-0, b. Bridgewater, of Sylvanus & Mary, Bridgewater, do.

64 Henry B., 10: 17: 56, canker rash, æ. 7-0-0, b. Ded., of Lemuel & Juliann.

36 Mary (Fairbanks), 10: 13: 50, old age, æ. 98-6-4, b. Wrentham, of Israel & Eliz.

12 Mary (Dean), w. of Josiah, 4: 20: 52, consumption, æ. 73-11-15, b. Ded., of Jonathan & Eliz.

108 Mary C., 10: 4: 61, cholera infantum, æ. 0-9-19, b. Ded., of Balch & Susan E., Ded., Gloucester.

158 Miriam D., 6: 9: 64, consumption, æ. 49-0-0, b. Ded., of Richard & Cally, Ded., do.

38 Lewis E., 8: 5: 46, bowel comp., æ. 2-8-0, b. Ded., of Lemuel & Julia A.

13 Louis E., 1: 8: 69, scarlet fever, æ. 3-4-25, b. Ded., of Wm. & Angenette, Ded., do.

49 Louisa W. (Whiting), 6: 10: 79, paralysis. æ. 63-1-0, b. Ded.. of Isaac & Thankful G., Dedham, Barre.

52 James, 7: 11: 77, consumption, æ. 65-9-8, b. Ded., of Josiah & Mary, Ded., do.

33 John, 10: 1: 47, fever, æ. 63-0-0, b. Ded., of John & Mary.

189 John, 5: 5: 64, old age, æ. 91-7-16, b. Ded., of John & Mary, Ded., do.

125 John, 9: 4: 64, consumption, æ. 53-6-7, b. Norton, of John & Betsey, Mansfield, do.

47 John W., 5: 22: 80, paralysis of heart, æ. 32-2-0, b. Ded., of John & Louisa, Norton, Ded.

55 Josiah, 7: 27: 78, obstruction of bowels, æ. 69-0-24, b. Ded., of Josiah & Mary, Ded., do.

3 Olive, 1: 8: 51, old age, æ. 77-0-0.

89 Oliver L., 8: 8: 83, cholera infantum, æ. 0-6-13, b. Ded., of Edgar H. & Abbie M., Canton, Machias Me.

168 Prudence (Fuller), 1: 10: 64, consumption, æ. 89-3-13, b. Ded., of Aaron & Abigail, Ded., do.

105 Susan J. (Whiting), w. of Josiah, 9: 3: 88, fatty degeneration of heart & kidneys, æ. 68-11-25, b. Ded., of Geo. & Sarah (Harris,) Ded., do.

DEBBINS.

90 Mary E., 9: 15: 87, obstruction of mitral valve, æ. 12-1-2, b. Ded., of Samuel H. & Eliz'h, P. E. I., Eng.

DeCORSEY.

43 Matilda (Fowler), 4: 26: 72, consumption, æ. 36-6-26, b. Boston, of —— & Diana, ——, N. Y. City.

DEER.

8 Kate, 1: 10: 90, marasmus, æ. 0-9-29, b. Sherborn, of Henry & Catharine (Cotter), Australia, Ire.

DEERING.

70 Jas. P., 8: 10: 85, consumption, æ. 27-2-11, b. Wakefield, of John & Margaret, Ire., do.

118 John F., 12: 13: 83, pneumonia, æ. 24-0-2, b. Malden, of John & Margaret, Ire., do.

3 Mary (Rial), 3: 6: 72, old age, æ. 82-0-0, b. Ire., of John & Mary.

DELANEY.

64 Jas., 8: 15: 80, stillborn, b. Ded., of Wm. & Ellen, Ire., Ded.

93 Matthew, 10: 30: 63, lung fever, æ. 42-0-0.

DELLMUTH.

40 Anna, 6: 10: 77, diphtheritis, æ. 5-10-11, b. Boston, of Wm. & Christine, Germ., do.

DEMAINE.

6 Christopher, 1: 15: 78, cirrhosis, æ. 41-6-0, b. Canada.

DEMPSEY.

17 Jas., 2: 27: 82, chronic disease of heart, æ. 30-0-0, b. Ire.

67 Michael, 11: 22: 61, typhoid fever. æ. 31-0-0, b. Ire.

DEMPSTER.[1]

17 ——, w. of ——, 10: 6: 46, fever, æ. 30-0-0.

DENEEF.

47 Ellie V., 6: 1: 85, phthisis, æ. 24-1-26, b. Ded., of Michael & Ann, Ire., do.

103 Michael, 10: 23: 83, phthisis, æ. 63-0-0, b. Ire., of Michael & Eliz'h, Ire., do.

111 Thos., 6: 24: 64, scarlet fever, æ. 4-3-8, b. Ded., of Michael & Ann, Ire., do.

77 Thos F., 10: 4: 70, croup, æ. 6-3-4, b. Ded., of Michael & Ann, Ire., do.

DENNEHY, DENAHEY.

50 James, 6: 18: 79, Bright's dis., æ. 45-2-0, b. Ire.

3 Margaret (Sullivan), 1: 5: 85, pneumonia, æ. 62-0-0, b. Ire., of Patrick & Mary, Ire., do.

DENNIN.

84 Eliza, 9: 26: 79, old age, æ. 70-0-0, b. Ire.

80 Margaret, 8: 13: 75, dropsy of brain, æ. 0-4-0, b. Ded., of John J. & Marg't, Taunton, Ire.

DERBY.

38 Henry, 5: 15: 78, consumption. æ. 47-7-0, b. Manchester N. H.

119 Lois (Smith), w. of Levi, 12: 7: 89, old age, æ. 94-7-22, b. Athol, of Eliab & Sarah (Humphrey), Athol, do.

DERVAN.

59 Eliz'h, 4: 27: 88, meningitis, æ. 1-0-15, b. Ded., of James H. & Margaret, W. Rox., do.

37 Mary, 3: 16: 90, difficult labor, b. Ded., of Luke & Belle (Carroll), Ire., do.

DESMOND.

83 John, 10: 5: 69, dysentery, æ. 0-0-29, b. Ded., of Dennis & Margaret, Ire., do.

1 Mary J., 1: 1: 85, septicaemia, æ. 22-2-0, b. Portland Me., of Daniel & Catherine, Ire., do.

70 Patrick, 6: 26: 89, insanity, æ. 23-0-0, b. Ire., of Timothy & Johanna (Sullivan), Ire., do.

DEVERAUX.

13 ——, 2: 28. 78, stillborn, b. Ded., of Jas. & Ann, Ire., do.

------

[1] Newspaper gives Oct. 4, 1846, Miss Mary J. Dempster, 25.

14 Ann (Cokely), 2: 28: 78, placenta praevia, æ. 25-0-0, b. Ire., of Thos. & Ann. Ire., do.

DEVLIN.
93 Jas., 10: 29: 85, marasmus, æ. 0-6-20, b. Ded., of Jas. & Sarah, Ire., Ded.
121 James McL., 11: 1: 88, convulsions, æ. 0-2-25, b. Ded., of James & Sarah J. (McLane), Ire., Ded.

DEWING.
1 Adah (Fisher), 1: 11: 53, consumption, æ. 83-1-22, b. Ded., of Jeremiah & Sarah.
44 Ebenezer, 11: 9: 52, consumption, æ. 72-1-2, b. Need., of Nath'l & Eliz'h.
30 George, 4: 3: 49, lung fever, æ. 31-0-0, b. Ded.

DEWOLF.
21 George, 6: 7: 44, colic, æ. 65-0-0, b. Bristol R. I.
91 Hannah (Talbot), 12: 10: 62, lung fever, æ. 76-9-15, b. W. Rox., of Nath'l & Mary, Stoughton, W. Rox.

DEXTER.
97 Anna, 6: 4: 53, consumption, æ. 29-0-0, b. Maine.
97 Clara F., 8: 7: 71, angina maligna, æ. 10-3-5, b. Ded., of Wm. W. & Harriet A., Valley Falls R. I., Wrentham.
94 Harriet A. (Blake), 7: 30: 71, heart dis., æ. 41-7-27, b. Wrentham, of Asa & Harriet, Wrentham, Franklin.
95 Hattie H., 7: 30: 71, angina maligna, æ. 12-3-24, b. Ded., of Wm. W. & Harriet A., Valley Falls R. I., Wrentham.
75 Roscoe M., 9: 21: 60, brain fever, æ. 2-0-28, b. Ded., of Nelson S. & Lydia K., Lisbon N. H., Maxfield Me.
92 Sarah F., 11: 1: 78, consumption, æ. 22-0-0, b. Ded., of Nelson S. & Lydia K., Littleton N. H., Maxfield Me.

DIGGS.
88 John, 4: 13: 64, cerebro spinal meningitis, æ. ——. [soldier.]

DILLINGHAM.
67 Catharine (Atherton), 9: 15: 73, paralysis, æ. 70-10-21, b. Ded., of Abner & Catharine, Sharon, Dover.
10 Catharine M. H., 3: 14: 58, consumption, æ. 27-4-20, b. Boston, of Thos. & Catharine.

DILLON.
60 Bridget F. (Mulvaney), 7: 4: 85, cancer, æ. 76-9-0, b. Ire., of Peter & Bridget, Ire., do.

DISBROW.
50 Theodore, 4: 15: 63, lung fever, æ. 20-0-0, b. Trenton N. J. [soldier.]

DIVINE.
57 Mary, 7: 2: 68, cholera infantum, æ. 0-3-2, b. Ded., of Richard & Ellen, Ire., do.

DIXON.
57 Eliza F. (Fales), 6: 29: 75, old age, æ. 84-7-4, b. Wrentham, of David & Abigail F., Wrentham, do.

35 George, 1: 19: 67, old age, æ. 85-6-4, b. Sterling Ct., of Robert & Sarah S., America, do.

DOGGETT.

20 Agnes G., 2: 14: 89, premature birth, æ. 0-0-18, b. Ded., of Thos. T. & Mary (Cox, Ded., Ire.

97 Ann E. (Cushing), w. of John, 10: 4: 49, dysentery, æ. 52-0-0, b. Boston, of Edw. & Mary.

83 Eliz'h, 3: 10: 74, bowel comp., æ. 0-0-11, b. Ded., of Jas. C. & Mary I., Ire.,do.

70 Ellen M., 11: 15: 55, whooping cough, æ. 0-6-12, b. Ded., of John & Mary.

75 Geo. F., 7: 25: 90, premature birth, æ. 0-0-1, b. Ded., of Thos. T. & Mary (Cox, Ded., Ire.

18 James, 2: 6: 75, ——, æ. 0-0-1, b. Ded., of Jas. C. & Mary I., Ded., do.

64 Jas. C., 5: 4: 88, pneumonia, æ. 39-8-0, b. Ded., of John & Mary, Ire., do.

74 Jane M., 10: 14: 68, consumption, æ. 61-10-1, b. Rox., of John & Sophia, Ded., Dorch.

38 John, 6: 17: 57, dis. of heart, æ. 76-9-2, b. Ded., of Samuel & Eliz'h.

68 John, 8: 16: 80, paralysis, æ. 55-8-20, b. Ire., of Chas. & Kate, Ire., do.

69 John A., 11: 14: 55, whooping cough, æ. 4-2-0, b. Ded., of John & Mary.

29 Margaret J., 4: 19: 57, fit, æ. 5-3-14, b. Ded., of John & Mary.

75 Margaret M., 9: 13: 84, phthisis, æ. 18-7-7, b. Ded., of John & Margaret, Ire., do.

5 Mary Holland, 2: 24: 61, childbirth, æ. 45-0-0, b. Ire., of Patrick & Catherine.

111 Mary A., 9: 6: 72, fits, æ. 0-0-9, b. Ded., of Jas. C. & Mary I., Ire., do.

71 Mary E., 11: 28: 55, whooping cough, æ. 0-6-25, b. Ded., of John & Mary.

DOHERTY, DOUGHERTY.

1 Cornelius, 1: 24: 70, whooping cough, æ. 0-11-16, b. Ded., of Daniel & Susan, Ire., do.

18 Edward, 11: 1: 71, hemorrhage of lungs, æ. 34-8-0, b. Ire., of Jas. & Honora.

48 Edward E., 2: 24: 70, ——, æ. 0-0-3, b. Ded., of Edward & Eliz'h, Ire., Ded.

DOLAN.

13 Ann (Riley), 2: 13: 85, pericarditis, æ. 40-0-0, b. Ire., of Philip & Mary, Ire., do.

6 Catharine, 1: 17: 59, lung fever, æ. 0-7-19, b. Ded., of Michael & Ellen.

24 Francis A., 3: 18: 82, croupal diphtheria, æ. 0-9-0, b. Ded., of John F. & Ann, Boston, Ire.

86 Michael, 6: 3: 61, intemperance, æ. 40-0-0, b. Ire.

6 Owen, 3: 24: 67, croup, æ. 0-0-6, b. Ded., of John & Rosanna, Ire., do.

35 Thos. F., 5: 23: 86, pneumonia, æ. 54-5-2, b. Ire., of Paul & Mary, Ire., do.

DONAHOE.

28 James, 8: 25: 52, cholera infantum, æ. 0-5-11, b. Ded., of Patrick & Sarah.

86 James, 8: 13: 65, cholera morbus, æ. 1-2-25, b. Ded., of Peter & Ellen.

11 Sarah (Heath), 4: 3: 63, lung fever, æ. 43-7-18, b. Ire., of Wm. & Mary.

DONLAN.

39 John, 6: 28: 57, lockjaw, æ. 13-9-13, b. Rox., of John & Bridget.

DONLEY, DONELLY.

127 Bernard, 2: 7: 65, consumption, æ. 28-0-0.

89 Bridget (Burke), w. of Patrick, 9: 8: 89, heart dis., æ. 60-0-0, b. Ire., of John & ——, Ire., do.

66 Daniel, 10: 17: 66, dropsy, æ. 57-0-0, b. Ire., of Wm. & Isabel.

104 Daniel, 12: 27: 67, consumption, æ. 20-2-19, b. Ire., of Daniel & Jane, Ire., do.

124 George, 9: 27: 61, ——, æ. 0-6-4, b. Ded., of Francis & Mary, Penn., N. B.

122 Georgiana, 9: 14: 61, cholera infantum, æ. 0-5-21, b. Ded., of Francis & Mary A., Penn., N. B.

3 John, 1: 2: 64, delirium tremens, æ. 22-0-0, b. Ire. [soldier.]

63 Margaret, 8: 13: 78, septic diphtheria, æ. 30-0-0, b. W. Rox., of Patrick & Bridget, Ire., do.

85 Mary A. (Bradley), 8: 20: 67, consumption, æ. 28-0-0, b. St. Johns, N. B., of Robert & Mary, Ire., N. S.

DONNER (*See Danner.*)

DONOR.

2 James, 1: 19: 50, spinal comp., æ. 60-0-0, b. Ire.

DONOVAN.

101 John, 8: 24: 61, inflam. of bowels, æ. 55-0-0, b. Ire. [soldier].

113 Margaret, 12: 20: 79, convulsions, æ. 0-4-9, b. Ded., of John & Hannah, Ire., do.

88 Mary (Long), 9: 14: 81, paralysis, æ. 56-0-0, b. Ire., of —— & Mary, Ire., do.

134 Michael, 7: 15: 63, lung fever, æ. 1-10-2, b. Ded., of John & Bridget, N. S., Ireland.

DOOLE.

100 ——, 10: 6: 49, ——, æ. 0-0-1, b. Ded., s. of Wm. & ——.

60 Andrew, 2: 7: 62, lung fever, æ. 36-0-0, b. Ire., of Frank & Bridget, Ire., do.

26 Andrew F., 8: 7: 51, scalded, æ. 2-4-21, b. Ded., of Andrew & Eliza.

33 Frederick, 5: 8: 57, consumption, æ. 0-6-8, b. Ded., of Andrew & Eliza.

98 George H., 12: 6: 63, consumption, æ. 11-2-25, b. Ded., of Andrew & Eliza, Ireland, do.

DOOLEY.

26 Margaret A., 3: 15: 81, typhoid fever, æ. 15-9-0, b. Eng., of John & Eliz'h, Ireland, do.

DOOLING.

43 Ellen (Ryan), 5: 15: 73, meningitis, æ. 45-0-0, b. Ire., of —— & ——, Ire., do.

DORMAN.

19 Bessie M., 3: 19: 79, scarlet fever, æ. 2-0-1, b. Pittsfield, of —— & Ellen C., ——, Canton Ct.

42 George, 6: 8: 86, congenital dis. of brain, æ. 0-7-0, b. Ded., of Daniel & Mary, N. S., P. E. I.

DORSHEIMER.

55 Wm. C., 9: 29: 58, cholera infantum, æ. 0-11-9, b. Ded., of Conrad & Mary.

DOUGHTY.

56 John, 3: 31: 64, ——, æ. ——. [soldier]

DOW.

9 Daniel, 3: 31: 48, consumption, æ. 49-9-0.

DOWD.

55 ——, 6: 13: 82, premature birth, b. Ded., d. of Thos. & Hannah, Ire., do.

57 Hannah (Mahar), 7: 23: 84, consumption, æ. 40-0-0, b. Ire., of Anthony & ——, Ire., do.

46 John, 6: 5: 73, meningitis, æ. 6-4-23, b. Ded., of Felix & Mary, Ire., do.

78 Mary (Furay), w. of Felix, 8: 4: 80, apoplexy, æ. 53-0 0, b. Ire., of Wm. J. & Ann (Robinson), Ire., do.

34 Mary A., 8: 4: 58, measles, æ. 1 4-21, b. Ded., of Felix & Mary.

34 Wm., 1: 29: 65, paralysis, æ. 38 0-0, b. Ire., of Patrick & Margaret.

6 Wm., 1: 27: 70, typhoid fever, æ. 17-0-12, b. Ded., of Felix & Mary, Ire., do.

DOWLING.

31 ——, 4: 14: 85, stillborn, b. Ded., s. of Dennis & Kate, Ire., Woonsocket R. I.

77 Mary E., 8: 11: 87, inanition, æ. 0-0-2, b. Ded., of Michael & Ellen, Ire., do.

55 Mary J., 9: 29: 74, cholera infantum, æ. 0-3-0, b. Ded., of Dennis & Catherine, Ire., Woonsocket R. I.

87 Thos. P., 7: 3: 88, convulsions, æ. 0-0-2, b. Ded., of Michael & Ellen, Ire., do.

DOWNEY.

77 Ann J., 7: 29: 67, consumption, æ. 0-0-9, b. Ded., of Andrew & Margaret, Ire., do.

DOWNS.

116 Agnes M., 8: 18: 61, diarrhoea, æ. 0-6-29, b. Ded., of Moses W. & Lucy E., Tamworth N. H., Industry Me.

20 John, 3: 8: 84, chronic diarrhoea, æ. 66-11-8, b. Eng., of John & Susan C., Eng., do.

DOYLE.

94 ——, 8: 3: 88, stillborn, b. Ded., d. of Jas. & Ellen, Ire., do.

66 Anna, 8: 31: 77, consumption, æ. 18-0-14, b. Ded., of John & Bridget, Ire., do.

17 James, 10: 14: 65, consumption, æ. 15-3-0, b. Ded., of Patrick & ——.

22 Michael W., 2: 10: 90, pneumonia, æ. 0-9-10, b. Ded., of Daniel & Fannie, Ire., do.

14 Patrick, 1: 31: 64, consumption, æ. 15-11-0, b. Ire., of John & Bridget.

105 Thos., 7: 8: 72, heart dis., æ. 45-0-0, b. Ire.

43 Thos., 4: 26: 83, consumption, æ. 30-2-4, b. Ded., of John & Bridget, Ire., do.

DRAKE.

66 (D. at Walpole) Ellen, 9: 12: 86, phthisis, æ. 23-5-0, b. Ded., of Richard & Ellen (Lane), Ire., do.

14 Hannah, 2: 2: 61, paralysis, æ. 75-0-9, b. Ded., of Peletiah & Catharine.

49 Mary C., w. of Willard, 9: 22: 46, ——, æ. 43-0-9.

91 Willard, 10: 21: 53, fever, æ. 51 0-0, b. Ded., of Willard & ——.

DRAPER.

49 Abbot W., 6: 17: 61, scarlet fever, æ. 1-8-0, b. Ded., of Francis & Louisa.

89 Abijah, 8: 28: 65, consumption, æ. 28-2-9, b. Ded., of Willard & Louisa.

74 Albert, 6: 17: 61, scarlet fever, æ. ——, b. Ded., of Francis & Louisa.

71 Amy (Bullard), 8: 20: 59, fever, æ. 66-0-0, b. Medfield.

78 Catharine, 12: 25: 59, consumption, æ. 37-0-0, b. Ded.

89 Edson, 9: 8: 53, fever, æ. 0–1–5, b. Ded., of Moses & Irene.

102 Edwin, 10: *23: 70, consumption, æ. 22-10-0, b. Ded., of Willard & Loisa, Ded., Walpole.

76 Eliz'h, 10: 4: 70, scald, æ. 2–1–25, b. Ded., of Geo. & Emma N., Ded., Addison Me.

72 Ernest N., 8: 19: 75, consumption of blood, æ. 1–2–0, b. Waltham, of Whiting S. & Delia F., Ded., do.

64 Francis W., 4: 12: 45, consumption, æ. 20-0-0, b. Dover.

49 George, 1: 4: 51, fit, æ. 59-0-0, b. Ded., of Joseph & ——.

83 George D., 5: 7: 66, consumption, æ. 34-4-0, b. Ded., of Jos. & Polly.

164 Hannah M., 9: 18: 64, consumption, æ. 24–5–0, b. Ded.. of Willard & Louisa S., Ded., Walpole.

100 Horace G., 9: 14: 65, ——, æ. 0–7–22, b. Ded., of Geo. & Emma N.

4 Joseph B., 1: 16: 81, marasmus, æ. 49–3-2, b. Ded., of Jos. & Amy (Bullard), Ded., Medfield.

85 Joseph L., 6: 22: 53, consumption, æ. 30-0-0, b. Dover, of Jos. & Polly.

21 Judith (Smith), 11: 27: 68, consumption, æ. 66 4-16, b. Ded., of Oliver & Olive, Ded., do.

70 Louisa (Smith), 6: 19: 83, paralysis, æ. 76 10-10, b. Walpole, of Abijah & Hannah (Whiting), Walpole, Ded.

84 Mamie, 5: 24: 66, humors, æ. 0–17–0, b. Ded., of Geo. D. & Fanny (Baker).

101 Martin, 11: 21: 79, old age, æ. 82-8-14, b. Ded., of Daniel & Hannah D., Ded.. do.

28 Mary E., 6: 1: 60, consumption, æ. 17–4–1, b. Ded., of Willard & Louisa, Ded., Walpole.

49 Mary L., 3: 23: 56, whooping cough, æ. 0–3–18, b. Ded., of Simeon W. & Nancy.

56 Mehitable, w. of Dr., 3: 26: 50, old age, æ. 81-0-0, b. Ded.

65 Nancy M., 8: 19: 72, cholera infantum, æ. 1–3–13, b. Ded., of Geo. & Emma, Ded., Addison Me.

90 Oren W., 1: 4: 69, dropsy on heart. æ. 10–10-0, b. Ded.. of Moses & Irene, ——, Wrentham.

85 Polly C. (Ellis), 6: 3: 66, urinary dis., æ. 74-0 0, b. Ded., of Phineas & Lucy.

46 Polly M., w. of Geo., 7: 26: 46, consumption, æ. 53-0-0. b. Franklin.

41 Willard, 3: 28: 77, consumption, æ. 76–5–0, b. Ded., of Daniel & Hannah D., Ded., do.

81 Willie H., 12: 30: 54, lung fever, æ. 0 9-16, b. Boxboro, of Lewis W. & Nancy.

DRAYTON.

62 Eliz'h L. (Adams), 6: 21: 65, consumption, æ. 61-8 2, b. Portsmouth N. H., of Benj. & Eliz'h.

12 John, 3: 28: 56, contraction of brain. æ. 53-8-17, b. Boston, of John & Nancy.

137 (D. at Boston) John H., 3: 18: 87, Bussey Bridge accident, æ. 61-6-22, b. Boston, of John & Eliz'h L., Boston, Portsmouth N. H.

62 Nancy (Hendley), 7: 18: 68, old age, æ. 86-0-25, b. Sharon, of Henry & Mary, Rox., do.

18 Nancy D. (Dorothy), 6: 2: 56, cancer, æ. 38-5-19, b. Snowhill Md., of Spencer & Hetty.

109 Nellie S., 12: 1: 81, consumption, æ. 25-0-27, b. Ded., of John H. & Mary K., Ded., Dorch.

102 Wm. H., 9: 1: 61, dysentery, æ. 56-0-0, b. Boston, of John & Nancy, Boston, Bridgewater.

DRESSER.

22 ——, 9: 30: 47, ——, æ. ——, b. Ded., —— of David J. & ——.

73 Hannah (Farnsworth), 12: 14: 53, dis. of heart, æ. 69-0-0, b. Fitchburg, of Jos. & Hannah.

DRIENAN.

57 Geo., 8: 1: 86, Bright's dis., æ. 65-0-0, b. Ire., of Morris & Ellen, Ire., do.

DRISCOLL.

7 Catharine, 7: 2: 65, inflam. of brain, æ. 4-4-28, b. *Boston, of Patrick & Mary F.

71 Thos., 7: 2: 83, diphtheria, æ. 6-3-6, b. Ded., of Timothy & Mary, Ire., do.

DRUGAN.

71 (D. at Westboro). Mary E., 7: 9: 90, melancholia & exhaustion, æ. 46-0-0, b. Boston, of Jos. & Sarah G. (Johnston), N. B., Pa.

DRUMMEY.

154 Joanna (Hennessey), 12: 11: 65, consumption, æ. 50-0-0, b. Ire., of Michael & Mary.

DRUMMOND.

59 Winnifred (Doyle). 5: 22: 67, fits. æ. 27-0-0, b. Ire., of Michael & Elizabeth, Ire., do.

DuBOIS.

29 Liza. 3: 11: 73, brain fever. æ. 2-2-14, b. Canada, of Felix & Loua, Ca., do.

DUCKWORTH.

21 Martha J., 2: 9: 66, lung fever, æ. 0-2-0, b. Ded., of Geo. & Eliza.

DUD.

15 Francis, [no date, Rec. 6: 24: 46], ——, æ. 50-0-0.

DUDLEY.

105 Lydia F. (Manly), 11: 19: 49, consumption, æ. 31-1-14. b. Putney Vt., of Amasa & Lydia.

DUFF.

21 Keziah (Cobb, 3: 11: 82, bronchial consumption, æ. 65-11-11, b. Sharon, of Jonathan & Sibbel (Holmes), Attleboro, Sharon.

DUFFY.

13 Samuel M., 2: 1: 80, convulsions, æ. 0-1½-0, b. Ded., of Owen E. & Hattie A., Boston, Ct.

DUGAN.

1 ——, 1: 2: 82, stillborn. b. Ded., d. of Cornelius & Honora, Webster, Woonsocket R. I.

105 ——, 11: 16: 82, stillborn, b. Ded., d. of Cornelius & Honora, Webster, Woonsocket R. I.

12 Honora A. (Maloney), 2: 16: 87, consumption, æ. 27-2-2, b. Woonsocket R.I.,
of Michael J. & Julia, Ire., do.
111 John F., 11: 19: 83, anus imperforatus, æ. 0-0 5, b. Ded., of Cornelius & Nora,
Webster, Woonsocket R. I.
43 Wm. J., 6: 10: 84, diphtheria, æ. 4-9-19, b. Ded., of Cornelius & Nora Webster, Woonsocket R. I.

DUNBAR.
6 Algernon S., 1: 21: 57, scarlatina, æ. 4-8-17, b. Ded., of Marvin & Sophia.
44 Alice H., 7: 28: 49, cholera infantum, æ. 0-11-0, b. Ded., of Thos. & ——.
43 Edward T., 7: 27: 49, dysentery, æ. 5-0-0, of Thos. & ——.
13 Henrietta, 2: 5: 57, scarlatina, æ. 1-6-13, b. Weatherstown, of Marvin &
Sophia.

DUNKIN.
71 John T., 7: 8: 67, dropsy on brain, æ. 2-3-0, b. Boston, of John & Catherine,
Rox., Oakham.

DUNLAP.
41 Thos. F., 8: 18: 58, cholera infantum, æ. 0-7-12, b. Boston, of Thos. & Mary.

DUNN.
39 Ann, 12: 23: 70, consumption, æ. 13-0-0, b. Ded., of John & Margaret. Ire.,do.
67 Edith F. M., 8: 8: 84, cholera infantum, æ. 0-8-0, b. Ded., of Walter H. &
Annie A., Dighton Me., Germ.
179 John, 3: 3: 64, ——, æ. 45-0-9, b. Ire., of David & ——, Ire., do.
39 Terrance J., 4: 6: 80, premature birth, æ. 0-1-0, b. Ded., of Jas. & Bridget,
Ire., do.
14 Thos., 2: 17: 81, pneumonia, æ. 59-0-0, b. Ire., of John & Hannah, Ire., do.

DUNPHY.
16 John, 7: 27: 72, cholera morbus, æ. 37-6-0, b. N. S., of Edward & Bridget.

DURSY.
70 Nicholas, 12: 2: 53, erysipelas, æ. 21-5-3, b. Germany.

DWYER.
37 Thos. O., 3: 5: 72, lung fever, æ. 63-0-9, b. Ire., of —— & ——, Ire., do.

DYER.
57 Bradbury, 8: 16: 73, old age, æ. 78-6-25, b. Andover N. H., of Wm. & Nancy.
132 (D. at Taunton) Daniel, 12: 12: 67, softening of brain, æ. 55-0-0, b. Ire.
138 James, 9: 24: 63, cholera infantum, æ. 0-11-0, b. Ded., of Daniel & Sarah,
Ire., do.
101 Melville E., 12: 12: 76, accident, æ. 23-9-12, b. Buxton Me., of Jas. E. & Mary
F., Baldwin Me., Buxton Me.

EAGAN, EGAN.
39 Henry, 6: 10: 61, membranous croup, æ. 4-4-0, b. Ded., of Patrick & Ann,
Ire., do.
50 Joseph P., 5: 22: 81, cerebro spinal meningitis, æ. 29-7-2, b. Boston, of Wm.
& Mary, Ire., do.
96 Wm. P., 10: 1: 89, abscess of liver, æ. 75-0-0, b. Ire., of —— & ——, Ire., do.

EARL.

117 Eliza (Colter), 12: 13: 82, pneumonia, æ. 36-8-21, b. Ire., of Jas. & Ann, Ire., do.

EARLEY.

31 Catharine Maguire, 5: 13: 86, pneumonia, æ. 78-0-0, b. Ire., of Philip & Bridget, Ire., do.

EARNES, EARNS.

5 Eli A., 1: 23: 76, congestion of brain, æ. 30-0-0, b. Blackstone, of John & Maria, Ire., do.

16 John C., 2: 1: 89, chronic diarrhoea, æ. 74-6-26, b. Ire., of Andrew & Mary, Ire., do.

EASTERBROOK.

102 Eliz'h (Willard), 11: 3: 79, cancer, æ. 63-4-1, b. Harrison Me., of Samuel & Sarah, Harrison Me., Sanford Me.

55 Harriet A. (Cobb), w. of Wm. E., 5: 21: 90, suicide, æ. 55-0-15, b. Barnstable, of Asa & Mercy G., Barnstable, Boston.

EATON.

5 ——, 2: 28: 48, cholera infantum, æ. 8-0-0, b. Ded., s. of Joel & ——.

66 (D. at Turner Centre, Me.), Abigail (Walker), 5: 14: 83, old age, æ. 72-10-19, b. S. Paris Me., of Micah & Eliz'h Edes, Petersham, Ded.

99 Caroline F. (Holmes), 10: 31: 79, ——, æ. 55-0-0, b. Milton, of Philip & Margaret, Milton, Me.

73 Caroline G., 12: 17: 55, disease of lungs, æ. 1-0-7, b. Ded., of William M. & Emeline P.

40 Eliza (Turner), w. of Luther, 9: 29: 44, scarlatina, æ. 42-0-0, b. Ded., of Jas. & Jemima.

4 Emma A., 1: 5: 79, Bright's dis., æ. 15-10-29, b. Ded., of Luther A. & Sarah E., Ded., Boston.

29 Hannah (Endicott), 6: 3: 60, old age, æ. 98-7-8, b. Canton, of James & Abigail, Canton, do.

103 Joel, 11: 25: 81, pneumonia, æ. 75-10-4, b. Ded., of Luther & Lucy (Ellis), Ded., do.

69 John, 7: 7: 90, heart failure, æ. 89-2-5, b. Ded., of John & Hannah (Endicott), Ded., Canton.

46 John E., 10: 7: 54, diseased throat, æ. 50-5-16, b. Ded., of Luther & Lucy.

32 Lucy (Ellis), w. of Luther, 2: 15: 47, fever, æ. 75-0-0, b. Ded., of John & Sibbel.

44 Luther, 5: 17: 76, pneumonia, æ. 73-10-0, b. Ded., of Luther & Lucy E., Ded., do.

103 Maria, 12: 20: 63, cancer, æ. 63-10-5, b. Ded., of Luther & Lucy, Ded., do.

EBBINGHAUS, EBBINGHOUSE.

42 Evangeline, 3: 8: 68, congestion of brain, æ. 0-5-13, b. Ded., of Fred & Mary, Germ., do.

96 Mary A. (McGowen), 11: 17: 78, syphilis, æ. 32-0-0, b. Ire., of Thos. & Eliz'h, Ire., do.

EBBS.
24 Ellen L., 2: 23: 73, conv'sions, æ. 0-6-1, b. Ded., of Thos. & Ellen, Ire., Eng.
42 Geo. R., 4: 19: 89, typhoid pneumonia, æ. 26-9-0, b. Ded., of Thos. & Ellen
   (Hull), Ire., Eng.
69 Thos. F., 12: 13: 74, convulsions, æ. 1-0-14, b. Ded., of Thos. & Ellen, Ire.,do.

EDDY.
73 Geo. W., 6: 11: 56, dis. of chest, æ. 72-0-0, b. Thompson Ct.
119 Seth W., 8: 13: 64, chronic dis.,æ. 26-0-0, b. Plymouth, of Henry H. & Abigail
   S., Plymouth, do. [soldier.]

EDES.
64 Lucy (Lewis), 11: 9: 53, liver comp., æ. 65-3-26, b. Need., of Joshua & Mary.

EDGERTON.
55 Sophia M. (Fisher), 7: 19: 77, consumption, æ. 55-9-6, b. Ded., of Eben'r, Jr.
   & Sophia M., Needham, Ded.

EDSON.
12 Esther G. (Stewart), 4: 2: 59, inflam. of bowels, æ. 62-0-0.

EDWARDS.
3 Ann, 3: 2: 65, diabetes, æ. 23-0-0, b. Ire., of John & Mary.

EIS.
124 Herman, 9: 1: 64, congestion of brain, æ. 3-3-18, b. Ded., of Chas. & Wilhelmine, Germ., do.
60 Lewis, 5: 31: 67, lung fever, æ. 1-10-0, b. Ded., of Charles & Wilhelmine,
   Germany, do.

ELDRIDGE.
19 Chas. H., 10: 7: 46, typhus fever, æ. 38-9-0, b. Boston.

ELKINS.
21 Harriet A. (Hall), 1: 24: 69, consumption, æ. 35-0-0, b. Gorham Me., of Chas.
   & Harriet.

ELLIOTT, ELLIOT, ELIOT.
18 Andrew, 2: 22: 83, paralysis, æ. 53-0-0, b. N. B., of Chas. & Ellen, N. B., do.
83 Jennie M., 7: 27: 83, consumption, æ. 21-3-21, b. Ded., of Wm. & Margaret,
   Ireland, do.
14 John, 2: 23: 80, consumption, æ. 20-7-24, b. Ded., of William & Margaret
   D., Ireland, do.
39 Josephine G., 3: 12: 72, scarlet fever, æ. 0-8-0, b. Ded., of Andrew & Jane,
   N. B., Ire.
40 Margaret (Donley), 5: 5: 76, consumption, æ. 38-2-0, b. Ire., of Daniel &
   Jane, Ire., do.
33 Sophia (Hedtlen), w. of Anthony, 9: 17: 51, consumption, æ. 21-8-1, b. N. S.,
   of John & Catharine.
85 Walter, 8: 25: 90, marasmus, æ. 0-4-27, b. Boston, of —— & Annie, ——, N.B.
85 Wm., 11: 1: 72, consumption, æ. 38-0-0, b. Ire., of Jas. & Jane, Ire., do.
3 Wm. H., 1: 11: 82, consumption, æ. 25-2-15, b. Boston, of Wm. & Margaret
   (Donley), Ire., do.

ELLIS.

28 ——, 9: 24: 47, dysentery, æ. 1-0-0, b. Ded., of Oliver & ——.

75 ——, 12: 25: 48, ——, æ. ——.

82 ——, 11: 16: 58, cholera infantum, æ. 0-0-36, b. Ded., d. of Alvin & Martha.

88 ——, 11: 22: 62, ——, æ. 0-9-3, b. Ded., s. of Calvin F. & Maria.

111 ——, 2: 15: 63, stillborn, b. Ded., —— of John & Harriet M., Ded., Walpole.

100 Abbie F., 1: 4: 72, consumption, æ. 27-3-8, b. Ded., of Alvin & Martha B., Dedham, do.

54 Abner, 12: 14: 44, consumption, æ. 75-0-0, b. Ded.

79 (D. at Walpole) Addie M., 9: 10: 58, cholera infantum, æ. 1-5-0, b. Walpole, of Isaac & Abby M.

36 Alfred B., 10: 10: 70, consumption, æ. 29-3-14, b. Walpole, of Alvin L. & Martha B., Ded., do.

68 Azuba, 11: 11: 47, paralysis, æ. 83-0-0.

40 Betsy, 7: 14: 55, dis. of heart, æ. 58-0-0, b. Ded., of Jos. & Eliz'h.

40 Betsey (Morse), 5: 29: 78, bronchitis, æ. 95-8-8, b. Ded., of David & Sybil.

20 Calvin F., 2: 23: 75, paralysis, æ. 68-3-23, b. Ded., of Jason & Susan D., Ded., do.

98 Caroline M., 8: 8: 71, consumption, æ. 24-0-8, b. Ded., of Alvin & Martha M., Ded., do.

38 Catherine (Whiting), 4: 12: 81, pneumonia, æ. 81-8-15, b. Ded., of Hezekiah & Mary, Ded., Walpole.

159 Colburn, 6: 14: 64, congestion, æ. 72-9-9, b. Ded., of Geo. & Mary G.

54 David, 11: 24: 46, old age, æ. 81-0-0, b. Ded.

102 (D. at Walpole) Elba J., 1: 15: 53, dropsy, æ. 6-2-9, b. Walpole, of Charles & Mary.

172 Francis, 2: 1: 64, dis. of spine, æ. 29-9-1, b. Ded., of Paul & Jane, Ded., do.

5 Frank A., 1: 19: 81, rupture of intestines, æ. 21-5-0, b. Ded., of Chas. H. & Abbie L. (Brooks), Ded., do.

49 & 116 Frank H., 8: 16: 49, dysentery, æ. 8-0-0, b. Ded., of Calvin F. & Julia.

72 Frank L., 8: 27: 59, dropsy on brain, æ. 0-7-0, b. Ded., of Lewis & Sarah.

32 Frederic J., 5: 13: 55, consumption, æ. 0-11-0, b. Ded., of Oliver & Hannah A.

59 George, 1: 26: 49, old age, æ. 87-0-0, b. Ded.

35 George, 6: 24: 55, dis. of heart, æ. 62-10-0, b. Medfield, of Geo. & Martha C.

94 Granville, 9: 15: 49, dysentery, æ. 4-8-0, b. Ded., of Calvin F. & Julia.

25 Hannah A. (Johnson), 7: 3: 54, consumption, æ. 35-7-2, b. Brookfield N. H., of Fred & Sophia.

91 Henry, 12: 9: 70, gastritis, æ. 70-4-2, b. Medway, of Henry & Azubah, Medway, do.

70 Isaac, 12: 30: 44, consumption, æ. 54-0-0.

113 Jane (Thayer), 12: 9: 84, paralysis, æ. 82-1-29, b. Easton, of Nath'l & Phoebe, Easton, do.

157 Jason, 5: 23: 64, general debility, æ. 86-0-0, b. Ded., of Ichabod & Sally N., Ded., Needham.

92 Jesse, 1: 14: 66, congestion of brain, æ. 75-4-2, b. Ded., of Joel & Azubah.

73 Joel, 2: 26: 52, inflam. of bowels, æ. 63-0-0, b. Ded., of Joel & Azubah.

36 Julia E., w. of Calvin F., 10: 10: 47, fever, æ. 36-0-0.

98 Leonore E., 9: 20: 68, infantile debility, æ. 0-1-28, b. Ded., of Alfred & Martha E., Ded., do.

105 (D. at Walpole) Louisa (Sumner), 11: 16: 68, consumption, æ. 77 10 21, b. Ded., of Geo. & Margaret.

110 Lucy (Ellis), 12: 10: 76, old age, æ. 79-0-0, b. Walpole, of John & Hannah, Walpole, do.

80 Lyman, 12: 12: 71, inflam. of liver, æ. 15-10-25, b. Ded., of Franklin & Mary A., Ded, Taunton.

103 M. Emily (Ellis), 10: 27: 68, consumption, æ. 25-3-11, b. Wrentham, of Alvin L. & Martha B., Ded., do.

54 Maria (Guild), 5: 16: 83, paralysis of heart, æ. 59-3-29, b. Ded., of Reuben & Olive, Ded., do.

113 Martha, 3: 2: 67, dis. of spine, æ. 30-0-22, b. Ded., of Paul & Jane, Ded., do.

79 Martha B. (Dean), 8: 15: 69, phthisis, æ. 47-0-21, b. Ded., of Dexter & Martha W., Ded., Boston.

10 Martha M. (May), 2: 15: 56, old age, æ. 87-7-0, b. Canton, of Samuel & Sarah.

58 Mary, 2: 27: 47, ——, æ. 69-0-0.

122 Mary, w. of Lemuel, 12: 24: 48, old age, æ. 83-0-0, b. Ded.

9 Mary A. E., 1: 31: 83, cancer, æ. 62-4-17, b. Medfield, of Jos. & Molly W., Ded., do.

103 Mary E. (Kingsbury), 9: 9: 63, ——, æ. 22-1-0, b. Ded, of Wm. & Betsy.

69 Merrill D., 9: 1: 78, paralysis, æ. 69-9-0, b. Ded., of Abner & Polly N., Ded., Needham.

87 Paul, 3: 23: 71, paralysis of lungs, æ. 32-3-11, b. Ded., of Paul & Jane, Ded., do.

46 Rebecca (Lewis), 1: 10: 56, old age, æ. 88-2-0, b. Ded., of Nath'l & Experience.

123 Rebecca N. (Ellis), w. of Merrill D., 12: 23: 89, paralysis, æ. 78-2-15, b. Ded., of Jason & Susan D. (Fairbanks), Ded., do.

58 Richard, 3: 10: 56, old age, æ. 79-0-0, b. Ded., of Wm. & Olive.

81 Rufus, 11: 12: 58, fistula, æ. 56-0-16, b. Ded., of John & Rebecca.

55 Rufus, 9: 16: 60, congestion of brain, æ. 26-10-8, b. Ded., of Rufus & Hannah, Ded., do.

1 Samuel, 3: 14: 51, dropsy, æ. 0-3-27, b. Ded., of Paul Jr. & ——.

29 (D. at Rox.) Sarah, 10: 3: 65, consumption, æ. 57-1-0, b. Walpole, of Jonathan & Mary.

33 Sarah A. (Gay), w. of Calvin F., 6: 21: 55, consumption, æ. 34 7-2, b. Ded., of Joel & Polly.

110 Sarah E., 10: 2: 88, heart failure, æ. 61 8-25, b. Ded., of Geo. & Catharine Whiting, Medfield, Ded.

29 Susan D. (Fairbanks), 7: 1: 71, old age, æ. 88 5-9, b. Ded., of Eben'r & Mary, Ded., do.

52 Walter, 8: 28: 60, diarrhœa, æ. 0 4-0, b. Ded., of Alvan L. & Martha B., Ded., do.

94 Willard, 3: 10: 66, lung fever, æ. 80 9-9, b. Ded., of Wm. & Olive.

77 Wm., 11: 27: 52, old age, æ. 72 7-9, b. Ded., of Wm. & Olive.

97 Wm. H., 12: 5: 76, congestion of brain, æ. 49-10-11, b. Medway, of Henry & Jane, Medway, Easton.

25 Willie H., 5: 11: 71, congestion of brain, æ. 0-11-19, b. Ded., of Wm. & Anna M., Walpole, New Orleans.

ELLSWORTH.

75 Ella M. (Page), w. of Cyrus, 5: 31: 88, spinal myelitis, æ. 32-2-15, b. Cambridge, of Freeman & Martha A. (Sargent), Wentworth N. H., Bow N. H.

ELY.

13 Eliza B. (Whittier), 2: 12: 81, gastric typhoid fever, æ. 36-10-8, b. Munroe Me., of Seth & Harriet E., Searsmont Me., Andover.

25 Fred'k D., 2: 13: 90, pneumonia, æ. 21-10-1, b. Ded., of Fred'k D. & Eliza B. (Whittier), Wrentham, Munroe Me.

82 Ida B., 11: 5: 70, croup, æ. 0-6-21, b. Ded., of Fred'k D. & Eliza B., [Wrentham, Munroe Me.]

EMERSON.

64 Ann, 5: --: 49, consumption, æ. ----, of Geo. & ----.

109 Geo., 9: 29: 72, old age, æ. 84-5-7, b. Thompson Ct., of Willard & Mary, Thompson Ct., do.

7 Jane H. (Mace), 1: 6: 77, Bright's dis., æ. 61-0-4, b. E. Redfield Me., of Andrew & Desire, E. Redfield Me., Liverpool.

60 Lucy A. (Fairbanks), 8: 21: 52, consumption, æ. 26-0-0, b. Ded., of Jesse & Boradil.

134 Nabby (Ellis), 2: 19: 62, ----, æ. 77-0-0, b. Ded., of Nathan & Elothea (Colburn).

ENDICOTT.

39 Henry B., 10: 5: 52, cholera infantum, æ. 1-3-12, b. Chelsea, of Augustus B. & Sarah.

10 John, 1: 31: 57, lung fever, æ. 93-0-0, b. Canton, of Jas. & Abigail.

35 Mary (Humphrey), w. of John, 3: 21: 45, lung fever, æ. 80-0-0, b. Ded.

26 Richard W., 4: 1: 85, premature birth, æ. 0-0-4, b. Ded., of Henry B. & Caroline W., Ded., do.

ENDRES.

114 Ann E., 3: 8: 63, croup, æ. 1-8-1, b. Ded., of Herman & Helena M., Germ., do.

ENGLEY.

53 Hannah E., 10: 29: 69, typhoid fever, æ. 20-1-17, b. Waldoboro Me., of Jacob & Abigail.

ERSKINE.

6 Fanny F., 7: 27: 69, dropsy, æ. 17-10-0, b. Rox., of Chas. & Maria F., Rox., Boston.

EVELETH.

61 Lucy C., 3: 25: 47, ----, æ. 4-0-0, of Daniel & ----.

EVERETT.

21 Abbie L. (Wight), w. of Aaron E., 2: 10: 88, bronchitis, æ. 72-7-17, b. Medway, of Aaron W. & Abigail R., Medway, Holliston.

38 Abby, 10: 26: 45, scarlet fever, æ. 7-0-0, b. Ded., of Nathan & Hepzibah.

15 (D. at Boston.) Abby M., 3: 28: 58, typhoid fever, æ. 9-4-0, b. Ded., of Isaac & [Matilda] J.

55 Alice S., 1: 22: 50, dysentery, æ. 1-5-0, b. Ded., of George & Julia.

25 **Chas. T.**, 3: 24: 78, consumption, æ. 19-0-9, b. Ded., of Nath'l H. & Lucy A., Ded., do.

32 **Edith M.**, 9: 3: 70, dysentery, æ. 2-11-4, b. Ded., of Francis E. & Clara, Ded., Newbury.

2 **Edw.**, 2: 9: 58, enlargement of brain, æ. 1-4-2, b. Ded., of Rufus S. & Rosella.

147 **Eleanor**, 12: 22: 63, paralysis, æ. 75-0-0, b. Ded., of Asa & Eleanor, Methuen, Dedham.

55 **Ellen A.**, 11: 24: 59, typhoid fever, æ. 10-10-4, b. Ded., of Francis & Mary N.

37 **Francis**, 5: 2: 84, cancer, æ. 80-0-14, b. Lunenburg Vt., of John & Salvina.

137 **Geo. F.**, 8: 23: 63, dysentery, æ. 8-0 16, b. Ded., of Geo. & Julia D., Ded., do.

31 (D. at Wash., D. C.) **Henry C.**, 1: 19: 65, chronic diarrhoea, æ. 21-11 0, b. Dedham, of Francis & Mary.

142 **Irene D.** (Smith), 11: 24: 63, congestion of lungs, æ. 33-11-2, b. Sharon, of Warren & Irene D., ——, Dedham.

62 **Joel**, 9: 8: 56, consumption, æ. 69-9-9, b. Ded., of Asa & Eleanor.

115 **Laura A.**, 8: 10: 61, cholera infantum, æ. 0-7-1, b. Ded., of J. Edw. & Irene, Dedham, do.

79 **Laura C.**, 7: 18: 52, dysentery, æ. 0-20-0, b. Ded., of Geo. & Julia.

197 **Lewis**, 7: 31: 64, paralysis, æ. 55-9-9, b. Ded., of Eben'r & ——, Ded., do.

74 **Lucy A.** (Pond), 11: 4: 53, consumption, æ. 26-0-0, b. Ded., of Frank & ——.

77 **Mary N.** (Pratt), 8: 29: 82, heart dis., æ. 69-0-12, b. Waterford Me, of Jos. & Lucy S., Me., Brighton.

98 **Moses**, 3: 17: 62, rheumatic dis. of heart, æ. 72-1-13, b. Ded., of Eben'r & Milly, Dedham, do.

22 **Nathan**, 1: 29: 49, consumption, æ. 55-9-0, b. Ded.

115 **Sarah** (Hill), 12: 7: 83, old age, æ. 87-7-28, b. Canton, of Nath'l & Abigail, Canton, do

17 **Seth**, 2: 26: 70, heart dis., æ. 78-1-13, b. Ded., of Asa & Eleanor, Ded., do.

5 **Willard**, 2d, 3: 18: 51, consumption, æ. 56-0-9, b. Ded., of Ebenezer & Sarah.

35 **Willard**, 11: 28: 56, consumption, æ. 71-3-1, b. Ded., of Wm. & Margaret.

83 **Willard**, 11: 27: 57, typhoid fever, æ. 35-0-0, b. Ded., of Willard & Lucy D.

EVERSON.

104 **Harriet R.** (Fales), w. of Erastus W., 9: 28: 87, paralysis, æ. 49-9 7, b. Wrentham, of Benj. H. & Rebecca Ellis, Wrentham, Dedham.

FAGAN.

35 ——, 5: 13: 79, stillborn, b. Ded., s. of John J. & Mary, Ire., Brookline.

36 ——, 5: 13: 79, stillborn, b. Ded., s. of John J. & Mary, Ire., Brookline.

55 **Ann**, 5: 28: 65, scrofula, æ. 5-5-3, b. N. Y. City, of Jas & Ann.

11 **Eliz'h**, 3: 18: 54, fit, æ. 0-0-7, b. Ded., of Patrick & Eliz'h.

126 **Eliz'h** (Clark), 12: 31: 90, gastro enteritis, æ. 70-0-0, b. Ire., of Thos. & Eliz'h (Wallace), Ire., do.

38 **Ellen** (Holton), 5: 1: 69, old age, æ. 78-9-9, b. Ire., of Patrick & Ann, Ire., do.

76 **Elliot L.**, 11: 2: 86, chronic diarrhoea, æ. 0-8-14, b. Ded., of John J. & Mary F., Ire., Brookline.

58 **John J.**, 5: 29: 90, heart dis., æ. 33-5-21, b. Ded., of Jas. & Ann Sheridan, Ireland, do.

34 **Mary** (Carlon), 3: 12: 66, consumption, æ. 40-0-0, b. Ire., of Thos. & Rose.

28 Peter, 4: 16: 75, typhoid fever, æ. 72-0-0, b. Ireland, of John & Catharine, Ireland, do.

FAIRBANKS.

  6 Abijah, 3: 1: 46, consumption, æ. 26-0-0, b. Ded., of Willard & Azubah.

95 Adda, 8: 31: 59, cholera infantum, æ. 1-5-4, b. Ded., of Jarvis & Lucy.

71 Adelaide M., 2: 18: 45, ——, æ. 0-1-7, b. Ded.

27 Ann (Duncan), 7: 20: 65, old age, æ. 83-0-0, b. Eng.

94 (D. at Walpole) Becca (Fetch), 9: 1: 58, numb palsy, æ. 87-0-0, b. Walpole, of Steven & Hannah.

23 Bessie H., 5: 26: 70, consumption, æ. 22-2-21, b. Ded., of Jarvis & Lucy, Ded., Dorch.

73 Boradil M. (Mason), 9: 16: 59, ——, æ. 58-0-0, b. Ded., of Wm. & ——.

17 Clarissa (Bird), 2: 5: 75, old age, æ. 78-3-8, b. Stoughton, of Asa & Betsey, Stoughton, Plymouth.

91 Cyrus E., 12: 23: 57, typhoid fever, æ. 37-0-0, b. Ded., of Samuel & Hannah.

22 Elmer W., 3: 11: 71, consumption, æ. 8-9-0, b. Ded., of Jesse & Phebe, Walpole, N. B.

184 Fanny E. (Lewis), 3: 26: 64, pneumonia, æ. 55-0-19, b. Walpole, of Jabez & Catherine, Ded., do.

  3 Francis E., 8: 15: 45, consumption, æ. 24-0-0, b. Ded., of Willard & Azubah.

67 Geo. S., 5: 7: 59, consumption, æ. 77-0-0, b. Boston.

118 Jas. G., 8: 23: 61, scrofula, æ. 28-2-15, b. Ded., of Jas. & Roxanna, Ded., Rox.

49 Jesse, 5: 20: 81, old age, æ. 80-7-0, b. Walpole, of Abner & Rebecca, Walpole, do.

112 Joshua, 10: 27: 65, dysentery, æ. 68-10-25, b. Ded., of Eben'r & Mary.

27 Lavina (Littlefield), 2: 28: 61, paralysis, æ. 79-0-0.

67 Lois S., 12: 24: 47, fever, æ. 29-0-0, b. Jefferson Me.

48 Marshall, 10: 14: 54, consumption, æ. 36-7-26, b. Ded., of Wm. & Mille.

85 Mary E. (Cole), 9: 26: 85, dropsy, æ. 54-5-0, b. Acton, of George B. & Eliza (Fletcher), Acton, do.

  4 Mary F., 12: 1: 45, fits, æ. 1-0-0, b. Ded., of Moses S. & Charlotte.

  8 Mille (Farrington), 3: 14: 54, consumption, æ. 66-2-0, b. Ded., of Ebenezer & Eliz'h.

43 Moses, 5: 28: 77, ossification valves of heart, æ. 83-0-0, b. Ded., of Wm. & ——, Ded., ——.

  2 Moses S., 7: 20: 45, inflammation, æ. 25-0-0, b. Ded., of Moses & Hannah.

  5 Nancy, 1: 19: 79, old age, æ. 84-4-16, b. Ded., of Ebenezer & Mary, Ded., Newton.

51 Prudence, 3: 26: 71, old age, æ. 89-11-12, b. Ded., of Ebenezer & Mary, Ded., Newton.

37 Sarah, 5: 20: 77, old age, æ. 87-3-25, b. Ded., of Eben'r & Mary, Ded., Newton.

69 Willard, 1: 21: 48, consumption, æ. 53-0-0.

38 Wm., 2: 10: 63, liver comp., æ. 77-6-18, b. Ded., of Eben'r & Mary.

130 Wm. H. H., 3: 13: 65, consumption, æ. 22-7-14, b. Ded., of Benjamin F. & Priscilla A.

FALES.

44 Addie M. (Allen), 5: 16: 82, ulcer of stomach, æ. 35-9-16, b. Mansfield, of Wm. B. & Fannie (Tolman), Mansfield, Sharon.

56 Chas. S., 9: 11: 57, dysentery. æ. 2-8-19, b. Ded., of Wm. & Mary.

71 Eliph't, 9: 5: 48, dysentery, æ. 68-0-0, b. Ded.

33 Frank H., 5: 6: 77, tetanus, æ. 14-2-24, b. Ded.. of Wm. & Mary J., Ded.. Georgetown Me.

66 Horace, 11: 17: 56, consumption, æ. 51-0-0, b. Ded., of Eliph't & Sybil.

45 James, 9: 30: 54, fall down stairs, æ. 62-14-0. b. Ded., of Nehemiah & Mary.

14 Joshua, 4: 26: 52, lung fever, æ. 67-5-4, b. Ded., of Joshua & Sarah.

27 Laura A., 8: 25: 44, scarlatina, æ. 10-0-0, b. Ded., of Joshua & ——.

89 Lucy, 9: 2: 59, cholera infantum, æ. 0-4-0, b. Ded., of Newman & Lucy.

128 (D. at Walpole) Lyman M., 2: 8: 65, consumption, æ. 27-1-21, b. Ded., of Horace & Hannah.

58 Mary (Fales), 6: 10: 65, rheumatism, æ. 81-2-4, b. New London N. H., of Nath'l & Mary.

69 Mary L. (Paul), 7: 22: 82, old age, æ. 88-10-9, b. Dorch., of Wm. & Anna' Ded., Attleboro.

50 Mary W., 10: 29: 53, old age, æ. 74-7-23, b. Ded., of Neh'h & Sarah.

21 Nehemiah, 3: 14: 57, consumption, æ. 72-3-0, b. Ded., of Nehemiah & Sarah.

10 (D. at Walpole) Olive M., 3: 21: 60, consumption, æ. 17-3-0, b. Milford, of Horace & Hannah.

106 Rebecca (Everett), 9: 7: 62, dysentery, æ. 81-4-3, b. Hanover N. H., of Nath'l & Rebecca, Ded., ——.

32 Rebecca E. (Ellis), 4: 9: 82, pneumonia, æ. 79-9-0, b. Ded., of Abner & Martha, Dorch., Canton.

25 Sarah. w. of Nehemiah, 5: 25: 45, old age, æ. 83-0-0, b. Ded.

90 Stephen, 12: 3: 60, paralysis, æ. 74-0-0, b. Ded., of Joshua & Sarah W., Ded., do.

128 (D. at Walpole), Sybil (Sumner), 11: 4: 67, old age, æ. 85-4-13, b. Ded., of Geo. & Margaret, Ded., do.

9 Willis, 1: 27: 61, congestion of brain, æ. 4-0-4, b. Ded., of Newman & Lucy (Weatherbee).

FALLON.

19 John, 3: 4: 84, dis. of liver, æ. 68-0-0, b. Ire., of John & Mary, Ire., do.

FANNING.

65 Sarah R. (Radcliffe), 8: 7: 84, phthisis, æ. 30-4-17, b. Ded., of Winslow & Sophia, Boston, W. Rox.

FARLEY.

119 John E. W., 11: 22: 87, hypostic pneumonia, æ. 72-8-16, b. Ipswich, of Jabez & Susanna, Ipswich, do.

61 Robert F., 8: 24: 73, convulsions, æ. 0-0-8, b. Ded., of Wm. H. & Caty, N.B., Boston.

FARNHAM.

127 (D. at Boston), Michael, 12: 23: 89, hemorrhage, æ. 75-0-0, b. Boothbay Me., of —— & Abigail, ——, Boothbay Me.

FARRELL.

81 Edw., 8: 14: 90, pneumonia, æ. 70-0-0, b. Ire., of —— & ——, Ire., do.

98 Margaret (Fitzpatrick), w. of Edw. E., 9: 11: 87, pneumonitis, æ. 65-0-0, b. Ire., of Michael & Honora, Ire., do.

FARREN.

106 Eliz'h (McGuinness), 12: 5: 85, paralysis of heart, æ. 37-0-0, b. Ire., of Arthur & Bridget, Ire., do.

95 Joseph, 10: 26: 85, ——, æ. 0-1-10, b. Ded., of Patrick & Eliz'h, Ire., do.

FARRINGTON.

25 Abby A., 5: 8: 53, scarlet fever, æ. 1-4-1, b. Ded., of Geo. O. & Abby D.

68 Abby A., 12: 4: 57, lung fever, æ. 2-0-0, b. Ded., of Geo. O. & Abby D.

104 Abby D. (Paul), 12: 16: 76, Bright's dis., æ. 50-8-7, b. Dorch., of John & Abigail D., Dorch., Westford.

20 Ambrose, 9: 1: 47, ——, æ. 70-0-0.

41 Annie R., 7: 11: 57, consumption, æ. 22-7-0, b. Ded., of Chas. & Lydia.

52 Caty (Colburn), 6: 29: 72, consumption of blood, æ. 72-5-21, b. Ded., of Isaac & Eliz'h, Ded., Marlboro.

28 Chas., 7: 14: 59, suicide, æ. 52-4-0, b. Ded., of Reuben & Eliz'h.

36 Chas. H., 4: 27: 82, apoplexy, æ. 50-6-9, b. Ded., of Chas. & Lydia D., Ded., do.

37 Charlotte, 5: 14: 78, dropsy, æ. 80-2-0, b. Ded., of Stephen & Lucy, Ded.,——.

82 David, 9: 17: 55, cancer, æ. 79-0-0, b. Ded., of Benj. & Sarah.

31 Desire (Whitney), 4: 27: 80, hydrothorax, æ. 87-2-18, b. Orange, of Jabez & Eliz'h, Rox., do.

46 Ebenezer, 4: 18: 48, old age, æ. 88-0-0, b. Ded.

85 Edward C., 8: 7: 65, consumption, æ. 28-2-11, b. Ded., of Chas. & Lydia D.

28 Eliz., w. of Reuben, 3: 24: 49, fever, æ. 68-0-0.

15 Eliz'h (Bent), 2: 6: 57, old age, æ. 90-5-6, b. Milton.

46 Emily A. (Alden), 4: 12: 65, consumption, æ. 45-7-0, b. Ded., of Francis & Sarah S.

51 Geo. M., 6: 22: 72, convulsion, æ. 0-15-0, b. Ded., of Geo. M. & Cleopatra K., Wrentham, Holliston.

18 Hannah (Kingsbury), 1: 21: 73, old age, æ. 94-9-21, b. Needham, of Nathan & Imaia, Needham, do.

12 Helena F., 9: 16: 48, inflam. of bowels, æ. 0-7-9, b. Ded., of Reuben & Emily.

141 James, 10: 17: 64, lung fever, æ. 82-0-19, b. Ded., of Benj. & Sarah, Ded., do.

74 Jesse, 12: 31: 57, inflam. of liver, æ. 77-0-8, b. Ded., of Benj. & Sarah.

41 Joseph N., 1: 8: 70, drowned, æ. 9-11-19, b. Salem, of Geo. M. & C. K., Wrentham, Holliston.

44 Lois (Holmes), 4: 1: 65, old age, æ. 84-6-5, b. Ded., of Wm. & Desire.

47 Lucy P., 3: 27: 68, old age, æ. 81-11-5, b. Ded., of Benj. & Sarah, Ded., do.

27 Lydia D. (Crehore), 3: 9: 69, consumption, æ. 62-2-9, b. Ded., of Elisha & Sarah, Milton, Canton.

40 Mary B, 2: 4: 67, paralysis, æ. 42-3-8, b. Ded., of Otis & Caty, Ded., do.

37 Mille, 6: 7: 57, old age, æ. 84-0-0, b. Walpole, of Eben'r & ——.

82 Nancy, 8: 7: 63, old age, æ. 80-10-0, b. Ded., of Stephen & Sarah, Dedham, Dorchester.

93 Otis, 12: 20: 70, accidental, æ. 73-4-20, b. Ded., of Ebenezer & Elizabeth, Dedham, Milton.

49 Rebecca (Metcalf), 5: 28: 80, paralysis, æ. 86-0-20, b. Ded., of Jos. & Rebecca (Fairbanks), Ded., do.

13 Reuben, 4: 6: 56, cancer, æ. 81-5-24, b. Ded., of Eben'r & Hannah.

81 Ruth (Gould), w. of David, 9: 29: 55, cancer, æ. 71-0-0, b. Greenfield N. H., of John & Mary.

5 Sarah, 10: 8: 52, old age, æ. 87-1-2, b. Dorch., of Stephen & Sarah.

95 Tirzah M. (Beckworth), 9: 13: 58, information on the brain, æ. 38-0-0, b. Lempster N. H., of Martin & Tirzah.

13 Wm. H., 3: 18: 58, apoplexy, æ. 37-1-6, b. Ded., of Ambrose & Lois.

FAVOR.

62 (D. at Boston) Benj. G. [adopted by F. F. Favor], 4: 18: 88, typhoid fever, æ. 25-2-0, b. Haverhill, of Charles C. & Anna Goodrich Cole, Norway Me., Haverhill.

FAY, FAHY, FEHEY.

46 Berbera, 2: 16: 70, ——, æ. 0-11-0, b. Ire., of Michael & Ellen, Ire., do.

130 Bridget (Burke), 6: 24: 63, lung fever, æ. 24-0-9, b. Ireland, of Patrick & Honora.

53 Bridget (Larkin), 4:2: 71, heart disease, æ. 62-9-0, b. Ire., of Darby & Mary, Ireland, do.

34 Cornelius, 5: 4: 49, consumption, æ. 32-0-0, b. Ire.

64 Lizzie, 6: 11: 89, consumption, æ. 31-7-10, b. Ire., of Michael & Ellen Joyce), Ireland, do.

22 Michael, 3: 5: 83, cystitis, æ. 78-0-0, b. Ire., of Richard & ——, Ire., ——.

1 Michael J., 1: 1: 90, consumption, æ. 27-3-23, b. Ire., of Michael & Ellen (Joyce), Ire., do.

FEARON.

46 Louisa A., 10: 16: 62, teething, æ. 1-0-11, b. Ded., of Edward & Eleanor, Ireland, Nova Scotia.

FELCH.

20 Vesubar, 2: 29: 76, teething, æ. 0-9-22, b. N. B., of George W. & Sadie A., Waterford Vt., Randolph.

FELIX.

107 Mary J., 10: 17: 89, ——, æ. 2-0-0, b. Boston, of Geo. & Catharine M. Taylor), W. Indies, Canada.

FELL.

5 Margaret C , 1: 15: 80, convulsions, æ. 0-11-0, b. Ded., of Chas. L. & Mary L., Ded., W. Rox.

27 Seibine (Grady), 4: 4: 87, heart dis., æ. 64-0-0, b. Ire., of Ferdinand & Kate, Ire., do.

FELTON.

66 Anna (Richards), 11: 26: 57, consumption, æ. 76-0-0, b. Ded., of —— & Abigail.

139 Chas. C., 10:9:64, consumption, æ. 55-10-24, b. Needham, of Isaac & Anna, Needham, do.

24 George, 8: 1: 51, bowel comp., æ. 0-2-15, b. Ded., of Chas. C. & Mary.

43 Horace, 3: 15: 65, consumption, æ. 15-10-21, b. Needham, of Chas. C. & Mary C.

30 Mary C. (Smith), 6: 10: 53, consumption, æ. 36-2-15, b. Lexington, of Chas. S. & Hannah.

91 Rosanna W., 10: 10: 63, brain fever, æ. 3-3-3, b. Ded., of Chas. C. & Mary W., Needham, Hingham.

53 Rosilla A., 11: 15: 59, croup, æ. 2-7-10, b. Ded., of Chas. & Mary W.

FERGUSON.

40 Andrew B, 5: 4: 82, heart dis., æ. 25-4-9, b. Scot., of John & Susanna, Scot., do.

FERNANDEZ, FERNANDIES.

23 Sarah E., 3: 17: 57, scarlatina, æ. 4-1-13, b. Andover, of Daniel & Sarah.

14 Wm. A., 4: 12: 59, dis. of brain, æ. 3-6-7, b. Ded., of Daniel & Sarah.

FERREL.

117 Catherine M., 8: 10: 64, dysentery, æ. 2-2-5, b. Manchester N. H., of Eugene & Margaret, Manchester N. H., Ire.

FERRIN.

23 Susanna (Edmunds), 3: 28: 71, old age, æ. 87-9-0, b. Saundus, N. H., of Thos. & Ruth, Newbury, ——.

FERRY.

74 Arthur V., 8: 29: 80, cholera infantum, æ. 1-0-5, b. Ded., of John & Ellen, Ire., do.

FESSENDEN.

57 John, 5: 11: 71, erysipelas, æ. 77-1-28, b. Lexington, of Thos. & [Lucy] (Lee), Lexington, Concord.

34 Nancy B. (Baker), 5: 18: 86, paralysis of lungs, æ. 82-7-15, b. Ded., of Eliph't & Anne E., Ded., do.

FETT.

86 Jacob, 12: 27: 57, typhoid fever, æ. 35-0-0, b. Germany.

FIELD.

105 Charlotte E. (Whiting), 11: 12: 83, rupture of heart, æ. 68-10-22, b. Boston, of Moses & Persis R. (Clark), Ded., Hubbardston.

45 Edwin H., 5: 30: 85, peritonitis, æ. 13-5-20, b. Ded., of Ferdinand C. & Eleanor T., Rox., Ded.

66 Eleanor L., 7: 27: 85, hemorrhage of bowels, æ. 16-11-7, b. Ded., of Ferdinand C. & Eleanor T., Rox., Ded.

127 Horace, 11: 12: 62, erysipelas, æ. 71-0-0, b. Mansfield, of Jos. & ——, Mansfield, ——.

19 Mary E., 1: 28: 90, Bright's dis., æ. 11-7-21, b. Ded., of Ferdinand C. & Eleanor T. (Clapp), Rox., Ded.

FILBRICK.

98 Catharina F., 11: 18: 58, tumor, æ. 52-0-0, b. Germany.

FINCH.

93 Sarah M. (Talmadge), w. of Alfred, 9: 8: 87, cerebral hemorrhage, æ. 75-1-5, b. Meriden Ct., of Daniel & Lucy, Mass., Ct.

FINN.

102 ——, 11: 9: 81, stillborn, b. Ded., of John W. & Maggie J., Ded., Walpole.

21 Annia, 12: 9: 72, slow fever, æ. 18–8–0, b. Ded., of Jas. & Mary.

126 Fannie, 12: 7: 87, pericarditis, æ. 8–7–17, b. Ded., of John W. & Maggie J., Ded., Walpole.

18 Frances (McLaughlin), 4: 21: 54, childbed, æ. 25–0–0, b. Ire., of John & Bridget.

87 Frances E., 10: 12: 80, diphtheria, æ. 4–3–17, b. Ded., of Jas. R. & Annie E., Ded., Ire.

19 James, 5: 15: 59, consumption, æ. 40–0–0, b. Ireland.

10 James V., 2: 12: 79, consumption, æ. 19–5–24, b. Ded., of Jas. & Mary, Ire., do.

109 (D. at Portsmouth Grove), John, 6: 13: 64, wound in arm, æ. 23–1–0, b. Ire., of John & Sarah, Ire., do. [soldier.]

69 Mary, 8: 10: 79, insufficiency of mitral valve, æ. 23–1–0, b. Ire., of Peter & Anna, Ire., do.

18 Mary A., 4: 9: 58, congestion of brain, æ. 2–10–3, b. Ded., of Patrick & Mary,

88 Mary A., 10: 17: 80, diphtheria, æ. 5–5–0, b. Ded., of Jas. R. & Annie E., Ded., Ire.

61 Patrick, 12: 23: 59, ——, æ. 33–0–0, b. Ire., of Richard & Ann.

42 Thos. J., 4: 16: 81, typhoid fever, æ. 25–0–0, b. Ded., of Patrick & Mary, Ire., do.

20 Wm., 4: 4: 60, lung fever, æ. 0–5–2, b. Ded., of Patrick & Mary.

90 Wm. P., 10: 20: 80, diphtheria, æ. 4–3–25, b. Ded., of James R. & Annie E., Ded., Ire.

FINNERTY.

11 Michael A., 7: 1: 72, diphtheria, æ. 34–5–0, b. Ire., of Anthony & Margaret, Ire., do.

FINNEY *(See also Phinney.)*

46 Mary H. (Harrington), 8: 2: 57, dysentery, æ. 56–7–2, b. Eastport Me., of Andred & Abigail.

FISH.

28 ——, 7: 10: 45, fever, æ. 2–0–0, b. Ded., —— of James & Frances.

21 Eli, 1: 24: 49, lung fever, æ. 65–0–0.

100 Frances M. (McIntosh), 12: 2: 80, progressive paralysis, æ. 60–0–9, b. Ded., of Elisha & Betsey, Dorch., Ded.

1 Sarah, 1: 13: 48, consumption, æ. 26–0–0.

FISHER.

61 ——, w. of Jeremiah, 4: —: 48, ——, æ. 80–0–0.

117 ——, 9: —: 49, dysentery, æ. 0–0–0, b. Ded., d. of Asa & ——.

98 ——, 4: 30: 64, dis. of brain, æ. ——, b. Ded., s. of Geo. & M. Estella, Ded., do.

135 Abijah, 11: 23: 67, old age, æ. 89–7–0, b. Ded., of Asa & Mary, Ded., do.

49 Albert, 6: 8: 87, enlargement of prostate gland, æ. 74–11–9, b. Bolton, of Jacob & Ann, Wrentham, Boston.

39 Alvan, 2: 13: 63, inflammation, æ. 70–6–0, b. Needham, of Aaron & Lucy S.

100 Alvan B., 8: 22: 61, dysentery, æ. 0–20–20, b. Ded., of Alvan J. & Martha C.

48 Alvan J., 4: 15: 63, congestion of lungs, æ. 34–10–0, b. Ded., of Alvan & Lydia, Needham, Ded.

60 Ann, 6: 13: 65, old age, æ. 89-8-0, b. Harvard.

89 Arvilla (Gray), w. of Albert, 7: 14: 88, cancer, æ. 80-2-10, b. Paris Me., of John & Naomi, Worcester, Paris Me.

83 Bertha C., 10: 3: 78, meningitis, æ. 3-1-21, b. Ded., of John B. & Helen S., Cook's Corner Vt., Ded.

3 Billings, 2: 4: 54, consumption, æ. 73-0-0, b. Ded., of Oliver & Sarah.

71 Chloe (Smith), 3: 24: 56, old age, æ. 84-0-0, b. Walpole, of Asa & Miriam.

51 (D. at Boston) Eben S., 4: 7: 67, consumption, æ. 43-7-0, b. Ded., of Eben & Sophia M., Need., Ded.

29 Ebenezer Jr., 1: 4: 47, consumption, æ. 56-0-0, b. Needham.

56 Ebenezer, 10: 12: 47, old age, æ. 96-0-0, b. Ded.

10 Edwin, 8: 29: 46, teething, æ. 1-0-0, b. Ded., of Amory & Eliz'h D.

7 Frank A., 1: 24: 57, croup, æ. 1-6-24, b. Ded., of Amory & Eliz'h D.

66 Freeman, 7: 8: 60, inflam. of kidneys, æ. 73-0-0, b. Need., of Aaron & Lucy, Need., do.

24 (D at Jamaica Plain) Freeman, 3: 14: 76, accident, æ. 33-2-11, b. Quincy, of Joshua & Eliza, Ded., ——.

50 Geo., 6: 8: 87, angina pectoris, æ. 56-6-21, b. Ded., of Jos. & Hannah, Ded., do.

99 Geo. W., 11: 22: 85, internal injury from accident, æ. 54-2-1, b. Rox., of Lewis W. & Lydia, Rox., Littleton.

80 Hannah (Parker), w. of Billings, 8: 29: 49, dysentery, æ. 60-0-0, b. Groton, of Imla & Hannah.

93 Hannah (Baker), 10: 29: 53, tumor, æ. 48-0-0, b. Ded., of Sabin & Hannah.

4 Hannah M. A., 3: 22: 52, consumption, æ. 23-4-0, b. Ded., of Billings & Hannah.

4 Henry F., 1: 14: 82, diphtheritic croup, æ. 6-7-0, b. Ded., of Freeman & Eliz'h D., Ded., do.

15 Herman, 2: 26: 61, heart dis., æ. 62-0-0, b. Southboro, of Joshua & Mary.

25 Jabez, 3: 13: 83, pneumonia, æ. 81-2-16, b. Ded., of Benj. & Abigail, Walpole, Ded.

98 Jeremiah, 12: 4: 73, chronic diarrhoea, æ. 70-0-0, b. Ded., of John & ——, Ded., do.

33 John, 4: 16: 49, lung fever, æ. 74-0-0.

76 John, 7: 29: 89, chronic enteritis, æ. 84-4-9, b. Ded., of John & Chloe, Ded., Walpole.

65 Joseph, 8: 13: 80, intussusception of bowels, æ. 75-0-19, b. Ded., of Benj. & Abigail, Ded., do.

88 Joshua, 8: 27: 90, gangrene of old age, æ. 83-3-0, b. Ded., of John & Chloe (Smith), Ded., Walpole.

46 Keziah (Billings), 8: 25: 53, liver comp., æ. 72-4-28, b. Canton, of Samuel & Hannah.

4 Leonard, 1: 18: 61, old age, æ. 76-0-14, b. Ded., of Oliver & Sarah (Billings), Ded., Sharon.

45 Lewis W., 2: 25: 71, consumption, æ. 75-0-0, b. Rox., of Lewis & Mary, Ded., Sharon.

73 Lydia (Patch), 8: 22: 70, paralysis, æ. 78-0-0, b. Littleton, of Abraham & Sarah.

85 Lydia (Ellis), w. of Alvan, 8: 21: 87, paralysis, æ. 82-5-25, b. Ded., of Abner & Martha, Ded., Canton.

36 Mary G. (Bronson), 4: 29: 85, old age, æ. 83-0-0, b. Mendon, of Willis & Sally (Godfrey), Mendon, Milford.

3 Mary M., 1: 25: 60, typhoid fever, æ. 15-0-0, b. Lindon Vt., of Ephraim & Laura.

34 May C., 4: 1: 83, diphtheritic croup, æ. 10-11-3, b. Ded., of Jos. & Mary E., Ded., Harrington Me.

8 Miriam B., 1: 22: 82, diptheritic croup, æ. 11-3-7, b. Ded., of Freeman & Eliz'h D., Ded., do.

42 Nancy (Farrington), 5: 15: 76, inflam. of bowels, æ. 72-6-0, b. Ded., of Abel & Hannah L., Canton, do.

130 Newell, 11: 18: 62, suicide, æ. 45-7-12, b. Walpole, of Asa & Sally, Walp., do.

88 Olive, 3: 21: 57, old age, æ. 82-0-0, b. Ded.

92 Olive (Smith), 4: 22: 57, old age, æ. 76-0-0, b. Ded.

22 Paul, 10: 27: 46, heart comp., æ. 70-0-0, b. Ded.

91 Persis H. (Howes), 10: 20: 76, cancer, æ. 71-1-1, b. Boston, of Elisha & Deborah, Dennis, Ashford.

67 Relief, w. of Eliphalet, 8: 23: 44, old age, æ. 76-0-0.

47 Sally (Pond), 5: 18: 82, old age, æ. 85-4-0, b. Ded., of Eliphalet & Prudence (Fairbanks), Ded., do.

37 Sophia M. (Smith), 5: 20: 49, consumption, æ. 51-0-0, b. Ded., of ——& Grace.

7 Susan A. (Lynde), 5: 17: 66, consumption, æ. 27-6-11, b. Melrose, of George & Harriet N.

49 Walter L., 9: 14: 53, affection of brain, æ. 0-9-17, b. Ded., of Eben S. & Ellen M. P.

FISKE.

77 Fanny (Field), w. of Abijah, 2: 22: 55, consumption, æ. 68-0-0, b. Foxboro, of Joseph & Elizabeth.

FITCH.

61 Edith M., 8: 5: 79, inflam. of brain, æ. 0-8-26, b. Yonkers N. Y., of James S. & Martha P. M., Albany Co. N. Y., Waltham.

FITCHELD.

75 ——, 9: 17: 70, ——, æ. 0-0-1, b. Ded., d. of Richard & Catharine, Ire., do.

FITZGERALD.

39 ——, 5: 18: 78, premature birth, æ. 0-0-1, b. Dedham, d. of John & Ellen, Boston, do.

110 ——, 12: 1: 81, stillborn, b. Ded., of Richard & Catharine, Ire., do.

141 Ellen (Donovan), w. of John, 12: 23: 88, apoplexy, æ. 47-9-8, b. Boston, of Robert & Catherine (Congdon), Eng., Ire.

102 Jas., 8: 24: 88, diarrhoea, æ. 72-0-0, b. Ire., of Patrick & Mary, Ire., do.

59 John M., 6: 19: 81, diphtheria, æ. 14-1-8, b. Boston, of John & Ellen, Boston, do.

125 Margaret, 1: 10: 65, diphtheria, æ. 3-10-10, b. Ded., of John & Mary.

126 Morris, 1: 18: 65, diphtheria, æ. 2-5-25, b. Ded., of John & Mary.
46 Patrick, 3: 9: 64, consumption, æ. 42-0-0, b. Ire.

FITZGIBBONS.

16 Julia A. (Murphy), w. of John, 1: 25: 88, consumption, æ. 30-4-16, b. N. Y.
　　City, of Thos. & Mary, Ire., do.
115 Mary, 12: 25: 84, consumption, æ. 25-2-5, b. Boston, of John & Margaret,
　　Ireland, do.

FITZHENRY.

41 Bridget, 4: 21: 75, whooping cough, æ. 5-0-0, b. Ireland, of Lawrence & Mary
　　A., Ireland, do.
68 Mary A. (Dunn), 12: 6: 74, consumption, æ. 40-0-9, b. Ire., of James & Mar-
　　garet, Ireland, do.

FITZPATRICK.

87 William H., 12: 24: 77, inherited syphilis, æ. 0-2-10, b. Ded., of John &
　　Mary, N. B., Boston.

FLAGG.

31 Charles, 2: 6: 47, erysipelas, æ. 60-0-0.

FLAVELL.

187 Hannah (Rotch), 4: 22: 64, consumption, æ. 29-0-0, b. St. John's, of Thomas
　　& Hannah, St. Johns, do.

FLEMING.

53 Douglass, 9: 20: 58, colic, æ. 54-0-0, b. Ire., of Chas. & Lilly.
30 Eliz., 8: 20: 51, whooping cough, æ. 1-8-10, b. Ded., of Douglass & Sarah.

FLUET.

79 Edmund A., 9: 5: 85, phthisis, æ. 25-10-1, b. Boston, of Louis & Eulalie
　　A., Canada, do.
54 Eulalie A. (Scheffer), 7: 26: 78, typhoid fever, æ. 53-5-14, b. Quebec, of —— &
　　Mary B., Quebec, do.
101 Louis, 10: 17: 83, apoplexy, æ. 69-1-19, b. Canada, of James & Mary L.,
　　Canada, do.
91 William A., 10: 26: 84, consumption, æ. 22-7-13, b. Boston, of Louis &
　　Eulalie, Canada, do.

FLYNN.

68 Daniel, 9: 8: 72, dysentery, æ. 2-7-11, b. Ded., of John & Hannah.
51 Thomas, 6: 6: 84, diphtheria, æ. 2-6-0, b. Ded., of George W. & Catherine,
　　Stoughton, Milton.

FOGER.

37 Martha, 8: 27: 59, cholera infantum, æ. 0-7-14, b. Ded., of Albert & Martha.

FOGERTY.

64 John, 6: 27: 65, heart dis., æ. 35-1-0, b. Ire., of Dennis & Joanna.

FOGG.

124 Mabel T., 12: 22: 62, scarlatina, æ. 5-1-7, b. Ded., of David S. & Mary B.,
　　Meredith N. H., New London Ct.
57 Mary M., 4: 27: 59, fever, æ. 1-3-0, b. Ded., of David S. & Mary.

FOLEY.

86 Hannah (McCarthy), 10: 8: 84, hip disease, æ. 68-0-0, b. Ire., of —— & ——, Ireland, do.

15 Honora, 9: 8: 71, consumption, æ. 21-0-0, b. Ireland, of Patrick & Johanna, Ireland, do.

77 James, 9: 16: 84, cholera infantum, æ. 0-8-14, b. Dedham, of John & Mary, Ireland, do.

94 Johanna (Sullivan), 10: 25: 85, consumption, æ. 70-0-0, b. Ireland, of John & Hannora, Ireland, do.

43 Julia, 7: 25: 55, consumption, æ. 0-6-0, b. Ded., of Patrick & Sarah.

193 Margaret, 6: 20: 64, scarlet fever, æ. 0-10-0, b. Ded., of Thomas & Margaret, Ireland, do.

59 Margaret, 6: 6: 70, consumption, æ. 18-1-0, b. Ire., of Patrick & Johanna, Ireland, do.

34 Patrick, 6: 21: 55, consumption, æ. 38-0-0, b. Ire., of Dennis & Mary.

103 Patrick, 11: 8: 79, pneumonia, æ. 29-0-0, b. Ireland, of Cornelius & Ellen, Ireland, do.

8 Patrick, 1: 26: 86, meningitis, æ. 0-4-0, b. Ded., of John & Mary, Ire., do.

FOLLANSBEE.

76 Louis H., 9: 3: 80, ——, æ. 0-0-3, b. Ded., of Sherman & Juliette, Brooklyn New York, Dedham.

FOLLETT.

49 Abby H., 4: 7: 88, endocarditis, æ. 11-3-2, b. North Attleboro, of E. M. & Jennie E., Wrentham, Ded.

FOLSOM.

10 Susan C. (Jackson), 6: 27: 71, peritonitis, æ. 29-7-0, b. Boston, of Charles & Susan C., Boston, do.

FORCE.

3 Eliza A., 1: 15: 61, inflam. of uterus, æ. 25-4-17, b. Ded., of George & Eliz'h B. (Dean), ——, Ded.

96 Emily L., 10: 24: 58, typhoid fever, æ. 15-0-0, b. Ded., of George & Eliza.

FORD, FOORD, FORDE.

18 Ann, 8: 2: 47, consumption, æ. 18-0-0, b. Dorch., of Nath'l & Ann.

86 Ann (Hickey), w. of John L., 7: 3: 88, paralysis, æ. 80-3-0, b. N. F., of Richard & Tabitha, ——, N. F.

169 Elizabeth, 1: 11: 64, whooping cough, æ. 2-4-2, b. Ded., of Thomas & Sarah, Ireland, do.

80 Enos, 4: 22: 61, inflam. of bladder, æ. 64-6-0, b. Milton, of James & Hannah, Milton, do.

120 (D. at Fall River) Esther, 12: 12: 90, exhaustion, æ. 90-2-0, b. Milton, of James & Hannah (Blake), Milton, do.

111 James G., 11: 18: 90, apoplexy, æ. 82-6-4, b. Ireland, of Charles & Jane (Graham), Ireland, do.

66 John, 11: 17: 74, consumption, æ. 20-2-4, b. Scot., of John & Jane, Scot., do.

69 Judith E. (Crosby), 7: 13: 65, childbirth, æ. 32-0-0, b. Nantucket, of Matthew & Elizabeth.

25 Sophia, 4: 1: 85, old age, æ. 82-9-24, b. Milton, of James & Hannah (Blake), Milton, do.

FORRIST.

15 Marcus A., 1: 28: 89, R. R. accident, æ. 24-3-26, b. Foxboro, of Marcus P. & Lucy M. (Howard), Foxboro, Easton.

FOSTER.

17 ——, 7: 11: 47, ——, æ. ——.

18 Hannah, 2: 2: 88, bronchitis, æ. 68-0-0, b. Ire., of Patrick & Ann, Ire., do.

34 John, 8: 26: 54, cholera infantum, æ. 0-4-7, b. Boston, of John & Ann.

FOULKNER.

77 Eliz'h W. (Whiting), 4: 17: 74, cancer, æ. 52-0-0, b. Ded., of James & Lucy, Ded., do.

FOWLER.

25 Esther S. (Young). w. of Wm. C., 2: 18: 88, apoplexy, æ. 69-9-24, b. Chatham, of Elisha & Esther, Chatham, do.

103 Wm., 10: 23: 90, ——, æ. 1-2-0, b. ——, of —— & Nina.

FOX.

82 Eliz'h A., 8: 14: 90, convulsions, æ. 0-8-25, b. Ded., of Patrick & Mary (McEntee), Ire., do.

FOXCROFT.

8 Betsey (Cook), 3: 9: 63, length of years, æ. 83-4-5, b. Boston, of Israel & Phebe, Boston, Malden.

FOY.

60 Susan, [no date, Rec. 1: 30: 51], consumption, æ. 35-0-0.

FRANCIS.

50 Benj. D., 3: 20: 64, ——, æ. ——. [soldier.]

FRANKLIN.

15 Chester, 2: 16: 64, pneumonia, æ. 18-0-0, b. Lyme N. H., of Ezra & Eliza. [soldier.]

FREEMAN.

21 ——, 4: 11: 86, stillborn, b. Ded., s. of Geo. & Cynthia, Warren, Me.

114 Danforth, 11: 3: 89, old age, æ. 65-0-0, b. W. Rox., of Geo. & ——.

FRENCH.

72 ——, w. of Benj., 8: 1: 54, old age, æ. 73-0-0.

36 Hannah (Johnson), 12: 5: 71, congestion of lungs, æ. 56-10-19, b. Walpole, of Comfort H. & Susan.

78 Hepzibeth, 10: 4: 56, consumption, æ. 34-0-0, b. Me.

77 Mary (Dascomb), 8: 8: 56, confined to bed 23 yrs., æ. 55-0-0, b. Rox.

70 Mary L., 7: 7: 54, poison, æ. 1-8-0, b. Ded., of Chas. & [Hepzibeth.]

134 Rufus, 6: 6: 67, gangrene, æ. 74-8-25, b. Ded., of Samuel & Mary, Ded., do.

100 Samuel, 12: 20: 55, consumption, æ. 69-0-0, b. Ded., of Samuel & Hannah.

47 Sophia J., 8: 16: 49, whooping cough, æ. 2-0-7, b. Ded., of Abram & Sophia J.

FRIERY, FRIARY.

19 John, 4: 23: 70, drowned, æ. 3-0-0, b. Ded., of Jas. & Bridget, Ire., do.

21 Margaret, 9: 15: 63, whooping cough, æ. 2-0-0, b. Ded., of Lawrence & Ann.
61 Mary (Guiney), 9: 19: 61, gastritis, æ. 35-0-0, b. Ire.

FRIZZELE.
62 Maria J., 8: 5: 72, consumption, æ. 1-2-0, b. P. E. I., of Daniel & Jane, P. E. I., do.

FROTHINGHAM.
55 Joanna (French, 7: 6: 72, consumption of blood, æ. 54-1-20, b. Boston, of Moses & Betsey, Hanover, do.
15 Mary E., 5: 25: 56, consumption, æ. 14-2-1, b. Boston, of Samuel P. & Joanna.
96 Samuel P., 12: 18: 72, dropsy, æ. 64-5-13, b. Boston, of Samuel & Lydia, Boston, do.

FULLER.
63 Aaron, 12: 18: 69, consumption, æ. 63-0-7, b. Ded., of Jesse & Lydia, Ded., Mendon.
11 Aaron, 2: 15: 79, consumption, æ. 28-4-0, b. Boston, of Aaron & Margaret S., Ded., Boston.
93 Abby E., 2: 26: 59, consumption, æ. 14-1-14, b. Walpole, of William E. & Priscilla S.
60 Abigail (Rutter), 12: 19: 59, lung fever, æ. 62-2-25, b. Wayland, of Thomas & Damarais.
103 Alvin E., 12: 3: 71, congestion of brain, æ. 1-8-12, b. Ded., of Alvin & Frances C., Ded., Saco Me.
73 (D. at W. Rox.) Anna, 10: 8: 68, old age, æ. 79-0-0, b. Ded., of Eliph't & Lydia, Ded., do.
106 Anna B., 8: 8: 72, heart dis., æ. 51-7-0, b. Pittsfield Vt., of Job M. & Rhoda, Sherborn Vt., Alston N. H.
39 Annie E., 5: 4: 82, peritonitis, æ. 12-6-22, b. Boston, of Naham & Annie (Ware), Walpole, Boston.
61 Betsey S. (Richards), 7: 11: 85, encysted dropsy, æ. 85-1-13, b. Ded., of Jos. & Abigail (Stowell), Ded., do.
24 Calvin, 6: 27: 54, paralysis, æ. 68-9-0, b. Ded., of Eliph't & Lydia.
151 Charles, 12: 11: 64, consumption, æ. 55-10-0, b. Ded., of Jesse & Lydia, Ded., do.
131 Chas., 12: 23: 87, old age, æ. 83-1-8, b. Shrewsbury Vt., of Jos. & Achsah, Dover, Sherborn.
21 Chas. R., 3: 8: 84, ——, æ. 0-0-10, b. Ded., of Henry & Clara R., Ded., do.
28 Eliz'h, 1:31: 64, ——, æ. 86-11-0, b. Ded., of Aaron & Abigail F., Ded., do.
10 Eliz'h F. (Ellis), 2: 2: 68, paralysis, æ. 61-0-0, b. Ded., of Joseph & [Molly] (Whiting), Ded., do.
68 Ellen, w. of Eliph't, 9: 23: 44, old age, æ. 86-0-0.
89 Ellis, 3: 23: 57, dropsy, æ. 69-10-13, b. Ded., of Eliph't & Eleanor.
13 Francis B., [no date, Rec. 6: 24: 46], ——, æ. 3-6-0.
61 George, 12: 11: 69, paralysis, æ. 50-2-2, b. Ded., of Jesse & Lydia, Ded., Mendon.
2 Greenwood, 1: 1: 88, paralysis, æ. 78-2-29, b. Shrewsbury Vt., of Joseph & Achsah, Dover, Sherborn.

9 Jesse, 3: 21: 50, gravel comp., æ. 80-7-0, b. Ded., of Aaron & Abigail.

96 Lucy (Gay), 6: 18: 68, gastritis, æ. 76-1-18, b. Ded., of Ichabod & Catharine.

82 Maria L. (Stone), 12: 19: 74, consumption, æ. 30-1-0, b. ——, of Isaac & ——.

6 Marthaetta, 1: 28: 60, fits, æ. 1-10-0, b. Ded., of Spencer & Sarah.

107 Mary, 10: 3: 61, infantile dis., æ. 0-0-11, b. Ded., of Geo. & Hannah, Ded., Walpole.

66 Peggy, w. of Samuel G., 5: 13: 44, consumption, æ 53-0-0.

99 (D. at Sharon) Sam'l, 6: 11: 53, consumption, æ. 66-0-0, b. Ded., of Jonathan & Annah.

43 Sarah (Gay), 11: 8: 52, lung fever, æ. 85-9-26, b. Ded., of Dan'l & Thankful.

121 Sarah (Dodge), 4: 14: 67, pneumonia, æ. 43-11-24, b. Edgecomb Me., of John & Sophia, Edgecomb, do.

75 Sarah (Fisher), 2: 24: 74, dropsy, æ. 53-11-0, b. Ded., of John & ——, Ded., do.

86 Spencer, 2: 24: 71, rheumatism, æ. 52-7-23, b. Mass., of Spencer & Sally, Ded., Dover.

80 Walter A., 12: 15: 66, fit, æ. 0-2-2, b. W. Rox., of Andrew J. & Annette.

GAFFNEY, GAFFY.

32 Bernard, 7: 19: 62, typhoid fever, æ. 22-6-0, b. Ire., of Michael & Ellen, Ire., do.,

13 Bridget, 8: 1: 67, ——, æ. 32-0-0, b. Ire.

41 Catherine (Dale), 5: 20: 84, apoplexy, æ. 62-2-0, b. Ire., of Luke & Sally, Ire., do.

66 Ellen, 10: 25: 55, consumption, æ. 1-6-18, b. Ded., of Michael & Ellen.

78 Ellen (Dorr), w. of Michael, 8: 11: 87, diarrhœa, æ. 70-7-22, b. Ire., of Edw. & Honora, Ire., do.

24 Lizzie B., 8: 24: 67, infantile, æ. 0-0-27, b. Ded., of Jas. & Bridget, Ire., do.

47 Margaret, 8: 7: 60, cholera infantum, æ. 1-0-0, b. Ded., of Peter & Margaret, Ire., do.

67 Mary E., 9: 19: 77, valvular dis. of heart, æ. 25-0-9, b. Montgomery N. Y., of Michael & Ellen, Ire., do.

102 Mary J. (McLane), w. of Frank D., 9: 23: 87, consumption, æ. 33-6-4, b. Ded., of James & Mary, Ire., do.

74 Peter D., 7: 17: 83, dropsy, æ. 57-4-25, b. Ire., of Patrick & Ellen, Ire., do.

94 Peter W., 11: 7: 80, pneumonia, æ. 0-1-0, b. Ded., of James J. & Mary G., Dedham, Ct.

GAGE.

65 Saloma (Snow), 10: 21: 61, apoplexy, æ. 71-11-0, b. Chatham, of Aaron & Abby.

GAHAGAN.

4 John, 6: 11: 69, scarlet fever, æ. 2-2-0, b. Methuen, of Mathew & Lucy, Ire., Charlestown.

GALE.

20 Anna (Bambauer), 1: 31: 73, phthisis, æ. 22-0-0, b. Boston, of Jacob & Catherine, Germany, do.

35 Mary (Lyford), 1: 18: 63, old age, æ. 74-0-0, b. New Market, N. H., of Francis & Mary, New Market, N. H., do.

GALHAR, GALHER.
15 Catharine, 4: 27: 59, dis. of heart, æ. 29-0-0, b. Ire., of Hugh & Mary.
57 Ellen, 9: 12: 55, canker, æ. 0-7-0, b. Ded., of Peter & Catharine.

GALLAGHER, GALLAHER.
33 ——, 4: 21: 85, premature birth, æ. 0-0-2, b. Ded., s. of P. Robert & Margaret V., Charlestown, Walpole.
97 John, 10: 9: 90, difficult labor, æ. 0-0-1, b. Ded., of Peter & Mary (Carroll), Ire., do.
45 Mary, 11: 9: 52, liver comp., æ. 32-0-0, b. Ire.
24 Peter, 3: 7: 81, consumption, æ. 32-0-0, b. Boston, of Patrick & Ann, Ire.,do.
16 Thos., 2: 21: 81, meningitis, æ. 0-7-0, b. Ded., of Peter & Mary, Boston., Ire.
54 Thos. A., 7: 16: 84, premature birth, æ. 0-0-3, b. Ded., of Patrick R. & Margaret V., Charlestown, Walpole.

GALLIGAN.
116 Barney, 12: 30: 82, alcoholism, æ. 33-0-0, b. Ire., of Jas. & Mary, Ire., do.

GALLIVAN.
15 Andrew J., 2: 13: 84, capillary bronchitis, æ. 0-1-11, b. Ded., of Andrew & Mary, Ireland, do.

GALUCIA.
9 Ambrose B., 1: 27: 78, cancer, æ. 66-9-24, b. Salem, of Simeon & Dorcas N., Salem, Lynnfield.
64 Edmund W., 7: 23: 70, congestion of brain, æ. 1-6-17, b. Ded., of Warren B. & Sarah W., Lynn, Boston.
31 Milton A., 11: 27: 44, water on brain, æ. 2-0-0, b. Ded., of Ambrose B. & ——.
28 Milton A., 4: 19: 74, brain fever, æ. 1-5-2, b. Ded., of Warren B. & Sarah W., Lynn, Boston.

GANTLEY.
73 Michael, 8: 7: 82, cerebro spinal meningitis, æ. 20-0-0, b. Ire., of Patrick & Catherine, Ire., do.

GARDNER.
88 Marcy (Stone), 3: 20: 71, old age, æ. 77-1-0, b. Providence R. I., of David & Elizabeth, Providence R. I., Seekonk.

GARGAN.
73 Joseph F., 9: 8: 78, cholera infantum, æ. 0-2-7, b. Ded., of John & Mary, Cambridge, Braintree.
76 Julia A. (Henry), w. of Patrick, 6: 3: 88, dilatation of heart, æ. 52-0-0, b. Ire., of Michael & ——, Ire., do.

GATELY.
64 John, 10: 16: 55, fit, æ. 35-0-0, b. Ireland.
72 Mary (McDonor), 8: 10: 81, homicide, æ. 42-0-0, b. Ireland, of Jeremiah & Winiford, Ireland, do.

GAY.
28 Albert, 3: 6: 89, general debility, æ. 69-9-4, b. Dedham, of Jason & Lucy (Pratt), Dedham, West Roxbury.
53 Bunker, 7: 22: 48, consumption, æ. 47-0-0, b. Ded., of Lusher & [Rebecca.]

93 Bunker, 7: 12: 57, dropsy, æ. 4-0-0, b. Ded., of Jere. & Hannah.

99 Charlotte (Colburn), 11: 1: 55, old age, æ. 88-9-0, b. Ded.

73 Clarissa (Colburn), 12: 7: 58, palsy, æ. 68-0-0, b. Ded., of Lewis & ——.

47 Daniel, 3: 30: 61, palsy, æ. 76-0-0, b. Ded., of Samuel & Grace.

101 Ebenezer F., 11: 15: 71, pleurisy fever, æ. 51-2-7, b. Ded., of Oliver & Mary, Dedham, Sharon.

35 Eliza C., 10: 10: 47, fever, æ. 44-0-0.

80 Elizabeth (Whiting), 4: 6: 53, old age, æ. 91-0-0, b. Ded.

114 Elizabeth, 12: 11: 81, ossification of mitral valve, æ. 86-8-0, b. Providence R. I., of Nathaniel & ——.

51 Ellis, 5: 30: 80, paralysis, æ. 69-7-0, b. Ded., of Lemuel & Lucy (Colburn), Thompson Ct., Dedham.

25 Elmira M. (Baker), 6: 3: 65, consumption, æ. 55-0-0, b. Ded., of Sabin & Nabby.

63 Erastus E., 7: 7: 87, æ. 52-9-8, b. Ded., of Ellis & Matilda, Ded., do.

8 Fisher, 2: 21: 60, numb palsy, æ. 75-0-0, b. Stoughton.

99 Frederick, 10: 7: 89, pyaemia, æ. 66-0-0, b. Ded., of William K. & Susan, Dedham, Greenfield N. H.

86 Hannah (French), 10: 8: 76, old age, æ. 84-7-0, b. Ded., of Benj. & [Hannah.]

117 Hannah S. (Dean), 11: 13: 62, dropsy, æ. 56-2-8, b. Dedham, of Joseph & Hannah, Dedham, do.

48 Henry, 5: 20: 61, consumption, æ. 42-0-0, b. Dedham, of William K. & Susanna.

77 Horace, 12: 16: 59, liver comp., æ. 68-0-0, b. Ded., of Luther & ——.

18 James A., 2: 14: 78, dropsy, æ. 68-0-0, b. Dedham, of Lemuel & Lucy C., Thompson, Dedham.

3 Jeremiah W., 1: 11: 86, paralysis of brain, æ. 81-4-11, b. Dedham, of William & Elizabeth, Dedham, do.

78 Jesse, 5: 19: 57, old age, æ. 77-0-0, b. Ded., of Jesse & [Sarah.]

63 Jesse, 1: 7: 59, old age, æ. 82-0-0, b. Ded., of Jeremiah & ——.

43 Joel, 2: 14: 67, old age, æ. 82-0-0, b. Ded.

94 Joseph A., 5: 27: 73, bilious fever, æ. 27-0-0, b. Ded., of Jeremiah W. & Hannah (Dean), Dedham, do.

2 Lemuel, 6: 2: 44, cancer, æ. 80-0-0.

76 Lemuel, 4: 16: 45, dropsy, æ. 41-0-0, b. ——, of Lemuel & ——.

17 Lizzie F., 3: 1: 87, consumption, æ. 18-1-4, b. Ded., of Eben'r & Adeline S., Stoughton, Walpole.

61 Lucy, 2: 8: 49, old age, æ. 84-0-0.

67 Lucy (Pratt), 1: 27: 58, palsy, æ. 57-0-0, b. Roxbury.

109 Lucy, 12: 8: 82, old age, æ. 85-2-16, b. Ded., of Wm. & Elizabeth (Whiting), Ded., do.

41 Martin, 11: 30: 45, fits, æ. 61-0-0, b. Ded., of Timothy & Abigail.

32 (D. at Walpole) Martin, 9: 3: 71, gravel, æ. 73-10 0, b. Ded., of Luther & Sally, Ded., do.

114 Mary (French), 10: 19: 62, old age, æ. 80-6-12, b. Sharon, of Phineas & Hannah, Sharon, ——.

118 Mary (Ellis), 12: 13: 82, old age, æ. 82-9-24, b. Ded., of Abner & Polly, Ded., do.

43 Mary L., 9: 24: 62, consumption, æ. 13-10-30, b. Ded., of Henry & Mary A.

85 Matilda (Baker), 10: 1: 76, pneumonia, æ. 75-1-0, b. Ded., of Aaron & Hannah G., Ded., do.

61 Mehitable (Holmes), 6: 15: 65, old age, æ. 88-12-0, b. Ded., of John & Esther.

15 Milly E. (Ellis), w. of Bunker, 2: 24: 87, accident, æ. 84-8-0, b. Ded., of Abner & Polly, Ded., do.

52 Moses, 6: 22: 48, old age, æ. 68-0-0, b. Ded.

79 Polly, 4: 14: 53, old age, æ. 80-0-0, b. Ded., of Daniel & ——.

93 Polly (Fuller), w. of Joel, 4: 16: 55, consumption, æ. 66-0-0, b. Francestown N. H., of Seth & ——.

59 Rufus, 5: 19: 51, tremens, æ. 35-0-0, b. Springfield, of Ellis & ——.

77 Sally, 3: 3: 53, old age, æ. 85-0-0, b. Ded., of Joseph & ——.

59 Sarah, 3: 12: 47, ——, æ. 61-0-0.

28 Sarah, 9: 24: 65, dysentery, æ. 88-0-0, b. Ded., of Jos. & Phebe.

68 Sarah A., w. of Eb. F., 6: 11: 48, puerperal fever, æ. 28-0-0, b. Ded.

70 Seth, 7: 26: 59, old age, æ. 79-0-0, b. Ded., of Seth & [Eliz'h].

20 Sophia, 1: 30: 71, old age, æ. 77-0-0, b. Ded., of Wm. & Mary, Ded., do.

57 Susan, w. of Wm. K., 4: 26: 45, cancer, æ. 53-0-0.

74 Susan M. (Wood), 8: 24: 85, paralysis, æ. 62-4-24, b. Newton, of Lemuel & Mary A. (Jones), Brighton, Ded.

75 Susanna E. T. (Tucker), 7: 18: 56, cancer, æ. 55-0-0, b. Milton, of Timothy & ——.

72 Theodore, 11: 26: 58, consumption, æ. 71-0-0, b. Ded., of Willard & Sally.

18 Theod'e, 2: 22: 81, paralysis, æ. 87-6-10, b. Ded., of Luther & Sally, Ded., do.

76 Theron C., 12: 6: 59, consumption, æ. 25-0-0, b. Ded., of Lemuel & [Eunice.]

18 Timothy, 10: 6: 46, old age, æ. 77-0-0, b. Ded., of Timothy & Abigail.

109 Walter L., 12: 4: 67, diphtheria, æ. 2-0-19, b. Ded., of Eben'r & Addie, Ded., Walpole.

68 Warren F., 10: 1, 52, dysentery, æ. 2-9-0, b. Ded., of Willard & Emeline.

14 William, 5: 19: 50, consumption, æ. 52-0-11, b. Boston.

27 Wm. K., 1: 6: 60, dis. of heart, æ. 68-0-0, b. Ded., of Wm. & Eliz'h.

GAYMOND.

114 ——, 11: 29: 83, premature birth, b. Ded., s. of George W. & Susan L., Utica N. Y., Waterboro Me.

GAYNOR.

51 Jos. P., 5: 10: 89, diphtheria, æ. 4-7-16, b. Ded., of Jos. P. & Honora, (Connare), Ireland, do.

50 Mary H., 5: 4: 89, diphtheria, æ. 2-9-3, b. Ded., of Jos. P. & Honora, (Connare), Ire., do.

GAYTON.

98 John A., 11: 11: 84, cerebro spinal meningitis, æ. 21-9-0, b. N. B., of John & Margaret, N. B., do.

GEGAN.

14 Patrick, 8: 4: 67, infantile, æ. 0-0-1, b. Ded., of Patrick & Betsy, Ire., do.

GEEN, GEHEN, GHEEN.

45 Mary A., 8: 21: 53, dysentery, æ. 0-11-9, b. Ded., of Moses & Margaret.
60 Mary A., 9: 20: 61, cholera infantum, æ. 1-2-19, b. Ded., of Moses & Marg't.
52 Moses, 7: 31: 61, typhus fever, æ. 42-0-0, b. Ire., of Patrick & Mary, Ire., do.
32 Thos., 8: 5: 59, cholera infantum, æ. 0-10-18, b. Ded., of Moses & Margaret.

GEENTY.

30 John, 12: 21: 63, convulsions, æ. 0-0-18, b. Ded., of John & Ellen (Kennedy), Ire., ——.

GEENTRY.

83 John, 12: 22: 71, pleurisy fever, æ. 53-0-3, b. Ire., of Thos. & Ellen, Ire., do.

GERRISH, GARISH.

19 Charles, 3: 18: 45, consumption, æ. 51-0-0.
68 Eley, 7: 27: 60, cancer, æ. 77-2-18, b. Ded., of John & Nancy, Ded., do.

GERRITSEN.

122 Anna C. (Koster), w. of Henry C., 11: 2: 88, disease of brain, æ. 70-11-4, b. Holland, of —— & Anna, Holland, do.

GERRY.

67 Daniel, 3: 3: 69, erysipelas, æ. 0-9-5, b. Ded., of John & Ellen, Ire., do.

GETHRO.

61 Alex'r, 8: 19: 77, teething, æ. 0-10-19, b. Ded., of Alex'r & Maggie, Canada, Taunton.
63 Fred'k, 7: 13: 81, heart dis., æ. 71-0-0, b. Canada, of Frank & Josephine, Canada, do.

GIBSON.

99 Robert, 5: 5: 64, small pox, æ. ——. [soldier]

GIFFORD.

72 Henry A., 7: 12: 65, ——, æ. 15-0-0, b. Lee. [soldier.]

GILES.

108 ——, 12: 16: 85, stillborn, b. Ded., s. of Wm. D. & Adelaide H., Manchester, do.
87 Abbie (Stevens), w. of John J., 8: 26: 90, phthisis, æ. 58-7-10, b. Stoughton, of Pelatiah & Myra (Wales), Mass., do.
1 Ophelia, 4: 6: 69, pneumonia, æ. 66-0-0.

GILL.

81 Margaret (Gill), 11: 2: 70, old age, æ. 86-11-0, b. Ire., of Michael E. & Ann, Ire., do.
39 Michael, 9: 17: 54, dysentery, æ. 63-0-0, b. Ire., of James & Alice.

GILROY.

45 Ann, 7: 28: 57, nervous fever, æ. 2-0-0, b. Forks Me., of Michael & Anne.
127 Joseph, 9: 5: 64, fits, æ. 0-0-15, b. Ded., of Michael & Ann, Ire., do.

GILSON, GILLSON.

36 ——, 6: 12: 74, stillborn, b. Ded., d. of Barney & Mary.
120 Aphia, (Skillings), 12: 16: 83, ossification of valves of heart, æ. 81-10-6, b. Cape Elizabeth Me., of Nath'l & Sarah (Doane).
75 Nellie T., 9: 25: 72, dysentery, æ. 3-7-7, b. Ded., of Barnard & Mary, Ire., do.

GLEASON.

43 Cornelia (Harrington), w. of Wm. C.. 5: 23: 87, chronic abscess, æ. 61-8-0, b. Eastport Me., of Andrew & Phoebe, Eastport, do.

81 Francis E., 8: 3: 65, consumption, æ. 30-0-29, b. Medfield, of Jon'a E. & Anna.

39 Mary F., 8: 28: 46, consumption, æ. 32-0-0, b. Medfield.

57 Michael, 8: 10: 77, heart dis., æ. 31-0-10, b. Ireland, of John & Sera. Ire., do.

GLISPIN.

113 Ann (Morris), w. of James, 11: 2: 89, heart disease, æ. 71-6-7, b. England, of George & Mary, Eng., Ire.

95 Mary F., 11: 15: 76, consumption of blood, æ. 3-6-0, b. Ded., of Thomas & Katy, ——, Lowell.

GLORA, GOLRA.

41 Ellen, 6: 9: 69, lung fever, æ. 52-0-0, b. Ire., of —— & ——, Ire., do.

4 James, 2: 16: 63, scarlet rash, æ. 2-0-3, b. Ded., of Miles & Ellen, Ire., do.

24 Lizzie, 4: 30: 62, lung fever, æ. 4-0-15, b. Ded., of Miles & Ellen, Ire., do.

GLOVER.

60 ——, w. of ——, 9: 4: 44, consumption, æ. 85-0-0, b. Ded.

23 Caroline J. (Whitney), 12: 3: 68, pleurisy, æ. 64-6-0, b. Newton, of Amasa & Abigail, Newton, do.

69 Edward, 2: 16: 56, pleurisy fever, æ. 70-0-0, b. Ded., of Edw. & Rebekah.

104 Samuel, 10: 31: 83, chronic pleurisy, æ. 61-2-1, b. Hyde Park, of Samuel & Charlotte, Marblehead, Walpole.

GLYNN.

49 Mary E., 9: 16: 69, teething, æ. 1-0-14, b. Boston, of Patrick & Catharine, Ireland, do.

GODING.

95 Edith M., 12: 17: 72, canker, æ. 0-0-28, b. Ded., of William B. & Annie E., Canton, New Bedford.

37 Isabelle M. (Locke), w. of George P., 4: 10: 89, Bright's dis., æ. 32-3-0, b. Boston, of Oliver B. & Martha A. (Gould), Lexington, W. Townsend.

7 Mabelle L., 1: 23: 84, meningitis tuberculosa, æ. 3-6-17, b. Ded., of George P. & Isabel M., Livermore Me., Boston.

66 Martha E., 8: 23: 78, canker, æ. 0-0-20, b. Ded., of George P. & Isabel M., Livermore Me., Boston.

51 Mary A., 6: 18: 79, diphtheria, æ. 5-0-0, b. Ded., of William B. & Annie E., Canton Me., New Bedford.

GOGHANS.

59 Margaret, 8: 23: 44, æ. 84-0-0.

GOLDEN.

74 Jeremiah A., 7: 13: 89, fracture of skull, æ. 45-0-0, b. Ire., of John & Bridget (Fannan), Ire., do.

6 John, 1: 16: 82, old age, æ. 75-0-0, b. Ire., of Martin & Sarah, Ire., do.

28 John E., 3: 26: 76, ——, æ. 4-0-0, b. Ded., of Martin & ——, Ire., do.

90 Laurie, 10: 25: 78, teething, æ. 0-8-2, b. Ded., of Martin & Ellen, Ire., do.

13 Thos., 1: 30: 77, ——, æ. 2-10- 0, b. Ded., of Martin & Ellen, Ire., do.

31 Thomas F., 3:30:81, typhoid fever, æ. 19–6–0, b. Rhode Island, of James & Alice (Cleary), Ire., do.

GOLDSMITH.
154 Emeline S., 12:20:63, typhoid fever, æ. 20–10–0, b. Hanover, of Hubbard & Helen, Litchfield Me., do.

GOOD.
97 Joseph, 8:11:88, premature birth, æ. 0–0–21, b. Ded., of Michael H. & Annie M. (Manning, Boston, do.

GOODWIN.
4 Hannah E. (Eldred), 1:5:77, puerperal convulsions, æ. 38–5–25, b. Wickford R. I., of Jas. & Hannah A., Newport R. I., Wickford R. I.
99 Susie F., 9:23:83, phthisis pulmonalis, æ. 20–3–24, b. Ded., of Horace H. & Abbie, Kennebunk Me., Boston.
54 Thos. J., 8:4:61, drowned, æ. 21–0–0. b. Fairfield Me., of Samuel & Eliza, Dresden Me., Falmouth.

GOOGINS, GOOKKINS.
33 ——. 9:1:45, scarlet fever, æ. 4–5–0, b. Ded.
69 (D. at Boston) Helen S., 5:13:62, consumption, æ. 17–6–7, b. Ded., of Philip C. & Susanna S., Waterboro Me., N. S.
13 Minnie E., 1:27:75, consumption, æ. 16–3–8, b. Ded., of John & Cynthia A., Waterboro Me., Roxbury Me.

GORDON.
18 Harriet D. (Dixon), 1:19:69, epithelial carcinoma, æ. 59–1–1, b. Sterling Ct., of Thos. & Ruth, Sterling, Plainfield Ct.
5 James A., 1:31:55, dis. of brain, æ. 0–6–2, b. Ded., of Jas. J. & Louisa H.
50 James J., 10:16:54, consumption, æ. 23–8–20, b. Ire., of Alex'r & Mary.

GORELY.
45 Geo. H., 5:18:76, valvular dis. of heart, æ. 40–0–0, b. N. Y., of Daniel & Elizabeth.

GOULD.
24 ——, 5:14:45,——, æ. 0–3–0.
65 Annie L., 8:18:78, cholera infantum, æ. 1–10–16, b. Ded., of Charles E. & Mary, Woonsocket R. I., Naugatuck Ct.
101 Jonathan, 12:14:67, old age, æ. 86–5–4, b. Ded., of Geo. & Rachel, Salem, Ded.
40 Samuel, 11:13:45, old age, æ. 75–0–0, b. Ded.
14 Sarah B., 2:9:84, hepatitis, æ. 61–0–0, b. Ded., of Jonathan & Sarah, ——, Weymouth.
38 Sarah K., 4:28:82, old age, æ. 72–0–0, b. Needham, of Samuel & Esther, Sutton, Needham.

GOWLAND.
1 Kate D. (Damrell), 1:18:60, consumption, æ. 24–2–0, b. Boston, of Wm. S. & Adeline A.

GRADEN.
37 Mary (Graden), 4:11:81, pneumonia, æ. 65–0–0, b. Ire., of John & Mary, Ire., do.

GRANT.

94 Annie, 9: 26: 90, cholera infantum, æ. 0-0-24, b. Ded., of William & Rachel (Morrison), N. S., do.

82 Granville, 10: 4: 76, phthisis, æ. 55-10-0, b. S. Berwick Me., of Moses & Sabina, S. Berwick Me., do.

GRAY.

42 Edward, 7: 26: 74, dysentery, æ. 0-9-0, b. Ded., of Wm. & Hannah, Ire., do.

135 Eliz'h (Bromily), 8: 2: 63, stoppage, æ. 41-6-21, b. Attleboro, of Jas. & Anna, Eng., do.

GREDEY.

62 Mary J., 6: 30: 60, scarlatina, æ. 0-6-4, b. Ded., of Peter & Mary J., Ire., do.

GREELEY.

38 Benjamin, 3: 10: 72, accidental, æ. 58-6-26, b. Haverhill, of Clement & Hannah, Haverhill, do.

47 Emma J. (Kingsbury), w. of Abner B., 4: 23: 89, pneumonia, æ. 28-0-27, b. Ded., of Warren & Sarah (Farrington), Ded., Milton.

GREEN.

39 Eldora P., 8: 11: 58, cholera infantum, æ. 0-6-22, b. Ded., of Leon'd & Lucy.

45 John, 3: 8: 64, lung fever, æ. ——. [soldier.]

49 John, 5: 14: 83, old age, æ. 81-0-0, b. Gloucester R. I., of Bradley & Esther, Ct., R. I.

28 John H., 8: 3: 44, cholera infantum, æ. 1-1-0, b. Dedham, of Elisha & Catharine.

28 John W., 10: 28: 67, convulsions, æ. 0-0-10, b. Ded., of John & Mary (Geddes), Ireland, do.

79 Joseph, 7: 23: 63, pneumonia, æ. 21-0-0 [soldier].

61 Katie, 6: 26: 75, scarlatina, æ. 7-0-9, b. W. Roxbury, of Thomas & Catherine, Ireland, do.

47 Lucy S. (Smith), 6: 29: 78, consumption, æ. 89-0-2, b. Ded., of Lemuel & Susanna, Dedham, Canton.

15 Owen, 8: 9: 67, cholera infantum, æ. 0-9-0, b. Dedham, of John & Mary, Boston, Ireland.

GREENER.

47 John C., 4: 14: 63, lung fever, æ. 0-10-14, b. Ded., of John N. & Catherine, Germany, do.

GREENLAW.

68 William E., 8: 2: 85, peritonitis, æ. 38-2-5, b. Deer Isle Me., of Levi & Ann, Maine, do.

GREER.

69 Amy V., 9: 2: 77, dysentery, æ. 2-5-0, b. Ded., of Alex'r & Annie, Ire., N. S.

78 John P., 8: 1: 90, pneumonia, æ. 0-5-7, b. Ded., of John & Bridget (McTegert), Ireland, do.

GREGG.

107 Daniel, 7: 14: 49, typhoid fever, æ. 70-9-9, b. Windham N. H., of Thomas & Mary.

19 Jasper, 2: 5: 83, bronchitis, æ. 0-5-0.

GREGORY.
110 Wallace, 11: 2 : 83, membraneous croup, æ. 0-9-0, b. Boston, of Charles & Mary.

GRIGGS.
121 (D. at Gloucester) Charles W., 8: 15: 81, drowned, æ. 10-10-14, b. Boston, of Charles R. & Mary E. (Lewis), Boston, do.
86 James, 11: 22: 86, hypertrophy of prostate gland, 78-2-27, b. Roxbury, of Moses & Margaret, Roxbury, Medfield.
19 Lewis E., 2: 16: 75, burn, æ. 4-0-22, b. Boston, of Charles R. & M. Emma, Boston, do.
30 Margaret, 8: 5: 45, old age, æ. 75-0-0.

GROOMS.
44 Walter, 4: 20: 81, valvular disease of heart, æ. 0-6-14, b. Sherborn, of —— & Mary, ——, Lowell.

GROSS.
73 Nathaniel, 7: 11: 63, pneumonia, æ. 22-0-0. [soldier]

GROVER.
43 Calvin, 4: 1: 66, congestion of brain, æ. 50-6-26, b. Foxboro, of Calvin & Ruth.
73 Frank D., 11: 13: 66, typhoid fever, æ. 26-9-0, b. Sudbury Vt., of Luther & Olive.
89 (D. at Gloucester) George C., 8: 15: 81, drowned, æ. 24-5-0, b. Foxboro, of Calvin & Hannah, Foxboro, Spencer.
140 Minnie I., 10: 30: 63, cholera infantum, æ. 0-0-22, b. Ded., of Manly & Charlotte E., Foxboro, Hopkinton.
30 Ruth B., 8: 5: 71, old age, æ. 84-5-26.

GROW.
47 Abby J., 8: 30: 53, cholera infantum, æ. 2-4-2, b. Dedham, of Nathaniel S. & Olive.

GUILD.
86 Adeline S. (Clapp), w. of N. H., 11: 2: 55, consumption, æ. 29-0-0, b. Ded., of Joseph & Mille.
26 Albert, 4: 2: 74, consumption, æ. 31-4-18, b. Ded., of Jason & Sarah E., Dedham, Dorchester.
56 Alice D., 5: 15: 63, typhoid fever, æ. 13-11-23, b. Ded., of Francis & Lauretta W.
42 Anna, 3: 5: 47, old age, æ. 90-0-0, b. Sharon.
48 Anna B. (Chase), 5: 24: 80, old age, æ. 75-10-0, b. Chester N. H., of Humphrey & Rebecca, Plaistow N. H., do.
58 Betsey, 8: 11: 78, diarrhoea, æ. 92-0-0, b. Ded., of Heman & Sarah.
24 Calvin, 4: 25: 58, malignant fungus, æ. 82-9-19, b. Ded., of Jos. & Miriam.
31 Caroline, 4: 9: 40, brain fever, æ. 11-0-21, b. Ded., of Joseph & [Sarah H.]
65 Chloe, w. of Jacob, 3: 27: 48, old age, æ. 83-0-0.
126 Curtis, 6: 26: 49, chronic diarrhoea, æ. 49-0-0, b. Ded., of Moses & [Abigail].
24 Eunice (Quincy), 8: 22: 56, consumption, æ. 36-3-6, b. Boston, of Nicholas & Eunice.

107 Francis, 12:3:82, progressive paralysis, æ. 81-2-29, b. Ded., of Calvin & Lendemine (Draper), Ded, do.
50 George, 9:3:56, consumption, æ. 38-11-29, b. Ded., of Jacob & Hannah.
12 George C., 1:5:09, scarlet fever, æ. 5-0-7, b. Ded., of George A. & Abby C., Ded., do.
32 Gustavus T., 9:7:52, dysentery, æ. 1-3-0, b. Ded., of Francis & Lauretta W.
9 Heman, 2:1:86, apoplexy, æ. 72-9-0, b. Needham, of Heman & Hannah, Ded, Me.
25 Henrietta, 3:25:74, cancer, æ. 58-0-0, b. Ded., of Abner & Sophia H., Ded., New Braintree.
15 Jacob, 2:14:70, pleurisy, æ. 89-0-17, b. Ded., of Jacob & [Chloe], Ded, ——.
27 Jason, 3:26:82, old age, æ. 82-9-26, b. Ded., of Amasa & Rebecca, Ded., do.
153 Joel, 12:3:65, insanity, æ. 69-9-22, b. Ded., of Joel & Hannah.
42 John, 12:2:47, fever, æ. 75-0-0, b. Ded.
20 Joseph, 1:2:49, consumption, æ. 54-[3-13], b. Ded., of [Amasa & Rebecca (Whiting).]
94 Katie, 10:31:53, old age, æ. 82-0-0, b. Ded., of Moses & [Rhoda].
37 Lauretta W. (Taft), 4:6:75, cancer, æ. 58-4-9, b. Ded., of Frederick A. & Amanda W., Uxbridge, Rehoboth.
125 Lucy, 3:7:49, consumption, æ. ——, b. Ded., of Moses & [Abigail].
100 Mark, 10:15:68, consumption, æ. 62-9-26, b. Ded., of Abner & Sarah, Ded., do.
70 Martha A., 5:27:62, consumption, æ. 1-10-0, b. Ded., of Franklin J. & Adelaide F., Ded., Boston.
129 Mary A., 11:13:61, dysentery, æ. 0-8-6, b. Ded., of N. H. & Sarah H.
116 Minnie F., 11:13:62, congestion of brain, æ. 1-0-13, b. Ded., of Moses E. & Sarah A., Ded., Walpole.
30 Miranda, 3:20:73, heart dis., æ. 74-6-10, b. Ded., of John & Rebecca E., Ded., do.
79 Moses, 7:27:57, apoplexy, æ. 65-0-0, b. Ded., of Moses & Abigail.
123 Moses D., 9:20:61, diarrhoea, æ. 0-10-0, b. Ded., of M. E. & Sarah A., Ded., Walpole.
32 Nathaniel, 8:28:45, consumption, æ. 70-0-0, b. Ded.
28 Nellie, 6:24:71, canker, æ. 1-2-0, b. Boston, of Edw. & ——, Ded., ——.
70 Olive (Cheney), 5:27:58, heart dis., æ. 59-0-0, b. Thompson Ct., of Joseph & ——.
61 (D. at Hall's Hill, Va.) Oscar S., 2:21:62, typhoid fever, æ. 17-0-0, b. Ded., of Heman & Eunice, Dedham, Boston. [soldier]
57 Rebecca (Whiting), 1:13:62, old age, æ. 90-6-8, b. Ded., of Joshua & Elizabeth, Dedham, do.
87 Rebecca E. (Eaton), 9:7:49, inflammation of bowels, æ. 77-0-0, b. Ded., of John & ——.
9 Reuben, 9:10:48, old age, æ. 86-0-0, b. Dedham.
19 Reuben, 3:3:82, pleuro pneumonia, æ. 88-5-11, b. Ded., of Joel & Hannah, Dedham, do.
89 Roxanna, 8:26:65, dysentery, æ. 83-1-17, b. Ded., of Heman & Sarah.

38 Sarah E. (Shepard), w. of Jason, 11: 5: 51, liver complaint, æ. 39-1-23, b. Dorchester, of Lemuel & Sarah.

98 Sarah H. (Smith), 11: 30: 80, typhoid pneumonia, æ. 72-8-19, b. Sudbury, of Abel & Sally, Sudbury, do.

41 Sophia, 2: 8: 67, paralysis, æ. 59-5-9, b. Ded., of Abner & Sophia, Dedham, New Braintree.

37 Sophia H. (Hand), 8: 8: 58, old age, æ. 84-6-3, b. New Braintree, of Percival & Margaret.

102 Susan (Hoskins). 12: 19: 63, old age, æ. 86-10-9, b. Boston, of William & Lydia, Boston, do.

94 Sybil (Hewins), 1: 26: 62, consumption, æ. 67-10-11, b. Sharon.

95 Theodore W., 3: 19: 66, scarlatina, æ. 4-6-24, b. Ded., of Lewis & Ann F.

46 Walter, 8: 14: 51, dis. of brain, æ. 0-0-18, b. Ded., of Mark & [Maria].

73 Warren, 11: 17: 48, apoplexy, æ. 41-0-0, b. Ded., of Joel & Hannah.

110 William, 1: 28: 63, insanity, æ. 72-10-6, b. Ded., of Aaron & Lydia, Dedham, Walpole.

GUINEY, GUINNAY.

11 Cornelius, 2: 2: 86, epilepsy, æ. 21-10-24, b. Boston, of Timothy & Julia, Ireland, do.

54 Julia (Curtin), 7: 24: 86, dysentery, æ. 63-9-0, b. Ireland, of Dennis & Margaret, Ireland, do.

2 Timothy, 1: 1: 90, heart dis., æ. 75-0-0, b. Ire., of Timothy & Hannah, Ire.,do.

GUINTNER.

10 Franciska (Hasanfus), 3: 2: 61, dropsy, æ. 59-0-0, b. Germ., of Kasmier & ——.

GUNTHER.

87 Henry, 8: 28: 67, consumption, æ. 43-0 4, b. Germany, of Henry & ——, Germany, do.

68 Louisa, 11: 7: 66, teething, æ. 1-1-0, b. Ded., of Henry & Margaret.

GUPTILL.

60 George W., 10: 22: 74, whooping cough, æ. 3-4-6, b. Needham, of John W. & Elizabeth M., N. Y., Eng.

47 Lillie E., 9: 2: 74, whooping cough, æ. 0-15-9, b. Ded., of John W. & Eliz'h M., New York, England.

GUY.

60 ——, 3: 5: 48, ——, æ. 6-0-0, d. of Timothy & ——.

55 Martin, 3: 22: 52, consumption, æ. 44-0-0, b. Dover, of Benj. & ——.

HAEBERER.

45 Emma, 5: 20: 73, cramp, æ. 2-7-5, b. Millbury, of William & Hermine, Germany, do.

HAGAR.

47 James, 2: 23: 46, railroad accident, æ. 20-0-0, b. Roxbury.

HAGUE.

96 John W., 7: 29: 61, cholera infantum, æ. 1-7-16, b. Portsmouth N. H., of Benjamin & Ellen, England, do.

HALBAUER.

51 Anna, 9: 18: 74, cholera infantum, æ. 0 11-18, b. Ded., of Ernest & Sarah, Germ., do.

6 Carl A., 1: 7: 90, paralysis, æ. 75-0-0, b. Germ., of John & Johanna C. (Schneider), Germ., do.

2 Ernst A., 1: 5: 80, diphtheria, æ. 3-2-0, b. Ded., of Ernest & Sarah, Germ.,do.

HALEY.

11 ——, 1: 14: 75, stillborn, b. Ded., s. of Denis & Mary, Ire., do.

41 Ann, 4: 15: 66, lung fever, æ. 0-6-0, b. Ded., of [Dennis] & Maria.

16 David, 6: 5: 63, scarlatina, æ. 1-3-6, b. Ded., of Dennis & Mary.

77 Helen F., 7: 29: 90, cholera infantum, æ. 0-4-4, b. Ded., of Jere'h F. & Marg't (Thompson), Ded., N. S.

99 John, 12: 10: 63, lung fever, æ. 24-0-0, b. Ire. [soldier.]

129 Nancy, 11: 27: 88, consumption, æ. 18-3-0, b. Ded., of Jere'h & Catherine (Kelly), Ire., do.

75 Susan G., 9: 20: 77, cholera infantum, æ. 0-1-0, b. Ded., of Dennis & Maria, Ire., do.

HALL.

1 ——, 1: 3: 80, stillborn, b. Ded., d. of Richard & Agnes, Ire., Ded.

68 Amos, 6: 26: 63, pleurisy, æ. 60-6-0, b. Salem N. H.

4 Arthur, 4: 5: 72, teething, æ. 0-10-2, b. Ded., of Charles O. & Emily L. Walpole, Taunton.

115 Eleanor (Donely), 11: 16: 65, consumption, æ. 27-5-13, b. Ire., of Daniel & Jane.

3 Esther W. (Whiting), 1: 4: 77, paralysis, æ. 69-7-0, b. Ded., of Isaac & Thankful, Ded., Barre.

103 John, 9: 22: 65, teething, æ. 2-0-0, b. Ded., of Richard & Ellen.

40 Lucy E., 3: 23: 88, convulsions, æ. 0-0-2, b. Ded., of Richard & Agnes (Doole), Ire., Ded.

8 Martha A. (Phipps), w. of. Jos. M., 3: 12: 50, consumption, æ. 37-10-3, b. Portsmouth N. H., of —— & M. A.

42 Mary E., 2: 12: 67, ——, æ. 0-0-6, b. Ded., of Stephen & Mary, Rockaway N. J., Scotland.

4 Sabina (Tilson), 1: 12: 58, pleurisy, æ. 54-9-0. b. Halifax, of Jos. & Lucinda.

132 Semanthy, w. of Chas. O., 12: 26: 87, paralysis, æ. 62-0-0, b. Royalston.

HALLORAN.

37 Edw., 5: 15: 87, broncho pneumonia, æ. 8-6-18, b. Ire., of Edw. B. & Catherine, Ire., do.

65 John, 7: 9: 87, meningitis, æ. 0-6-9, b. Ded., of Jas. & Bridget, Ire., do.

40 John J., 5: 18: 87, broncho pneumonia, æ. 5-11-27, b. Ire., of Edward B. & Catherine, Ire., do.

5 Mary (Martin), w. of Jas., 1: 4: 88, consumption, æ. 45-0-9, b. Ire., of Edw. & Katharine, Ire., do.

7 Mary A., 1: 10: 90, gastro-intestinal catarrh, æ. 1-5-18, b. Ded., of James & Bridget (Nooman), Ire., do.

39 Sarah J., 5: 17: 87, broncho pneumonia, æ. 7-2-10, b. Ire., of Edward B. & Catherine, Ire., do.

HALTHAUF.
20 Mary, 6: 19: 52, lung fever, æ. 66-0-0, b. Germany.

HAMILTON.
89 Alex'r, 10: 16: 80, heart dis., æ. 56-9-9, b. N. Scituate, of Leonard & Ruth, Vt., Scituate.
28 Almeda E., 4: 18: 57, dropsy, æ. 5-1-2, b. Franklin, of Alex'r & Sophronia E.
28 Clara M. (Coolidge), 5: 7: 86, pleuro pneumonia, æ. 38-7-15, b. Ded., of Curtis & Lydia, N. H., Wrentham.
13 Edw. W., 1: 20: 90, heart dis., æ. 0-1-8, b. Concord, of Fred'k E. & Ida M. (Doty), Portland Me., Fall River.
10 Elmer W., 1: 29: 82, croupal diphtheria, æ. 4-7-9, b. Ded., of Geo. W. & Delia, Franklin, Woodstock Ct.
106 Frances M. (Page), 12: 28:76, phthisis, æ. 27-8-3, b. Orono Me., of Elijah & Nancy, Orono Me., Garland Me.
27 Geo. W., 4: 24: 79, consumption, æ. 28-11-22, b. Franklin, of Wm. M. & Jane, Scituate, Me.
28 Herbert O., 2: 2: 72, scarlet fever, æ. 3-4-17, b. Ded., of Wm. M. & Clara M., Scituate, Ded.
7 Jas. A. G., 1: 17: 85, meningitis, æ. 4-8-10, b. Ded., of Wm. M. & Clara, Scituate, Ded.
95 Jos. O., 12: 21: 70, bronchitis, æ. 0-2-25, b. Ded., of Wm. M. & Clarria, Scituate, Ded.
57 Sophronia E. (Osborn), 8: 11: 66, heart dis., æ. 37-7-1, b. Scituate, of Jos. & Sophronia.
24 Wm. M., 3: 12: 83, Bright's dis., æ. 56-7-10, b. Scituate, of Leonard & Ruth, Scituate, do.

HAMMER.
10 Wm. P., 1: 18: 77, ——, æ. 4-3-0, b. Albany N. Y., of Wm. & Annie K., Germ, do.

HANBURY.
39 John J., 7: 8: 60, scarlatina, æ. 1-8-21, b. Watertown, of Jas. & Catharine, Ire., do.
37 Mary, 7: 3: 60, scarlatina, æ. 3-11-0, b. Watertown, of Jas. & Catharine, Ire., do.

HANDY.
56 William, 6: 29: 55, erysipelas, æ. 27-0-0, b. R. I.

HANLON.
5 ——, 1: 13: 86, premature birth, æ. 0-0-1, b. Ded., d. of —— & Mary,——, Ire.

HANNON.
2 Catharine, 2: 28: 75, inflam. of lungs, æ. 1-9-0, b. Ded., of Thos. & Annie, Ire., do.
62 James, 8: 20: 86, scirrhus of liver, æ. 71-0-0, b. Ire., of Henry & Rose, Ire., do.
67 Johnny, 8: 7: 79, teething, æ. 0-7-0, b. Ded., of Thos. & Ann, Ire., do.
111 Mary (Sheridan), w. of Jas., 10: 4: 88, cancer, æ. 64-0-0, b. Ire., of Walter & Mary, Ire., do.

83 Matthew, 9: 21: 85, teething, æ. 0-8-21, b. Ded., of Thos. & Ann, Ire., do.

90 Walter, 6: 3: 70, fever congestion, æ. 11-0-0, b. Ded., of Jas. & ——, Ire., ——.

HANSL.

36 Annah C., 4: 30: 61, brain fever, æ. 0-8-23, b. Ded., of Chas. & Mary, Germ., do.

HANSON.

41 Bridget, 9: 21: 54, consumption, æ. 0-9-0, b. Randolph, of Edw. & Maria.

HAPGOOD.

13 Catharine (Conant), 4: 5: 59, dis. of heart, æ. 73-5-15, b. Concord, of Locke & Hannah.

134 Henry, 11: 4: 61, suicide, æ. 65-0-0.

HARDY.

21 (D. at Taunton) Ambrose, 3: 4: 76, hemorrhage of lungs, æ. 48-10-11, b. Assonet, of Wm. & Mary, (Gloucester, Assonet.

153 Eliza S. (Macy), 12: 28: 64, consumption, æ. 34-2-0, b. Nantucket, of Josiah & Eliza, Nantucket, do.

HARLAND.

7 Joan, 3: 4: 54, measles, æ. 5-0-0, b. Ire., of Michael & Ellen.

6 John, 3: 1: 54, measles, æ. 1-9-0, b. Ire., of Michael & Ellen.

HARM.

11 Christian, 12: 16: 73, congestion of brain, æ. 51-7-21, b. Germany, of —— & ——, Germany, do.

59 Christian, 8: 2: 79, consumption, æ. 21-9-15, b. Roxbury, of Christian & Catherine, Germany, do.

HARNEL.

38 John, 7: 4: 74, lung fever, æ. 18-0-9, b. Canada, of John & Sarah, Canada, do.

HARRINGTON.

53 Gertie E., 5: 14: 89, diphtheria, æ. 9-2-0, b. Riverside, of William H. & Lucy V. (Thornton), Bath Me., Gill.

32 James F., 5: 3: 78, infantile, æ. 0-1-24, b. Boston, of James F. & Lena. Hartford Ct., Boston.

80 Mima (Urry), w. of Joseph D., 8: 15: 87, consumption, æ. 41 10-18, b. Eng., of Urias & Jane, England, do.

HARRIS.

25 ——, 9: 18: 47, cholera infantum, æ. ——.

141 Cora T., 9: 1: 65, murdered, æ. 10-0-0, b. Danville Vt., of Warren & Annie E. T.

43 Enoch, 10: 9: 44, old age, æ. 80-0-0, b. Dedham.

52 George S., 6: 11: 87, diphtheria, æ. 3-8-27, b. Ded., of Charles A. & Mary E., Boston, Milton.

51 Gertrude E., 6: 10: 87, diphtheria, æ. 7-5-12, b. Ded., of Chas. A. & Mary E., Boston, Milton.

54 Sarah C. (Simpson), 7: 19: 77, paralysis, æ. 72-3-4, b. Cape Neddick Me., of Wm. & Dolly, Cape Neddick, do.

HARRISON.
83 George, 12: 19: 68, heart disease, æ. 67-11-2, b. Dover, of Jacob & Lydia, Dedham, Needham.
38 Hannah E. (Lewis), 5: 25: 77, gangrene, æ. 72-7-15, b. N. C., of John & Elizabeth.
93 Jacob, 7: 17: 61, congestion of lungs, æ. 52-3-25, b. Ded., of Jacob & Lydia, Dedham, Needham.
84 Lydia (Richardson), 9: 26: 76, pneumonia, æ. 96-5-0, b. Needham.

HART.
5 Beezy (Kilcoin), 3: 17: 71, disease of womb, æ. 26-0-0, b. Ireland, of John & Mary, Ireland, do.
47 Daniel, 4: 17: 90, diphtheria, æ. 12-3-7, b. Dedham, of Dominick & Mary (Wade), Ireland, do.
35 Margaret, 4: 20: 76, consumption, æ. 62-0-0, b. Ireland.
81 Mary (Very), 12: 15: 66, typhoid fever, æ. 46-0-0, b. East Greenwich, of Elijah & Esther.
112 Peter, 10: 5: 88, softening of brain, æ. 86-0-0, b. Ireland, of James & Mary, Ireland, do.

HARTIG.
121 John F., 12: 13: 62, ——, æ. 2-5-12, b. Ded., of John P. & Mary, Germany, Ireland.
125 Louiza, 5: 23: 63, teething, æ. 0-5-0, b. Ded., of John & Mary, Germany, Ireland.

HARTLEY.
86 James, 8: 27: 67, congestion of brain, æ. 17-0-0, b. England, of James & Harriet, England, do.

HARTNETT.
116 Ann, 12: 6: 90, bronchitis, æ. 0-2-29, b. Ded., of John F. & Mary A. (Connaughton), Dedham, W. Roxbury.
124 Catherine (Kenney), 12: 18: 65, pleurisy, æ. 36-0-0, b. England, of Patrick & Catherine.
45 George F., 3: 9: 67, lung fever, æ. 0-2-10, b. Dedham, of Edward & Mary, Ireland, do.
13 Johanna, 8: 27: 66, dysentery, æ. 0-11-0, b. Ded., of W. J. & Catharine.
75 John, 7: 18: 83, cholera infantum, æ. 0-4-12, b. Ded., of George & Maggie, Dedham, Norfolk.
79 Joseph, 7: 26: 83, cholera infantum, æ. 0-4-20, b. Ded., of George & Margaret, Dedham, Norfolk.
22 Katherine, 4: 27: 62, lung fever, æ. 2-3-0, b. Ded., of William & Katherine, Ire., Eng.
37 Michael, 3: 23: 66, consumption, æ. 24-6-0, b. Ire., of John & Catherine.

HARTNEY.
41 Bridget, 7: 13: 60, scarlatina, æ. 0-8-10, b. Ded., of Morty & Rosey, Ire., do.
1 Catharine, 1: 24: 54, infantile dis., æ. 0-0-6, b. Ded., of Thos. & Catharine.
6 Catharine (Heath), 1: 22: 84, old age, æ. 75-0-0, b. Ire., of William & Mary, Ire., do.

44 Eliz'h, 6: 28: 60, scarlet fever, æ. 8-0-18, b. Ded., of Morty & Rosa, Ire , do.
3 Ellen, 1: 24: 63, consumption, æ. 13-9-7, b. Ded., of Thomas & Catherine,
   Ire., do.
32 Mortimer, 5: 13: 86, cancer, æ. 54-11 0. b. Ire., of Michael & Mary, Ire., do.
60 Rose (Doyle), w. of Mortimer, 5: 29: 89, pneumonia, æ. 56-0-0, b. Ireland, of
   Michael & Lizzie, Ire., do.
82 Thos., 9: 24: 80, heart dis., æ. 67-0-0, b. Ire., of Patrick & Bridget, Ire., do.

HARTSHORN.
93 Daniel, 7: 21: 71, old age, æ. 84-4-8, b. Walp., of Samuel & Mary. Walp., do.
24 Ida E. (Taft), 3: 25: 85, heart dis., æ. 29-11-3.
75 Mary E. (Rhoades), 4: 16: 54, consumption, æ. 43-0-0, b. Ded., of Lewis &
   Hannah.
101 Ross H., 2: 15: 72, whooping cough, æ. 0-0-24, b. Ded., of Fred. H. & Isabella
   S., Boston, Sagharbor N. H.

HARTWELL.
2 Lydia A. (Fisher), 1: 28: 54, consumption, æ. 24-5-27, b. Rox., of Lewis W. &
   Lydia.

HARTY.
39 Margaret, w. of Thos., 7: 1: 55, dropped dead, æ. 27-0-0, b. Ire.

HASE.
86 Benj., 9: 21: 63, shot wound, æ. 22-0-0, b. Phila. [soldier.]

HASKELL.
42 Carrie E., 1: 10: 70, consumption, æ. 1-7-0. b. Digerson N. Y., of Martin N.
   & Angeline, Digerson N. Y., Waltham Vt.
64 Chas. C., 7: 29: 64, drowned, æ. 25-6-0, b. Salem, of John A. & Cynthia.
96 Joseph, 8: 3: 73, dropsy, æ. 75-0-0.
93 Nancy S. (Stearns), 11: 5: 78, old age, æ. 72-4-0, b. Lancaster, of Eli & Mary,
   Lancaster, ——.
49 Otis, 7: 4: 86, consumption, æ. 79-11-0, b. Harvard, of Josiah & Rhoda, Harvard, Still River.
53 Sarah, 11: 27: 44, consumption, æ. 75-0-0.

HASKINS.
45 Sarah L., 9: 21: 59, cholera infan'm, æ. 1-4-0. b. Ded., of Henry S. & Sarah A.
33 (D. at Rox.) Shiverick, 2: 2: 61, paralysis, æ. 71-10-3, b. Hardwick, of Shiverick & ——, Hardwick, Provincetown.

HASSON.
5 Catharine, 1: 17: 56, teething. æ. 1-5-18, b. Ded., of Barney & Ellen.
62 Ellen (Fikeley), 9: 28: 66, lung fever, æ. 42-0-0, b. Ire., of Thos. & Catharine.

HASTINGS.
88 (D. at Rox.) Ida E., 2: 5: 55, ——. æ. 1-9-0, b. Rockland Me., of S. E. &
   Emeline C.
98 Wm. A., 10: 5: 49, dysentery, æ. 3-8-0, b. Canton, of Josiah & Clarissa.

HASTY.
111 Jennie, 1: 21: 67, scrofula, æ. 0-8-14, b. Leicester, of A. J. & Lucy C., Port
   land Me., Walpole.

HATCH.

48 Nancy, 8: 18: 49, cancer, æ. 56-0-0, b. Maine.

HATFIELD.

92 Theodore, 9: 15: 89, diphtheria, æ. 8-1-6, b. W. Rox., of Jos. H. & Catharine (Como), N. S., do.

HATHEWAY.

25 ——, 3: 21: 80, stillborn, b. Ded., d. of Berton & Caroline, ——, N. B.

24 Caroline E. (Logan), 3: 21: 80, childbirth, æ. 34-7-11, b. N. B., of John & Hannah, N. B., do.

HATTON.

85 (D. at Antietam, Md.) Edw. E., 9: 17: 62, killed in battle, æ. 22-9-0, b. ——, of Henry & Susan M., Eng., Holland. [soldier.]

44 Geo. E., 5: 16: 73, lung fever, æ. 29-0-0, b. Guiana, of Henry & Susan, Eng., Vt.

52 Henry, 6: 12: 66, dis. of heart, æ. 69-0-0, b. Eng.

21 Susan M. (Gellup), w. of H., 3: 24: 55, tumor, æ. 45-6-21, b. Woodstock Vt., of Elias & Susan M.

HAVEN.

58 John A., 1: 20: 62, typhoid fever, æ. 90-8-26, b. Lancaster, of Asa & Eunice.

71 (D. at Rox.) Samuel, 9: 5: 47, dysentery, æ. 76-0-0, b. Ded., of Jason & Katherine.

HAVEY.

16 Geo. H., 2: 17: 84, inflam. of stomach, æ. 16-4-0, b. Quincy, of John & Margaret, N. S., Boston.

3 John H, 1: 7: 80, meningitis, æ. 8-9-7, b. Boston, of John H. & Margaret, N. S., Boston.

79 Mary A., 11: 23: 73, congestion of liver, æ. 11-7-19, b. Dorch., of John & Margaret, N. S., Rox.

HAWES.

1 Caroline, 7: 14: 45, consumption, æ. 22-0-0, b. Ded., of Timothy & Hannah.

84 Geo. M., 12: 23: 57, congestion of brain, æ. 5-0-0, b. Ded., of Jos. & Lucy.

79 Increase, 4: 7: 64, ——, æ. 79-0-0, b. Walpole, of Benj. & Mary S., Sharon, Ded.

104 (D. at Prov., R. I.) Jane S., 8: 6: 53, dysentery, æ. 1-4-9, b. Prov., of William & Sophia.

16 John D., 2: 22: 70, ——, æ. 0-0-5, b. Ded., of Jas. E. & Esther D. H.

79 Jonathan, 10: 6: 56, consumption, æ. 74-0-0, b. Canton, of John & ——.

76 Joseph F., 10: 10: 52, dysentery, æ. 0-16-0, b. Ded., of Joseph & Lucy.

103 (D. at Prov., R. I.) Sophia, 2: 2: 53, consumption, æ. 26-11-22.

45 Timothy, 9: 7: 51, heart comp., æ. 74-0-0, b. Walpole.

HAWKINS.

12 ——, 5: 11: 47, ——, æ. ——, b. Ded., of Charles & ——.

105 Chas., 9: 19: 61, consumption, æ. 43-1-0, b. Ded., of Geo. & Dorcas B., Pawtucket R. I., Andover.

5 Chas., 3: 16: 70, debility, æ. 0-0-2, b. Ded., of Chas. & Mary A., Ded., W. Rox.

91 Dorcas B. (Townsend), 8: 28: 65, dropsy on heart, æ. 78-0-24, b. Andover, of
—— & Alice.

92 Edward, 4: 18: 64, consumption, æ. 17-0-0, b. Ded., of Jas. & Harriet A.,
Ded., Needham.

51 George, 4: 27: 46, consumption, æ. 21-0-0, b. Ded., of Chas. & Dorcas.

20 Harriet A. (Bullard), 3: 19: 61, consumption, æ. 40-9-16, b. Sherborn, of
Richard & Jemima.

67 Harriet I., 8: 25: 78, cholera infantum, æ. 0-4-6, b. Ded., of Wm. N. & Ellen
L., Ded, W. Rox.

13 Henry C., 3: 1: 55, consumption, æ. 24-11-11, b. Ded., of Geo. & Dorcas.

50 James J., 11: 3 or 4: 62, accidental, æ. 25-3-0, b. Scotland, of James &
Catharine R.

40 James J., 2: 15: 63, consumption, æ. 42-4-7, b. Ded., of Geo. & Dorcas B.

93 Lizzie, 9: 20: 90, heart disease, æ. 65-10-24, b. Dedham, of George & Dorcas,
Pawtucket R. I., Andover.

7 Mary A. (Standish), w. of Charles, 3: 31: 52, consumption, æ. 31-0-0, b.
Standish Me., of Jonathan & ——.

104 William, 11: 11: 49, consumption, æ. 33-3-3, b. Ded., of Geo. & Dorcas.

HAYDEN.

28 Michael, 3: 27: 82, chronic cystitis, æ. 77-7-0, b. Wrentham, of Isaac &
Sarah.

25 Thornton, 1: 25: 64, lung fever, æ. 25-0-0. [soldier]

HAYES, HAYS.

53 Arvilla, 12: 25: 56, lung fever, æ. 0-6-17, b. Ded., of John & Maria.

7 Catharine, 2: 4: 56, croup, æ. 0-0-15, b. Ded., of John & Ann.

30 John, 2: 29: 88, consumption, æ. 60-0-0, b. Ire., of Michael & Ann Mead,
Ireland, do.

100 William P., 8: 17: 88, intussusception, æ. 0-4-9, b. Ded., of Wm. J. & Maggie
J. (Kelliher), Ire., do.

65 Willie, 6: 23: 90, meningitis, æ. 1-1-4, b. Ded., of Wm. J. & Maggie J.
(Kelliher), Ire., do.

HAYFORD.

11 Abba E. (Clark, 3: 2: 61, pleuro pneumonia, æ. 46-7-0, b. Prov. R. I., of
Calvin S. & Freelove (Edwards).

1 Maria T., 1: 7: 84, pneumonia, æ. 67-3-9, b. Paris N. Y., of Harvey & Prudence, N. S., Franklin.

HAYMAN.

108 Mary, 10: 4: 62, diphtheria, æ. 0-7-27, b. New York, of Henry & Mary,
Germany, do.

HAYNES.

146 Catherine, 1: 12: 88, tuberculosis, æ. 32-0-19, b. Ireland, of Meyer & Mary,
Ireland, do

131 Clara A. (Nevers), 9: 22: 64, consumption, æ. 46-10-2. b. Boston, of Benj. &
Lucy, Burlington, Lexington.

57 Clara E., 5: 2: 70, consumption, æ. 21-8-0, b. Roxbury, of Wm. F. & Clara
A., Dorchester, Boston.

17 Ophir, 2: 22: 81, pneumonia, æ. 61-5-26, b. Roxbury, of Ophir & Harriet (Mallard), Roxbury, ——.

HAYWARD.
52 Ebenezer, 7: 14: 77, peritonitis, æ. 74-9-13, b. Bedford, of Mather & Lucy P., Boxboro, Bedford.
54 Mary L., 9: 27: 53, dysentery, æ. 8-10-0, b. Boston, of Charles L. & Emmeline G.

HAZELTINE.
86 Chauncey, 2: 6: 68, disease of brain, æ. ——, b. Rockingham Vt., of William & Dolly.
80 Cordelia (Drown), 9: 14: 69, consumption, æ. 42-0-2, b. Calais Vt., of Seneca & Asenath, R. I., Woodbury Vt.

HEALBAN.
54 Wm., 11: 23: 69, teething, æ. 0-6-5, b. Ded., of —— & ——, Germ., do.

HEALEY.
10 David, 3: 15: 62, inflam. of lungs, æ. 0-1-1, b. Ded., of Daniel & Honora. ·
1 Eliz'h, 1: 12: 61, croup, æ. 0-6-0, b. Ded., of John & Catharine, Ire., do.
51 John, 5: 6: 65, consumption, æ. 60-11-7, b. England, of John & Ann.

HEAMANN.
114 George, 7: 24: 64, inflam. of brain, æ. 1-5-0, b. New Brunswick N. J., of Geo. & Eliz'h, New Brunswick N. J., do.

HEATH.
102 Anna E., 9: 15: 65, cholera infantum, æ. 1-11-11, b. Lowell, of William W. & Julia.
29 Julian G. (Merrow), 4: 12: 87, cancer, æ. 56-0-22, b. Auburn Me., of Reuben & Camelia, Minot Me., Harpswell Me.
42 Venorah, 4: 23: 72, canker, æ. 0-2-10, b. Ded., of Simeon A. & Mercy, Salem, Kennebeck Me.
73 (D. at Hall's Hill, Va.) Wm., 12: 7: 61, accidental shooting, æ. 26-0-0, b. Ire., of Michael & ——. [soldier.]
50 Wm. W., 2: 26: 70, apoplexy, æ. 38-9-20, b. Enfield N. H., of Dorset & Sarah, Enfield N. H., ——.

HEATON.
9 Chas. W., 9: 9: 69, phthisis, æ. 27-0-0, b. Alton Ill., of Geo. & Sarah B., Thetford Vt., Kennebunk Me.

HEFFERNAN, HEFFRON.
19 Johanna J., 2: 8: 88, convulsions, æ. 20-10-0, b. Ded., of Thos. & Ellen, Ire., do.
99 John, 10: 19: 82, cyanosis, æ. 0-4-0, b. Ded., of Thos. & Ellen, Ire., do.
15 Lizzie, 2: 7: 77, ——, æ. 0-0-21, b. Ded., of Thos. & Ellen, Ire., do.
58 Michael, 10: 30: 58, congestion of lungs, æ. 26-0-0.

HEFNER.
98 Sarah D. (Adams), w. of Lewis, 8: 16: 88, ascites, æ. 67-6-16, b. Southbridge, of Joseph & ——, ——, Ct.

HEIL.

93 ——, 11: 24: 60, weakness, &c. ——, b. Ded., s. of Francis & Catharine, Germ., do.

89 Louezer, 7: 1: 58, consumption, &c. 0-5-0, b. ——, of Francis & Catharine.

HEIN, HEYN.

100 Chas. O., 10: 19: 82, typhoid fever, &c. 7-9-10, b. Ded., of Oscar & Bertha, Germany, do.

48 Emma, 6: 5: 87, convulsions, &c. 0-9-11, b. Ded., of Oscar L. & Bertha A., Germany, do.

108 Frank, 11: 28: 84, pneumonia, &c. 69-0-0, b. Germ., of —— & ——, Germ., do.

91 Henry O., 9: 25: 81, eclampsia infantum, &c. 0-11-12, b. Ded., of Oscar L. & Bertha A., Germ., do.

88 Louis O., 9: 8: 89, ——. &c. 1-3-18, b. Ded., of Oscar L. & Aususta B. (Wingler), Germ., do.

56 Oscar, 7: 31: 79, convulsions, &c. 0-10-10, b. Ded., of Oscar & Bertha, Germ., do.

HEINIG.

16 Alice R., 2: 21: 86, scarlet fever, &c. 2-2-0, b. Boston, of Wm. O. R. & Louisa M., Germ., Switz.

15 Sophia L., 2: 16: 86, scarlet fever, &c. 4-1-3, b. Brooklyn N. Y., of Wm. O. R. & Louisa M., Germ., Switz.

HELFRICH

50 Geo., 5: 28: 76, convulsions, &c. 1-7-8, b. Ded., of Geo. & Theresa, Boston, Germany.

HEMMELL.

15 John, 1: 19: 60, congestion of brain, &c. 34-0-9, b. Ire., of Jas. & Esther.

HENDERSON.

94 ——, 9: 30: 81, stillborn, b. Ded., s. of John B. & Margaret J., Ire., do.

129 ——, 12: 14: 87, stillborn, b. Ded., d. of John B. & Nellie, Ire., Ded.

135 Jas. E., 12: 13: 88, consumption, &c. 34-0-0, b. Scot., of Jas. & Catherine, Scot., do.

26 Jas. F., 3: 1: 89, abscess of brain, &c. 0-5-1, b. Ded., of Jas. E. & Catherine M. (Powers), Scot., Boston.

38 Jos. S., 3: 16: 90, heart dis., &c. 80: 1: 18, b. Waterboro Me., of John & Lydia (Sanborn), Waterboro Me., do.

103 Lizzie A., 12: 1: 85, marasmus, &c. 0-1-29, b. Dedham, of John B. & Maggie J., Ireland, do.

98 Maggie J. (Gannon), 11: 18: 85, phthisis, &c. 31-8-4, b. Ire., of Thos. & Sarah, Ire., do.

109 Rebecca, 21: 19: 83, consumption, &c. 14-0-0, b. Boston, of Vincent & Lydia, Va., do.

75 Seth. J., 8: 27: 85, cholera infantum, &c. 0-2-27, b. Hyde Park, of Seth J. & Maggie M., Westboro Me., Albion R. I.

40 Wm., 4: 20: 75, scrofula, &c. 0-2-18, b. Ded., of Walter & Ellen, Ire., Ded.

HENDRICK.

7 Maria B. (Barnes), 5: 16: 74, cancer, &c. 37-0-9, b. Holland, of Gerat & Johanna, Holland, do.

HENIHAN.
43 ——, 1: 15: 70, stillborn, b. Ded., of Thomas & Margaret, Ire., do.
25 James T., 2: 25: 73, spinal meningitis, æ. 7-4-21, b. Ded., of James & Mary, Ire., do.
32 John, 3: 24: 73, dis. of brain, æ. 6-11-0, b. Ded., of Thos. & Marg't, Ire., do.
72 John C., 12: 11: 61, croup, æ. 3-6-6, b. Ded., of Thos. & Margaret.
36 John T., 4: 10: 81, typhoid fever, æ. 21-3-21, b. Hudson, of James & Mary, Ire., do.
27 Thos. F., 1: 23: 72, typhoid fever, æ. 10-8-17, b. Ded., of Thos. & Margaret, Ire., do.

HENNESSEY.
24 Abigail, 6: 1: 70, croup, æ. 3-1-14, b. Ded., of John & Ellen, Ire., do.
98 Catharine (Kenslor), 12: 10: 76, consumption, æ. 48-0-0, b. Ire., of Jas. & ——, Ire., ——.
56 Dennis, 9: 16: 60, diarrhoea, æ. 0-0-22, b. Ded., of Michael & Ellen, Ire., do.
22 Dominick, 6: 14: 59, croup, æ. 7-0-7, b. Ded., of Daniel & Catharine.
23 Dominick, 9: 22: 63, cholera infantum, æ. 1-1-0, b. Ded., of John & Marg't.
16 Dominick, 10: 16: 65, spasms, æ. 0-0-6, b. Ded., of John & Margaret.
41 Eliza (Nolan), 5: 9: 82, cancer, æ. 38-0-0, b. Ire., of Patrick & ——, Ire., ——.
12 John, 12: 27: 73, accident, æ. 36-0-0, b. Ire., of Michael & Mary, Ire., do.
26 John J., 5: 20: 60, scarlet fever, æ. 4-11-26, b. Ded., of Daniel & Catharine.
123 Margaret (Aspal), 12: 13: 65, old age, æ. 68-0-0, b. Ire., of Thos. & Nancy.
21 Margaret (Aspen), 12: 15: 65, old age, æ. 68-0-0, b. Ire., of Walter & ——.
9 Margaret E., 1: 29: 82, convulsions, æ. 0-0-3, b. Ded., of Daniel & Eliza, Ire., do.
7 Mary (Powers), 2: 10: 60, old age, æ. 73-0-0, b. Ire., of James & Honora.
147 Mary, 9: 30: 65, dysentery, æ. 1-3-0, b. Ded, of John & Ellen.
97 Michael, 7: 9: 60, croup, æ. 2-10-0, b. Ded., of Michael & Eleanor.
37 Wm., 8: 8: 62, congestion of brain, æ. 3-2-0, b. Ded., of John & Ellen (Tobin), Ire., do.

HENSEL.
128 Chas. H., 12: 1: 62, consumption, æ. 39-9-24, b. Germ.

HERBERT.
108 Lulu, 12: 6: 82, umbilical hemorrhage, æ. 0-0-6, b. Ded., of John L. & Mary E., Dover N. H., Canada.

HERBST.
90 Frank E., 12: 6: 70, membranous croup, æ. 3-9-9, b. Dorch., of Henry & Anna, Germ., do.

HERMBERG.
63 John, 7: 23: 68, consumption, æ. 37-0-0, b. Germ., of John & Mary, Germ., do.

HERRICK.
1 Georgianna, 1: 13: 57, teething, æ. 1-0-19, b. Boston, of George & Lydia.

HERRING.
67 Edwin J., 6: 14: 63, consumption, æ. 29-10-21, b. Ded., of Nath'l & Hannah, [soldier.]
70 Hannah K. (Kingsbury), 7: 12: 65, heart dis., æ. 65-8-0, b. Ded., of Moses & Hannah.

56 Joseph, 4: 22: 45, ——, æ. 76-0-0.

HERSEY.

36 Geo. C., 8: 8: 62, executed, æ. 29-7-6, b. Hingham, of Jas. & Sarah (Gardner), Hingham, Boston.

HESS.

22 Catharine, 12: 27: 65, teething, æ. 1-3-0, b. Lynn, of Wm. & Juliet.

HEWINS.

124 ——, 12: 3: 87, stillborn, b. Ded., s. of Geo. & Harriet W., Boston, Ded.

88 Carrie E. (Sparrell), 10: 21: 76, typhoid fever, æ. 39-3-0, b. Boston, of Wm. & Caroline F., S. Scituate, Rox.

67 Carrie F., 4: 19: 62, dropsy on brain, æ. 1-8-8, b. Ded., of Alfred & Carrie E.

78 Chas. C., 8: 3: 67, slow fever, æ. 3-0-0, b. Ded., of Geo. & Hattie W., Boston, Ded.

78 Eliz'h (Alden), 10: 4: 62, lung fever, æ. 63-11-20, b. Newton, of Paul & Rebeckah, Needham, do.

55 Fisher A., 9: 8: 57, consumption, æ. 28-0-2, b. Ded., of Nath'l A. & Hannah.

99 Gertrude N., 8: 16: 88, inflam. of stomach, æ. 7-10-25, b. Ded., of Geo. & Harriet W. (Carroll), Boston, Ded.

127 Hannah (Hersey), w. of Nath'l A., 12: 11: 87, paralysis, æ. 82-7-26, b. N. Bridgewater, of Elijah & Laurana (Packard), Hingham, N. Bridgewater.

19 Nath'l A., 12: 11: 48, consumption, æ. 45-0-0, b. Sharon.

9 Otis W., 1: 14: 77, ——, æ. 67-2-0, b. Sharon, of Philip & Lucy.

HICKEY, HICKIE.

11 Chas. H., 1: 13: 90, consumption, æ. 42-0-0, b. Ire., of Matthew & Catherine, Ire., do.

97 Timothy F., 10: 3: 89, consumption, æ. 23-5-5, b. Dorch., of Timothy & Ellen (Hallahan), Ire., do.

HICKS.

25 Cyrus, 2: 24: 89, heart dis., æ. 75-6-7, b. Taunton, of Jonathan C. & Hannah (Tisdale), Rehoboth, Taunton.

HIGGINS.

120 ——, 4: 18: 63, ——, æ. 0-0-1, b. Ded., of Patrick & Catharine.

26 Bridget, 11: 27: 63, childbirth, æ. 35-0-0, b. Ire.

5 Dennis, 1: 22: 62, ——, æ. 1-5-6, b. Ded., of Michael & Hannah.

73 Hannora, 6: 9: 69, congestion of brain, æ. 0-9-16, b. Ded., of Dennis & Ellen, Ire., do.

52 Mary, 11: 12: 62, congestion of brain, æ. 4-2-10, b. Ded., of Dennis & Mary, Ire., do.

144 Mary, 9: 14: 65, dysentery, æ. 1-2-15, b. Ded., of Patrick & Catharine.

76 Nelly, 6: 27: 69, pneumonia, æ. 0-7-10, b. Ded., of Patrick & Catharine, Ire., do.

HILDRETH.

19 Edward F., 1: 17: 66, teething, æ. 1-3-0, b. Ded., of Henry O. & Cornelia S.

HILL.

34 Edith B., 5: 12: 77, diphtheria, æ. 7-9-0, b. Ded., of David S. & Mary, Milford N. H., N. S.

74 Ellis M., 12:23:53, worms, æ. 1-8-5, b. Ded., of Geo. W. & Martha A.
95 Emily F., 7: 26: 61, consumption, æ. 17-5-25, b. Ded., of Geo. & Lenda, Canton, Ded.
 1 George, 6:2:48, erysipelas, æ. 47-0-0, of Nath'l & ——.
91 Georgianna B. (Brown), 4:26:71, drowned, æ. 44-5-27, b. Wilmot N. H., of David & Mary, ——, Mass.
52 Hannah J. (Swain), 5: 12: 65, cancer, æ. 39-11-20, b. Hill N. H., of Chase & Emily.
62 Lenda (Whiting), 6: 24: 70, consumption, æ. 68-0-14, b. Ded., of Lemuel & Mary, Dedham, do.

HILTON.
108 Sophronia (Luce), w. of Alden, 10: 17: 89, paralysis, æ. 63-0-0, b. New Sharon Me., of Ezekiel & Nancy (Norcross), Me., do.

HINKLEY.
147 Ambrose, 11:23: 64, poison, æ. 33-0-0. [soldier.]

HIRSCH.
 57 Geo. S., 6: 19: 76, phthisis, æ. 43-8-0, b. Germ., of John M. & Mary, Germ.,do.

HITCHINGS.
 70 Amanda E. (Taft), 8:21: 76, consumption, æ. 49-0-11, b. Ded., of Fred'c A. & Amanda, Uxbridge, Rehoboth.
104 *Betsey (Wade), 12:20:63, inflam. of bowels, æ. 75-11-0, b. Malden, of Edw. & Rebecca, Charlestown, do.
 63 Edw. T., 6: 11: 89, meningeal dis. of brain, æ. 4-11-6, b. Ded., of Henry & Mary F. (Taft), Boston, Medford.
 63 Martha, 11: 9: 53, consumption, æ. 32-11-7, b. Malden, of Daniel & Betsy.

HITTL.
 60 Bertha, 7: 1: 87, stillborn, b. Ded., of Julius J. & Louise M., Germ., Boston.
 21 Frances M. (Lorence), 3: 12: 87, apoplexy, æ. 61-11-24, b. Bohemia, of Frank J. & Anna, Bohemia, do.

HOAR.
 38 James, 8: 9: 58, canker rash, æ. 9-3-9, b. Eng., of David & Mary.
 63 Mary, 11: 1: 61, cholera infantum, æ. 0-7-7, b. Dedham, of David & Mary.

HOBART.
 41 Eliz'h, 4: 11: 81, pneumonia, æ, 0-4-0.

HODGDEN.
 82 Oliver, 10: 28: 72, typhoid fever, æ. 30-0-0, b. Hiram Me., of Geo. & ——.

HODGES.
 83 Abel B., 10: 30: 72, typhoid fever, æ. 23-7-25, b. Taunton, of William V. & Elioendi, Taunton, do.
 10 Lurania W. (Lane), 7: 27: 74, chronic pleurisy, æ. 68-8-17, b. Norton, of David & Lurania, Norton, do.
  9 Mary F., 1: 7: 88, apoplexy, æ. 53-0-27, b. Ded., of Charles & Mary T. (Farrington), ——, Dedham.
 53 Mary T. (Farrington), 4: 12: 67, consumption, æ. 64-7-3, b. Ded., of Stephen & Lucy, Dedham, Milton.

HODGKIN.

48 Frank J., 8: 19: 60, diphtheria, æ. 4-7-0, b. Auburn Me., of A. B. & Harriet M., Lewiston Me., Auburn Me.

HODSON.

29 Gertrude F., 2: 29: 88, whooping cough, æ. 0-3-13, b. Ded., of William T. & Kitty E., Lancaster Pa., W. Roxbury.

HOFFMAN.

92 Constantine, 12: 18: 70, ——, æ. 59-9-0, b. Germany, of Frederick & ——, Germany, do.

122 (D. at Boston) Ernestina (Oehler), w. of Chas., 12: 3: 87, consumption, æ. 29-0-0, b. Saxony, of Gottfried & Ernestina, Saxony, do.

43 John, 6: 6: 78, consumption, æ. 69-0-0, b. Germany, of —— & Mary J., Germany, do.

HOGAN.

4 Anna, 1: 26: 55, congestion of brain, æ. 1-6-6, b. Ded., of John & Catharine.

4 Edward, 1: 15: 62, ——, æ. 0-2-14, b. Ded., of Patrick & Betsy.

40 Edward, 1: 5: 70, convulsions, æ. 0-0-5, b. Dedham, of John & Catharine, Ireland, do.

62 Margaret, 6: 4: 67, lung fever, æ. 22-0-0, b Boston, of Patrick & Anastatia, Ireland, do.

138 Mary, 8: 20: 65, dysentery, æ. 2-9-4, b. Ded., of Edw. & Catherine.

26 Thomas, 7: 8: 70, pneumonia, æ. 2-0-0, b. Dedham, of Patrick & Eliza H., Ireland, do.

HOLLAND.

67 ——, 6: 19: 67, ——, æ. 0-0-1, b. Ded., s. of Patrick & Mary, Ire., do.

92 Patrick, 8: 29: 65, diarrhoea, æ. 1-1-22, b. Ded., of Patrick & Mary.

HOLLINGSWORTH.

31 Agnes S. (Thompson), w. of David H., 3: 20: 80, enlargement of heart, æ. 54-2-27, b. N. S., of John B. & Sarah, Scot., do.

HOLMES.

46 ——, 6: 28: 78, stillborn, b. Ded., s. of Walter & Sarah F., Dorch., Boston.

26 Augustus N., 8: 21: 44, dysentery, æ. 3-0-0, b. Ded., Edw. B. & ——.

35 Caroline (Buttrick), 8: 31: 54, consumption, æ. 48-8-26, b. Lancaster, of Horatio & ——.

36 Chas. H., 3: 28: 45, inflammatory fever, æ. 8-0-0, b. Ded., of Edw. B. & ——.

117 Daniel C., 11: 16: 89, pericarditis, æ. 62-4-0, b. Hanson, of Luther & Nancy (Baker), Dorch., Hanson.

152 (D. at Rockville, Ct.) Edw. B., 12: 24: 64, paralysis, æ. 73-11-19, b. Canton, of Jos. & ——.

69 Elijah J., 6: 29: 67, inflam. of bowels, æ. 43-1-17, b. Winthrop Me., of John & Dolly, Peterboro N. H., Candia N. H.

34 Eliza, 2: 5: 68, consumption, æ. 74-8-16, b. Dorch., of Issachar & Mary, Canton, Rox.

74 Jane (Thompson), 10: 24: 86, old age, æ. 72-9-0, b. N. S., of James & Sarah, N. S., do.

62 Jeremiah, 1: 6: 59, old age, æ. 80-0-0, b. Sharon, of John & ——.

8 Jos., 2:4:56, consumption, æ. 27-7-8, b. N. Yarmouth Me., of Jos. & Sarah.

7 Lucy, 3:14:48, dropsy, æ. 70-0-0.

53 Mabel L., 6:2:76, diphtheria, æ, 7-8-18, b. Boston, of Walter & Sarah F., ——, Dorch.

70 Mary A., 7:5:67, canker, æ. 0-2-0, b. Ded., of Fred. H. & Agnes A., Gardiner Me., Scot.

80 Nath'l A., 8:2:65, consumption, æ. 51-5-25, b. Monmouth Me., of John & Dolly.

87 Oliver, 6:4:61, consumption, æ. 39-0-1, b. Portsmouth N. Y., of Benjamin & Mary, Portsmouth N. H., Rye N. H.

10 Sarah, 3:18:54, consumption, æ. 22-10-6, b. N. Yarmouth Me., of Joseph & Sarah.

136 Sarah (Kenney), 10:6:64, liver comp., æ. 69-0-16, b. N. Yarmouth Me., of Samuel B. & Hannah, Nottingham N. H., Yarmouth Me.

HOLT.

12 Mary M. (Beal), 2:15:83, consumption, æ. 46-11-15, b. Boston, of Thatcher & Lydia, Boston, do.

HOLTHAM.

9 Stella M., 1:8:75, scarlet fever, æ. 3-9-20, b. Ded., of Alfred & Elizabeth J., Eng., do.

HOMER.

90 Elnathan L., 4:14:64, pneumonia, æ. ——. [soldier.]

31 Nellie F., 1:24:68, putrid sore throat, æ. 11-0-3, b. Haverhill, of Wm. P. & Lucy H., Hawley, Berlin.

HOOBAN.

71 Ann V., 8:9:81, cholera infantum, æ. 0-1-9, b. Ded., of John & Maria, Ire., do.

125 John, 12:5:87, consumption, æ. 41-11-0, b. Ire., of Thos. & Mary, Ire., do.

95 Maria (Goonan), 9:27:82, consumption, æ. 36-7-0, b. Ire., of Jere'h & Mary, Ire., do.

22 Maria T., 4:10:79, tuberculosis, æ. 7-0-18, b. Ded., of John & Maria, Ire., do.

61 Maria T., 8:2:80, cholera infantum, æ. 0-2-8, b. Ded., of John & Maria, Ire., do.

HOOKER.

145 Jerusha B. (Holmes), 11:19:64, liver comp., æ. 58-11-10, b. Milton, of Eben'r & Charlotte, Stoughton, Canton.

26 Joseph E., 4:26:61, pleurisy, æ. 17-11-0, b. Ded., of James & Jerusha.

7 Miriam H., 8:17:48, dysentery, æ. 2-0-0, b. Ded., of James & [Jerusha].

HOPKINS.

94 Lydia A. (Allen), 11:15:78, consumption, æ. 65-6-0, b. Taunton, of John & Betsey, ——, Taunton.

9 Mary A. (Gibbons), 2:12:59, consumption, æ. 25-11-25, b. N. Y., of John & Mary.

HORGAN.

116 Honora, 3:13:63, scarlet fever, æ. 2-9-11, b. Ded., of Jeremiah & Margaret, Ire., do.

139 Jeremiah, 9: 23: 63, cholera infantum, æ. 1-0-2, b. Stoughton, of Jere'h & Margaret, Ire., do.

HORN.

44 Henry, 6: 10: 84, paralysis, æ. 73-2-6, b. Watertown, of Wm. & Martha S., Framingham, Watertown.

102 Mary A. (Hibbard), 12: 15: 78, pneumonia, æ. 66-2-1, b. Prov. R. I., of Benj. D. & Lydia L., Claremont N. H., Prov. R. I.

HORTON.

24 Frank V., 3: 22: 74, typhoid fever, æ. 3-0-12, b. Ded., of Albert G. & Anna A., Eng., Wis.

70 Fred'k G., 10: 10: 73, congestion of brain, æ. 0-4-0, b. Ded., of Albert G. & Anna A., Eng., Wis.

46 Walter F., 9: 4: 58, cholera infantum, æ. 0-6-0, b. Ded., of Geo. C. & Eliza.

HOUGHTON.

16 Agnes (McEneny), 5: 25: 56, consumption, æ. 23-7-26, b. Ded., of Arthur & Nancy.

27 Edw. C., 6: 20: 71, inflam. of liver, æ. 4-9-0, b. Ded., of Jos. & Mary.

9 Ephraim, 2: 7: 79, paralysis, æ. 83-11-20, b. Winchendon, of Robert & Sarah, Leominster, Lunenburg.

107 Geo. W., 12: 28: 76, peritonitis, æ. 52-4-0, b. Putney Vt., of Amos & Almira.

36 Polly (Bonney), 2: 29: 72, congestion of lungs, æ. 65-0-0, b. Hanson, of Ezekiel & ——, Hanson, do.

66 Wm., 7: 27: 68, old age, æ. 79-9-2, b. Winchendon, of Robert & Sarah, Leominster, Lunenburg.

HOWARD.

110 Adeline B. (Baker), 12: 14: 67, neuralgia, æ. 60-0-0, b. Ded., of Sabin & Abigail, Ded., Ashford.

80 Eliza G. (Barrows), 9: 23: 78, paralysis, æ. 63-5-0, b. Dover N. H., of Amos C. & Abigail, Dover N. H., do.

35 Martin, 4: 7: 81, consumption, æ. 41-5-0, b. Ire., of Anthony & Ellen, Ire., do.

84 Mary L., 9: 29: 75, marasmus, æ. 0-1-21, b. Ded., of Martin & Eliz'h C., Ire., do.

138 Oramel, 10: 10: 64, chronic diarrhœa, æ. ——. [soldier.]

4 Seth, 1: 8: 57, gangrene, æ. 54-0-0.

HOWARTH.

122 Jane (Fagan), 12: 21: 83, ——, æ. 54-0-0, b. Ire., of Thos. & Ellen, Ire., do.

98 John E., 10: 29: 81, cyanosis, æ. 0-0-1, b. Ded., of Thos. & Ellen, Ded., Ire.

HOWE.

52 ——, w. of Joseph, 4: 30: 46, consumption, æ. 66-0-0, b. Ded.

80 Alice G., 11: 22: 75, paralysis, æ. 27-0-0, b. Ded., of Josiah D. & Hannah, Marlboro, Barre.

99 Elijah, 11: 30: 80, pneumonia, æ. 88-1-9, b. Ded., of Thos. 3d & Hannah Withington, Ded., Dorch.

69 Francis, 5: 18: 59, apoplexy, æ. 72-0-0, b. Framingham.

107 Francis E., 10: 7: 65, dysentery, æ. 1-2-4, b. Ded., of Elijah Jr. & Julia A.

13 Joseph, 5: 21: 47, consumption, æ. 76-0-0.

50 Josiah D., 5: 4: 65. consumption, æ. 26-8 21, b. Princeton, of Josiah D. & Hannah.

65 Josiah D., 6: 10: 67, consumption, æ. 60-11-24, b. Oakham, of Josiah & Phebe, Oakham, do.

103 Julia A. (Gay), 12: 12: 80, pneumonia. æ. 77-4-7, b. Ded., of Moses & Mehitable Holmes, Ded.. Sharon.

31 Lucy (Gay), 5: 23: 78, old age, æ. 85-10-0, b. Ded., of Lemuel & Lucy C., Ded., do.

74 Mary II., 8: 30: 76, pneumonia, æ. 31-9-23, b. Lexington, of Josiah D. & Hannah, Marlboro, Barre.

37 Mattie R., 2: 15: 65, congestion of brain, æ. 0-7-26, b. Wolfboro N. II., of Allen L. & Lizzie.

24 Sarah J. (Mullen), w. of Patrick, 2: 15: 88, consumption, 30-7-8, b. Ded., of Michael & Margaret, Ire., do.

HOWELL.

132 (D. at Boston), John, 12: 6: 88, R. R. accident, æ. 69-3-16, b. Eng., of Daniel & Mary (Sinister), Eng., do.

42 Wm. II., 9: 9: 59, typhus fever, æ. 15-8-6, b. Eng., of John & Eliza.

HOWES.

76 Hannah, 5: 18: 58, cancer, æ. 76-0-0, b. Walpole.

63 Nelly F., 10: 25: 57, cholera infantum, æ. 0-9-0, b. Charlestown, of Reuben & Mary D.

HOWLAND.

139 (D. at Boston) Jos., 3: 3: 87, accident, æ. 45-0-0, b. P. E. I., of Wm. & Ann, Ire., do.

HOWLETT.

80 Annie V., 10: 28: 79, chronic catarrhal pneumonia, æ. 18-1-14, b. Charlestown, of Thos. & Catherine, Ire., do.

52 Jas. A., 6: 5: 80, phthisis, æ. 22-7-0, b. Charlestown, of Thos. & Catherine (Keating), Ire., do.

80 Mary V., 10: 13: 84, consumption, æ. 25-5-0, b. Charlestown, of Thos. & Catherine, Ire., do.

HUBBARD.

66 Frank, 12: 22: 51, dropsy, æ. 0-9-0, b. Ded., of John S. & ——.

106 Frank K., 10: 7: 87, convulsions, æ. 0-0-4, b. Ded., of Frank K. & Julia E., Marlboro N. II., Loray N. Y.

12 Jane G. (Golding), 11: 22: 83, phthisis pulmonalis, æ. 69-0-0, b. Lowell, of John & ——, Templeton, do.

87 John S., 8: 19: 65, dysentery, æ. 55-5-6, b. Candia N. II., of Jos. & Mary.

44 Samuel A., 12: 13: 56, dropsy, æ. 18-1-2, b. Rox., of John S. & Jane G.

HUDSON.

9 Henry A., 2: 4: 64, typhoid fever, æ. 13-0-0, b. Fitchburg, of Wm. & ——.

HUGHES.

1 John, 1: 15: 76, consumption, æ. 65-0-0, b. Ire., of —— & ——, Ire., do.

33 Mary (Grady), 5: 5: 78, consumption, æ. 32-11-0, b. Ire., of Patrick & Mary, Ire., do.

HUMPHREY, HUMPHREYS.

91 Betsey H. (Deveraux), 10: 18: 85, cancer, æ. 87-5-10, b. Marblehead, of John & Betsey (Leach), Marblehead, do.

12 Frank R., 2: 18: 78, bronchitis, æ. 0-6-0, b. Ded., of Nickerson G. & Sarah, Washington D. C., Ct.

55 Henry R., 4: 16: 88, premature birth, æ. 0-0-2, b. Ded., of Henry D. & Lena R., W. Rox., Gloucester.

95 James, 11: 13: 80, diabetes, æ. 50-7-13, b. Athol, of James & Sarah, Athol, do.

74 Lena R. (Witham), w. of Henry D., 7: 19: 90, multiple neuritis, æ. 24-5-8, b. Gloucester, of Sidney & Susan E. (Saunders), Gloucester, do.

11 Sarah (Kendall), 2: 9: 85, cerebral hemorrhage, æ. 87-11-0, b. Athol, of Joel & Mary, Athol, ——.

HUNKINGS, HUNKINS.

44 Charlotte (Dean), 9: 20: 54, spinal complaint, æ. 39-5-26, b. Ded., of Eben'r & Louisa.

42 Henry W., 10: 30: 52, typhoid fev.,æ. 15-1-4, b. Ded., of Thos. J. & Charlotte.

HUNNEWELL.

72 Charles, 5: 19: 56, dis. of heart, æ. 78-0-0.

HUNT.

39 Lizzie H., 7: 16: 74, consumption, æ. 14-1-12, b. Medfield, of Thomas E. & Hannah J., Marlboro, Medway.

11 Oliver, 2: 6: 76, disease of brain, æ. 66-2-8, b. Douglas, of Oliver & Phebe, Douglas, do.

80 Persis G. (Forbush), 9: 7: 85, constriction of colon, æ. 77-6-16, b. Upton, of Samuel & Lydia, Upton, Hopkinton.

71 Susanna (Eaton), 9: 3: 78, paralysis, æ. 79-6-11, b. Haverhill, of —— & Rebecca, Haverhill, do.

40 Thos., 9: 13: 62, convulsion, æ. 0-0-6, b. Ded., of Michael & Ann, Ire., do.

HUNTING.

90 C. Valentine, 1: 19: 73, rupture of blood vessel, æ. 6-11-5, b. Rox., of Reuben & Louisa (Pratt), Rox., Boston.

124 Mary A. (Freeman), w. of Reuben, 12: 26: 90, chronic bronchitis, æ. 79-8-26, b. Rox., of Leonard & Eliz'h (Horton), Bellingham, Sherborn.

HUPFER.

71 Johanna C. (——), 8: 16: 75, dysentery, æ. 81-5-18, b. Germ., of Goddfreed & Johanna, Germ., do.

HURD.

60 Eliz'h, w. of Joseph, 3: 12: 47, ——, æ. 22-0-0.

124 Sarah C., 5: 10: 63, consumption, æ. 19-10-8, b. Galveston Tex., of Alvin & Relief H., Orleans, Boston.

HURLEY, HERLEY.

59 ——, 6: 28: 87, stillborn, b. Ded., s. of Patrick H. & Hannah B., Dedham, Depere Wis.

43 Edw. M., 6: 16: 86, cerebro spinal meningitis, æ. 3 8-23, b. Ded., of Patrick & Hannah, Ded., Depere Wis.

18 John S., 3:2:82, diphtheria, æ. 4-5-1, b. Ded., of Charles J. & Mary A. J., Ire., do.

17 Jos., 2:20:83, pneumonia, æ. 3-0-0, b. Ded., of Jos. & Margaret, Ire., do.

60 Mary A., 7:17:68, cholera infantum, æ. 1-0-0, b. Ded., of Jos. & Margaret, Ire., do.

HURST.
104 John, 8:17:62, drowning, æ. 25-0-0, b. Germ., of Geo. & Catharine, Germ.,do.

HUSSEY.
67 Geo. W., 7:16:87, drowning, æ. 29-3-29, b. Milton N. H., of Jos. & Susan E., Milton N. H., Lebanon Me.

HUSTON.
22 Geo. L., 8:9:50, cholera infantum, æ. 1-1-16, b. Ded., of Wm. R. & Susan E.

HUTCHINS.
38 Emma F., 7:16:53, cholera infantum, æ. 1-6-4, b. Ded., of Thomas F. & Ruth T.

20 Geo. H., 1:8:64, chronic dis., æ. 28-4-4, b. Ded., of Jos. S. & Sarah.

65 Henry, 10:25:55, ——, æ. 0-0-2, b. Ded., of Thos. F. & Ruth T.

82 Sarah (White), 12:21:71, debility, æ. 72-9-3, b. Ded., of Luther & Rebecca, Ded., do.

HUTCHINSON.
37 Rachel A. (Willard), 11:13:70, apoplexy, æ. 76-4-4, b. Lancaster, of John & Lucy A., Lancaster, do.

HUTT.
76 Alice, 9:27:72, dysentery, æ. 0-5-4, b. Ded., of Wm. H. & Mary A., N. S., Boston.

HYDE.
7 John, 4:15:71, consumption, æ. 71-5-5, b. Newton, of John & Abigail, Newton, do.

ICHLER.
56 Chas., 10:6:53, croup, æ. 1-5-0, b. Germany, of Chas. & ——.

IDE.
132 Sybil J., 12:13:61, typhoid fever, æ. 31-2-0, b. Ded., of Nath'l & Sybil, Ded., Sharon.

INCHES.
29 ——, 6:3:53, scarlet fever, æ. 0-1-0, b. Ded., s. of Martin B. & Mary W.

INGALLS, INGELS.
11 ——, 5:11:47, ——, æ. ——.

31 Eleanor B. (Cuthbert), 2:16:72, heart dis., æ. 54-2-19, b. N. S., of Abram & ——, Eng., do.

57 John C., 5:18:63, paralysis, æ. 61-2-24, b. Canada, of Henry & Margaret, England, do.

INGERSOLL.
46 Aden, 6:21:77, tumor, æ. 18-2-0, b. Poughkeepsie N. Y., of S. H. & Anna, N. Y., Ill.

INGRAHAM.
106 Mary E., 9: 26: 66, cholera infantum, æ. 0-2-16, b. Ded., of George L. & Nancy A. T.
47 Wm. O., 10: 13: 51, lung fever, æ. 0-1-5, b. Dedham, of Geo. L. & ——.

IVES.
30 Eliz'h (Tourgee), 1: 20: 68, consumption, æ. 31-0-0. b. Natick R. I., of Benj. & Sally A.

JACKSON.
44 ——, 4: 26: 83, stillborn, b. Ded., s. of Robert S. & Nellie M., N. Y., Vt.
22 John P., 1: 13: 64, old age. æ. 95-6-11, b. Dover N. H., of Wm. & Sarah.

JACOB.
117 Maximilian, 12: 12: 83, injury from a fall, æ. 42-0-0, b. France, of Wm. & Leaner, France, do.

JEFFERSON.
82 Austin, 4: 1: 64, ——, æ. ——. [soldier.]

JESSER.
20 Ann (Sheridan), 3: 4: 82, anaemia, æ. 52-5-0, b. Ire., of John & Mary, Ire..do.
48 Peter, 6: 7: 77, heart dis., æ. 41-0-0, b. France, of —— & ——, France. do.

JEWETT.
32 Franklin M., 1: 22: 65, pneumonia, æ. 26-0-0. [soldier.]

JOHN.
16 Cain, 7: 11: 47, consumption, æ. 26-0-0, b. Dedham.

JOHNSON.
23 Alfred, 4: 19: 60, consumption, æ. 23-0-0, b. Walpole, of Noel & Lucy A.
4 Alfred E., 1: 12: 86, cerebral meningitis, æ. 1-1-13, b. Ded., of Alfred E. & Ida, Norway, do.
19 Anna L., 2: 17: 74, inflation of bowels, æ. 17-8-15, b. New Hampton N. H.
21 E. A., 1: 10: 64, pneumonia, æ. 35-0-0. [soldier.]
19 Edwin, 6: 11: 56, consumption, æ. 31-5-10, b. Charlestown, of Marshall & Hannah.
59 Eugene N., 6: 4: 83, diphtheria, æ. 26-6-0, b. Green Garden Ill., of Silas & Lestina, Shrewsbury Vt., Plymouth Vt.
10 Francis, 9: 15: 48, consumption, æ. 29-0-0, b. Charlestown.
41 George, 3: 4: 64, pneumonia, æ. ——. [soldier.]
85 George R., 4: 9: 64, small pox, æ. ——. [soldier.]
21 Henrietta, 6: 13: 59, consumption, æ. 24-0-9, b. Charlestown, of Marshall & Alice.
81 Jas. G., 10: 26: 72, ——, æ. 60-3-0, b. Eng., of —— & ——, Eng., do.
10 John H., 6: 26: 72, encephaloid tumors, æ. 9-11-22, b. Boston, of John H. & Julia J., Baltimore, St. Johns.
3 (D. at Boston) John H., 1: 3: 88, heart dis., æ. 53-0-0, b. Baltimore Md., of John & Mary, Southern State, do.
48 (D. at Boston) Josiah B., 10: 16: 59, consumption, æ. 29-9-24, b. Charlestown, of Marshall & Hannah.
105 Louisa (Slack), 12: 30: 78, pleurisy fever, æ. 53-0-0, b. Eng., of Jas. & Maria, Eng., do.

88 Lucy A. (Smith), w. of Noel M., 9: 3: 87, old age, æ. 78–11–6, b. Bridgton Me., of Abner & Fanny, Beverly, Baldwin Me.

13 Lydia (Winslow), 4: 18: 63, consumption, æ. 73–6–0, b. Deer Isle Me., of —— & Lydia, Deer Isle, do.

46 Mary, 5: 31: 79, Bright's dis., æ. 65–7–0, b. Eng.

58 Noel, 5: 15: 71, accidental, æ. 63–10–0, b. Coventry R. I., of Elisha & Betsy, Coventry, do.

132 (D. at Walpole) Rebecca R., 12: 10: 62, dropsy, æ. 5–6–6, b. Walpole, of Samuel & Margaret.

82 Robert, 8: 17: 87, cholera infantum, æ. 1–2–26, b. Boston, of Robert D. & Mary T., Boston, do.

104 Samuel, 12: 19: 71, imperfect development, æ. 0–0–1, b. Ded., of Edw. & Catharine, Portland Me., Ded.

35 Wm., 10: 8: 70, diabetes, æ. 67–6–7, b. Hartford Ct., of Reuel & Lucretia, Woburn, Hartford Ct.

6 Wm. N., 6: *15: 65, teething, æ. 2–4–8, b. Blackstone, of John & Harriet.

JONES.

71 Chas., 8: 12: 79, hydrothorax, æ. 30–0–0.

40 Elijah, 6: 9: 61, accidental shooting, æ. 55–0–0, b. Needham, of John & Sylvia, Dorch., Framingham.

84 Harriet T., 12: 23: 68, consumption, æ. 58–0–0, b. Newburyport, of Richard & Abigail, Eng., Woburn.

33 Helen M., 3: 2: 45, convulsion fits, æ. 2–0–0, b. Ded. (Foundling.)

111 Jas., 12: 4: 84, phthisis, æ. 29–0–0, b. Ire., of Patrick & Rose, Ire., do.

82 Lurana (Sawin), 4: 18: 66, consumption, æ. 67–0–0, b. ——, of Levi & ——.

76 Mary C. (Hill), w. of John, 8: 6: 87, dysentery, æ. 71–5–3, b. Ire., of Stephen & Mary (Blackwell), Ire., Scot.

34 Patrick, 8: 16: 59, dysentery, æ. 22–0–0, b. Ire., of Patrick & Rose.

129 Rose, 9: 13: 64, typhoid fever, æ. 17–0–0, b. Ire., of Patrick & Rose, Ire., do.

JONIO.

15 Roselee, 1: 16: 73, brain fever, æ. 0–7–1, b. Ded., of Jos. & Cordelia, Canada, do.

JORDAN.

15 Albert H., 10: 8: 62, diphtheria, æ. 2–7–20, b. Ded., of Dedrick & Susan, Wareham, Stoddard N. H.

29 Caty, 7: 10: 62, consumption, æ. 49–10–6, b. Canton, of John & Catharine.

24 Chas. A., 2: 28: 60, railway accident, æ. 26–2–18, b. Portland Me., of Tristam & Martha, Bridgton Me., Portland Me.

111 Emma A., 10: 12: 62, diphtheria, æ. 6–2–19, b. Marlow N. H., of Dedrick & Susan, Wareham, Stoddard N. H.

64 Geo. W., 7: 16: 81, ossification of valves of heart, æ. 80–5–0, b. Needham.

22 Hannah (Alden), 3: 15: 57, old age, æ. 89–0–0, b. Need., of Samuel & Susanna.

84 Joseph, 10: 3: 55, consumption, æ. 34–0–0, b. Buxton Me., of Samuel & Abigail.

113 Mariah L., 10: 15: 62, diphtheria, æ. 11–11–12, b. Peterboro N. H., of Dedrick & Susan, Wareham, Stoddard N. H.

21 Martha C. (Mayo), 3: 8: 71, paralysis, æ. 71-3-0, b. Brewster, of James & Abigail, Brewster, do.

16 Selina (Farrington), 2: 26: 61, dropsy, æ. 78 0-0, b. Pomfret Ct., of Ephraim & Elizabeth.

JOSSELYN.

50 Deborah, 5: 5: 47, ——, æ. 81-0-0.

69 Ira O., 8: 4: 81, congestion of brain, æ. 0-7-11, b. Ded., of Joseph H. & Nellie E., Hanson, Hanover.

JOYCE.

104 James, 9: 25: 65, liver comp., æ. 32-0-0, b. Ire., of Jas. & Eliz'h.

21 Maggie A., 2: 16: 89, exhaustion, æ. 13-7-10, b. Millbury, of John & Mary (Fitzpatrick), Ire., do.

27 Mary J., 3: 15: 81, consumption, æ. 26-0-12, b. Boston, of Patrick & Mary, Ireland, do.

KAALLY.

55 Mary H., 8: 16: 61, cholera morbus, æ. 0-8-0, b. Ded., of James & Ellen H., Ireland, do.

KAHLMEYER.

80 George H., 10: 31: 70, lung fever, æ. 48-6-17, b. Germany.

KANE.

5 Catharine A., 4: 13: 66, croup, æ. 1-0-26, b. Sharon, of Wm. & Alice.

3 Hannah, 4: 5: 66, croup, æ. 3-10-0, b. Sharon, of Wm. & Alice.

113 Lizzie, 10: 9: 88, tubercular meningitis, æ. 1-4-18, b. Sherborn, of —— & Mary, ——, Lowell.

104 Patrick, 10: 24: 90, heart disease, æ. 42-0-0, b. Ireland, of Dennis & Margaret (Toban), Ire., do.

148 Paul, 11: 27: 64, drowned, æ. 50-0-0, b. Ireland. [soldier]

KATZENMEIER.

88 Frank, 12: 28: 69, convulsions, æ. 0-1-8, b. Ded., of Peter & Margaret, Germany, do.

100 Peter, 11: 13: 79, cerebro-spinal meningitis, æ. 48-0-0, b. Germany, of George & ——, Germany, do.

KEARNEY, KARNEY.

62 Bridget (Golding), 7: 2: 81, marasmus, æ. 66-0-0, b. Ireland, of Martin & Sarah, Ireland, do.

15 James, 1: 21: 90, pneumonia, æ. 75-0-0, b. Ireland, of James & Margaret, Ireland, do.

28 James, 2: 14: 90, heart disease, æ. 70-0-0, b. Ireland, of Mark & Bridget, Ireland, do.

12 Patrick F., 3: 19: 54, infantile dis., æ. 0-0-2, b. Ded., of Walter & Ann.

6 Walter, 2: 25: 61, convulsions, æ. 5-10-13, b. Ded., of Walter & Ann.

KEATING.

26 Catharine (Lynding), 3: 6: 69, childbirth, æ. 34-0-0, b. Ireland, of Martin & Mary, Ireland, do.

1 James A., 1: 20: 63, lung fever, æ. 1-6-17, b. Ded., of James & Catharine, Ireland, do.

94 James J., 10: 2: 82. typhoid fever, æ. 19-1-25, b. Ded., of James & Catharine, Ireland, do.

83 Mary A., 9: 25: 80, disease of heart, æ. 22-9-0, b. Ireland, of Michael & Eliza, Ireland, do.

44 Mary C., 8: 1: 55, consumption, æ. 0-6-6, b. Ded., of Jas. & Catharine.

42 William E., 6: 17: 69, ——, æ. 0-3-11, b. Dedham, of James & Catherine, Ireland, do.

KEEFE, KEEF, KEEFFE.

126 Ann, 8: 31: 67, consumption, æ. 33-0-0, b. Ireland, of James & Bridget, Ireland, do.

77 Elenia (Drinan), 7: 25: 83, phthisis, æ. 21-0-0, b. Ire., of George & Margaret, Ireland, do.

84 Johanna, 1: 23: 71, cancer, æ. 47-0-0, b. Ire., of —— & ——, Ire., do.

152 Peter, 11: 27: 65, consumption, æ. 25-4-28, b. Ire., of James & Bridget.

7 Timothy, 11: 19: 68, canker, æ. 1-3-0, b. Ded., of Timothy & Mary, Ire., do.

KEEGAN.

90 Catherine (Casserly), w. of Peter, 9: 4: 87, inflam. of bowels, æ. 50-0-0, b. Ire., of Owen & Catherine, Ire., do.

120 (D. at Boston) Hannah (O'Brien), w. of Patrick, 12: 8: 89, heart disease, æ. 60-0-0, b. Ire., of Patrick & ——, Ire., do.

6 Margaret, 2: 8: 62, dysentery, æ. 66-0-0, b. Ireland.

98 Margaret, 9: 6: 65, typhoid fever, æ. 10-0-27, b. Ded., of Patrick & Mary.

55 Margaret, 5: 21: 68, bowel comp., æ. 1-1-9, b. Ded., of Peter & Catharine, Ire., do.

90 Mary (Fagan), 9: 24: 82, dysentery, æ. 67-0-0, b. Ire., of Jas. & Mary, Ire., do.

53 Mary A., 8: 2: 61, diarrhoea, æ. 1-2-0, b. Ded., of Peter & Catharine.

KEELAN.

41 Thos. F., 9: 18: 62, inflam. of brain, æ. 0-11-5, b. Ded., of Michael & Catherine E., Ire., do.

KEENE.

8 (D. at Boston), Nahum, 1: 12: 89, heart dis., æ. 69-9-20, b. Duxbury, of Solomon & Lucia, Pembroke, do.

KEENER.

6 Brian, 2: 2: 55, consumption, æ. 40-0-0.

KEEP.

110 Wm., 6: 13: 49, cholera, æ. 51-0-0, b. Prov. R. I.

KELLEHER.

93 John, 12: 28: 62, delirium tremens, æ. 36-0-0, b. Ire.

KELLER, KELLAR.

137 ——, 8: 20: 65, stillborn, b. Ded., s. of Fred. & Eliz'h.

100 John, 11: 25: 85, pneumonia, æ. 35-0-0, b. Ire., of —— & ——, Ire., do.

139 Peter, 8: 30: 65, cerebral meningitis, æ. 9-0-0, b. Germ., of Fred. & Eliz'h.

KELLOGG.

59 Elliot E., 7: 21: 75, consumption, æ. 56-0-0, b. Jamaica Vt., of Alpheus & Augusta B., Vt., do.

KELLY, KELLEY.

30 Bridget, 5:10:86, phthisis, æ. 37-0-0, b. Ire., of Robert & Ann, Ire., do.

10 Catherine, 9:13:69, dis. of brain, æ. 0-4-0, b. Ded., of Philip & Catherine, Ire., do.

23 Ellen (Green), 4:6:77, suicide, æ. 45-0-0, b. Ire., of Wm. & Margaret, Ire., do.

39 Ellen (Finnerty), w. of John, 3:23:88, apoplexy, æ. 80-0-0, b. Ire., of Wm. & Mary, Ire., do.

48 Geo., 5:17:81, R. R. accident, æ. 35-0-0.

25 Hannah (McLaughlin), 4:20:79, heart dis., æ. 64-0-0, b. Ire., of Thomas & Catherine, Ire., do.

19 James, 1:20:69, scarlet fever, æ. 4-0-0, b. Ded., of Jas. & Bridget, Ire., do.

95 Jas., 10:18:81, typhoid fever, æ. 9-7-0, b. Ded., of Jas. & Bridget E., Ire., do.

84 Jas. F., 7:28:83, cholera infantum, æ. 0-11-0, b. Ded., of James & Sarah A., Ire., do.

18 (D. at Bridgewater) John, 3:15:64, consumption, æ. 14-0-0, b. Ire., of John & Ann.

45 John, 7:16:69, liver complaint, æ. 61-0-0, b. Ire., of Patrick & Mary, Ire., do.

93 John J., 9:23:82, stillborn, b. Ded., of Edw. P. & Nora E., Walpole, Ire.

14 Margaret, 3:28:53, fit, æ. 0-0-10, b. Ded., of Michael & Mary.

32 Margaret, 4:2.81, consumption, æ. 21-6-0, b. Ded., of Thos. & Mary, Ire., do.

93 Margaret E. (McGuiness), 8:25:83, typhoid fever, æ. 27-0-10, b. Ded., of Bernard & Mary, Ire., do.

115 Mary, 8:6:64, dysentery, æ. 1-2-6, b. Ded., of Jas. & Catherine, Ire., do.

39 Michael, 10:31:47, consumption, æ. 50-0-0.

60 Michael, 6:20:81, heart dis., æ. 68-0-0, b. Ire., of Edw. & Margaret, Ire., do.

36 Nellie, 4:9:83, diphtheria, æ. 10-11-11, b. Ded., of John & Johanna, Ire., do.

9 Nora E. (Grady), 2:6:84, puerperal peritonitis, æ. 24-0-0, b. Ire., of Ferdinand & Nora, Ire., do.

99 Patrick G., 11:13:84, drowning, æ. 41-7-0, b. Ire., of Peter & Bridget, Ire., do.

47 Robert, 6:27:86, consumption, æ. 75-0-0, b. Ire., of —— & ——, Ire., do.

81 Sarah A., 7:27:83, cholera infantum, æ. 0-11-0, b. Ded., of Jas. H. & Sarah A., Ire., Ded.

84 Thos., 5:25:61, intemperance, æ. 38-0-0, b. Ire.

38 Thos., 5:25:61, delirium tremens, æ. 36-0-0, b. Ire., of Patrick & Mary, Ire., do.

109 Thos., 12:—:76, consumption, æ. 35-0-0, b. Ire., of Robert & ——.

40 Thos., 3:20:90, leucocythaemia, æ. 67-0-0, b. Ire., of Edw. & Margaret (Martin), Ire., do.

15 Thos. F., 1:13:69, scarlet fever, æ. 1-0-0, b. Ded., of Jas. & Bridget. Ire., do.

69 Wm., 12:1:61, lung fever, æ. 0-3-0, b. Ded., of Philip & Catharine.

KELSCH.

56 John, 6:10:76, tuberculosis, æ. 47-10-14, b. Germ., of John & Ann M., Germ., do.

KENELLY.

12 James, 2:4:64, typhoid fever, æ. ——. [soldier.]

KENNARD.

50 Frank H., 4: 29: 68, consumption, æ. 27-3-21, b. Cunningham Ct., of Jas. B. & Catharine, Nashua N. H., Newburyport.

KENNEDY.

100 Ann (Cannon), 3: 29: 86, cerebral hemorrhage, æ. 68-0-0, b. Ire., of Thos. & Bridget, Ire., do.

69 Ann E., 8: 4: 85, cholera infantum, æ. 0-5-22, b. Ded., of Wm. J. & Mary E., Prov. R. I., Ded.

106 Eliza J. (Ebbs), w. of Jas. A., 10: 26: 90, typhoid pneumonia, æ. 32-2-14, b. Ded., of Thos. & Ellen (Hull), Ire., Eng.

91 Geo. W., 9: 10: 90, lockjaw, æ. 2-11-8, b. Ded., of Wm. J. & Mary E., Prov. R. I., Ded.

51 John, 10: 19: 69, teething, æ. 1-1-14, b. Ded., of John & Mary, Ire., do.

72 John H., 7: 8: 83, convulsions, æ. 0-1-7, b. Ded., of J. A. & Eliza J., Eng., Ded.

22 Lewis, 2: 1: 69, scarlet fever, æ. 5-4-25, b. Ded., of John & Mary, Ire., do.

40 Maggie, 7: 22: 74, consumption, æ. 23-2-0, b. Boston, of Michael & Margaret, Ire., do.

35 Mary I. (Ewer), 5: 10: 78, consumption, æ. 33-6-21, b. Boston, of Chas. B. & Charlotte B., ——, Ded.

43 Michael J., 5: 14: 82, ——, æ. 2-6-11, b. Ded., of John 2d & Mary, Ire., do.

33 Sarah, 4: 10: 82, albuminuria, æ. 6-8-0, b. Ded., of John 2d & Mary, Ire., do.

92 Sarah J., 10: 18: 85, scarlatina, æ. 6-0-0, b. Ded., of Stephen & Rosanna, Ireland, do.

62 Thomas H., 7: 2: 87, hydrocephalus, æ. 0-10-16, b. Ded., of James A. & Eliza J., England, Ireland.

106 William, 11: 23: 84, heart disease, æ. 65-0-0, b. Ireland, of William & Margaret. Ireland, do.

KENNEY.

119 Joseph C., 12: 9: 90, drowning, æ. 1-8-20, b. West Roxbury, of Malachi & Maria A. (Gately), Roxbury, Ireland.

46 Louisa K., 10: 24: 44, dysentery, æ. 0-13-0.

79 (D. at Boston) Patrick, 8: 14: 87, drowning, æ. 23-0-0, b. Ireland, of James & Bridget, Ireland, do.

47 Thomas, 3: 15: 67, bleeding of stomach, æ. 40-0-0, b. Ireland, of John & Ann, Ireland, do.

KENWORTHY.

3 Elizabeth A., 1: 9: 56, convulsion fits , æ. 0-2-0, b. Ded., of Wm. & Ann.

KEOUGH.

88 Mary A., 10: 11: 85, phthisis, æ. 57-1-6, b. P. E. I., of James & Grace, Ireland, do.

KERESY.

30 Mary, 7: 11: 62, lung fever, æ. 3-7-0, b. Boston, of Thos. & Kate, Ire., do.

KERN.

111 Joseph T., 12: 10: 79, meningitis, æ. 0-6-8, b. Dedham, of Joseph & Mary, France, do.

43 Maria J., 8: 3: 74, cholera infantum, æ. 0–3–0, b. Ded., of Huen & Frances.

31 Therese, 3: 20: 73, croup, æ. 0–4–18, b. Dedham, of Michael & Eugene, France, do.

KERRIGAN.

99 ——, 12: 5: 67, stillborn, b. Ded., d. of James & Mary, Ireland, do.

19 James, 4: 7: 62, lung fever, æ. 0–11–0, b. Ded., of Jas. & Mary.

5 Lizzie F., 1: 10: 85, phthisis, æ. 22–6–0, b. Ded., of Jas. & Mary, Ire., do.

KERSTEIN.

77 Antonia (Ressel), 9: 30: 77, consumption, æ. 21–0–0, b. Bohemia, of Anthony & Caroline, Bohemia, do.

KEYES.

17 Benjamin F., 4: 8: 58, disease of heart, æ. 58–1–1, b. Westford, of Jonathan & Martha.

30 Catharine (Wight), 2: 11: 72, paralysis, æ. 73–5–14, b. Ded., of Ebenezer & Catharine, Dedham, do.

48 Hortense E. (White), 9: 11: 58, disease of heart, æ. 22–10–24, b. Belfast Me., of James & Lydia.

KIERNAN, KEIRNON.

19 Catharine, 7: 25: 63, consumption, æ. 11–6–0, b. Ded, of John & Catherine.

100 John, 11: 13: 84, softening of brain, æ. 58–11–15, b. Ireland, of Frank & N., Ireland, do.

68 Margaret J., 7: 16: 82, anaemia, æ. 25–6–0, b. Ded., of John & Katherine, Ireland, do.

KIESSLING.

39 Alfred R., 2: 22: 65, lung fever, æ. 5–10–0, b. Dedham, of Frank J. & Enestine P.

127 Amelia, 12: 31: 90, scarlet fever, æ. 8–5–15, b. Ded., of Frederick G. & Agnes L. (Shubert), Germ., do.

60 Bruno, 5: 27: 71, scarlet fever, æ. 3–10–5, b. Ded., of Fred. G. & Agnes, Germany, do.

63 Charles, 8: 24: 77, marasmus, æ. 0–4–0, b. Ded., of Frederick & Agnes, Germany, do.

31 Chr. Frederica (Stroldel), 4: 6: 76, old age, æ. 81–3–27, b. Germany, of —— & ——, Germany, do.

43 Geo. F., 3: 12: 68, cancer, æ. 74–0–0, b. Germ., of —— & ——, Germ., do.

41 Herman B., 2: 24: 65, cramp, æ. 0–9–19, b. Ded., of Frank J. & Enestine P.

74 Louis, 9: 11: 78, cholera infantum, æ. 0–1–7, b. Ded., of Fred G. & Agnes, Saxony, do.

KILBURN.

87 ——, 8: 8: 83, premature birth, b. Ded., s. of Albert A. & Clara J., W. Salisbury Vt., Boston.

59 Edmund F., 7: 30: 80, convulsions, æ. 0–6–22, b. Ded., of Albert A. & Clara J., Vt., Lowell.

KILIAN.

177 Wm., 2: 27: 64, consumption, æ. 39–7–10, b. Germ., of —— & Christine, Germ., do.

KILLDUFF.
61 James, 5: 5: 64, consumption, æ. 46-7-0, b. Ire., of Jas. & Margaret.

KILLIKELLY.
50 Anastatia, 7: 3: 66, water on brain, æ. 2-0-5, b. Ded., of Thos. & Bridget.
79 Bridget A. (Kelley), 10: 8: 77, hemorrhage of lungs, æ. 47-0-0, b. Ire., of Thos. & Bridget, Ire., do.
58 Charles, 12: 7: 69, diphtheria, æ. 3-3-24, b. Ded., of Thos. & Bridget, Ire., do.
108 Eliz'h J., 9: 23: 88, inanition, æ. 0-0-27, b. Ded., of Thomas W. & Ellen C. (Leary), Ded., Dorch.
50 Harriet, 8: 25: 60, scarlatina, æ. 1-8-0, b. Ded., of Thos. & Bridget, Ire., do.
12 Hattie, 2: 15: 79, typhoid fever, æ. 17-7-15, b. Ded., of Thomas & Bridget, Ire., do.
8 Hysinth, 1: 23: 51, croup, æ. 0-7-26, b. Ded., of Thos. & Bridget.

KILMARTIN.
51 John, 6: 24: 75, dropsy, æ. 68-0-0, b. Ire., of Timothy & Mary, Ire., do.

KILPATRICK.
27 (D. at Worcester) David, 2: 23: 66, accident, æ. 26-8-0, b. Scot., of James & Sarah.
33 Sarah (Brown), 1: 17: 67, consumption, æ. 63-0-0, b. Scot., of John & Sarah, Scot., do.
42 Wm., 4: 12: 66, drowned, æ. 28-4-12, b. Scot., of Jas. & Sarah.

KIMBALL.
97 Carrie L., 11: 1: 84, peritonitis, æ. 29-2-12, b. Ded., of Franklin & Elmira, Ded., do.
73 (D. at sea off Portsmouth N. H.) Edw. W., 7: 14: 90, drowning, æ. 27-5-4, b. Ded., of Franklin & Elmira (Guild), Ded., do.
49 Elsie M., 6: 7: 85, tubercular meningitis, æ. 24-9-23, b. Temple N. H., of Chas. F. & Juliet A., Temple N. H., Attleboro.
47 (D. at Boston) Mabel F., 5: 29: 87, peritonitis, æ. 22-9-9, b. Ded., of Chas. F. & Juliet A., Temple N. H., Attleboro.
61 Susan (McIntosh), 10: 25: 57, consumption, æ. 41-0-0, b. Ded., of Elisha & Betsy.
54 Walter F., 1: 2: 62, inflam. of bowels, æ. 0-3-19, b. Ded., of Franklin & Elmira, Ded., do.
62 Wm. D., 10: 25: 57, consumption, æ. 0-10-24, b. Dorch., of John T. & Susan.

KING.
88 (D. at Saratoga Springs N. Y.) Lucy A. (Bingham), w. of John, 7: 7: 88, schirrus of liver, æ. 66-0-0, b. Ded., of Pliny & Jerusha (Avery), Ct., Ded.

KINGSBURY.
3 ——, w. of Moses, 7: 8: 46, dropsy, æ. 75-0-0.
131 Catherine S. (Baker), 11: 29: 62, consumption, æ. 24-7-8, b. Ded., of Alford & Julia A., Ded., Springfield.
11 Chas., 3: 15: 53, freezing, æ. 38-0-0, b. Ded., of Moses & Hannah.
116 Chas. F., 1: 6: 67, spotted fever, æ. 14-7-14, b. Ded., of Geo. & Cordelia K., Ded., do.
13 Chas. J., 8: 16: 71, chol. infantum, æ. 0-6-0, b. Ded., of Edgar H. & Maria F.

98 Cynthia (Rhoades), 3: 15: 70, old age, æ. 88–6–0, b. Sharon, of Daniel & ——.

34 Edgar H., 4: 3: 89, heart dis., æ. 71–9–12, b. Canandaigua N. Y., of Caleb & Irene Buck, Mass., N. Y.

48 Edw. L., 6: 4: 75, hemorrhage of lungs, æ. 24–0–0, b. Ded., of Lewis H. & Eunice H., Walpole, Boston.

11 Eliz. C., 4: 26: 50, scarlet fever, æ. 1–6–9, b. Ded., of Lewis H. & Eunice H.

53 Eunice (Haven), 6: 4: 82, anasarca, æ. 62–11–8, b. Boston, of John A. & Susanna (Hooper), Lancaster, Charlestown.

91 Ezekiel, 1: 22: 69, palsy, æ. 76–6–0, b. Ded., of Ezekiel & Mary, Ded., do.

52 Flora M., 11: 9: 59, congestion of lungs, æ. 0–0–3, b. Ded., of Lewis H. & Eunice.

23 Geo. W., 6: 11: 54, dis. of heart, æ. 52–9–0, b. Walpole, of Solomon & Keziah.

11 Gertrude V., 8: 18: 74, cholera infantum, æ. 0–7–0, b. Ded., of Edgar H. & Maria F., N. Y., Ire.

88 Henry W., 8: 24: 66, dysentery, æ. 2–0–0, b. Ded., of Warren & ——.

30 Ida J., 9: 15: 50, whooping cough, æ. 1–0–18, b. Ded., of Geo. & Cordelia.

82 Jabez, 1: 19: 54, old age, æ. 79–0–0, b. Ded., of Jabez & Rebecca.

40 Joshua L., 9: 9: 59, consumption, æ. 54–8–0, b. Ded., of Moses & Hannah.

58 Margaret (Byrne), 4: 3: 64, consumption, æ. 33–6–0, b. Ire., of Owen & Margaret.

24 Mary E., 8: 20: 50, stoppage, æ. 2–10–0, b. Ded., of Chas. & Abigail.

68 Melzar, 7: 30: 71, consumption, æ. 67–10–0, b. Ded., of Moses & Hannah, Ded., do.

13 Mercy (Philbrook), 4: 9: 68, paralysis, æ. 63–0–0, b. Livermore Me., of Eben'r & ——.

8 Moses, 3: 25: 48, jaundice, æ. 75–0–0.

48 Moses, 4: 7: 88, old age, æ. 85–10–8, b. Needham, of Moses & Cynthia, Natick, Sharon.

80 Rebecca (Dean), 2: 11: 59, old age, æ. 81–0–0, b. Ded., of Benj. & Eliz'h.

56 Sally (Fisher), 7: 23: 84, old age, æ. 75–1–13, b. Walpole, of Asa & Sally (Gay), Walpole, do.

103 Wm., 5: 27: 62, heart dis., æ. 60–11–16, b. Ded., of Jabez & Rebecca, Ded., do,

KINSALLEA.

119 Jos., 9: 30: 82, premature birth, æ. 0–0–2, b. Ded., of Terrence W. & Maggie A., Ire., do.

120 Wm., 9: 30: 82, premature birth, æ. 0–0–2, b. Ded., of Terrence W. & Maggie A., Ire., do.

KIRBY.

94 Philip, 9: 4: 83, chronic pneumonia, æ. 70–0–0, b. Hampton Va., of Jack & Rachel.

KITTSON.

12 Margaret (Shores), 4: 11: 63, spinal affection, æ. 75–4–16, b. Portsmouth N.H., of Peter & Lucy, Portsmouth N. H., do.

KLEMM.

103 Ann (Hartnett), 11: 16: 84, cancer, æ. 52–0–0, b. Ire., of —— & ——, Ire., do.

45 F. D., 5: 16: 82, convulsions, æ. 0–0–3, b. Ded., of Fred'k D. Jr. & Elizabeth A., Ded., do.

112 Fred'k D., 12: 1: 84, dis. of brain, æ. 60-7-3, b. Germ., of Fred'k & Katharine, Germ., do.
121 Sadie F., 12: 26: 83, meningitis, æ. 0-7-29, b. Ded., of Fred'k D. Jr. & Eliz'h A., Ded., do.

KNIGHT.
  12 Abby E., 2: 25: 51, inflammation of bowels, æ. 28-5-21, b. Smithfield R. I., of Thos. & Sarah.

KNOBEL.
  43 Alice L., 5: 5: 75, marasmus, æ. 0-2-0, b. Ded., of Edw. & Fannie, Germ., Boston.
108 Frank W., 11: 30: 79, membraneous croup, æ. 2-11-0, b. Ded., of Edw. & Fannie L., Prussia, Boston.
  92 Sarah, 8: 19: 83, meningitis, æ. 0-7-0, b. Ded., of Edw. & Fannie, Germ., Boston.
109 William O., 12: 2: 79, diphtheria, æ. 1-9-0, b. Ded., of Edw. & Fannie L., Prussia, Boston.

KREIS.
  84 Frank L., 9: 13: 81, diphtheria, æ. 2-7-22, b. Dedham, of Frank & Bertha, Germany, Austria.

KREUTEL.
  66 Henry E., 8: 7: 84, cholera infantum, æ. 0-3-28, b. Ded., of Hugo & Eliz'h, Saxony, do.
  74 Otto O., 5: 27: 88, diphtheria, æ. 0-7-4, b. Ded., of Ernst H. & S. Elizabeth, Germ., do.

KULT.
109 Anna F., 9: 30: 66, congestion of brain, æ. 0-6-19, b. Ded., of Lawrence & Frances.

LAFFERTY.
  34 Catharine, 6: 18: 60, ——, æ. 5-0-0, b. Charlestown, of Barney & Fanny, Ireland, do.

LAGAR.
  54 William H., 6: 8: 82, diphtheria, æ. 2-6-0, b. Boston, of Peter & Josephine, Sweden, do.

LAMBERT.
109 Matthew, 12: 1: 84, old age, æ. 65-0-0, b. Ire.

LAMSON.
113 Alvan, 7: 13: 64, apoplexy, æ. 71-8-0, b. Weston.
107 Frances F. (Ward), 11: 29: 81, pneumonia, æ. 88-2-20, b. Weston, of Artemas & Catherine M. (Dexter), Shrewsbury, ——.

LANCASTER.
  43 Henry, 9: 18: 59, canker, æ. 0-0-17, b. Ded., of John & Eliza.

LANDER, LANDERS.
100 Margaret, 5: 5: 64, dis. of heart, æ. 2-7-19, b. Ded., of Wm. & Ellen, Ire., do.
  53 Mary, 9: 6: 60, croup, æ. 0-8-22, b. Ded., of Wm. & Ellen, Ire., do.

LANE.
  87 ——, 9: 1: 87, stillborn, b. Ded., s. of Walter J. & Sarah, Eng., do.

5 Eliz. B., 7: 27: 48, dysentery, æ. 3-9-0, b. Ded.

93 Emily L., 9: 30: 81, cholera infantum, æ. 0-7-26, b. R. I., of Walter J. & Sarah A.

39 John B., 12: 5: 50, heart comp., æ. 51-2-7, b. Sanbornton N. H., of John & Hannah.

96 Thos. F., 11: 29: 67, consumption of bowels, æ. 5-8-0, b. Ded., of Thos. & Ann, Ire., do.

LAPOINT.

24 Anna, 1: 4: 72, fits, æ. 1-8-0, b. Canada, of Mitchell & Maria, Canada, do.

49 Delphine, 6: 7: 72, congestion of lungs, æ. 16-0-0, b. Canada, of Mitchell & Salyria, Canada, do.

LARIN (*See also Lowing.*)

77 Ephime, 11: 23: 71, scarlet fever, æ. 2-10-0, b. Ded., of Lewis & Delphine, Canada, do.

LARKIN.

73 James, 8: 27: 75, chronic cystitis, æ. 52-0-0, b. Ire., of Darby & Mary R., Ire., do.

94 John, 11: 9: 67, consumption, æ. 34-4-16, b. Ire., of Kerren & Honora, Ire., do.

2 John J., 1: 27: 63, rheumatic fever, æ. 11-3-0, b. Boston, of P. K. & Nancy, Ire., do.

80 Mary A. (Scully), w. of James. 8: 18: 89, consumption, æ. 65-0-0, b. Ire., of Bartholomew & Johanna (Falvey), Ire., do.

12 Mary E., 2: 10: 84, typhoid fever, æ. 27-2-0, b. Ded., of James & Mary, Ire., do.

LARY.

56 Dennis, 11: 19: 54, consumption, æ. 22-0-0, b. Ireland.

LATHROP.

105 (D. at Alexandria La.) Julius M., 4: 26: 64, gun shot, æ. 23-11-21, b. Bordentown N. J., of John P. & Maria M., Boston, Poughkeepsie N. Y. [soldier.]

87 Maria M. (Long), 10: 16: 76, malignant disease of bowels, æ. 74-5-0, b. Poughkeepsie N. Y., of Thos. & Frances G., W. Indies. N. Y. City.

LAUKE.

101 Fred'k G., 12: 7: 78, cancer, æ. 59-7-0, b. Germ.

LAWLER.

53 Agnes, 6: 17: 75, convulsions, æ. 0-8-0, b. Ded., of Patrick & Ann, Ire., Halifax.

54½ Annie M., 7: 26: 86, marasmus, æ. 0-0-16, b. Ded., of Wm. H. & Lizzie, St. Johns, Ded.

55 Margaret, 8: 8: 73, cholera infantum, æ. 0-1-14, b. Ded., of Patrick & Ann, Ire., do.

53 Patrick, 7: 22: 78, consumption, æ. 50-0-0, b. Ire.

LAWLESS.

31 Arthur P., 5: 12: 77, acute nephritis, æ. 2-10-0, b. Ded., of Michael & Ann, Ire., do.

30 Bridget (Barrett), 4: 24: 57, disease of heart, æ. 47-0-0, b. Ire., of Michael & Catherine.

24 Mary J., 4: 28: 77, diphtheria, æ. 7-3-0, b. R. I., of Michael & Ann, Ire., do.

LAWRENCE, LORENZ.

48 Albert A., 7: 1: 78, congestion of brain, æ. 14-8-0, b. Ded., of Francis & Mary, Germ., do.

90 Ellis, 9: 24: 66, dropsy. æ. 79-3-0, b. Sharon, of David & Chloe.

25 Sally (Turner), 12: 8: 68, paralysis, æ. 75-0-0, b. Ded., of Hezekiah & ——, Ded., ——.

98 Wm., 12: 4: 67, lung fever. æ. 1-5-0, b. Ded., of Francis & Mary, Germ., do.

LAWTON.

100 Alice (Gill), w. of John, 10: 7: 89, leucocythaemia, æ. 61-0-0, b. Boston, of Michael & Margaret, Ire., do.

LEACH.

35 Ferdinand, 10: 1: 50, bowel comp., æ. 0-10-15, b. Boston.

93 Mary S., 12: 14: 72, lung fever, æ. 79-0-0. b. Boston, of Wm. & Eliz'h.

87 Robert, 10: 23: 54, dropsy, æ. 57-0-0, b. Dover N. H.

LEARY. (*See also O'Leary.*)

112 Dennis, 12: 21: 66, phthisis, æ. 26-0-0, b. Ire., of Daniel & Mary.

63 John, 7: 17: 64, sunstruck, æ. 2-0-0, b. Boston, of Jas. & Ellen.

LEE.

63 ——, 7: 2: 60, fit, æ. 0-0-1, b. Ded., d. of John & Mary J., Eng., Limerick Me.

90 ——, 6: 25: 61, convulsions, æ. 0-0-1, b. Ded., d. of John & Mary J., Eng., do.

97 Alfred, 4: 28: 64, lung fever, æ. 22-0-0. [soldier.]

74 John, 7: 12: 63, pneumonia, æ. 30-0-0. [soldier.]

75 Mary (Cardon), 7: 24: 65, dysentery, æ. 30-0-0, b. Ire., of Michael & ——.

77 Samuel, 7: 18: 63, congestion of lungs, æ. 30-0-0. [soldier.]

LEFTON.

61 Hope, 4: 30: 88, meningitis, æ. 1-0-15. [Foundling.]

LEGALLEE.

114 Ann R. (Thomas), w. of Ellis B., 11: 29: 90, dis. of liver, æ. 84-11-16, b. Charlestown, of John & Rebecca (Robinson), Charlestown, Boston.

18 Anna L., 4: 2: 53, typhoid fever, æ. 8-11-5, b. Ded., of Ellis B. & Ann R.

38 Jane W. (Willis), 7: 4: 60, cancer, æ. 43-3-0, b. Boston, of Deane & Jane, Easton, ——.

59 Thos. W., 7: 13: 52, rheumatism, æ. 66-0-0.

LEHANE.

50 Daniel, 9: 20: 69, consumption, æ. 54-0-0, b. Ire., of Jeremiah & Margaret, Ire., do.

4 Julia, 1: 20: 76, whooping cough, æ. 2-7-0, b. Ded., of John & Margaret, Ire., do.

6 Margaret (Cronin), 4. 13: 75, heart dis., æ. 49-0-0, b. Ire., of Jeremiah & Mary, Ire., do.

LEIBOLD.

52 Caroline (Morhoff), 6: 5: 82, heart dis., æ. 40-10-29, b. Germ., of Christian & Caroline, Germ., do.

63 Mary, 6: 7: 67, lung fever, æ. 1-1-0, b. W. Rox., of George & Caroline, Germ., do.

LELAND.

72 Hannah (Cobb), 8: 26: 71, old age, æ. 82-2-0, b. Walpole, of Jabez & Deliverance.

119 Hannah M., 10: 26: 61, consumption, æ. 22-10-16, b. Ded., of Charles & Caroline, Ded., Jefferson Me.

54 Richard, 9: 21: 58, rheumatism, æ. 72-1-20, b. Ded., of Isaac & Deborah.

LEMIRE.

84 Grace (Coats), 10: 30: 72, consumption, æ. 51-0-0, b. Scot, of John & Grace, Scot., do.

22 Leopold L., 3: 10: 84, inflam. of bowels, æ. 74-0-0, b. France.

LEMOTE.

58 Louisa L., 5: 25: 89, diphtheritic croup, æ. 1-3-7, b. Boston, of Joseph F. & Lucy G. (Avery), Boston, Newbury Vt.

90 Lucy G., 9: 10: 90, cardiac dilatation, æ. 6-7-0, b. Boston, of Joseph F. & Lucy G. (Avery), Boston, Newbury Vt.

LEONARD.

28 ——, 3: 24: 84, stillborn, b. Ded., s. of Philip H. & Mary E., Ded., Ire.

31 ——, 3: 29: 84, stillborn, b. Ded., d. of Wm. & Luetta, Plymouth, Ded.

87 Ann (Clark), 10: 21: 78, consumption, æ. 60-0-0, b. Ire., of Thomas & Betsey, Ire., do.

26 Asa, 2: 22: 66, consumption, æ. 63-4-19, b. Taunton, of Benj. & Lurana.

20 Bridget, 9: 3: 67, whooping cough, æ. 7-0-0, b. Ire., of John & Catharine, Ire., do.

8 Chas. M., 4: 17: 71, measles, æ. 0-8-2, b. Walpole, of Geo. & Eliz'h, Germ.,do.

15 Eliz'h (Allen), 2: 3: 62, paralysis, æ. 58-2-7, b. Taunton, of John & Betsy.

46 John, 8: 17: 55, dysentery, æ. 1-1-7, b. N. Y. City, of Philip & Margaret.

68 John, 6: 19: 83, consumption, æ. 74-0-0, b. Ire., of John & Susan, Ire., do.

76 John, 7: 25: 90, consumption, æ. 1-4 10, b. Ded., of John F. & Mary J. (Hickey), Ire., do.

45 John J., 8: 31: 58, cholera infantum, æ. 0-11-14, b. Ded., of Martin & Ann.

31 Martha R. (Day), 9: 2: 70, poison from paint, æ. 30-3-18, b. Ded., of Joseph & Hanna E., Walpole, Ded.

2 Mary, 1: 2: 85, old age, æ. 95-0-0, b. Ire., of —— & ——, Ire., do.

4 Mary A. (McGlone), 1: 17: 84, puerperal fever, æ. 29-0-0, b. Ded., of Patrick & Kate, Ire., do.

49 Mary E., 8: 9: 57, dysentery, æ. 1-3-1, b. Ded., of Philip & Margaret.

29 Mary E. (O'Brien), 3: 24: 84, childbirth, æ. 22-0-7, b. Ire., of Wm. & Annie, Ire., do.

8 Mary G., 1: 7: 88, consumption, æ. 25-0-4, b. Ded., of Philip & Margaret, Ire., do.

60 Minnie H., 5: 31: 90, convulsions, æ. 27-4-7, b. Walpole, of Geo. & Eliz'h (Schulz).

113 Patrick, 2: 25: 63, scarlet fever, æ. 1-11-13, b. Ded., of Michael & Bridget, Ire., do.

21 Patrick, 9: 6: 67, whooping cough, æ. 5-6-0, b. Ire., of John & Catherine, Ire., do.

9 Robert, 4: 8: 71, consumption, æ. 17-0-0, b. Ire., of Felix & Mary, Ire., do.

22 Sarah A., 2: 28: 75, whooping cough, æ. 0-3-13, b. Ded., of Philip & Margaret, Ire., do.

22 Thos., 9: 9: 67, whooping cough, æ. 1-3-0, b. Ire., of John & Catherine, Ire., do.

27 Thos., 10: 21: 67, infantile, æ. 0-0-4, b. Ded., of Martin & Ann, Ire., do.

58 Wm. H., 12: 6: 54, lung fever, æ. 1-1-8, b. Ded., of Asa & Charlotte.

36 Willie E., 1: 29: 67, inflam. of lungs, æ. 6-6-7, b. Ded., of Asa & Charlotte F., Taunton, do.

LEWIS.

84 Levi C., 11: 19: 77, chronic pleurisy, æ. 72-9-14, b. Brunswick Me., of Nathan C. & Margaret, Ct., Brunswick Me.

66 Margaret A. (Estes), 8: 7: 79, hypertrophy of heart, æ. 74-11-24, b. Brunswick Me., of Edw. & Margaret, Durham Me., Brunswick Me.

81 Nancy, 4: 10: 53, old age, æ. 90-0-0, b. Ded.

30 Submit, 1: 12: 47, old age, æ. 78-0-0, b. Ded., of Samuel & ——.

LINCOLN.

13 Mariah M. A., 5: 7: 50, lung fever, æ. 0-8-0, b. Ded.

96 Mary A. (Bennett), 9: 6: 65, dropsy, æ. 43-4-21, b. Boston, of *Baslee & Emma.

LINNEHAN.

1 Julia (Sullivan), 1: 18: 72, childbirth, æ. 28-0-0, b. Ire., of Timothy & Ellen.

LIPS.

52 Augusta, 7: 14: 86, cholera infantum, æ. 0-5-0, b. Ded., of Fred'k & Dora, Germ., do.

71 Chas., 8: 17: 71, diarrhoea, æ. 0-0-21, b. Ded., of Fred: & Dorohe, Germ., do.

68 Chas., 9: 25: 73, teething, æ. 0-10-0, b. Ded., of Fred'k & Dora, Germ., do.

79 Chas. J., 10: 28: 70, accident, æ. 32-4-26, b. Germ.

50 Charlie, 6: 5: 82, convulsions, æ. 0-0-1, b. Ded., of Fred'k & Doretta, Germ., do.

LITTLE.

104 Sarah L., 11: 24: 81, heart dis., æ. 82-5-0, b. Marshfield, of Luther & Hannah Lovell, Marshfield, Weymouth.

LITTLEFIELD.

10 Bridget (Kelley), w. of Albert, 1: 11: 88, Bright's dis., æ. 75-0-0, b. Ire., of Martin & Mary, Ire., do.

LOCKE.

102 Eliza C. (Dawes), 10: 16: 68, consumption, æ. 28-4-2, b. Duxbury, of Allen & Lydia, Duxbury, Pembroke.

103 Harriet, 7: 11: 70, lung fever, æ. 12-11-0, b. Ded., of Calvin S. & [Annie], Acworth N. H., Hingham.

LOCKLIE.

64 E., 6: 5: 63, consumption, æ. 24-0-0. [soldier.]

LOLLON.

67 Henry G., 11: 26: 56, consumption, æ. 24-0-0, of Job & Patience.

LONG.

43 Alvin J., 4: 20: 84, congestion of lungs, æ. 0-0-21, b. Ded., of John & Catherine, P. E. I., do.

32 Charles A., 4: 21: 80, cyanosis, æ. 0-0-2, b. Ded., of John A. & Catherine, P. E. I., do.

23 Eva A., 2: 21: 69, scrofula, æ. 0-7-10, b. Ded., of William B. & Nancy W., P. E. I., Bath Me.

LONGLEY.

86 George C., 9: 13: 81, diphtheria, æ. 2-1-1, b. Waterford Me., of Chas. M. & Abbie S., Waterford Me., Boston.

LORD.

12 Hannah, 9: 14: 65, consumption, æ. 19-0-0, b. St. Johns N. Q., of John & Ann.

130 William H., 9: 14: 64, run over by cars, æ. 43-5-0, b. Kennebunk Me., of Jeremiah & Lydia.

LORING.

101 Clarissa (Withington), 11: 29: 85, old age, æ. 77-7-11, b. Dorch., of Daniel & Anne, Dorch., do.

21 Jonathan H., 3: 3: 81, heart dis., æ. 72-11-18, b. Marblehead, of Henry & Sally (Stewart), Boston, do.

LORIO.

9 Elizabeth (Roup), w. of John, 1: 10: 90, ascites, æ. 80-5-19, b. Germ., of John & ——, Germ., do.

15 George, 2: 3: 80, diphtheria, æ. 2-0-21, b. Dedham, of George & Regular, Germany, ——.

7 Jacob W., 1: 30: 80, diphtheria, æ. 2-5-6, b. Ded., of Jacob & Catharine, Germany, do.

125 John, 12: 28: 90, pneumonia, æ. 76-9-27, b. Germany, of John & Mary, France, do.

6 John F., 1: 29: 80, diphtheria, æ. 1-3-14, b. Ded., of Jacob & Catharine, Germany, do.

38 Lilly E., 5: 4: 84, convulsions, æ. 3-0-15, b. Ded., of Jacob & Catherine, Germany, do.

110 Olga C., 10: 15: 87, difficult birth, æ. 0-0-4, b. Ded., of Jacob & Caterina, Germany, do.

LOUNGER.

75 John, 8: 10: 62, convulsion fits, æ. 0-2-21, b. W. Rox., of John & Catharine.

LOVELOCK.

36 William, 5: 15: 49, consumption, æ. 66-0-0.

LOVEWELL.

195 Sarah B. (Reed), 6: 24: 64, ——, æ. 36-3-29, b. Sanford Me., of Jacob & Dorothy, Berwick Me., Sanford Me.

LOWDEN.

33 George K., 4: 1: 84, consumption, æ. 18-3-28, b. Ded., of James & Jane, Ireland, do.

27 Mary J., 4: 15: 77, consumption, æ. 19-1-15, b. Ded., of James & Jane, Ireland, do.

LOWE.
   18 Arthur C., 2: 21: 84, hemorrhage, æ. 19-5-21, b. Canton, of Thos. & Anne, England, do.

LOWELL.
   87 Alice F., 12: 10: 69, small pox, æ. 1-0-10, b. Ded., of Leonard & Frances J., Abbot Me., Ded.

LOWERY, LOWEY.
   40 George F., 1: 31: 71, inflammation of lungs, æ. 0-1-5, b. Ded., of James C. & Isabella, Ireland. Ded.
   29 Harriet, 7: 28: 59, fit, æ. 0-0-24, b. Ded., of Andrew & Margaret.
   88 James L., 9: 9: 67, scald, æ. 1-1-12, b. Minn., of James L. & Isabella, Ireland, do.
   2 Jane (Griffin), 1: 4: 56, liver comp., æ. 59-0-0, b. Ire., of Jos. & Sarah.
   43 John, 3: 14: 56, liver comp., æ. 70-10-0, b. Ire., of Robert & Sarah.
   35 Joseph M., 2: 26: 72, congestion of lungs, æ. 3-5-3, b. Dedham, of James & Isabella, Ire., do.

LOWING. *(See also Larin.)*
   48 Delphine, 6: 2: 72, consumption, æ. 15-0-4, b. Canada, of Lewis & Delphine, Canada, do.

LUCAS.
   13 Philip, 1: 20: 88, cancer, æ. 43-3-26, b. Eng., of Chas. & Mary, Eng., do.

LUCE.
   39 Chas. A., 5: 3: 76, consumption of blood, æ. 1-6-9, b. Hyde Park, of David W. Jr. & Clara A., New Bedford, Boston.

LUDWIG.
   85 Wm. F., 9: 30: 80, suicide, æ. 39-4-23, b. Germ., of Henry & ——, Germ., ——.

LUNA.
   55 Jerome, 6: 18: 87, ——, æ. 1-2-0.

LUND.
   9 Eliz'h A. (Lund), 5: 26: 66, ——, æ. ——, b. Ded., of Nicholas M. & Luanna M.

LUTHER.
   87 Jas. M., 11: 14: 62, consumption, æ. 42-6-12, b. Warren R. I., of Barnabas & Sabra.

LUTZ.
   60 Chester W. B., 8: 3: 78, cholera infantum, æ. 0-11-0, b. Ded., of Geo. & M. Ella, P. E. I., Dorch.
   64 Geo. O., 9: 5: 73, ——, æ. 0-2-7, b. Ded., of Geo. & Ella M., P. E. I., Dorch.
   60 Wm. M., 7: 30: 80, meningitis, æ. 0-4-0, b. Ded., of Geo. & [Ella] M., P. E. I., Milton.

LYMAN.
   55 Mary A., 10: 4: 53, dysentery, æ. 1-8-28, b. Ded., of Jas. K. & Lavina.

LYNCH.
   28 Ann (Eagan), 3: 15: 69, lung fever, æ. 69-0-0, b. Ire., of Michael & Nancy, Ire., do.
   38 Catherine, 9: 8: 62, ——, æ. 25-0-0, b. Ire., of Timothy & Mary, Ire., do.

65 Edward, 8: 30: 86, convulsions, æ. 0-2-10, b. Ded., of Daniel A. & Mary A., Ded., W. Rox.

11 John, 4: 19: 52, dropped dead, æ. 34-0-0, b. Ire., of Morris & Mary.

65 John F., 7: 26: 85, convulsions, æ. 0-10-3, b. Ded., of Stephen F. & Mary, Ded., Ire.

101 Margaret, w. of John, 10: 12: 49, dysentery, æ. 29-0-0, b. Ire.

58 Mary (Ryan), w. of Patrick, 4: 24: 83, paralysis, æ. 80-0-0, b. Ire., of John & Margaret (Davis), Ire., do.

2 Patrick, 1: 27: 70, dis. of lungs, æ. 70-0-0, b. Ire., of Martin & Susan, Ire., do.

12 Timothy, 7: 7: 72, old age, æ. 82-0-0, b. Ire., of Martin & ——, Ire., do.

82 Wm., 12: 7: 68, gravel, æ. 70-0-0, b. Ire., of —— & ——, Ire., do.

57 Wm. F., 12: 1: 69, consumption, æ. 25-10-18, b. Ded., of Wm. & Ann, Ire., do.

LYNDA.

55 Abigail, 9: 5: 47, fever, æ. 90-0-0.

LYONS.

18 Abigail H. (Harding), 5: 15: 59, inflam. of bowels, æ. 67-0-6, b. Rox., of Wm. & Sarah.

81 Bridget, 8: 16: 87, dysentery, æ. 81-0-0, b. Ire., of —— & ——, Ire., do.

53 Catherine, 5: 22: 83, epistaxis, æ. 26-0-0, b. Ire., of Jerry & Julia, Ire., do.

9 Edw., 1: 31: 83, meningitis, æ. 5-7-0, b. Ded., of Thos. & Mary, Ire., do.

42 Ellen H., 5: 19: 85, phthisis, æ. 16-1-14, b. Ire., of Thos. & Mary, Ire., do.

69 John, 7: 1: 63, old age, æ. 75-0-0, b. Ireland.

50 John, 4: 4: 67, consumption, æ. 43-0-0, b. Ire., of Chas. & Winifred, Ire., do.

62 Margaret, 8: 11: 78, cholera infantum, æ. 0-5-19, b. Ded., of Maurice & Bridget, Ire., do.

10 Mary J. (Jones), w. of John, 4: 11: 52, dis. of heart, æ. 67-0-0, b. Dorch., of Elijah & Jerusha.

1 Michael, 1: 3: 83, consumption, æ. 17-7-0, b. Ire., of Thos. & Mary, Ire., do.

125 Patrick, 11: 14: 88, internal injuries, æ. 26-0-0, b. Ire., of John & Hannah (Murphy), Ire., do.

MABBETT.

20 ——, 3: 31: 79, stillborn, b. Ded., s. of Wm. L. & Sarah E., R. I., Eng.

15 Sarah (Lucas), 2: 12: 82, paralysis, æ. 65-9-0, b. Eng., of William & Sarah, Eng., do.

McAFEE.

13 Albert C., 7: 16: 72, cholera infantum, æ. 0-1-0, b. Ded., of Jos. & Rosanna, Ire., do.

16 Joseph A., 9: 16: 71, marasmus, æ. 0-9-12, b. Ded., of Joseph & Rosanna, Ire., do.

McALEER.

30 Rose (McAleer), w. of John, 3: 14: 80, dysentery, æ. 97-0-0, b. Ire., of Lawrence & ——, Ire., do.

McALLISTER.

66 Geo. W., 7: 3: 65, inflam. of bowels, æ. 2-11-26, b. Ded., of Robert & Jane C.

26 James, 7: 11: 59, consumption, æ. 43-0-0, b. Ire.

79 Jane (Carlisle), 9: 1: 81, consumption, æ. 50-0-0, b. Ire., of Hugh & ——,
Ire., ——.

6 Maggie, 10: 23: 75, tuberculosis, æ. 20-8-5, b. Ded., of Robert & Jane, Ire.,do.

118 Robert, 12: 6: 80, heart dis., æ. 68-0-0, b. Eng., of —— & Mary (Hill), Scot.,
England.

26 Sarah R., 8: 16: 52, dysentery, æ. 0-8-8, b. Ded., of John & Jane.

McAULIFFE, McCAULIFF.

51 Bridget (Moniray), 11: 11: 62, hernia. æ. 40-0-0, b. Ire., of William & Mary,
Ire., do.

13 Delia T. (Fitzpatrick), w. of Lawrence J., 1-27-89, typhoid fever, æ. 29-11-0,
b. Ire., of Jas. & Margaret (Vagban), Ire., do.

124 Ellen F. (Curry), w. of Thos., 12: 25: 89, pneumonia, æ. 32-0-0, b. Waltham,
of Jas. & Bridget, Ire., do.

37 John, 1: 18: 71, accident, æ. 40-0-0, b. Ire, of Lawrence & Mary, Ire., do.

44 Lawrence, 4: 24: 66, fits, æ. 0-0-1, b. Ded., of Lawrence & Honora.

47 Margaret, 7: 24: 69, ——, æ. 0-0-17, b. Ded., of Edw. & Bridget, Ire., do.

McCAFFRY.

46 Mary (McGuire), w. of Thos., 4: 5: 88, pneumonia, æ. 41-0-0, b. Ire., of Owen
& Bridget (Farry), Ire., do.

9 Thomas F., 5: 20: 67, drowned, æ. 5-7-0, b. N. B., of Bernard & Margaret,
Ire., do.

McCALL.

29 Robert, 10: 10: 55, dropsy, æ. 27-9-10, b. Scot., of Duncan & Janet.

McCALLUM.

8 Mabel, 1: 8: 77, umbilical hemorrhage, æ. 0-0-2, b. Ded., of Daniel & Katie,
Scot., Ire.

McCANDLISH.

71 John, 8: 14: 76, premature birth, æ. 0-0-5, b. Ded., of John & Elizabeth L.
Boston, do.

McCANN.

31 Bernard, 4: 9: 82, cholera infantum, æ. 0-5-10, b. Lowell, of —— & Kate.

McCARTHY, McCARTY.

72 Ann, 9: 30: 64, fits, æ. 4-4-0, b. Ded., of Michael & Margaret, Ire., do.

96 Chas., 11: 27: 76, leucocythemia, æ. 15-7-14, b. Lowell, of John & Joanna,
Ire., do.

125 Daniel, 7: 25: 67, consumption, æ. 17-0-0, b. Ire., of Michael & Elizabeth,
Ire., do.

77 Francis, 11: 3: 86, inflam. of bowels, æ. 0-2-1, b. Ded., of John & Mary A.,
Ire., Walpole.

133 Hannah M., 9: 30: 64, fits, æ. 4-4-2, b. Ded., of Michael & Margaret, Ire., do.

82 Jeremiah, 10: 17: 62, mania a potu, æ. 45-0-0, b. Ire. [soldier.]

81 John, 11: 11: 86, cirrhosis of liver, æ. 83-0-0, b. Ire.

50 Josephine, 5: 14: 83, typhoid fever, æ. 10-5-0, b. Worcester, of Wm. & Ann,
Rox., P. E. I.

7 Margaret (Hyde), 11: 28: 73, paralysis, æ. 85-0-0, b. Ire., of Henry & Hannah,
Ire., do.

35 Margaret (Murphy), 5: 3: 79, consumption, æ. 48-0-0, b. Ire., of Jas. & ——,
Ire., ——.

56 Margaret T., 6: 28: 82, consumption, æ. 19-2-25, b. Ded., of Michael & Margaret, Ire., do.

7 Mary E., 1: 11: 89, difficult labor, æ. 0-0-1, b. Ded., of Thos. F. & Abby T. (Sullivan), Boston, Ded.

109 Michael, 11: 13: 90, apoplexy, æ. 73-0-0, b. Ire., of John & Margaret Hyde), Ire., do.

22 Nellie, 2: 12: 73, inflam. of stomach, æ. 0-7-3, b. Ded., of Michael & Margaret, Ire., do.

McCASLIN.

88 Ellen (White), 12: 3: 86, dis. of heart, æ. 56-9-0, b. Ire., of Wm. & Margaret, Ire., do.

55 Henry, 3: 27: 64, teething, æ. 0-11-25, b. Ded., of Andrew & Ellen, Ire., do.

McCAULEY.

31 Margaret, 6: 14: 53, consumption, æ. 30-0-0, b. Ireland.

McCONNELL.

25 ——, 4: 15: 61, fits, æ. 0-0-1, b. Ded., s. of Alexander & Mary.

McCORMICK.

66 Catherine, 7: 13: 87, apoplexy, æ. 58-0-0, b. Ire., of Andrew & Mary, Ire., do.

McCOUGHLIN.

78 James, 2: 1: 49, brain fever, æ. 24-0-0, b. Ire.

McCUE.

6 Andrew, 1: 22: 79, pneumonia, æ. 46-0-0, b. Ire., of Andrew & Mary A., Ire., do.

57 John, 11: 30: 54, dis. of brain, æ. 0-3-2, b. Ded., of Andrew & Ann.

McDERMOTT.

91 James, 12: 17: 86, suicide, æ. 48-0-0, b. Ire., of Cornelius & Catherine, Ire., do.

McDONALD.

126 Jas., 11: 17: 88, obstruction of mitral valve of heart, æ. 57-0-19, b. Augusta Me., of Jas. & Mary (Lacy), Me., do.

66 John, 7: 11: 82, enteritis, æ. 1-2-24, b. Sherburn, of Alex'r & Barbara, Scot., do.

56 John, 7: 13: 72, cholera infantum, æ. 0-2-10, b. Boston, of —— & Mary.

McDONOUGH.

95 John, 12: 17: 53, inflam. of bowels, æ. 45-0-0, b. Galway.

17 John, 8: 17: 67, diarrhoea, æ. 0-5-14, b. Ded., of John & Susan, Ire., do.

18 Katie E., 3: 4: 85, consumption, æ. 20-3-0, b. Amesbury, of Peter & Mary, Ire., do.

8 Martin, 12: 9: 68, scarlet fever, æ. 3-1-2, b. Ded., of Patrick & Margaret, Ire., do.

5 Michael, 6: *7: 65, intermittent fever, æ. 2-8-18, b. Ded., of Patrick & Margaret.

14 Patrick, 3: 26: 62, consumption, æ. 4-11-16, b. Ded., of John & Hannah.

79 Patrick, 9: 24: 76, accident, æ. 56-2-0, b. Ire., of Martin & Catherine, Ire., do.

104 Thos., 5: 15: 64, scarlet fever, æ. 0-6-0, b. Ded., of John & Julia, Ire., do.

McELWIE, McELWEE.

99 Edw., 8: 21: 61, cholera infantum, æ. 0-3-11. b. Ded., of John & Mary, Scot., W. Rox.

46 John, 5: 10: 72, lung fever, æ. 48-4-10, b. Scot., of Wm. & Agnes, Scot , do.

87 Mary E. (Richards), 9: 29: 63, erysipelas, æ. 33-11-9, b. W. Rox., of Danforth & Cyrene, Dover. Sudbury.

McENENY.

17 Arthur, 2: 27: 45, consumption, æ. 42-0-0.

23 Matthew, 2: 10: 49, consumption, æ. 19-0-0, b. Ded.

29 Nancy (Doole), 1: 16: 68, cancer, æ. 66-0-0, b. Ire.

McENTEE.

41 ——, 3: 27: 88, stillborn, b. Ded., d. of Patrick & Rose, Ire., do.

17 ——, 2: 9: 89, stillborn, b. Ded., s. of Patrick & Rose (Dearoe), Ire., do.

McGEE.

37 ——, 4: 29: 76, stillborn, b. Ded., s. of John & Ellen, Ire., do.

68 ——, 9: 1: 77, stillborn, b. Ded., s. of John & Ellen, Ire., do.

103 ——, 9: 27: 87, stillborn, b. Ded., s. of John & Eliza, Ire., do.

4 Catherine (McGuire), 1: 12: 80, heart dis., æ. 73-0-0, b. Ire., of John & Rose, Ireland, do.

33 Catherine, 4: 10: 80, infantile convulsions, æ. 0-9-7, b. Ded., of John & Ellen, Ire., do.

29 Ellen (Haley), 3: 26: 83, consumption, æ. 38-0-0, b. Ire., of Robert & Ann, Ireland, do.

97 John, 3: 26: 86, bronchial pneumonia, æ. 4-4-10, b. Ded., of John & Ellen, Ireland, do.

12 Kate, 1: 20: 88, diphtheria, æ. 1-0-28, b. Ded., of Daniel J. & Julia E., Boston, W. Rox.

McGINNIS. (*See McGuiness.*)

McGLONE.

20 Barnard, 4: 22: 58, fits, æ. ——, b. Ded., of Barnard & Mary.

76 Catharine, 7: 28: 67, dysentery, æ. 1-4-0, b. Ded., of Patrick & Catharine, Ireland, do.

34 Sarah, 5: 9: 57, croup, æ. 0-3-13, b. Ded., of Patrick & Catherine.

McGLOSHEN, McGLASHAN.

11 Arthur N., 1: 21: 77, meningitis, æ. 1-3-0, b. Ded., of Richard & Mary, Scotland, do.

54 Jenet (McCole), 5: 21: 65, typhoid fever, æ. 34-0-0, b. Scot., of —— & Jenet.

McGLYNN.

23 Bryan, 3: 28: 62, falling down cellar, æ. 46-0-0, b. Ireland, of Michael & Mary, Ireland, do.

McGOEAVAN.

35 Catharine, 2: 13: 65, consumption, æ. 60-0-0, b. Ire.

McGOORAN.

2 Catharine (Gormany), 2: 13: 65, consumption, æ. 62-0-0, b. Ire., of Francis & Mary.

McGOWAN, McGOWEN.
55 Michael C., 5: 17: 89, heart malformation, æ. 0-2-0, b. Ded., Michael & Mary (Hoey), Ire., do.
81 William, 4: 1: 64, ——, æ. 60-0-0, b. Scot. [soldier].

McGRATH.
107 Mary, 11: 18: 83, paralysis, æ. 70-0-0, b. Ireland, of Michael & Mary, Ireland, do.

McGREGOR.
77 Eugene K., 11: 29: 66, accidental, æ. 16-6-25, b. Milo Me., of William W. & Eliza A.

McGUINESS, McGINNIS.
16 Ann (Hixon), 2: 14: 57, consumption, æ. 30-0-0, b. Ire., of Thos. & Agnes.
54 Catharine (Connor), 7: 31: 66, cancer, æ. 66-9-0, b. Ireland, of Barnard & Mary.
35 Edward H., 9: 19: 52, cholera infantum, æ. 1-11-0, b. Boston, of Edward & Ann.
20 Eliza (Riely), 3: 10: 87, phthisis, æ. 68-0-0, b. Ire., of Patrick & Ellen, Ire.,do.
38 Ellen, 5: 16: 87, membranous croup, æ. 6-8-1, b. Ded., of John F. & Bridget L., Blackstone, Ire.
47 Fred'k H., 8: 3: 57, consumption, æ. 0-7-15, b. Ded., of Edw. & Ann.
39 Mary, 4: 12: 81, diphtheria, æ. 10-5-0, b. Ded., of Bernard & Mary, Ire., do.
17 Mary E., 7: 7: 63, scarlatina, æ. 0-7-0, b. Ded., of Matthew & Eliz'h.
33 Wm., 3: 30: 81, pneumonia. æ. 5-9-0, b. Ded., of Bernard & Mary, Ire., do.

McILROY.
81 Elsie V., 8: 9: 77, dysentery, æ. 1-7-0, b. Ded., of Fred'c A. & Martha E., Boston, Ded.

McINTOSH. (*See Mackintosh.*)

MACK.
1 John, 2: 16: 68, consumption, æ. 19-0-0. b. N. B., of John & Marg't, Ire., do.
82 Thos., 4: 29: 53, ——, æ. 3-0-0, b. Ded.

McKEE.
33 ——, 4: 17: 76, marasmus, æ. 0-0-30, b. Ded., s. of James & Margaret, Brookline, Ire.
20 Frances, 4: 29: 78, convulsions, æ 0-5-0, b. Ded., of John A. & Sarah, Brookline, Ire.
81 Geo., 10: 2: 76, marasmus, æ. 0-1-7, b. Ded., of John A. & Sarah, Brookline, Ireland.
92 Mabel F., 9: 30: 81, meningitis, æ. 1-9-0, b. Ded., of John A. & Sarah, Brookline, Ire.
20 Martha J. M., 3: 19: 81, convulsions, æ. 0-3-0, b. Ded., of John A. & Sarah, Brookline, Ire.
20 Wm. J., 3: 31: 76, abscess, æ. 1-7-0, b. Ded., of John A. & Sarah, Brookline, Ireland.

McKEON.
91 Thos., 9: 21: 67, canker, æ. 1-3-0, b. Ded., of John & Bridget, Ire., do.

McKERRY.
40 John H., 5: 24: 69, convulsions, æ. 6-5-6, b. Waterford, of John N. & Cath'e.
59 Judith H., 8: 27: 78, cholera infantum, æ. 0-11-0, b. Ded., of John N. & Catherine E., Scot., Eng.
121 Mary, 12: 7: 65, diphtheria, æ. 4-3-22, b. Woonsocket R. I., of John N. & Catharine.

MACKEY.
4 Arthur H., 3: 16: 75, pulmonary consumption, æ. 31-5-0, b. at sea, of Wm. & Letitia, Scot., do.

MACKINTOSH, McINTOSH.
6 Augustus B., 8: 2: 48, fits, æ. 2-7-0, b. Ded., of Elisha & ——.
62 Chas. A., 6: 9: 89, hypertrophy of liver, æ. 35-9-15, b. W. Rox., of Charles G. & Harriet A. (Richards), Canton, Ded.
66 Elisha, 4: 13: 62, apoplexy, æ. 78-0-18, b. Dorch., of Jeremiah & Susanna, Dorch., Franklin.
74 Henry N., 12: 31: 55, consumption, æ. 2-4-19, b. Dorch., of Elisha & Pelina R.
34 Mary, 6: 25: 53, erysipelas, æ. 64-8-11, b. Dorch., of Jer'h & Susanna.
20 Phebe A. (Morrill), w. of Andrew, 6: 25: 51, consumption, æ. 25-9-20, b. Natick, of Samuel & Sarah.
31 Polina R. (Whiting), w. of E., 5: 8: 55, typhoid fever, æ. 44-10-11, b. Ded., of Moses & Abigail.
40 Rebecca (Damon), 9: 17: 54, rheumatic fever, æ. 72-3-17, b. Ded., of Jonathan & Mary.

McKIRDY.
21 Ann (Blackburn), 2: 27: 75, pleurisy fever, æ. 66-9-12, b. Scotland, of Wm. & Ann.
16 John, 1: 29: 75, pleurisy fever, æ. 65-0-0, b. Scot., of —— & ——, Scot., do.

McLANE.
66 Jas., 6: 15: 89, heart dis., æ. 68-0-0, b. Ire., of John & Mary Laverty), Ire.,do.
79 Sarah, 6: 8: 88, meningitis, æ. 1-0-0, b. Ded., of John J. & Maria J., Ded., W. Roxbury.

McLAUGHLIN.
82 Mary A., 11: 12: 86, typhoid fever, æ. 8-10-12, b. Eng., of Thomas & Kate, England, Ireland.
39 Thos., 9: 11: 62, consumption, æ. 1-0-26, b. Ded., of Jas. & Eliz'h.

McLAY.
84 Agnes, 8: 18: 67, consumption, æ. 0-8-0, b. Ded., of John & R., Scot., Eng.
14 John E., 8: 30: 66, cancre, æ. 1-0-0, b. Ded., of John & Rhodeacher.

McLEAR.
66 Lily, 7: 30: 70, cholera infantum, æ. 0-7-0, b. Boston, of Frank & Rosa, Ire., Vt.

McLEOD.
81 ——, 9: 19: 80, stillborn, b. Dedham, d. of John D. & Mary (Conant), Brit. Prov., do.
57 Angus, 6: 27: 85, pernicious anæmia, æ. 36-9-0, b. P. E. I., of Daniel & Betsy, Scot., do.

48 David, 11 : 17 : 51, accident, æ. 21-0-0, b. Nova Scotia.

86 Mary (Conant), 10 : 4 : 80, puerperal convulsions, æ. 32-11-0, b. Turner Me., of —— & Blanche (Turner), Bridgewater, Turner Me.

McMANUS, McMANNUS.

82 Bridget, 3 : 9 : 59, —— æ. 70-0-0, b. Ire.

47 Catherine, 5 : 27 : 66, water on brain, æ. 5-3-16, b. Ded., of John & Mary.

101 Chas., 9 : 6 : 66, teething, æ. 0-11-15, b. Ded., of Patrick & Catherine.

11 Chas., 9 : 21 : 69, typhoid fever, æ. 41-0-0, b. Ire., of Bryan & Rose, Ire., do.

107 John, 11 : 27 : 84, cancer, æ. 59-0-0, b. Ire., of Jas. & Mary, Ire., do.

83 Rose (McLaughlin), 11 : 19 : 60, bilious fever, æ. 64-0-0, b. Ire., of Chas. & Margaret, Ireland, do.

McMULLEN.

110 Hugh, 12 : 5 : 79, accident R. R., æ. 50-0-0.

113 Mary, 11 : 1 : 65, dysentery, æ. 0-10-0, b. Ded., of Wm. & Hannah.

McNABB.

74 Catherine (Tinney), 8 : 27 : 75, paralysis, æ. 69-0-0, b. Ire., of Frank & Alice, Ireland, do.

51 Mary, 6 : 5 : 82, heart dis., æ. 36-0-0, b. Ire., of Edw. & Catherine, Ire., do.

McNAMARA.

31 John, 8 : 20 : 51, dysentery, æ. 37-0-0, b. Ire., of John & Margaret.

MACOMBER.

59 Emma A. (White), w. of Chas. F., 5 : 28 : 89, meningitis, æ. 28-8-25, b. Charlton, of Washington W. & Mercyette (Clemence), Charlton, Southbridge.

29 John L., 6 : 20 : 58, scarlet fever, æ. 7-9-5, b. Ded., of Amos & Sarah.

51 Louisa M. (Holmes), w. of Winchester S., 4 : 9 : 88, old age, æ. 85-11-22, b. Monmouth Me., of John & Dolly (Bayley).

85 Winchester S., 12 : 13 : 73, Bright's dis., æ. 60-10-2, b. Jay Me., of Winchester & Polly, Bridgewater, Charlestown.

McPHERSON.

56 Mary J., 4 : 24 : 67, burnt, æ. 2-8-0, b. Mich., of John & Jane, P. E. I., Canada.

McSWEENEY.

53 Jeremiah, 3 : 14 : 70, convulsions, æ. 0-3-4, b. Ded., of Timothy & Mary, England, Ireland.

McTAGART.

60 Chas. J., 7 : 29 : 84, convulsions, æ. 4-4-3, b. Ded., of Jas. & Lizzie, Ire., do.

MADDEN.

71 Rose, 12 : 12 : 61, apoplexy, æ. 32-0-0, b. Ire., of Patrick P. & Bridget.

112 Thos., 12 : 11 : 79, ——, æ. 70-0-0, b. Ire., of Patrick & Mary, Ire., do.

MAGUIRE.

20 Hugh, 8 : 31 : 63, inflam. of bowels, æ. 40-0-0, b. Ire., of Michael & Margaret, Ire., do.

3 Rose, 2 : 14 : 71, heart dis., æ. 70-0-0, b. Ire., of Thos. & Mary, Ire., do.

144 Theresa, 11 : 6 : 64, rheumatic fever, æ. 6-3-0, b. Dorch., of Hugh & Margaret, Ire., Scot.

MAHAN.

96 Geo. R., 10: 30: 84, cystitis, æ. 45-0-0, b. Needham, of Robert & Mary Jones,
—, Ded.

1 John, 1: 1: 89, marasmus, æ. 0-8-0, b. Boston, of John & Mary (King), Ire., do.

10 Mary A. (Jones), w. of Robert G., 1: 16: 89, pneumonia, æ. 83-7-26, b. Ded.,
of Lewis & Martha (Miles), Ded., N. H.

MAHAR, MAHER. (See also Marr.)

25 Margaret, 8: 5: 51. bowel complaint, æ. 0-12-18, b. Ded., of Michael & Mary.

101 Margaret, 10: 24: 82, consumption, æ. 46-0-0, b. Ire., of Anthony & Johanna,
Ire., do.

MAHERN.

51 John L., 4: 29: 90, pneumonia, æ. 14-4-5, b. Cambridge, of Anthony & Mary
R. (Fell), Ire., Ded.

MAHONEY.

83 Anna, 11: 10: 70, heart dis., æ. 20-0-0, b. Ire., of Wm. & Catherine, Ire., do.

23 Catherine (McKeon), 3: 11: 84, valvular disease of heart, æ. 73-0-0, b. Ire., of
John & Margaret, Ire., do.

76 Daniel, 4: 8: 57, accidental, æ. 35-0-0, b. Ire., of Thos. & Joanna.

24 John, 3: 19: 87, stillborn, b. Ded., of John F. & Eliz'h, Ded.. R. I.

7 Mary A., 3: 6: 63, scarlatina, æ. 5-0-25, b. Ded., of Michael & Cella.

14 Michael, 2: 13: 76, phthisis, æ. 32-0-0, b. Ire., of John & Catherine, Ire., do.

16 Patrick, 2: 18: 76, ——, æ. 67-0-0, b. Ire., of Michael & Mary, Ire., do.

114 Thos., 11: 2: 55. dis. of throat, æ. 3-4-19, b. Ded., of Michael & Celia.

MAIER. See Meyer.)

MAKER.

8 Ethel F., 1: 23: 84. eclampsia infantum, æ. 0-0-22, b. Ded., of Geo. L. &
Martha E., Chatham, Ded.

MALBY.

78 Martin, 7: 19: 63, pneumonia, æ. 24-0-0. [soldier.]

MALONEY.

19 Daniel W., 11: 13: 65, teething, æ. 1-0-0, b. Ded., of Michael & Susan.

61 Mary A., 6: 28: 60, scarlatina, æ. 5-5-23, b. Greenville R. I., of Peter & Ann,
Ire., do.

MALPUS.

66 Nellie R., 5: 11: 88, tubercular meningitis, æ. 1-9-17, b. Ded., of Geo. H. &
Mary A. (Ryan), Eng., do.

MANDEVILLE.

11 Ambrose, 2: 3: 82, phthisis, æ. 20-8-8, b. Ded., of Richard & Bridget,
N. F., Ire.

135 (D. at Boston) Eliz'h C., 3: 14: 87, Bussey Bridge accident, æ. 18-2-7, b. Ded.,
of Richard & Bridget, N. F., Ire.

11 Ellen, 7: 16: 67, purpurea hemorrhagica, æ. 0-0-14, b. Ded., of Richard &
Bridget, [N. F.,] Ire.

103 Mary J., 10: 30: 82, phthisis, æ. 23-5-24, b. Ded., of Richard & Bridget, [N. F.,]
Ireland.

133 Richard, 12: 7: 88, pneumonia, æ. 67-9-5, b. N. F., of Thos. & Ellen Shield, [N. F.,] Ire.

62 Thos., 5: 19: 64, teething, æ. 1-3-14, b. Ded., of Richard & Bridget.

MANEY.

57 Walter B., 7: 31: 80, cholera infantum, æ. 0-10-5, b. Lewiston Me., of John & Johannah, Boston, Ire.

MANN.

49 Charlotte B. (Billings), 6: 27: 66, paralysis, æ. 73-8-0, b. Ded., of Richard & Mary.

42 Franklin D., 9: 7: 44, scrofula, æ. 9-0-0.

80 George II., 7: 27: 63, consumption, æ. 12-7-0, b. Ded., of Henry H. & Mercie R., Ded., Chatham.

40 Herman, 11: 26: 51, heart complaint, æ. 56-7-18, b. Walpole, of Herman & Sarah.

72 Ruthy (Skillings), 12: 14: 57, consumption, æ. 59-0-0, b. Boston, of John & Mary.

40 Samuel C., 3: 3: 64, paralysis, æ. 61-0-3, b. Ded., of Herman & Sarah, Wrentham, Boston.

58 Sarah (Whiting), 3: 31: 83, old age, æ. 81-2-6, b. Ded., of Joshua & Mary, Dedham, do.

105 Warren E., 9: 19: 66, consumption, æ. 0-2-0, b. Dedham, of Elijah T. & Sarah J.

42 William H., 3: 7: 64, chronic diarrhoea, æ. 66-2-0, b. Dedham, of Herman & Sarah, Wrentham, Boston.

MARCOUX.

33 Cordelia, 2: 23: 72, lung fever, æ. 6-10-0, b. Canada, of Joseph & Mary, Canada, do.

MARDEN.

6 ——, 3: 7: 48, ——, æ. 5-0-0, — of Aaron & ——.

12 Emily J. (Haynes), 2: 4: 86, pneumonia, æ. 62-2-0, b. Chichester N. H., of —— & Lois (Proctor), Chichester, do.

36 Frederick, 11: 2: 51, dysentery, æ. 0-6-22, b. Ded., of Aaron & Mary.

37 Mary L. (Bodge), 5: 26: 86, pulmonary dis., æ. 86-11-0, b. Needham, of David O. & Sally (Blake).

96 Mary P. (Webster), w. of Ellis, 9: 9: 87, heart dis., æ. 70-5-7, b. Kennebunkport Me., of Nath'l & Sarah, Gilmanton N. H., S. C.

16 Mary T. (Cox), 5: 12: 51, consumption, æ. 32-4-22, b. Dedham, of John & Lucretia.

MARKWARD.

86 Isabella (Matthews), w. of Carl L. T., 8: 25: 90, heart dis,, æ. 52-2-2, b. Eng., of Wm. M. & Maria (Lander), Eng., do.

MARONEY.

117 Ann (Kilduff), 9: 7: 66, consumption, æ. 38-0-0, b. Ire., of John & ——.

3 George, 8: 22: 73, general debility, æ. 14-5-0, b. Ded., of Wm. & Ann.

10 Mary E., 8: 3: 66, consumption, æ. 17-0-0, b. Lowell, of Wm. & Ann.

23 Wm. E., 7:30:51, bowel comp., æ. 0-6-0, b. Ded., of Wm. & Ann.

57 Wm. H., 10:13:53, cholera infantum, æ. 1-6-0, b. Ded., of Wm. & Ann.

MARR *(See also Mahar.)*

75 Henry A., 11 : 22 : 66, consumption, æ. 18-11-17, b. N. B., of Wilson & Bridget.

34 Jenneate E., 1 : 18 : 67, typhoid fever, æ. 16-5-2, b. N. B., of Wilson & Bridget, N. B., Ireland.

MARS.

23 Julia A. (Hastings), 4:5:55, consumption, æ. 32-11-4, b. Needham, of Josiah & Clarissa.

MARSH.

34 ——, 9:22:45, fever, æ. 0-14-0, b. Ded., of Francis & Eliza.

77 Charles, 9: 13: 78, consumption, æ. 24-11-0, b. Ded., of Francis & Eliza, Dedham, do.

52 Daniel, 3: 24: 64, heart dis., æ. 73-9-15, b. Hingham, of Lot & Lydia, Hingham, Weymouth.

85 Elizabeth (Metcalf), 12: 31: 68, old age, æ. 90-9-19, b. Ded., of Jonathan & Elizabeth, Dedham, do.

70 Fanny (Hersey), 8: 5: 81, old age, æ. 80-3-25, b. Ded., of Elijah & Lurana Hingham, ——.

90 Frances, 12: 9: 62, consumption, æ. 18-8-28, b. Ded., of Daniel & Fanny Hingham, Ded.

33 Francis, 5: 4: 79, chronic diarrhœa, æ. 72-6-28, b. Ded., of Martin & Eliz'h Hingham, Ded.

31 Franklin W., 5: 28: 74, dis. of bowels, æ. 0-6-21, b. Ded., of Francis & Emma L., Ded., Boston.

123 Geo., 12: 25: 90, chronic dis. of brain, æ. 52-6-1, b. Ded., of Daniel & Fanny (Hersey), Hingham, Ded.

114 Jane, 11: 15: 48, consumption, æ. 19-0-0, b. Ded., of Daniel & Fanny.

78 Martin, 7: 26: 65, old age, æ. 88-3-11, b. Hingham, of Thos. & Lillis.

73 Martin M., 9: 14: 72, catarrhal consumption, æ. 22-11-30, b. Ded., of Francis & Eliza, Ded., do.

MARSHALL.

103 Levi, 5: 14: 64, lung fever, æ. ——. [soldier.]

MARSTON.

142 Carlos, 9: 1: 65, murdered, æ. 42-0-0, b. Sutton N. H., of Asa & Mary.

141 Cora T., 9: 1: 65, murdered, æ. 10-0-0, b. Danville Vt., of Warren & Annie E. T. Harris.

140 Susanna E. (Tenney), 9: 1: 65, suicide, æ. 36-0-0, b. Hanover N. H., of Harvy & Judith D.

MARTIN, MARTYN.

35 ——, 4: 27: 69, stillborn, b. Ded., d. of Robert & Mary, Scot., do.

63 ——, 7: 8: 70, ——, æ. 0-0-1, b. Ded., d. of Robert & Mary, Scot., do.

79 ——, 12: 6: 71, stillborn, b. Ded., d. of Robert & Mary, Scot., do.

11 Chas. H., 9: 16: 48, summer comp., æ. 0-5-0, b. Ded.

101 Edw., 10: 7: 89, old age, æ. 89-9-0, b. Ire., of Patrick & Catharine Conway), Ire., do.

73 Emma, 12: 25: 57, croup, æ. 0-2-21, b. Ded., of John & Barbara.

8 James D., 1: 13: 76, consumption, æ. 25-0-0, b. Dorch., of John & Mary, P. E. I., do.

10 John, 2: 23: 59, lung fever, æ. 0-4-0, b. Ded., of John & Barbara.

5 Mary, 1: 14: 58, croup, æ. 0-0-28, b. Ded., of John & Mary.

34 Sarah T., 3: 29: 73, convulsions, æ. 1-0-0, b. Boston, of Frank E. & Millie E., New Orleans, do.

15 William, 1: 29: 75, convulsions, æ. 0-7-19, b. Ded., of Wm. & Caroline, Albion R. I., Prov. R. I.

MASON.

49 Annie H., 4: 16: 63, diphtheria, æ. 4-11-13, b. Ded., of Wm. H. & Mary F., Ded., Medfield.

20 Chas., 6: 12: 56, paralysis, æ. 61-7-5, b. Ded., of Thaddeus & Abigail.

22 Edward B., 9: 14: 63, fall from horse, æ. 26-2-12, b. Boston, of Wm. P. & H. (Rogers). [soldier.]

106 Ellen A., 12: 25: 63, lung fever, æ. 3-1-0, b. Foxboro, of Wm. A. & Amelia, Salem, Ohio.

74 Leonard, 12: 20: 58, bowel comp., æ. 71-0-0, b. Ded., of Wm. & -

13 Lugarda L., 9: —: 44, fever, æ. 4-0-0, b. Ded.

18 Sally H. [no date, Rec. 6: 24: 46], ——, æ. 51-0-0.

123 Tabitha N. (Eldridge), 5: 5: 63, consumption, æ. 51-5-25, b. Orleans, of Obadiah & Patience, Harwich, do.

82 Wm. H., 5: 4: 61, consumption, æ. 35-8-14, b. Ded., of Eliph't T. & Mary F., Dedham, do.

46 (D. at Boston) Woodbury J., 4: 9: 90, hydrophobia, æ. 36-9 15, b. Tamworth N. H., of John B. & Mary A., Tamworth, Elizabethtown N. Y.

MASSEY.

40 Samuel, 4: 18: 89, heart dis., æ. 55-0-0, b. Ire.

MASTERSON.

26 Margaret, 5: 8: 53, consumption, æ. 14-0-0, b. Ire., of John & Ann.

65 Michael, 7: 4: 60, ——, æ. 32-0-0, b. Ire., of John & Ann, Ire., do.

MATTA.

7 Henry, 1: 2: 75, paralysis, æ. 70-5-28, b. France, of Henry & Theresa France, do.

MATTHEWS.

54 Mary *(Campbell), 6: 17: 80, enlargement of heart, æ. 41-8-16, b. N. S.

112 Wm., 2: 17: 67, lung fever, æ. 75-3 19, b. Isle of Jersey, of Chas. & Eliz'h, Eng., do.

MATTHEWSON.

74 Albert S., 11: 13: 66, typhoid fever, æ. 11-8-3, b. Prov. R. I., of Israel & Sarah.

83 Edw. D., 9: 1: 49, dysentery, æ. 2-2-21, b. Chelmsford, of Jas. & Susanna.

[MATZ] METZ.

39 Susan F., 2: 14: 68, consumption, æ. 1-4 4, b. Ded., of Florian & Catherine Germ., Ire.

MAY.
2 Alice D., 1:3:77, scarlet fever, æ. 3-4-0, b. Ded., of Wm. & Anna M., Woodstock Ct., do.

MAYNARD.
19 Joanna, 3:7:87, pneumonia, æ. 80-3-21, b. Jaffrey N. H., of Elias & Joanna (Winship, Jaffrey N. H., Lexington.
18 Waldo, 9:28:72, ——, æ. 61-0-0, b. Boston, of Elias & Joanna.

MAYNES.
138 Jos. E., 12:20:88, drowning, æ. 11-7-9, b. W. Rox., of Jas. H. & Jane E., Ire., do.

MAYO.
19 Abigail (Rogers), 4:23:54, pleurisy, æ. 74-7-0, b. Chatham, of Crisp & Deborah.
47 James, 1:14:45, lung fever, æ. 67-0-0.

MEAD.
63 Charles, 9:21:51, bleeding, æ. 27-0-0.
129 Irene, 11:7:62, consumption, æ. 38-0-0, b. Tamworth N. H., of Wm. & Mary, Barton N. H., Sandwich N. H.
63 Nancy, w. of Alpheus, 3:10:49, consumption, æ. 22-0-0.
92 Sarah L., 3:4:55, stoppage, æ. 3-4-0, b. Ded., of Chas. & Sarah.

MEIGHAN, MEHAN.
122 Catharine, 12:12:65, heart dis., æ. 21-0-0, b. Ire., of Martin & Margaret.
9 Heiram, 12:3:73, heart dis., æ. 25-0-0, b. Ire., of Martin & Margaret, Ire., do.
52 James E., 6:25:75, scarlet fever, æ. 1-5-0, b. Ded., of Edmond & Catherine, Ire., Canada.
14 John M., 10:6:65, diarrhœa, æ. 0-11-0, b. Ded., of Edmund & Catherine.
4 Margaret (Lemouge), 4:7:74, paralysis, æ. 59-0-0, b. Ire., of Keoran L. & Honora, Ire., do.
60 Martin, 5:21:75, scarlet fever, æ. 6-4-10, b. Ded., of Edmond & Catherine, Ire., Canada.
38 Martin, 4:14:83, dropsy, æ. 70-0-0, b. Ire., of Thos. & Ellen, Ire., do.
61 Philip, 8:4:72, dysentery, æ. 0-10-6, b. Ded., of Edmund & Catharine, Ire., do.

MEINERSHAGEN.
64 Jos. H., 6:10:83, dysentery, æ. 32-6-27, b. Germ., of John & Clara E., Germ., do.

MELLEN.
6 ——, 8:13:46, dysentery, æ. 4-0-0, b. ——, of Geo. & ——.
31 Lewis D., 9:15:50, drowned, æ. 10-7-25, b. Canton, of Geo. W. & Sophia.

MENAHAN. (See also *Minnehan*.)
4 Bridget, 3:3:65, infantile debility, æ. 0-0-1, b. Ded., of Michael & Honora.

MERRILL.
106 (D. at Taunton) Hayden A., 10:16:89, paresis, æ. 46-0-0, b. Merrimac, of —— & ——, N. H., do.

MESSER.

115 Anna M., 11:9:62, consumption, æ. 0-6-6, b. Tewksbury, of Chas. & Jane, Holland, N. Y.

51 (D. at Wrentham) Geo. C., 8:23:60, typhoid fever, æ. 29-2 18, b. Ded., of Geo. W. & Nancy, New London N. H., Sharon.

METCALF.

14 ——, 2:22:87, stillborn, b. Ded., s. of Eugene H. & May H. (Lewis), Charlestown, Ded.

15 Hannah (Smith), 2:15:81, paralysis, æ. 83-11-29, b. Ded., of Nathaniel & Nancy, Ded., do.

64 Joseph, 10:26:57, old age, æ. 92-6-6, b. Ded., of Jos. & Ruth A.

14 Rebecca, 9:26:48, bowel comp., æ. 84-4-0.

METZLER.

8 John, 7:8:65, colic, æ. 0-0-9, b. Ded., of John & Mary.

MEYER, MAIER, MYERS.

84 Alfred, 8:22:89, convulsions, æ. 0-3-29, b. Ded., of Chas. P. & Charlotte (Emerson), Germ., Eng.

44 Barbara L., 6:16:77, convulsions, æ. 5-0-0, b. Ded., of Adolph & Barbara, Germ., do.

13 Bertha E., 2:10:84, diphtheritic croup, æ. 2-6-13, b. Ded., of Christian A. & Melinda A., Germ., Boston.

11 Julius J., 2:8:84, convulsions, æ. 0-0-19, b. Dover, of Augustus A. & Salman, Germ., do.

96 Peter, 11:16:59, fits, æ. 0-7-10, b. Ded., of Peter & ——.

MEYERHOFF, MYERHOOF.

69 Annie F., 12:4:57, consumption, æ. 57-0-0, b. Germany.

64 Margaret, 11:8:74, consumption, æ. 38-3-0, b. Germ., of Clouse & Anna F., Germ., do.

MIGNAULT.

86 D. R., 11:10:62, delirium tremens, æ. 28-0-0, b. France, [soldier.]

MILES.

66 Wm., 7:24:81, valvular dis. of heart, æ. 69-5-13, b. Boston, of Thos. & Maria, Boston, do.

MILEY.

3 John, 2:26:52, infantile dis., æ. 0-4-12, b. Cambridge, of Dan & Marg't.

MILLER.

90 Andrew F., 9:29:53, whooping cough, æ. 1-10-8, b. Ded., of Allen H. & Hannah R.

16 Chas. D., 2:28:60, drowning, æ. 7-0-0, b. Boston, of Jos. R. & Mary B.

80 Frank A., 9:6:81, paralysis of heart, æ. 8 1-3, b. Springfield, of Chas. & Louisa, Germ., Ded.

71 Hannah R. (Radloff), 9:19:64, childbirth, æ. 41-11-10, b. Seekonk, of Jas. & Mary, Seekonk, ——.

89 John F. R., 9:25:53, whooping cough, æ. 0-2-13, b. Ded., of Allen H. & Hannah R.

123 Lewis A., 12: 18: 62, consumption, æ. 23-6-0, b. N. Y., of Fred'k & Lydia, Denmark, Mass.

63 Maud, 10: 3: 66, weakness, æ. 0-1-0, b. Ded., of Arthur L. & Lydia C.

MILLS.

27 Bathsheba (Bates), w. of Hiram, 3: 5: 89, old age, æ. 84-4-22, b. Webster, of Alanson & Comfort (Robinson), Webster, do.

15 Eliz'h A. (Alden),[3: 28: 53, old age, æ. 90-7-0, b. Need., of Silas & Margaret.

82 John A. B., 9: 27: 84, cholera infantum, æ. 0-3-4, b. Ded., of C. P. & Sarah A., Canada, do.

MINNEHAN. *(See also Menahan.)*

3 John, 2: 3: 62, dropsy of brain, æ. 0-11-2, b. Ded., of Michael & Mary (Hayes).

MITCHELL.

4 Bridget (Kennedy), 3: 2: 70, childbirth, æ. 37-1-0, b. Ire., of John & Mary, Ire., do.

11 Eliza J., 9: 3: 65, cholera infantum, æ. 1-1-0, b. Ded., of Terence & Ann M.

51 Jas. T., 5: 18: 83, cervical abscesses, æ. 1-6-28, b. Ded., of Thos. & Margaret, Scot., Milton.

64 Margaret A. (Deneef), 8: 4: 84, consumption, æ. 27-5-20, b. Milton, of Michael & Ann, Ire., do.

36 Mary J., 4: 16: 84, consumption, æ. 0-6-11, b. Ded., of Thos. S. & Margaret A., Scot., Milton.

MONAGAN, MONAHAN, MONEHAN, MONIHAN. *(See also Menahan.)*

102 Ellen (Haberlin), 10: 29: 82, typhoid fever, æ. 55-0-0, b. Ire., of John & Bridget, Ire., do.

5 John, 3: 7: 67, diarrhoea, æ. 3-9-9, b. Ded., of Terence & Anastatia, Ire., do.

30 Mary (Fagan), 10: 10: 56, dysentery, æ. 70-0-0, b. Ire., of Simeon & Mary.

83 Mary A., 9: 22: 75, consumption, æ. 17-0-0, b. Ded., of Terence & Stacy W., Ire., do.

68 Rose, 8: 27: 78, consumption, æ. 50-0-0, b. Ire., of Patrick & Mary, Ire., do.

5 Terence, 7: 5: 69, liver comp., æ. 36-0-0, b. Ire., of Patrick and Mary, Ire., do.

MONTAGUE.

41 Virginia W., 8: 11: 53, cholera infantum, æ. 0-1-24, b. Ded., of George L. & Cath. F. W.

MONTGOMERY.

80 Esther R., 9: 18: 84, canker, æ. 0-4-0, b. Ded., of Frank H. & Anna I., St. George Me., Portland Me.

71 Nathan F., 8: 23: 60, canker, æ. 0-5-10, b. Ded., of Francis W. & Sarah, Halifax, Abington.

MONTIVIRO.

68 Manuel, 8: 3: 75, tuberculosis, æ. 35-0-0, b. Cuba.

MOODY.

23 Blanche E., 3: 25: 78, bronchitis, æ. 1-1-22, b. Milford, of Eben N. & Pamelia, Maine, Ct.

MOONAY, MOONEY.

7 Francis, 2: 8: 55, dis. of brain, æ. 1-6-14 b. Ded., of John & Margaret.

77 Margaret (Malloy), w. of Martin, 6: 6: 88, old age, æ. 94-0-9, b. Ire., of John
& Mary, Ire., do.

MOORE.

7 Chas. B., 1: 26: 81, paralysis, æ. 44-7-3, b. Framingham, of John & Susanna,
Gerry, Boston.

57 Fred., 7: 8: 79, ——, æ. 0-0-0.

MORAN.

58 Catharine (Leonard), 7: 8: 68, consumption, æ. 26-11-0, b. Ire., of John &
Ann, Ire., do.

140 John F., 12: 22: 88, R. R. accident, æ. 25-10-12, b. Ded., of Dominick & Catherine (Leonard). Ire., do.

60 John J., 8: 14: 77, cholera infantum, æ. 0-10-0, b. Ded., of John & Mary, Ire.,do.

MORGAN.

101 Chas. D., *6: 24: 70, softening of brain, æ. 37-10-0, b. Ded., of John & ——,
——, Ded.

75 (D. at Charlestown), Mary F., 2: 24: 58, dropsy on brain, æ. 1-0-24, b. Charlestown, of Chas. & Mary G.

70 Michael J., 7: 24: 82, consumption, æ. 64-9-9, b. Ire., of Matthias & Honora,
Ire., do.

MORHOFF.

95 Christian, 11: 10: 67, suicide, æ. 62-0-0, b. Germ.

MORRILL, MORRELL.

82 Chas. E., 10: 2: 69, congestion of brain, æ. 0-4-15, b. Dedham, of Edw. H.
& Jane E., Andover, Manayunk Pa.

62 Edwin H., 10: 16: 61, dropsy of brain, æ. 1-0-23, b. Boston, of Simon S. &
Leanor.

65 Freddie W., 8: 7: 79, basilar meningitis, æ. 0-6-7, b. Hyde Park, of Wm. A.
& Jennie E., Boston, Dorchester.

43 Helen, 12: 10: 47, fever, æ. 12-0-0.

182 Sarah B. (Tidd), 3: 20: 64, metritis, æ. 31-11-28, b. Woburn, of Wm. &
Luthera, Woburn, Charlestown N. H.

MORRISON.

13 ——, 9: 1: 46, dysentery, æ. 4-0-0, b. Ded., of Wm. & ——.

40 Charlotte P., 12: 18: 56, consumption, æ. 18-2-12, b. Ded., of Wm. & Olive.

102 Francis L., 10: 7: 89, cholera infantum, æ. 0-2-3, b. Ded., of Frank J. &
Nellie (McNeill), Austria, P. E. I.

9 Mary A., 2: 16: 55, consumption, æ. 22-7-9, b. Ded., of Wm. & Olive.

43 Michael, 7: 2: 61, ——, æ. 4-6-0, b. Ded., of Wm. & Johanna, Ire., do.

92 Wm., 10: 4: 67, lung fever, æ. 67-0-0, b. Ded., of Wm. & Nancy, Dedham,
Wrentham.

MORRISSEY.

29 Cornelius, 8: 14: 70, cholera infantum, æ. 0-1-24, b. Ded., of Wm. & Bridget,
Ire., do.

98 Katy J., 10: 28: 79, diphtheria, æ. 13-0-0, b. Ded., of Daniel & Catherine,
Ireland, do.

129 Margaret, 3: 13: 65, pneumonia, æ. 0-6-8, b. Ded., of Wm. & Joanna.

57 Mary. 8: 29: 61, dysentery, æ. 1-6-0, b. Wrentham, of John & Johanna, Ireland, do.

121 Patrick, 12: 9: 89, consumption, æ. 32-11-8, b. Ded., of Daniel & Catharine (Tynan), Ireland, do.

3 Thos. J., 1: 16: 84, meningitis, æ. 4-6-0, b. Boston, of Thos. J. & Mary A., N. F., do.

MORROW.

100 Geo. L., 12: 11: 76, asthma, æ. 7-7-0, b. Boston, of Wm. H. & Susan, Salem, Hyannis.

26 Wm. H., 3: 14: 83, heart dis., æ. 79-7-0, b. Boston, of Wm. H. & Lucy, Scot., Cambridge.

MORSE.

3 ——, 1: 24: 53, infantile dis., æ. 0-0-1, b. Ded., d. of Jesse & Nancy.

66 Abby R. (Shackley), 2: 21: 63, cancer, æ. 33-11-24, b. Norway Me., of Aaron & Margaret, Kennebunk Me., ——.

83 Abigail C. (Colburn), 2: 10: 54, consumption, æ. 37-0-0, b. Ded., of Eliph't & Cynthia.

69 Abigail C. (Colburn), 3: 18: 69, phthisis, æ. 45-11-19, b. Ded., of Nath'l & Anna, Dedham, do.

124 Alvin H., 5: 29: 67, consumption, æ. 31-8-18, b. Ded., of Ezra & Sally, Dedham, do.

41 Azuba, 10: 28: 46, consumption, æ. 72-6-0, b. Sharon.

196 (D. at Holliston) Benj. D., 7: 28: 64, liver comp., æ. 57-8-21, b. Ded., of Seth & ——, Dedham, do.

62 Caroline A., 6: 21: 47, consumption, æ. 22-0-0.

91 Chas. E., 12: 29: 59, consumption, æ. 44-0-0, b. Ded., of Ezra & Hannah.

37 Cynthia, 5: 5: 61, consumption, æ. 43-1-1, b. Ded., of Ezra & Sally, Ded., do.

109 (D. at Walpole) Cynthia J., 1: 22: 63, consumption, æ. 24-8-20, b. Walpole, of Jos. & Roxa M., Walpole, Dedham.

74 David, 9: 5: 52, diseased kidneys, æ. 65-0-0, b. Ded., of David & Sibbel.

83 David, 4: 10: 59, consumption, æ. 32-0-0, b. Walpole, of David & Nancy G.

53 Deborah, 3: 9: 52, old age, æ. 93-6-0, b. Dover.

80 Edwin F., 7: 26: 55, dysentery, æ. 2-0-0, b. Ded., of John & Hannah W.

122 Ella M., 12: 16: 62, typhoid fever, æ. 9-9-0, b. Ded., of Dean & Sybil E., Ded., do.

22 Eva A., 3: 16: 76, congestion of lungs, æ. 0-7-0, b. Ded., of Jos. & Martha K., Ded., Medfield.

33 Howard, 6: 17: 60, consumption, æ. 28-8-14, b. Ded., of Ezra & Sally, Ded., do.

11 Irene, 3: 2: 59, old age, æ. 81-2-5, b. Ded.

113 Jesse, 6: 14: 61, dropsy, æ. 72-10-0, b. Ded., of Seth & Mary, Ded., do.

52 John, 4: 21: 61, paralysis, æ. 69-6-19, b. Ded., of John & Mary, Ded., ——.

176 John L., 2: 26: 64, lung fever, æ. 49-8-6, b. Ded., of Lewis & Nabby F., Ded., do.

7 Joseph, 5: 23: 51, consumption, æ. 50-0-0, b. Ded., of Geo. & Rene.

92 Julia (Sumner), 7: 28: 59, consumption, æ. 35-0-0, b. Ded., of Moses & Catharine.

99 (D. at Walpole) Levina (Ellis), 11: 30: 58, old age, æ. 87-0-0, b. Ded., of Jos. & Marian.

96 Lewis, 10: 5: 82, R. R. accident, æ. 58-8-26, b. Canton, of Joseph & Ruth (Taunt), Canton, do.

51 Lucy (Whiting), 9: 2: 55, typhoid fever, æ. 70-9-19, b. Ded., of Solomon & Luca.

54 Luther T., 4: 6: 71, apoplexy, æ. 49-3-21, b. Canton, of Jos. & Ruth, Canton,do.

102 Maria B. (Bullen), 4: 2: 86, dis. of liver, æ. 70-0-0, b. Medway, of David & Patty (Harding), Medway, do.

6 (D. at Norton) Mark, 1: 16: 85, old age, æ. 64-9-13, b. Rumny N. H., of Joel & Ajubah H., Ded., Rumny N. H.

121 Mary (Wilbur), 9: 12: 61, consumption, æ. 74-6-0, b. ——, of Nathan & Rhoda, Salisbury, do.

84 Mary A. (Snow), 3: 17: 54, inflam. of bowels, æ. 30-0-0, b. Brewster, of Obed & Tempest.

93 Mary E. (Dean), 4: 27: 68, phthisis, æ. 68-1-23, b. Salisbury, of Eben'r & Lois, Ded., ——.

64 Metcalf, 2: 22: 54, chronic dis., æ. 38-0-0, b. Medway.

173 Nabby F. (Fisher), 2: 11: 64, pneumonia, æ. 76-4-12, b. Ded., of Eliph't & Judith, Dedham, Medfield.

44 Osborn, 4: 25: 47, drowned, æ. 27-0-0, b. Ded., of Ezra & Sally.

16 Phebe A. (——), w. of ——, 2: 28: 87, paralysis, æ. 65-8-0, b. Georgetown, of John & Naomi, Georgetown, do.

98 (D. at Walpole), Richard, 6: 10: 53, old age, æ. 84-0-0, b. Ded., of John & Rebekah.

69 Roxa F., w. of John, 12: 25: 44, dropsy, æ. 50-0-0.

83 Ruth S. (Taunt), 9: 4: 82, paralysis, æ. 87-8-4, b. Canton, of John & Hannah, Canton, do.

101 Seth, 10: 6: 53, dis. of heart, æ. 73-0-0, b. Ded., of Seth & Mary.

96 Sybil E. (Lewis), 1: 1: 62, typhoid fever, æ. 53-10-10, b. Ded., of Joseph & Sybil, Ded., do.

MORST.

95 Caroline, 10: 27: 84, dropsy, æ. 34-0-7, b. Germ., of —— & ——, Germ., do.

MOSS.

67 Ellen E., 8: 26: 64, convulsions, æ. 0-0-6, b. Dedham, of John & Ellen, Germany, do.

MOULTON.

28 Mabel R., 3: 18: 80, basilar meningitis, æ. 0-8-13, b. Brookline, of Edw. B. & Carrie E., Woonsocket R. I., Cumberland Me.

MULCARY.

8 Bridget, 2: 8: 59, croup, æ. 0-5-8, b. Ded., of Patrick & Margaret.

MULKERN.

44 Ellen, 2: 13: 70, consumption, æ. 19-4-1, b. Dedham, of Timothy & Mary, Ireland, do.

52 James, 9: 2: 55, consumption, æ. 9-0-0, b. Ire., of Timothy & Mary.

46 Martin, 5: 9: 83, consumption, æ. 62-0-0, b. Ireland, of Martin & Mary, Ireland, do.

74 Mary, 7: 17: 67, consumption, æ. 18-1-7, b. on the ocean, of Timothy & Mary, Ireland, do.

74 Timothy, 9: 13: 84. ossification of heart, æ. 65-0-0, b. Ireland, of Michael & Mary, Ire., do.

MULLEN.

48 Bridget, 9: 7: 74, heart disease, æ. 6-2-28, b. Dedham, of Michael & Ann, Ireland, do.

58 Catharine, 7: 28: 72, lung fever, æ. 2-0-15, b. Dedham, of Michael & Ann, Ireland, do.

3 John, 1: 31: 67, heart disease, æ. 32-0-0, b. Ireland, of John & ——, Ire., do.

9 Margaret (Clements), 3: 8: 62, consumption, æ. 25-0-0, b. Ireland, of James & Elizabeth.

MULLIGAN.

1 Mary, 1: 10: 55, consumption, æ. 70-0-0, b. Ireland.

MULROONEY.

33 William, 2: 10: 64, typhoidis, æ. 39-0-0, b. Ireland, of Thomas & Dora, Ireland, do. [soldier.]

MULVERHILL.

8 Margaret (Shei), 4: 12: 67, dropsy, æ. 68-0-0, b. Ireland, of Dennis & Mary, Ireland, do.

95 Mary V., 4: 4: 83, measles, æ. 13-1-13, b. Ded., of Dennis & Eliza, Ire., do.

MUNIER.

70 Catherine M., 8: 20: 80, hydrocephaloid, æ. 0-1-21, b. Boston, of Joseph & Catherine, Boston, N. S.

MUNROE.

50 ——, 9: —: 50, ——, æ. 9-0-0, b. Ded., of Hiram & ——.

78 William, 9: 15: 75, old age, æ. 85-10-8, b. Northboro, of Abraham & ——, Northboro, ——

MURDOCK.

64 Mary (Cummings), w. of John, 6: 17: 90, hydrothorax, æ. 80-6-10, b. Boston, of Andrew & Susan (Weld), ——, Newton.

24 Sarah (Eustis), 4: 15: 61, consumption, æ. 85-9-28, b. Ded., of William & Mary.

MURDY.

2 Eliz'h Vavian, 2: 23: 72, dropsy, æ. 49-3-22, b. Ire., of John & Eliz'h.

46 Josephine, 5: 27: 87, scrofula and phthisis, æ. 15-3-27, b. Ded., of James & Maria, Eng., Ire.

20 Samuel J., 3: 14: 78, hemorrhage of lungs, æ. 31-11-12, b. Eng., of Samuel & Eliz'h, Eng., Ire.

67 Warren, 9: 13: 86, tubercular meningitis, æ. 7-4-3, b. Ded., of Jas. & Maria, England, Ireland.

MURPHY.

145 Frank, 12: 30: 88, ——, æ. 0-4-16, b. Ded., of John & Margaret (Clifford), Ireland, do.

12 George, 9: 24: 74. emphysema, æ. 46-0-0, b. Ireland, of John & Margaret, Ireland, do.

35 Honora, 5: 13: 57, whooping cough, æ. 2-1-6, b. Ded., of Thos. & Mary.

118 James, 12:23:81, cerebro spinal meningitis, æ. 2-0-15, b. Ded., of John & Margaret, Ire., do.

63 Johanna M., 8:5:79, consumption, æ. 22-5-5, b. Ded., of Timothy & Eliz'h, Ire., do.

17 John, 3:9:64, dysentery, æ. 21-0-0, b. Ire., of John & Mary. [soldier.]

80 John, 8:29:82, dysentery, æ. 40-0-0, b. Ire.

126 Julia, 9:5:64, dysentery, æ. 0-0-14, b. Ded., of John & Sarah, Ire., do.

97 Margaret (Brown), 10:26:81, cancer, æ. 76-6-0, b. Ire., of Edw. & Margaret, Ire., do.

94 Margaret (Clifford), w. of John, 9:27:89, valvular disease of heart, æ. 42-0-0, b. Ire., of Jas. & Mary, Ire., do.

7 Mary, 5:9:90, scarlet fever, æ. 7-4-1, b. Me., of John & Ellen, Ire., do.

72 Olive (Blake), 12:14:53, bilious fever, æ. 24-0-0, b. New Glaston Me., of Jos. & Rebekah.

91 Patrick A., 11:27:72, water on brain, æ. 8-0-4, b. Newburyport, of Thos. & Ann, Ire., do.

5 Wm., 1:25:83, consumption, æ. 45-0-0, b. Ire., of John & ——, Ire., do.

20 Wm. T., 3:6:86, scarlet fever, æ. 3-5-0, b. Ded., of John M. & Mary A., Ded., Lowell.

MURRAY, MURREY.

11 Arthur W., 3:16:58, croup, æ. 0-3-22, b. Ded., of Walter & Jane.

118 Bridget, 11:20:65, dysentery, æ. 1-11-0, b. Ire., of Thos. & Bridget.

48 Margaret (Conlon), w. of Daniel, 4:23:89, chronic disease of liver, æ. 60-11-13, b. Ire., of [Owen] & Ann, Ire., do.

21 Patrick, 4:23:62, whooping cough, æ. 1-1-6, b. Ded., of Daniel & Margaret.

93 Walter, 8:31:65, dysentery, æ. 34-0-0, b. N. S., of Jas. & Margaret.

MUSCHE.

66 Isabella, 7:24:75, dysentery, æ. 0-4-0, b. Ded., of Frederic & Margaret, Prussia, Ire.

74 Lizzie, 8:16:81, cholera infantum, æ. 0-5-0, b. Ded., of Fred'k & Margaret, Germ., Ire.

MUXWORTHY.

24 Henry, 4:17:86, phthisis, æ. 53-0-0, b. Eng., of Geo. & Mary, Eng., do.

20 Mabel J., 2:8:90, phthisis, æ. 15-5-20, b. Ded., of Henry & Mary, Eng., do.

115 Rose E., 11:30:90, consumption, æ. 19-11-17, b. Ded., of Henry & Mary (Dunn), Eng., do.

77 Studley W., 7:29:89, consumption, æ. 28-0-16, b. Eng., of Henry & Mary (Dunn), Eng., do.

32 (D. at Asheville N. C.) Wm. H., 3:9:90, phthisis pulmonalis, æ. 22-0-0, b. Eng., of Henry & Mary (Dunn), Eng., do.

MYERHOOF. (See *Meyerhoff.*)

MYERS. (See *Meyer.*)

MYLOD.

65 Mary C., 12:23:44, spinal dis., æ. 0-6-0, b. Ded., of Wm. & ——.

88 Roxanna (Hammond), 12: 15: 54, consumption, æ. 23-0-0, b. Buckfield Me., of Wm. P. & ——.

90 Wm. A., 12: 19: 59, dis. of heart, æ. 60-0-0, b. Franklin, of Wm. & ——.

NASH.

63 Charity (Pond), 4: 7: 62, paralysis, æ. 73-0 0, b. Ded., of Ebenezer & Mary, ——, Newton.

NAVIN. (*See also Nevin.*)

48 John F., 6: 1: 82, epilepsy, æ. 23-0-0, b. Boston.

NEAS.

15 Barbara C., 7: 25: 72, epilepsy, æ. 21-11-7, b. Boston, of Rochat & Augusta, Germ., do.

1 Bonaparte, 1: 1: 77, old age, æ. 74-7-0, b. Germ., of —— & ——, Germ., do.

88 Eliz'h (Gramer), 8: 8: 83, valvular dis. of heart, æ. 77-8-18, b. Germ., of —— & ——, Germ., do.

4 Joseph, 9: 11: 68, old age, æ. 80-0-0, b. Germ., of —— & ——, Germ., do.

83 Lucy E., 6: 18: 88, meningitis, æ. 0-11-12, b. Ded., of Frank & Mary, Germ., Boston.

3 Mary A., 4: 6: 68, inanition, æ. 0-7-0, b. Rox., of Thomas & Lizzie M. F., Germ., do.

NEEDHAM.

72 Joseph, 10: 4: 68, dropsy, æ. 57-0-0, b. Ire., of Jos. & Mary, Ire., do.

NELSON.

12 Eva, 2: 7: 76, consumption, æ. 3-0-0, b. Boston, of Terance & Martha, Baltimore, do.

NEVIN. (*See also Navin.*)

45 David W., 12: 19: 56, scarlet fever, æ. 3-0-0, b. Ded., of John & Margaret.

59 John, 12: 11: 54, fits, æ. 0-0-4, b. Ded., of John & Margaret.

105 John, 12: 22: 63, typhoid fever, æ. 28-0-0, b. Ire., of Michael & Mary, Ire., do. [soldier.]

NEWBURY.

95 Susana, 9: 9: 87, diarrhœa, æ. 0-2-7, b. Taunton, of Daniel & Jennie (Kelley), Ire., Taunton.

NEWELL.

17 Bertha H., 1: 7: 66, gastric fever, æ. 2-10-17, b. Ded., of Francis & Sophia.

58 Dorcas, w. of Calvin, 12: 6: 59, old age, æ. 83-0-0, b. Acton.

80 Eliza, 8: 28: 74, old age, æ. 83-9-0, b. Belchertown, of Nathan & Annie, Belchertown, Ded.

40 Ida M., 5: 5: 73, lung fever, æ. 0-6-8, b. Ded., of Francis E. & Sophia E., Dover, W. Rox.

35 Montgomery, 7: 1: 53, consumption, æ. 65-6-0, b. Need., of Josiah & ——.

113 Sophia E. (Hall), w. of Francis E., 11: 23: 90, Bright's dis., æ. 48-0-22, b. W. Rox., of Geo. & Sarah C. (Webber), Barrington N. H., Boscawen N. H.

NEWSOME.

66 Ada L., 8: 13: 80, infantile debility, æ. 0-0-28, b. Ded., of Thos. & Hannah, Eng., do.

93 Ann (Lockwood), 10: 22: 84, hepatic abscess, æ. 74-7-28, b. Eng., of Charles & Betty, Eng., do.

63 Ellen, 7: 10: 82, stillborn, b. Ded., of Thos. & Hannah, Eng., do.

55 Fred. C., 7: 23: 79, canker, æ. 0-0-17, b. Ded., of Thos. & Hannah, Eng., do.

61 Geo. L., 7: 23: 76, inflam. of brain, æ. 0-5-0, b. Ded., of Thomas & Hannah, Eng., do.

64 Hilda, 7: 10: 82, stillborn, b. Ded., of Thos. & Hannah, Eng., do.

24 Jas., 2: 12: 90, congestion of lungs, æ. 79-8-13, b. Eng., of William & Nancy (Bennett), Eng., do.

NEWTON.

17 Maria R., 4: 17: 54, consumption, æ. 20-6-19, b. Rox., of Leonard & Louisa.

NICHOLS.

66 Eliz'h G. (Stow), 12: 25: 58, nervous fever, æ. 22-1-2, b. Reading, of John & Caroline.

51 Frances L., 6: 18: 85, premature birth, æ. 0-0-1, b. Ded., of John H. & Caroline E., Barrington N. H., Boston.

40 John, 7: 1: 49, consumption, æ. 40-0-0, b. Germ.

12 Martha H., 1: 23: 77, dropsy, æ. 36-4-23, b. Barrington N. H., of Samuel & Mary B., S. Reading, do.

NICHOLSON.

42 Elizabeth R., 6: 1: 78, accident, æ. 78-2-22, b. Boston, of Samuel & Elizabeth, Md., ——.

4 Maria, 1: 10: 59, paralysis of brain, æ. 65-0-0, b. Boston, of —— & Mary.

NICKERSON.

112 Atkins, 7: 8: 64, dropsy, æ. 75-5-0, b. Chatham, of Moses & Rebecca, Chatham, do.

34 Atkins, 4: 7: 80, pleuro pneumonia, æ. 66-8-27, b. Chatham, of Atkins & Zipporah, Chatham, do.

72 Edith A., 8: 24: 60, ——, æ. 0-1-0, b. Ded., of Atkins & Emily, Chatham, do.

73 Edward A., 9: 19: 77, consumption, æ. 37-0-0, b. Ded., of Myrick & Eunice, Chatham, Dorch.

77 Emily (Eldridge), 9: 3: 80, heart dis., æ. 59-0-8, b. Chatham, of Atkins & Esta, Chatham, do.

80 Freddie, 11: 23: 73, ——, æ. 0-0-1, b. Ded., of Alphonso L. & Catharine, Ded., Germ.

75 Mary A., 9: 11: 78, albuminuria, æ. 2-2-18, b. Ded., of Alphonso L. & Catherine, Ded., Germ.

63 Myrick, 8: 6: 76, chronic cystitis, æ. 67-4-0, b. Chatham, of Leonard & Ann C., Cape Cod, do.

2 Priscilla, 2: 5: 71, ——, æ. 31-1-20, b. Dennis, of Levi & Myra, Dennis, Yarmouth.

44 Rebecca (Jordan), 8: 20: 74, paralysis, æ. 74-7-14, b. Needham, of Jesse & Hannah, Needham, do.

NIGHTINGALE.

92 ——, 11: 28: 60, stillborn, b. Ded., d. of Geo. E. & Lucy A., Dorch., Needham.

NIHAN.
128 Hannah, 11 : 26 : 88, tumor, æ. 55-0-0, b. Ire., of Jas. & Ellen, Ire., do.

NILES.
68 Eliza, 4: 22 : 62, old age, æ. 88-10-27, b. Braintree, of Jeremiah & Abigail, Braintree, Weymouth.

NOLAN.
54 Francis, 9: 9: 60, aptha, æ. 0-1-14, b. Ded., of Patrick & Hannah, Ire., do.
13 John F., 2: 12: 76, membraneous croup, æ. 4-2-26, b. Hyde Park, of John F. & Eliz'h, Ire., Woonsocket.
67 Mary, 8: 3: 68, cholera infantum, æ. 0-8-0, b. Ded., of Patrick & Hannah, Ire., do.
64 Sarah M., 4: 12: 62, lung fever. æ. 0-9-3, b. Ded., of Malachi & Sarah J., Ire., do.

NOOMAN.
27 Rosy (Donahoe), 3: 23: 76, phthisis, æ. 41-0-0, b. Ire., of —— & Mary, Ire.,do.

NOONAN.
2 Bridget P. (Brown), w. of Michael, 1: 1: 89, puerperal peritonitis, æ. 28-0-0, b. Ire., of Morris & Margaret (Phelan), Ire., do.
106 James, 10: 3: 65, dysentery, æ. 74-0-0, b. Ire., of John & Bridget.
7 Mary (Cary), 5: 6: 72, bronchitis, æ. 58-0-0, b. Ire., of John & Eliz'h, Ire., do.
6 Mary V., 1: 6: 77, convulsions, æ. 0-7-24, b. Ded., of David & Margaret, Ire., Vt.

NORRIS.
136 (D. at Boston), Edw. E., 3: 14: 87. Bussey Bridge accident, æ. 26-7-11, b. Ded., of Andrew J. & Harriet E., Dorchester N. H., Charlton.
76 Frank E., 9: 25: 60, canker, æ. 0-0-22, b. Ded., of Samuel H. & Isabella, Dorchester N. H., Boston.
76 Fred. T., 11: 21: 71, accident, æ. 9 4-7, b. Ded., of Samuel M. & Isabella, Dorchester N. H., Boston.
52 Martha (Everett), 10: 28: 69, lung fever, æ. 70-6-6, b. Chesterfield N. H., of Richard & ——, Chesterfield N. H., ——.
23 Mary E., 3: 6: 81, rachitis. æ. 15-0-5, b. Ded., of Samuel & Isabella, Dorch., [N. H.], Boston.
135 Zebulon, 10: 6: 64, dropsy, æ. 69-2-28, b. Dorchester N. H., of Nathaniel & Lucy, Pembroke N. H., Hebron N. H.

NOYES.
5 Catharine (Dean), 1: 13: 59, old age, æ. 82-0-0, b. Ded., of John & Mary.
23 Eliz'h (Morrill), 4: 24: 53, lung fever, æ. 64-8-25, b. Natick, of Eliakim & Ruth.
95 Martha (Colburn), 9: 10: 83, paralysis, æ. 71-8-18, b. Ded., of Danforth & Clarissa Coolidge, Ded., Sherborn.
50 Nancy G. (Cummings), 9: 16: 74, old age, æ. 71-8-24, b. Ded., of John & Polly.
116 Nath'l, 11: 12: 89, old age, æ. 79-8-2, b. Ded., of Samuel & Catharine.
45 Otis, 6: 23: 78, suicide, æ. 75-10-5, b. Dedham, of Nathaniel & Catherine, Dedham, do.

NUNN.

83 Martha M. (Driver), 9: 18: 79, consumption, æ. 30-11-18, b. Eng., of George & Elizabeth, Eng., do.

54 Olive, 7: 13: 79, convulsions, æ. 0-5-18, b. Boston, of Thomas & Martha M., England, do.

OAKS.

92 Matthew, 12: 17: 62, delirium tremens, æ. 50-0-0, b. Eng.

OBER.

108 Albert A., 1: 20: 63, consumption, æ. 0-4-20, b. Dedham, of Albert G. & Rebecca, Sedgwick Me., Machias Me.

O'BRIEN, O'BRIAN.

12 ——, 5: 5: 50, infantile dis., æ. 0-0-7, b. Ded.

68 ——, 3: 1: 69, ——, æ. 0-0-0, b. Ded., of Timothy & Mary, Ire., do.

58 Ellen, 6: 27: 82, brain disease, æ. 0-8-6, b. Sherburn, of —— & Margaret, ——, Scot.

58 Hannah, 9: 4: 61, typhoid fever, æ. 18-0-0, b. Ire.

51 James H., 7: 19: 78, cholera infantum, æ. 0-4-0, b. Ded., of Thomas H. & Mary V., Ded., do.

82 Lawrence, 9: 21: 75, consumption, æ. 35-0-0, b. Ireland, of James & Margaret, Ire., do.

54 Margaret (Lynch), 6: 3: 76, dropsy, æ. 45-0-0, b. Ireland, of James & Ann, Ireland, do.

67 Mary E., 10: 18: 66, gravel, æ. 13-9-9, b. Boston, of Patrick & Mary.

27 Morris, 3: 30: 80, cystitis, æ. 80-0-0, b. Ire., of Geo. & Eliz'h, Ire., do.

43 Thomas, 12: 10: 51, consumption, æ. 35 0-0, b. Ire., of Delly & Ellen.

O'CALLAGHAN. (See also Callahan.)

35 Timothy L., 3: 12: 90, apoplexy, æ. 53-10 41, b. Webster, of John & Mary (Sanger), Ire., Mass.

O'CONNELL.

121 Catharine, 12: 14: 90, heart disease, æ. 62-0-0, b. Ire., of John & Bridget (Delay), Ire., do.

101 Patrick, 10: 14: 90, pneumonia, æ. 52-7-0, b. Roxbury, of John & Bridget (Delay), Ire., do.

O'CONNOR.

54 Margaret A., 6: 18: 87, convulsions, æ. 2-0-15, b. Roxbury, of Charles J. & Mary E., Eng., Scot.

O'DONNELL.

84 Alexander, 10: 4: 78, valvular disease of heart, æ. 50-0-0, b. Ire., of John & Mary, Ire., do.

17 Daniel, 5: 31: 56, lung fever, æ. 0-1-11, b. Ded., of Alex'r & Joanna.

128 Edw. J., 12: 12: 87, diphtheritic croup, æ. 2-4-27, b. Ded., of Jas. F. & Sarah, Norwich Ct., Springfield.

20 John, 3: 24: 55, fit, æ. 0-3-10, b. Ded., of Alex'r & Jane.

118 Mary, 8: 12: 64, scarlet fever, æ. 0-10-0, b. Ded., of Alexander & Joanna, Ireland, do.

OEHLER.

101 Moritz, 9: 18: 87, gunshot wound, æ. 32-8-17, b. Germ., of Gottfried & Ernestine, Germ., do.

O'HARA.

16 Dennis, 2: 17: 80, worms, æ. 1-4-0, b. Ded., of Terence & Rosy, Ire., do.

3 Rose (Snow), w. of Terence, 1: 3: 90, consumption, æ. 52-0-0, b. Ire., of Dennis & Ann (McGee), Ire., do.

O'HARE.

45 John H., 8: 7: 60, cholera infantum, æ. 0-8-5, b. Ded., of Patrick & Mary, Ire., do.

41 Mary (——), w. of ——, 4: 3: 72, childbirth, æ. 41-0-0, b. Ire., of Alexander & Mary, Ire., do.

16 Patrick, 1: 17: 73, dis. of heart, æ. 58-0-0, b. Ire., of Jas. & Ann, Ire., do.

O'KEEFE.

99 Timothy, 12: 4: 78, consumption, æ. 45-0-0, b. Ire., of John & Margaret, Ire., do.

O'LAUGHLIN, O'LOUGHLIN.

18 James, 8: 25: 67, consumption, æ. 42-0-0, b. Ire.

4 Mary (McNally), w. of Jas., 1: 3: 90, heart dis., æ. 67-0-0, b. Ire., of Terence & Nancy (Dunn), Ire., do.

OLDHAM.

133 Richard, 12: 26: 61, found dead, æ. 0-5-2, b. Ded., of Richard & Mary, Ire.,do.

O'LEARY. (*See also Leary.*)

93 ——, 9: 20: 89, premature birth, b. Ded., d. of Peter J. & Eliz'h M. (McKey), Rox., Ire.

113 Annie, 11: 26: 83, convulsions, æ. 4-7-4, b. Ded., of Peter J. & Eliz'h, Boston, Ireland.

85 Dennis, 9: 8: 82, croupal diphtheria, æ. 1-10-19, b. Ded., of Dennis & Mary, Ire., do.

84 Edward, 9: 8: 82, croupal diphtheria, æ. 4-7-17, b. Ded., of Dennis & Mary, Ire., do.

5 Ellen (Branan), 4: 28: 74, childbirth, æ. 23-7-0, b. Ire., of Wm. & Ann.

46 Rose (Gaffney), 2: 28: 71, diphtheria, æ. 22-5-23, b. Ded., of Patrick & Catharine, Ire., do.

OLFENE.

68 ——, 6: 23: 89, premature birth, æ. 0-0-1, b. Ded., s. of Chas. M. & Mary E., Lewiston Me., N. S.

OLMSTEAD.

34 Amanda, 4: 23: 85, stillborn, b. Ded., of Moses & Amanda, Va., do.

O'NEIL, O'NEAL.

63 Ann (Burns), w. of John, 6: 13: 90, pneumonia, æ. 68-1-2, b. Ire., of —— & ——, Ire., do.

6 Catherine, 4: 8: 71, scarlatina, æ. 6-2-10, b. Ded., of Martin & Mary A., Ire., Canton.

70 Eliz'h N., 8: 10: 79, teething, æ. 0-8-0, b. Fitchburg, of John H. & Eliza, N. Y., Ire.

78 Jas. P., 9: 11: 80, teething, æ. 0-6-0, b. Ded., of Jas. & Ellen, Ire., do.

19 John, 3: 24: 55, found dead, æ. 35-0-0, b. Ire.

82 Margaret, 12: 6: 73, ——, æ. 0-2-0, b. Ded., of John & Sarah, Ire., N. S.

66 Martin, 11: 12: 64, infantile disease, æ. 0-0-2, b. Ded., of Martin & Mary A. (Brannen).

108 Martin, 10: 11: 65, croup, æ. 2-9-0, b. Ded., of Matthew & Margaret.

36 Matthew, 3: 13: 88, scarlet fever, æ. 8-6-10, b. Ded., of Martin & Mary A., Ire., do.

137 Michael J., 12: 19: 88, typhoid fever, æ. 32-3-25, b. Ded., of Matthew & Margaret, Ire., do.

76 Neil, 8: 28: 85, empyema, æ. 38-0-0, b. Ire.

35 Thos. H., 6: 11: 74, ——, æ. 0-2-20, b. Ded., of John & Eliz'h, N. Y., Ire.

105 Wm., 11: 19: 79, membraneous croup, æ. 5-2-6, b. Ded., of Martin & Mary A., Ire., do.

ONION.

90 (D. at Milton), Catharine (Fisher), 8: 31: 53, old age, æ. 84-0-0, b. Sharon, of Asa & ——.

58 Elihu, 6: 15: 48, old age, æ. 88-0-0.

97 Hezekiah, 12: 4: 63, epileptic fit, æ. 83-7-19, b. Dedham, of Joseph & Anna, Dedham, do.

24 Joseph, 2: 15: 66, old age, æ. 79-7-12, b. Ded., of Jos. & Hannah.

34 Philinda, w. of Joseph, 3: 14: 45, paralysis, æ. 50-0-0.

ORCUTT.

63 Eliza, 3: 6: 45, ——, æ. 17-0-0.

O'REILLY.

23 Mary E., 3: 6: 83, diphtheria, æ. 4-3-0, b. Dedham, of Patrick & Margaret, Ire., do.

58 Willie, 8: 4: 77, marasmus, æ. 0-9-0, b. Ded., of John & Dora, Ire., do.

OSGOOD.

8 Martha (Fox), 3: 5: 62, typhoid fever, æ. 77-1-6, b. Dracut, of Charles & Martha.

O'SULLIVAN (*See also Sullivan.*)

56 J. Frank, 6: 26: 85, marasmus, æ. 0-9-0, b. Ded., of P. O. & Mary A., Ire., Boston.

21 Margaret, 3: 21: 78, dropsy, æ. 0-0-4, b. Ded., of Patrick & Mary A., Ire., Boston.

OTIS.

69 Jenks H., 8: 27: 64, kick of horse, æ. 34-8-0, b. Dorchester, of George A. & Lucinda S., Scituate, Boston.

OTTO.

57 Emma (Ahlborn), 7: 21: 82, childbirth, æ. 26-0-0, b. Germany, of John & Christina, Germ., do.

59 Frank, 7: 30: 72, cholera infantum, æ. 0-0-8, b. Dedham, of Frank & Emma, Germ., do.

OVENS.
21 Mime, 3: 11: 85, gastritis, æ. 0-1-14, b. Dedham, of William & Sarah J., England, do.
89 William, 12: 6: 86, inanition, æ. 0-3-9, b. Dedham, of William & Sarah J., England, do.
63 William J., 7: 14: 85, consumption, æ. 15-10-21, b. Eng., of Wm. & Jemima Theophilus, Eng., do.
OWEN, OWENS.
154 Elizabeth (Colburn), 3: 16: 64, lung fever, æ. 84-0-0, b. Ded.,of Lewis & Mary O., Ded., do.
47 John, 4: 13: 65, malignant sore throat, æ. 18-0-0, b. Leominster. [soldier]
3 Nathaniel, 1: 6: 58, old age, æ. 81-2-12, b. Ashford Ct., of Ebenezer & Deborah.
149 Phebe (Champney), 8: 29: 63, old age, æ. 71-0-0, b. ——, of Jonathan & ——.
50 William N., 10: 4: 46, ——, æ. 74-0-0, b. Eng.

PACKARD.
71 Sarah (Dyer), 12: 9: 53, dropsy, æ. 53-3-27, b. Randolph, of Samuel & Sarah.
PAECH.
53 Louisa (Voit), w. of Theodore, 5: 11: 90, heart dis., æ. 42-11-11, b. Germ., of Wm. & Fannie (Heidler), Germ., do.
PAGE.
107 Addy W., 9: 11: 62, congestion of brain, æ. 0-7 14, b. Ded., of Samuel & Emily, Hampden Me., Ded.
94 Eliz'h (Farrington), 5: 12: 68, dis. of heart, æ. 66-8-17, b. Ded., of Eben'r & Eliz'h F., Ded., ——.
131 Herbert W., 4: 10: 65, ——, æ. 0-0-18, b. Ded., of Samuel & Emily B.
6 Mary C. (Drake), 1: 13: 87, cancer, æ. 66-10-16, b. Canton, of Bethuel & Harriot (Crane), Easton, Canton.
PAINE.
81 Jerusha W. (Wild), 10: 16: 78, dropsy, æ. 79-0-22, b. Braintree, of Jonathan & Deborah, Braintree, do.
PARK, PARKS.
135 (D. at Fortress Monroe) Henry M., 6: 6: 64, wounded in battle, æ. 21-11-26, b. Walpole, of H. G. & Eliz'h. [soldier.]
100 Montgomery N., 9: 5: 66, phthisis, æ. 21-6-29, b. Westfield, of H. G. & Eliz'h.
PARKER.
31 ——, 8: 25: 45, ——, æ. 5-0-0, b. Ded.
29 ——, 9: 25: 47, dysentery, æ. 2-0-0.
104 ——, 12: 18: 78, stillborn, b. Ded., d. of Wm. & Jane K., Boston, do.
53 Abijah, 4: 10: 88, fatty degeneration of heart, æ. 81-0-21, b. Ded., of Abijah & Lydia (Hosley), Shirley, Pepperell.
47 Amanda L., 10: 10: 54, consumption, æ. 12-6-13, b. Ded., of Asher & Louisa.
112 Chas. E., 12: 3: 81, alcoholism, æ. 32-0-0.
70 Clemie E. (Aldridge), 8: 15: 70, dysentery, æ. 25-10-15, b. Blackstone, of Rowland & Mary C., Blackstone, Charleston S. C.

53 Hannah, w. of Wm., 8: 1: 47, consumption, æ. 35-0-0.

14 Josephine, 10: —: 44, ——, æ. 1-0-0.

79 Louisa (Morse), 7: 28: 65, dysentery, æ. 62-7-0, b. N. S., of John & Eliza.

112 Mary A. R. C. (Davis), w. of Richard G., 8: 21: 48, consumption, æ. 48-0-0, b. Boston.

84 Rhoda (Hoyle), 5: 3: 59, consumption, æ. 55-0-0, b. Eng., of Josiah & Debo'h.

5 Sally (Kilburn), 1: 3: 64, congestion of lungs, æ. 79-0-0, b. Pepperell.

16 Sally, 1: 28: 78, congestion of lungs, æ. 79-4-0, b. Pepperell, of Abijah & Sally, Pepperell, do.

45 Theresa, 4: 3: 90, lack of vitality, æ. 0-0-7, b. Boston, of Geo. & Theresa.

90 Woods, 1: 6: 55, apoplectic fit, æ. 52-0-0, b. Ded., of Abijah & ——.

PARSONS.
105 Herbert B., 9: 28: 65, dysentery, æ. 5-7-24, b. Ded., of Fisher & Harriet.

8 Nath'l S., 9: 20: 44, typhus fever, æ. 26-0-0, b. Ded., of Leonard & ——.

PARTRIDGE.
65 (D. at Boston) Chas. O., 6: 29: 65, cancer, æ. 20-8-6, b. Woolwich, of Horatio & Rebecca.

2 Margaret, 6: 21: 48, old age, æ. 81-0-0.

PATCH.
2 David, 1: 24: 53, accident, æ. 59-0-0, b. Hamilton, of Aaron & Mercy.

PATTEN.
115 Mary, 6: 19: 49, fits, æ. 1-5-0, of John & ——.

PATTERSON.
4 Edw. E., 1: 25: 60, brain fever, æ. 3-8-0, b. Ded., of C. W. & Maranda J.

12 Enoch, 3: 17: 58, old age, æ. 85-5-17, b. Northboro, of David & Beulah.

143 Joseph B., 11: 26: 63, ——, æ. 3-0-17, b. Ded., of Chauncey & Mirand J., Montpelier Vt., Hopkinton.

24 Mary (Adams), 5: 19: 58, lung fever, æ. 71-11-0, b. Newton, of Roger & Hepzibah.

61 Mary B. (Fairbanks), 11: 1: 53, consumption, æ. 40-1-11, b. Ded., of Wm. & Mille.

120 Miranda J. (Colburn), 4: 7: 67, consumption, æ. 31-4-7, b. Hopkinton, of David G. & Calista, Holliston, do.

97 Wm. H., 10: 29: 58, congestion of brain, æ. 0-10-0, b. Ded., of C. W. & Maranda J.

PAUL.
120 Abigail (Pratt), 12: 30: 81, softening of brain, æ. 81-8-26, b. Mansfield, of Josiah & Jane, Mansfield, do.

11 Albert A., 2: 12: 78, consumption, æ. 1-0-15, b. Ded., of Edwin F. & Huena A., Dorch., Scot.

60 Chas. H., 6: 10: 70, inflam. of bowels, æ. 10-10-4, b. Milton, of James & Elizabeth E., Eng., do.

80 Eliz'h, 8: 7: 67, consumption, æ. 0-3-11, b. Ded., of Jas. & Eliz'h, Eng., do.

66 Hiram, 9: 8: 73, carbuncle, æ. 69-6-14, b. Dorch., of Wm. & Anna D., Ded., Attleboro.

9 Isaac, 4: 4: 52, lung fever, æ. 77-7-14, b. Ded., of Eben'r & Abigail.

81 James, 8: 8: 67, consumption, æ. 0-3-12, b. Ded., of Jas. & Eliz'h, Eng., do.

35 Jas. W. D., 2: 11: 64, scarlet fever, æ. 10-1-23, b. Medford, of Jas. & Esther E., Eng., do.

20 Lydia (Tucker), 5: 5: 54, lung fever, æ. 75-9-13, b. Milton, of Jeremiah & Rebecca.

72 Nancy M. (Smith), 7: 10: 67, consumption, æ. 29-6-16, b. Rehoboth, of —— & Lydia.

80 Susan B. (Sampson), w. of Hiram, 6: 9: 88, paralysis, æ. 82-0-22, b. Middleboro, of Samuel & Mary, Middleboro, do.

35 Susan F., 8: 24: 59, dysentery, æ. 1-5-0, b. Ded., of Edwin & Nancy.

81 Susan F., 10: 12: 62, cholera infantum, æ. 1-4-18, b. Ded., of Eben'r & Susan, Ded., Lunenburg.

94 Wm., 9: 3: 87, paralysis of heart, æ. 85-11-1, b. Dorch., of Wm. & Annie (Damon), Ded., Attleboro.

42 Wm. F., 12: 20: 56, consumption, æ. 27-0-26, b. Dorch., of Wm. & Abigail.

PAULSON.

31 ——, 3: 6: 90, stillborn, b. Ded., s. of Peter & Mary (Anderson), Denmark, do.

PEABODY.

59 Annie E. (Robinson), 9: 3: 61, consumption, æ. 33-0-13, b. N. B., of Thomas & Mary, N. B., Cowhegan Me.

PECK.

82 Adelaide (Payton), w. of Edw., 8: 21: 89, alcoholism, æ. 29-0-0, b. N. Y. City, of Wm. & Catherine (Lysaght), Ire., do.

55 Edwin E. F., 7: 27: 86, spinal caries, æ. 19-0-4, b. New Haven, of Thos. H. & Annie L., Prov. R. I., N. S.

20 Minnie L., 3: 2: 83, pneumonia, æ. 0-11-0, b. Ded., of Thos. H. & Annie L., Prov. R. I., N. S.

PECKHAM.

78 Herbert W., 9: 17: 84, cholera infantum, æ. 0-10-1, b. Sherborn, of Chas. W. & Annie, Ct., Eng.

PEDRICK.

81 ——, 12: 16: 71, ——, æ. 0-0-1, b. Ded., s. of W. Edward & Addie L., Charlestown, Boston.

PELTON.

55 Florentine W., 6: 25: 85, chronic peritonitis, æ. 57-2-2, b. Somers Ct., of Asa & Lois, Ct., do.

95 Mary F., 9: 27: 90, phthisis, æ. 22-9-18, b. Boston, of Florentine W. & Mary R. (Whitney), Somers Ct., Waltham.

PENDERGAST, PENDERGRAST.

20 Eliz'h A., 5: 4: 70, pneumonia, æ. 2-3-19, b. Ded., of Jas. & Mary, Ire., do.

78 Ellen M., 8: 6: 69, phthisis, æ. 12-3-19, b. Ded., of Jas. & Mary, Ire., do.

27 John, 7: 11: 70, imperfect development, æ. 0-0-3, b. Ded., of James & Mary, Ire., do.

73 Nelly, 8: 26: 60, bowel compl't, æ. 1-3-0, b. Abington, of Isaac H. & Nancy, Randolph, Groton.

PENNIMAN.

12 Harriet A., 3: 23: 53, croup, æ. 8-3-0, b. Ded., of Edw. L. & Sarah A.

76 Sarah, 12: 26: 48, old age, æ. 76-0-0.

PEPPER.

3 Hugh, 1: 8: 89, Bright's dis., æ. 40-0-0, b. Ire., of Hugh & Eliz'h Roundtry, Ire., do.

PERKINS.

188 (D. at Walpole) Isaac, 4: 23: 64, palsy, æ. 66-9-0, b. Ashford Ct., of Wm. & Mary, Ashford Ct., Lysburn Ct.

28 John T., 8: 12: 51, consumption, æ. 28-7-22, b. Edgecomb Me., of Ebenezer & Eliz.

62 Lizzie L., 8: 5: 76, cholera infantum, æ. 0-2-14, b. Natick, of John & Susie, Boston, Dedham.

119 Mary (Lee), 4: 9: 63, influenza, æ. 91-11-25, b. Lisbon Ct., of Andrew & Eunice, Lynn, Wallingford Ct.

PERRY.

53 ——, —: —: 62, bleeding, æ. 0-0-10, b. Ded., — of Geo. G. & Mary M.

102 ——, 12: 8: 80, stillborn, b. Ded., d. of Louis & Minnie, N. B., do.

49 Ellen E. (Tracy), 6: 25: 84, typhoid fever, æ. 36-0-0, b. Ire., of Jas. & Mary, Ireland, do.

80 Geo. E., 10: 18: 58, heart comp., æ. 0-5-0, b. Ded., of Geo. G. & Mary M.

80 (D. at Walpole) Huldah M. (Achorn), 10: 11: 54, consumption, æ. 24-10-9, b. Waldoboro Me., of Henry & Harnel.

106 Martha B. (Thomas), 12: 24: 80, paralysis, æ. 76-2-16, b. Mansfield, of Calvin & Martha B. King, Middleboro, Norton.

23 Mary (Quincy), 2: 20: 89, cardiac asthma, æ. 72-0-18, b. Boston, of John W. & Abigail, Boston, do.

105 Nath'l, 10: 20: 53, consumption, æ. 69-2-15, b. Quincy, of Louman & —— Boutell.

PETERS, PETER.

85 Armond A., 5: 25: 61, croup, æ. 1-0-11. b. Tewksbury, of Armond A. & Phillipena, Germany, do.

64 Dhobold, 10: 3: 66, drowned, æ. 17-1-20, b. Northampton, of Dhobold & Catharine.

PETERSON.

46 ——, 5: 18: 76, stillborn, b. Ded., s. of Wm. H Jr., & Nellie, Canton, Boston.

47 ——, 5: 19: 76, premature birth, æ. 0-0-2. b. Ded., s. of Wm. H. Jr., & Nellie, Canton, Boston.

143 Chas. F., 10: 24: 64, chronic diarrhoea, æ. ——. [soldier.]

15 (D. at Boston), Johanna E. (Bjoikman), w. of Heinrich M., 1: 25: 88, pelvic abscess, æ. 50-0-0, b. Sweden, of Nicholas & Marie, Sweden, do.

19 John, 9: 19: 72, typhoid fever, æ. 23-11-0, b. Denmark.

58 Maria E., 6: 26: 87, scarlatina, æ. 10-10-8, b. Gloucester, of Martin H. & Johanna E., Norway, Sweden.

PETTEE.

90 Charlotte E. (Ellis), 12: 11: 80, old age, æ. 87-0-0, b. Walpole, of Oliver & Margaret.

92 Helen L., 10: 27: 53, canker, æ. 13-0-0, b. Dedham, of Jas. & ——.

9 Jas., 1: 26: 68, old age, æ. 81-6-0, b. Ded., of Samuel & [Catharine], Ded.,——.

45 James E., 4: 15: 50, consumption, æ. 21-0-0, b. Ded., of James & ——.

65 Lucy A., 3: 14: 59, consumption, æ. 32-0-0, b. Ded., of Jas. & ——.

43 Maria, 5: 26: 85, scirrhus of mesenteric glands, æ. 63-10-21, b. Ded., of Jas. & Lucy (Ellis), Dedham, Walpole.

3 Mary E., 6: 6: 44, fever, æ. 8-0-0, b. Dedham, of James & Charlotte.

10 Silas, 12: 23: 46, ——, æ. 56-0-0, b. Dedham.

PETTENGILL.

67 Augustus T., 5: 12: 88, heart & liver dis., æ. 67-1-18, b. Salem, of Thomas & Elizabeth, Newburyport, do.

55 Frances H., 4: 8: 71, hemorrhage of lungs, æ. 20-5-29, b. Boston, of Jonᵃ. M. & Emeline H., Methuen, Boston.

36 Fred'k A., 8: 6: 58, croup, æ. 3-6-0, b. Ded., of Augustus T. & Sarah D.

4 Laura, 6: 22: 48, consumption, æ. 26-0-0.

78 Mabel, 10: 15: 70, ——, æ. 0-1-0, b. Hyde Park, of E. M. & Lizzie H.

23 Sarah D. (Snell), 3: 24: 80, cancer, æ. 59-8-18, b. Milton, of Geo. & Mary, Bridgewater, W. Rox.

PHELPS.

99 Dorcas (Chamberlain), 11: 2: 81, old age, æ. 83-11-0, b. Bedford, of Phineas & Dorcas, Chelmsford, do.

28 Timothy, 3: 24: 83, old age, æ. 89-10-13, b. Tewksbury, of Jos. & Isabelle, Andover, Tewksbury.

PHILLIPS.

18 Francis, 6: 5: 52, fit, æ. 31-8-16, b. Ded., of Nathan & Mehitable.

186 Geo., 4: 14: 64, consumption, æ. 56-0-0, b. Germ., of —— & ——, Germ., do.

92 Mary (Hulen), 12: 8: 72, inflam. of bowels, æ. 56-9-21, b. France, of John & Mary, France, do.

72 Nathan, 8: 21: 79, old age, æ. 86-1-18, b. E. Bridgewater, of Mark & Celia, E. Bridgewater, ——.

102 Roland, 8: 1: 62, scrofula, æ. 9-10-12, b. Ded., of Geo. & Mary, Germ., do.

PHINNEY. *(See also Finney.)*

94 Nath'l M., 7: 22: 61, consumption, æ. 61-5-0, b. Machias Me., of Nath'l & Mary, Machias Me., do.

PHIPPS.

99 (D. at Walpole) Benj. F., 7: 17: 66, sunstroke, æ. 24-6-9, b. Ded., of Loammi & Lurana.

32 Chas. W., 4: 9: 69, scarlet fever, æ. 4-3-0, b. Ded., of Albert L. & Mary E.

43 Laura M., 3: 6: 63, scarlet fever, æ. 6-5-0, b. Ded., of Lamia W. & Lorrana, Ded., Bridgewater.

60 Lewis W., 8: 21: 66, inflam. of bowels, æ. 0-0-18, b. Ded., of Albert L. & Mary E.

18 Loammi W., 4: 20: 70, consumption, æ. 62-2-4, b. Ded., of Wm. & Lucretia. Holliston, ——.

58 Lorana (Pincen), 7: 23: 76, phthisis, æ. 64-4-0, b. Bridgewater, of —— & Lorana, Bridgewater, do.

PIERCE.

83 Chas. R., 8: 19: 67, sore mouth, æ. 0-2-2, b. Ded., of Abel M. & Mary R., Rehoboth, Prov.

3 Chester F., 1: 4: 57, scarlatina, æ. 2-6-5, b. Ded., of Wm. F. & Sarah A.

100 Eben'r S., 10: 9: 83, paralysis, æ. 74-6-16, b. Natick, of Eben'r & Nancy R.

58 Frances, 5: 27: 70, consumption, æ. 22-11-0, b. Ded., of Eben'r S. & Nancy E., Rox., Fall River.

60 Harriet E., 10: 20: 57, inflam. of bowels, æ. 13-4-0, b. Ded., of Eben'r S. & Nancy E.

60 Mary A. (Chipman), w. of Oliver B., 4: 28: 88, cerebral hemorrhage, æ. 69-8-17, b. Wellfleet, of Eben'r & Martha (Higgins), Wellfleet, Castine Me.

36 Nancy, 4: 27: 69, paralysis, æ. 81-1-0, b. Natick.

PIKE.

26 Alfred A., 9: 3: 50, cholera infantum, æ. 0-11-22, b. Boston, of Jacob & Harriet.

21 Chas. E., 4: 4: 79, scarlet fever, æ. 16-2-12, b. Boston, of Geo. H. & M. B., Saugus, Boston.

PILSTER.

24 (D. at Walpole) Joanna L. (Schlusemeyer), 5: 3: 71, consumption, æ. 35-2-0, b. Germ., of Enos & Duror, Germ., do.

PIPER.

11 George, 8: 11: 44, cholera morbus, æ. 69-0-0, b. Eng.

66 Harry H., 7: 23: 71, cholera infantum, æ. 0-6-26, b. Boston, of Harry S. & Eliza J., Farmington Me., Boston.

PIPPING.

136 Caroline D., 12: 18: 88, meningitis, æ. 0-0-13, b. Ded., of Henry & Hannah M. (Hanson), Ded., Boston.

121 Chas. F., 11: 25: 87, dilatation of heart, æ. 60-8-5, b. Germ., of Chas. F. & Eleanor, Germ., do.

PITCHER.

77 Sarah J. (Logan), 8: 30: 75, valvular dis. of heart, æ. 44-0 11, b. Eng., of —— & ——, England, do.

PITTS.

28 Lavinia (Bell), 4: 30: 79, Bright's dis., æ. 62-3-8, b. Newbury N. H., of —— & Susan.

PLACE.

87 Hannah, 8: 15: 52, fever, æ. 8-6-0, b. Dedham, of Aurelius & Hannah.

83 (D. at Walpole) John S., 1: 1: 58, ——, æ. 0-0-11, b. Walpole, of Geo. H. & Louisa.

PLIMPTON.

51 Nancy, 8: 12: 46, consumption, æ. 40-0-0, b. Dedham.

POLLARD.
26 Martha A. (Bouton), w. of Thos., 2: 19: 88, fibroid tumor, æ. 44-7-0, b.
    Goshen N. Y., of Shubel & Hannah (Dickenson), N. Y. State, do.
33 Susan (Weatherbee), w. of Abel, 3: 3: 88, accidental fall, æ. 100-1-17, b.
    Boxboro.

POLLEY.
199 John, 9: 9: 64, dis. of heart, æ. 82-1-4, b. Framingham, of Nath'l & Anna,
    Medford, Framingham.

POLLOCK.
16 George J., 8: 13: 67, diarrhoea, æ. 0-11-17, b. Ded., of John S. & Catharine,
    N. S., Ireland.
26 Mary J., 10: 16: 67, effusion of brain, æ. 3-6-0.

POMMEROKE.
55 Herman, 8: 4: 66, cholera morbus, æ. 0-4-0, b. Ded., of Chas. F. & Crisennis.

POND.
6 Chas. D., 1: 24: 58, inflam. of heart, æ. 0-3-8, b. Ded ,of Nath'l D. & Flora M.
5 Chas. T., 2: 6: 46, congestion of brain, æ. 29-0-0, b. Walpole, of Thurston &
    Susanna.
100 Edwin W., 9: 13: 71, scrofula, æ. 26-2-27, b. Dedham, of Nathaniel W.
    & Lucy A., Franklin, Wrentham.
44 Fanny (Cheney), 7: 23: 57, dropsy, æ. 60-0-0, b. Dover, of John & Hannah.
19 Fanny, 10: 10: 68, dropsy, æ. 34-0-0, b. Ded., of Samuel & Fanny, Ded., Dover.
128 Fanny F., 6: 12: 63, croup, æ. 3-0-0, b. Dedham, of James M. & Elsie E.,
    Wrentham, Waldoboro Me.
78 Fanny G. (Dean), w. of J. M., 4: 6: 55, fever, æ. 29-0-0, b. Ded., of
    Dexter & Martha.
87 Flora M. (Tower), 10: 27: 60, consumption, æ. 40-2-27, b. Peacham Vt., of
    Daniel & Mary, Peacham Vt., ——.
12 Francis T., 2: 10: 81, acute Bright's dis., æ. 74-5-3, b. Norfolk, of Samuel
    & Catherine (Smith), Wrentham, Sterling.
15 Frank E., 6: 16: 68, congestion of brain, æ. 2-7-22, b. Dedham, of James F.
    & Abby, Dedham, do.
81 (D. at Pomfret Ct.) Julia A., 11: 20: 68, consumption, æ. 47-0-26, b. Dedham,
    of Eliphalet & Ann, Dedham, Hartford Ct.
127 Leila C., 6: 4: 63, croup, æ. 5-3-28, b. Dedham, of James M. & Elsie E.,
    Wrentham, Waldoboro Me.
52 Mary E., 5: 8: 68, consumption, æ. 14-9-4, b. Dedham, of Nath'l D. & Flora
    M., Dedham, Dover Me.
110 Melissa D. (Dinslow), 10: 12: 66, ——, æ. 40-9-0, b. Boonville N. Y., of
    Jeremiah & Charlotte D.
81 Nath'l D., 4: 20: 61, consumption, æ. 35-7-9, b. Dedham, of Eliphalet &
    Ann, Dedham, Hartford Ct.
76 Samuel, 3: 3: 74, dropsy, æ. 76-0-9, b. Dedham, of Samuel & ——, ——, Ded.

POPE.

48 Curtis H., 3: 27: 67, congestion of lungs, æ. 3-10-27, b. Rox., of Holley K. & Josephine L., Boston, Roxbury.

25 Wm., 8: 28: 56, consumption, æ. 0-5-15, b. Dedham, of Wm. & Hannah.

PORTER.

91 Helen T., 9: 5: 87, marasmus, æ. 0-9-21, b. Boston, of Wm. & Catherine, ——, Ire.

POTTS.

96 John, 12: 2: 63, dysentery, æ. 54-0-0, b. Ire., of Jas. & Sarah, Ire., do.

POWER, POWERS.

102 Francis J., 10: 20: 90, consumption, æ. 46-0-0, b. N. F., of Thos. & Mary A. (O'Brien), N. F., Ire.

38 Hilda G., 3: 20: 88, dis. of brain, æ. 0-7-4, b. Ded., of Patrick J. & Mary E., N. F., do.

79 Margaret E., 9: 12: 80, eclampsia infantum, æ. 1-11-0, b. Ded., of James & Bridget, Ire., do.

39 Wm., 5: 9: 85, suicide, æ. 35-0-0.

POYEN.

40 Louis F., 3: 26: 66, consumption, æ. 28-7-3, b. Sumner Me., of Louis F. & Lucy A.

PRATT.

128 Albert E., 9: 6: 64, chronic diarrhoea, æ. ——. [soldier.]

87 Effie T., 2: 11: 68, croup, æ. 9-8-19, b. Lincoln Me., of Jos. W. & Joanna P., St. George Me., Ded.

55 Eliza P., 5: 2: 63, consumption, æ. 44-9-4, b. Waterf'd Me., of Jos. & Lucy S., Harvard, Brighton.

— Geo. H., 2: 8: 49, congestion of brain, æ. 3-0-0.

65 John H., 8: 23: 52, dysentery, æ. 1-0-0, b. Ded., of Simeon & Charlotte.

84 Juliana (Page), w. of Jos. W., 2: 24: 58, dis. of heart, æ. 32-0-0, b. Handor Me., of Chas. & Sarah.

61 Lucy S. (Coolidge), 10: 26: 74, consumption of bowels, æ. 89-6-0, b. Brighton, of Henry & Mary, Brighton, do.

66 Martha, 9: 4: 52, dysentery, æ. 3-0-0, b. Ded., of Simeon & Charlotte.

89 Naomi G. (Leonard), 12: 26: 69, smallpox, æ. 75-8-0, b. Taunton, of Joseph & ——.

109 Walter H., 10: 8: 62, croup, æ. 1-9-17, b. Ded., of Simeon & Charlotte, W. Rox., Ded.

PRAY.

46 Catherine (Kerrigan), 5: 21: 80, consumption, æ. 31-5-5, b. Ded., of Jas. & Mary, Ire., do.

70 Henry A., 8: 12: 60, typhoid fever, æ. 5-10-9, b. Thompson Ct., of Wm. H. & Angeline F., Foster R. I., Hamilton Ct.

PRESBRY.

53 Adeline M., 11: 16: 46, ——, æ. 2-0-0, b. Ded., of Alpha & ——.

52 Orlando T., 11: 11: 46, ——, æ. 8-0-0, b. Ded., of Alpha & ——.

PRESLEY.
25 Sarah, 3: 25: 82, ossification of valves of heart, æ. 80-0-0, b. N. S.

PRICE.
81 Abraham, 8: 6: 63, typhoid fever, æ. 23-0-0. [soldier.]
72 Rebecca G., 5: 20: 69, phthisis, æ. 15-9-5, b. Waltham, of Thos. G. & Mary, Eng., do.
76 Thos. J., 9: 21: 54, consumption, æ. 15-0-0, b. Eng., of Thos. G. & Mary A.

PRIEST.
38 Emma S., 9: 11: 54, dysentery, æ. 5-3-2, b. Rox., of Wm. E. & Harriet S.
69 Fanny, w. of Joseph, 8: 31: 48, dropsy, æ. 35-0-0.
53 Joseph, 8: 25: 50, consumption, æ. 38-0-0, b. Ded., of —— & Harriet.

PRINCE.
26 Amelia A. (Langdon), w. of Wm. G., 2: 13: 90, heart and cerebral arteries, æ. 80-0-0, b. Charlestown, of John W. & Rebecca (Cordis), Boston, Charlestown.
9 Geo. H., 1: 29: 57, croup, æ. 3-4-29, b. Ded., of Jas. H. & Lucy A.
107 Henry, 12: 26: 63, cholera morbus, æ. 4-10-0, b. Ded., of Jas. H. & Lucy, Boston, Dover.
46 Lucy M. (Newell), 3: 26: 63, congestion of brain, æ. 37-1-25, b. Dover, of Jesse & Permelia.
62 (D. at Milford) Nathan, 5: 31: 63, whooping cough, æ. 1-0-21, b. Ded., of Jas. H. & Lucy M.

PROCTOR.
105 Mary A., 11: 20: 81, heart dis., æ. 31-6-0, b. Eng., of Samuel & Mary, Eng., do.

PRUDEN.
111 Israel R., 12: 14: 72, old age, æ. 78-8-8, b. Castine Me., of William & Sarah, Eng., do.

PULLEN.
35 Arthur S., 4: 27: 61, scarlet fever, æ. 6-3-20, b. E. Winthrop Me., of Sumner B. & Elvira W., Winthrop Me., do.
116 Etta S., 12: 27: 66, ulceration of intestines, æ. 27-10-27, b. Winthrop Me., of S. B. & E. W.
60 Helen E., 6: 7: 56, typhoid fever, æ. 20-0-0, b. Livermore Me., of S. B. & E. W.

PURBECK.
37 William, 8: 4: 46, cancer, æ. 76-0-0, b. Salem.

PUTNAM.
56 Howard, 4: 17: 88, premature birth, æ. 0-0-1, b. Ded., of Waldo D. & Minnie S. (Howard), Northbridge, Frostburg Md.

QUIGLEY.
43 Emma, 9: 24: 54, bowel comp., æ. 1-4-0, b. Ded., of Thomas & Catharine.
62 James, 7: 19: 85, drowning, æ. 18-0-0, b. N. B., of David & Matilda.

QUINCY.
27 Arthur B., 3: 15: 49, scarlatina, æ. 2-0-0, b. Ded., of Edmund & [Lucilla P.]
36 Edmund, 5: 17: 77, apoplexy, æ. 69-3-16, b. Boston, of Josiah & E. S. M., Boston, N. Y.

81 Lucilla P. (Parker), 11: 6: 60. apoplexy, æ. 50-0-20, b. Boston, of Daniel P. & Mary, Southboro, do.

24 Morton, 3: 10: 49, scarlatina, æ. 3-0-0, b. Ded., of Edmund & [Lucilla P.]

QUINLAN.

64 Johanna, 8: 16: 78, meningitis, æ. 3-8-21, b. Ded., of Wm. & Johanna,Ire.,do.

69 Johanna C. (Reardon), w. of Wm., 6:24: 80, peritonitis, æ. 42-0-0, b. Ire., of Daniel & Ellen (Crimmins), Ireland, do.

QUINN.

77 ——, 10: 28: 68, ——, æ. 0-0-1, b. Ded., s. of Felix & Isabella, Ire., do.

45 Lucy E., 5: 8: 83, diphtheria, æ. 7-8-0, b. Ded., of Felix & Isabella, Ire., do.

27 Mary A., 1: 9: 68, whooping cough, æ. 0-2-7, b. Dedham, of Felix & Eliz'h.

96 Terrance, 3: 25: 86, pneumonia, æ. 20-7-24, b. Ded., of Felix & Isabella, Ireland, do.

QUIRK.

49 Catherine (Skelley), 7: 25: 77, dysentery, æ. 66-0-0, b. Ire., of —— & Catherine, Ire., do.

RABS.

19 Chas., 3: 5: 85, phthisis, æ. 32-0-0, b. Germany, of Fred'k & Rosine,Germ.,do.

RADFORD.

28 Jeremiah S., 7: 22: 54, consumption, æ. 62-0-0, b. Ipswich, of Benj. & Mary.

84 Lydia (Field), 11: 11: 70, paralysis, æ. 72-1-0, b. Quincy.

RAFFERTY.

83 (D. at Cohasset) Catharine (Tierney), w. of John, 8: 22: 80, heart dis., æ. 74-0-0, b. Ire., of Thomas & Mary, Ire., do.

64 John, 8: 8: 76, consumption, æ. 69-0-0, b. Ire., of John & Ellen, Ire., do.

82 John M., 8: 11: 67, teething, æ. 0-11-22, b. Dedham, of Michael & Catherine, Dedham, do.

43 Margaret, 6: 23: 69, consumption, æ. 0-9-16, b. Hyde Park, of Michael & Catharine, Ireland, do.

52 Richard J., 4: 10: 88, consumption, æ. 33-1-7, b. Dedham, of John & Catherine, Ireland, do.

RAMSDALE.

76 Eunice (Roby), 5: 7: 54, consumption, æ. 21-4-0, b. Danbury N. H., of Joseph & Mehitable.

RAND.

16 Eliz. A., 5: 22: 52, dis. of heart, æ. 10-9-23, b. Boston, of Edw. S. & Eliz. A.

RANKIN.

45 Eliz'h, 3: 27: 68, congestion of brain, æ. 4-0-11, b. Ire., of Robert & Ann.

RASGER.

39 Charles, 8: 3: 53, inflam. of bowels, æ. 3-5-18, b. Ded., of Peter & Catharine.

RATCHFORD.

18 Ellen, 7: 21: 63, dis. of brain, æ. 3-7-5, b. Ded., of Thos. & Mary, Ire., do.

30 John D., 1: 17: 65, consumption, æ. 1-3-14, b. Ded., of Thos. & Mary.

120 Thos., 10: 28: 88, mitral insufficiency, æ. 57-10-0, b. Ire., of Patrick & Mary, Ire., do.

RAUSCH.
111 Conrad, 10: 22: 66, accidental, æ. 34-4-27, b. Germ., of Geo. & Margaret.

RAYMOND.
87 Addie F., 9: 12: 82, consumption, æ. 22-9-0, b. Prov. R. I., of Roland & Adeline N., N. Y., Ded.
3 Elmina, 1: 7: 78, paralysis, æ. 71-2-0, b. Westford, of John & Phebe, Westford, do.
38 Emeline (Savil), 2: 11: 68, consumption, æ. 62-6-9, b. Quincy, of John & Esther, Quincy, do.
48 Frederick, 4: 22: 48, scrofula, æ. 10-0-0.
79 Jepthah, 10: 9: 72, heart dis., æ. 75-0-0, b. Westford, of John & Phebe, Westford, do.

RAYNOR.
60 Edna G., 8: 3: 79, infantile, æ. 0-9-4, b. Boston, of Horace R. & Mabel, Boston, do.
64 Effie G., 8: 6: 79, infantile, æ. 0-9-7, b. Boston, of Horace R. & Mabel, Boston, do.

READER.
52 Geo. J., 4: 20: 63, lung fever, æ. 36-0-0, b. Granby Ct. [soldier.]

REARDON, READON.
22 James, 3: 31: 61, consumption, æ. 20-0-0, b. Ire., of Wm. & Mary.
145 Mary, 9: 19: 65, dysentery, æ. 1-0-10, b. Ded., of John & Mary.

REDDING.
139 Mary Mullen, w. of Morris, 12: 21: 88, heart disease, æ. 76-0-0, b. Ire.
54 Maurice, 5: 20: 68, rheumatism, æ. 53-0-0, b. Ire., of Jas. & ——, Ire., do.
58 Rebecca (Eldridge), 8: 15: 66, cancerous humour, æ. 45-1-6, b. Chatham, of John H. & Faloma.

REDHOUGH.
16 Eliz'h A., 2: 14: 77, inflam. of bowels, æ. 9-6-4, b. Eng., of Thos. & Ellen, Eng., do.
74 James W., 8: 25: 79, typhoid fever, æ. 18-0-14, b. Eng., of Thos. & Ellen, Eng., do.

REED, READ.
88 Carrie M., 9: 12: 82, marasmus, æ. 0-3-10, b. Boston, of —— & Jennie, ——, Bangor Me.
85 Daniel, 9: 22: 75, chronic enteritis, æ. 1-3-0, b. Ded., of Jas. & Katie, Scot., Boston.
72 James, 12: 26: 74, pneumonia, æ. 45-0-0, b. Scot., of John & Mary, Scot., do.
59 James A., 7: 16: 76, purpura, æ. 3-10-15, b. Ded., of Jas. & Katie, Scot., Boston.
16 Katie, 3: 5: 79, old age, æ. 102-0-0, b. Va.

REENBOLD.
32 Rehme, 10: 27: 56, dysentery, æ. 1-5-0, b. Ded., of Fred & Charlotte.

REEVES.
46 Adeline L., 6: 25: 86, entro colitis, æ. 0-7-6, b. Ded., of David W. and Harriet (Baker), Eng., do.

87 Lucy, 10: 12: 84, inanition, æ. 0-4-7, b. Ded., of David W. & Harriett B., Eng., do.

REGAN.

1 Patrick, 1: 2: 64, ——, æ. 71-0-0, b. Ire.

REIDEL, READEL, RIDDLE.

9 Anna (Reineck), 2: 24: 60, childbirth, æ. 32-0-0, b. Germ.. of Philip & Eva K.

143 Joseph L., 12: 20: 88, consumption, æ. 27-3-10, b. Boston, of Joseph & Catherine (Echer), Germ., do.

174 Lebet, 2: 12: 64, whooping cough, æ. 8-2-24, b. Ded., of Peter & Anna L., Germany, do.

REILLY. (*See Riley.*)

REIM.

116 Otto, 8: 0: 64, fracture of skull, æ. 22-0-0, b. Germ. [soldier]

REISER.

44 Benedict, 4: 1: 90, exhaustion, æ. 67-0-12, b. Germany, of —— & Julia, Germany, do.

REMINGTON.

26 Lydia M. (White), 9: 9: 56, consumption, æ. 31-5-6, b. Northbridge, of Washington & Lydia M.

REVELL.

66 Lucretia, 8: 23: 72, cholera infantum, æ. 0-1-14, b. Ded., of Chas. & Eliza, England, do.

RHOADES, RHODES.

7 Aaron, 12: 25:45, ——, æ. 65-0-0, b. Dedham.

6 Abigail C., 4: 5: 51, consumption, æ. 37-0-0, b. Ded., of Aaron & Betsy.

102 Chas. E., 8: 3: 66, phthisis, æ. 28-0-0, b. Ded., of Moses & Nancy.

65 Ellen H., 11: 17: 56, typhoid fever, æ. 16-0-0, b. Burlington Vt., of William B. & Harriet D.

86 Freddie A., 8: 29: 87, pneumonia, æ. 0-8-5, b. Brockton, of B. F. & Mary R., ——, Boston.

5 Geo. H., 1: 27: 60, typhoid fever, æ. 17-7-0, b. Dorch., of Aaron W. & Ruth.

79 Hannah E. (Ellis), 9: 1. 54, consumption, æ. 69-8-12, b. Ded., of Oliver & Mary.

118 Harriet E. (Thompson), 2: 18: 67, dis. of uterus, æ. 43-8 15, b. Brooks Me., of Robert & Theodosia, N. H., Prospect Me.

34 Hattie E., 9: 30: 70, cholera infantum, æ. 1-0-22, b. Ded., of A. E. & E. A., Walpole, N. Y.

72 Henry D., 2: 24: 45, ——, æ. 0-0-15, b. Ded.

75 Maggie F., 8: 5: 87, meningitis, æ. 0 7-12, b. Brockton, of B. F. & Mary, ——, Boston.

70 Martha M., 12: 21: 52, scarlatina, æ. 4-0-0, b. Boston, of John & ——.

77 Nancy, 3: 17: 57, sciatic rheumatism, æ. 54-0 0, b. Walpole.

77 & 124 Olive D. (Lewis), w. of N. A., 1: 20: 49, consumption, æ. 34-0 0, of —— & Sybil.

201 Ruth (Small), 9: 7: 64, consumption, æ. 46 0-28, b. New Sharon Me.. of Nathaniel & Hannah P.

141 Willard F., 11: 3: 63, shot, æ. 25-5-23, b. Dedham, of Lewis S. & Harriet F., Sharon, Upton. [soldier.]

80 Willie E., 10: 27: 60, asthma, æ. 0-1-0, b. Dedham, of Aaron W. & Ruth, Roxbury, New Sharon Me.

RICHARDS.

54 ——, 9: —: 48, ——, æ. 0-0-0, d. of Augustus & ——.

47 Abel, 8: 13: 46, rheumatism, æ. 67-0-0, b. Dedham, of Abel & [Mary.]

81 Abiathar, 9: 23: 84, old age, æ. 88-7-10, b. Newport N. H., of Sylvanus & Lucy (Richardson), Dedham, Newton.

70 Abigail, 3: 12: 56, old age, æ. 88-0-0.

85 Betsy (Pitcher), 5: 15: 59, fever, æ. 73-0-0, b. Sharon, of Wm. & Jemima.

32 (D. at Taunton) Catharine (Newell), 2: 18: 72, softening of brain, æ. 68-0-0, b. Dedham, of Reuben & Catharine, Needham, do.

2 Catharine, 1: 4: 87, old age, æ. 89-6-17, b. Dedham, of Abiathar & Eliz'h, Dedham, do.

19 Charles, [no date, Rec. 6: 24: 46], ——, æ. 52-0-0, b. ——, of Abel & ——.

79 Clarissa (Gay), 8: 13: 74, old age, æ. 82-9-0, b. Dedham, of Ebenezer & [Sarah,] Dedham, ——.

54 Curtis A., 6: 25: 85, tuberculosis pulmonalis, æ. 3-2-0, b. Boston, of George B. & Bessie, Pa., Va.

33 Danforth, 3: 21: 47, consumption, æ. 35-0-0, b. Ded., of Sam'l & ——.

91 Ebenezer, 10: 2: 79, old age, æ. 80-7-3, b. Ded., of Abiathar & Elizabeth, Dedham, do.

67 Edward F., 7: 15: 82, Bright's disease, æ. 45-8-2, b. Ded., of Edward M. & Rebecca G., Boston, Ded.

45 Edward M., 4: 3: 65, paralysis, æ. 69-8-3, b. Boston, of Samuel & Mary.

18 Eliza (Lyon), 3: 17: 79, old age, æ. 81-11-0, b. W. Rox., of Benj. & Elizabeth, W. Rox., Eng.

16 Eliza C. (Cobb), 2: 23: 85, cancer, æ. 43-4-7, b. Barnstable, of Asa & Mercy G., Chatham, Boston.

47 Elizabeth, 4: 18: 48, old age, æ. 88-0-0.

8 Frank, 8: 26: 46, throat distemper, æ. 1-2-0, of Abiathar & Julia.

35 Henry W., 5: 16: 77, suicide, æ. 51-2-0, b. W. Roxbury, of Lemuel & Eliza, Dover, W. Rox.

163 Ira, 8: 1: 64, disease of kidney, æ. 80-0-0, b. Ded., of Abiathar & Sally S., Dedham, do.

33 Jeremiah F., 9: 7: 52, fit, æ. 53-3-18, b. Ded., of Reuben & Sarah.

37 Joel, 10: 11: 47, tumor, æ. 58-0-0, b. Ded., of Jesse & ——.

62 (D. at Chicago, Ill.), John H., 10: 22: 46, inflammation of brain, æ. 42-0-0, b. Ded., of Samuel & Mary.

79 Julia (Colburn), w. of Abiathar, 8: 5: 89, tuberculosis, æ. 83-3-28, b. Ded., of Isaac & Elizabeth (Dexter), Ded., Marlboro.

91 Lemuel, 4: 15: 64, lung fever, æ. 69-5-17, b. Dover, of Joseph & Choley, Dedham, do.

72 Maria (Colburn), 8: 25: 80, uterine tumor, æ. 57-8-0, b. Ded., of Isaacus & [Louisa] (Fisher), Ded., Wendell.

54 Martha E., w. of Lewis, 3: 9: 52, consumption, æ. 45-0-0.

11 Mary, [no date, Rec. 6 : 24 : 46], ——, æ. 93-0-0, b. Ded.

67 Mary F. (Gragg), 8 : 14 : 80, shock from parturition, æ. 41-1-15, b. Milton, of Moses & Rebecca N., Groton, Newton.

23 Mason, 2 : 14 : 66, lung fever, æ. 76-8-17, b. Ded., of Samuel & Olive.

56 Moses, 3 : 30 : 52, consumption, æ. 71-0-0, b. Ded., of Abel & [Mary.]

71 Polly, 9 : 24 : 58, cancer, æ. 73-0-0, b. Ded.

19 Polly (Battelle), 2 : 27 : 61, old age, æ. 86-6-22, b. Dover, of Ebenezer & Hannah.

100 Polly, 6 : 19 : 64, general debility, æ. 72-0-0, b. Ded., of Abel & Mary W.

65 Reuel, 6 : 9 : 63, diphtheria, æ. 23-2-21, b. Ded., of Eb: & Catharine, Ded., do.

78 Roxana L., 9 : 18 : 76, typhoid fever, æ. 61-9-12, b. Ded., of Mason & Eliza W., Ded., Prov. R. I.

4 Samuel, 8 : 28 : 44, old age, æ. 87-0-0.

97 Samuel, 6 : 18 : 66, old age, æ. 89-5-6, b. Sharon, of Wm. & Ann.

52 Sarah, w. of Reuben, 4 : 24 : 45, dropsy, æ. 83-0-0, b. Needham.

4 Sarah, 2 : 6 : 48, lung fever, æ. 84-0-0.

108 Sarah, 10 : 7 : 49, old age, æ. 94-0-0, b. Rox.

79 Sarah E., 9 : 17 : 84, dysentery, æ. 45-4-28, b. Ded., of Edw. M. & Rebecca G., Boston, Ded.

12 Susan (Bird), w. of Joel, 8 : 30 : 46, affection of heart, æ. 41-0-0, b. Stoughton, of Asa & ——.

115 Sybil (Packard), 12 : 26 : 66, old age, æ. 68-5-26, b. Bridgewater, of Jos. & ——.

53 Wm. F., 7 : 19 : 73, consumption, æ. 20-9-21, b. Boston, of Fred'k & Sarah L., Ded., Webster.

RICHARDSON.

117 ——, 3 : 20 : 63, stillborn, b. Ded., of Joseph & Sophia, Denmark Me., ——.

89 Chas. B., 10 : 7 : 63, drowned, æ. 2-2-12, b. Ded., of Thos. B. & Mary J., Dixfield Me., Castine Me.

104 Demaria, 10 : 28 : 70, dropsy, æ. 58-0-0, b. Me., of Hezekiah & Dorcas, Me., do.

25 James, 6 : 7 : 58, old age, æ. 86-8-0, b. Medfield, of James & Hannah.

93 Joseph, 9 : 2 : 69, Bright's dis., æ. 41-3-9, b. Medway, of Horace & Catharine, Medway, Ded.

73 Moses, 8 : 28 : 84, cerebro spinal sclerosis, æ. 61-10-28, b. Medfield, of Simon & Abigail, Medway, Medfield.

91 Samuel, 1 : 24 : 73, cancer, æ. 66-5-0, b. Portland Me., of John & Lydia (Sibly), Wrentham, Portland Me.

118 Sophia (Obin), 3 : 28 : 63, internal inflammation, æ. 38-0-0, b. Ded., of Henry & Sophia.

14 Warren E., 1 : 28 : 75, canker, æ. 0-0-13, b. Ded., of Warren A. & Eliza F., Milford, Boston.

RIDDLE. (*See Reidel.*)

RILEY, REILLY.

61 Ann (McNnab), 7 : 5 : 82, consumption, æ. 43-0-0, b. Ire., of Edw. & Catharine, Ire., do.

32 Annie (Sullivan), w. of John F., 3 : 21 : 89, cancer, æ. 36-0-19, b. Nashua N. H., of David & Julia (Doyle), Ire., do.

22 Edw. J., 2:11:88, consumption, æ. 16–11–16, b. Eagle Wis., of Patrick & Ann, Ire., do.

58 Ella M., 7:21:84, meningitis, æ. 18-1-1, b. Ded., of Patrick & Ann, Ire., do.

143 Ellen, 9:13:65, dysentery, æ. 2–11–13, b. Ded., of Jas. & Ellen Kaally.

57 Ellen, 7:29:78, abscess in lung, æ. 42–0–0, b. Ire., of Patrick & Ellen, Ire., do.

6 Ellen M., 3:1:63, whooping cough, æ. 0–4–0, b. Ded., of Patrick & Bridget.

54 John, 4:25:63, delirium tremens, æ. 50-0-0, b. Ire.

42 Katy E., 6:3:84, consumption, æ. 16–8–20, b. Ded., of Patrick & Ann, Ire.,do.

76 Margaret, 8:19:82, hydrocephalus, æ. 1-0-0, b. Boston, of Thos. & Julia, Ire., Lakeville.

86 Mary, 10:15:78, consumption, æ. 60–0–0, b. Ire.

48 Mary A., 4:20:68, consumption, æ. 17-9-11, b. Ded., of Michael F. & Mary, Ire., do.

25 Michael, 11:11:63, convulsions, æ. 0–0–6, b. Ded., of Jas. & Catherine.

4 Michael F., 4:11:66, gravel, æ. 42–0–0, b. Ire., of Thomas & Mary.

71 Thos., 12:23:74, killed by cars, æ. 45–0–0, b. Ire., of Patrick & Ellen, Ire.,do.

84 Wm., 10:18:62, fracture of skull, æ. 24–0–0, b. Ire., of Thos. & Mary, Ire., do.

64 William F., 10:30:61, dropsy on heart, æ. 13–3–21, b. Ded., of Michael F. & Mary.

RITTERHOUSE.

107 Emma, 9:26:66, dysentery, æ. 0–10–26, b. Ded., of Jacob & Sibbel.

RITZ.

85 Mary (Dorst), 10:4:78, consumption, æ. 67-5-0, b. Germ., of H. & Catherine, Germ., do.

ROACH, ROCHE.

50 ——, 6:27:84, stillborn, b. Ded., d. of Jas. & Bridget, Ire., do.

29 Hannah M., 5:8:86, diphtheria, æ. 3–11–1, b. Ded., of James & Bridget, Ire., do.

52 Margaret (Cummings), 7:20:78, paralysis, æ. 75-0-0, b. Ire., of —— & ——, Ire., ——.

101 Mary (O'Bryne), 5:11:64, erysipelas, æ. 53–11–0, b. Ire.

4 Mary E. G., 1:3:88, tubercular meningitis, æ. 4–1–3, b. Ded., of Edward & Maria, Ire., do.

33 Morris, 5:14:86, old age, æ. 80-0-0, b. Ire., of Patrick & Ellen, Ire., do.

ROBBINS.

53 Edw. H., 6:8:80, enlargement of heart, æ. 59–5–0, b. Ded., of Joseph & Venus (Thacher), N. J., Dorch.

30 Eliz'h F. (Rhoads), 4:21:77, valvular dis. of heart, æ. 49–6–17, b. Walpole, of Moses & Mandy.

97 Emily A., 7:14:68, consumption, æ. 21–3–3, b. Boston, of John M. & Tamon R., Stratton Vt., Whitingham Vt.

25 Fanny (Cole), 3:5:69, heart dis., æ. 69–9–8, b. Boston, of Seth & Fanny, Philipston, W. Cambridge.

34 John, 4:9:84, cystitis, æ. 67–0–0, b. Ded., of Jos. & Venus, N. J., Dorch.

38 Joseph, 10:2:52, palsy, æ. 82–9–2, b. Princeton N. J.

70 Lydia, 5:25:88, heart dis., æ. 72–4–16, b. Ded., of Jos. & Venus, N. J., Dorch.

14 Sarah E., 3: 25: 54, consumption, æ. 16-3-20, b. Ded., of —— & Lydia.
74 Seth, 8: 28: 70, consumption, æ. 60-0-0, b. Ded., of Joseph & Venus, N. J., Dorch.

ROBERTS.
17 Abraham, 2: 5: 78, suicide, æ. 62-6-4, b. Walpole, of Abraham & Lydia H., Walpole, do.
95 Angeline (Soule), w. of A., 5: 15: 55, consumption, æ. 35-0-0, b. Ded., of Ephraim & Sally.
2 Geo. E., 1: 7: 81, diphtheria, æ. 4-1-15, b. Ded., of Ellis M. & Mary, Wales.do.
95 Sarah M. (Fisher), 3: 22: 86, heart dis., æ. 71-0-0, b. Ded., of Oliver & ——.

ROBERSON.
76 Silas, 7: 16: 63, lung fever, æ. 22-0-0. [soldier.]
53 Wm., 4: 23: 63, lung fever, æ. 21-0-0. [soldier.]

ROBERTSON.
66 David, 10: 3: 47, mortification, æ. 75-0-0, b. Scot.
151 Edwin H., 11: 14: 65, consumption, æ. 27-6-11, b. Broomfield Me., of James & Betsey.

ROBINSON.
87 Betsey (Atkingson), 3: 12: 58, consumption, æ. 62-0-0, b. Buckstone Me., of John & Olive.
55 Deborah C. (Upton), 7: 23: 84, apoplexy, æ. 72-3-6, b. Athol, of James & Deborah, ——, Athol.
26 Eldridge G., 7: 11: 54, erysipelas, æ. 49-0-17, b. Concord, of Wm. & Martha.
46 Esther, 11: 11: 52, fit, æ. 15-7-26, b. Ded., of Samuel D. & Deborah C.
150 Geo. E., 10: 2: 63, cholera infantum, æ. 0-5-0, b. Ded., of Chas. W. & Ann.
77 Herbert A., 10: 6: 60, cholera infantum, æ. 0-9-10, b. Dedham, of Albert W. & Elizabeth, Providence R. I., Dedham.
51 James, 5: 3: 47, ——, æ. 34-0-0, b. England.
106 Martha C. (Jones), w. of Shadrick, 9: 3: 88, old age, æ. 80-0-0, b. Md., of —— & ——, Southern State, do.
30 Shadrach, 5: 1: 79, old age, æ. 80-4-6, b. Va., of Edward & ——.

ROBLEY.
57 George, 9: 26: 57, dis. of spine, æ. 5-5-19, b. Dedham, of Robert C. & Laura P.

ROBY.
67 Isabel, 9: 19: 52, drowned, æ. 3-0-0, b. Dedham, of Joseph & Elizabeth.
114 M. A. E. (Weatherbee), 12: 26: 66, dis. of stomach, æ. 36-2-5, b. Dedham, of Joel & Betsy.
90 (D. at Medway), Mehitable (Pray), 7: 13: 58, stoppage, æ. 64-0-0, b. N. H., of William & ——.

ROCK.
14 Thos., 1: 16: 73, fever, æ. 0-5-0, b. Canada, of Natty & Lizzie, Canada, do.

RODMAN.
1 Edw. M., 1: 28: 58, burnt, æ. 7-1-3, b. Ded., of Alfred & Anna L.

ROGERS, RODGERS.
114 Eliz'h, 12: 29: 82, diphtheritic croup, æ. 3-4-23, b. Ded., of Terence & Mary, Ireland, Scotland.

83 Margaret J., 9: 28: 84, cholera infantum, æ. 0-2-0, b. Dedham, of Terence & Mary, Ireland, Scotland.

71 Mary E. J. (McCaffrey), 8: 21: 84, pneumonia, æ. 34-4-21, b. Scotland, of Bernard J. & Catherine, Ireland, do.

105 Susan (Snow), w. of Warren, 10: 2: 87, paralysis, æ. 70-5-19, b. Orleans, of Thatcher & Mercy, Orleans, do.

90 Wm. R., 9: 9: 80, consumption, æ. 28-8-24, b. Georgetown Me., of Francis & Susan (Rowe), Georgetown Me., do.

ROLLAND.

75 Harry II., 8: 28: 79, accident, æ. 11-7-5, b. Chelsea, of John E. & Mary L., Boston, do.

RONAN.

36 Thomas, 5: 14: 57, jaundice, æ. 3-8-0, b. Lawrence, of James & Bridget.

ROSE.

33 Charles B., 5: 8: 87, diphtheria, æ. 5-0-6, b. Dedham, of Benj. & Cora H., Staten Island N. Y., Worcester.

31 Frank, 4: 9: 69, lung fever, æ. 29-3-26, b. Eng., of Benj. & Mary A., Eng., do.

84 John E., 9: 25: 80, consumption, æ. 22-9-18, b. Ded., of Samuel & Agnes (Hooker), England, Ireland.

48 Samuel, 6: 10: 66, inflam. of lungs, æ. 31-4-4, b. Eng., of Benj. & Mary II.

ROSS.

84 Andrew J., 8: 19: 87, apoplexy, æ. 51-0-0, b. Prussia. of Bernard & Catherine, Prussia, do.

38 Bernard, 5: 2: 76, consumption, æ. 57-0-0, b. Germany, of Bernard & Catherine, Germany, do.

56 Bernard, 6: 19: 80, old age, æ. 82-6-0, b. Prussia.

16 Chas. L., 1: 22: 90, diphtheria, æ. 15-10-22, b. Central Falls R. I., of Andrew J. & Abby (Dunlap), Prussia, Boston.

22 Josephine A., 3: 19: 80, consumption, æ. 19-5-0, b. Boston, of Bernard & Mary, Germany, do.

17 Lillian J., 2: 13: 80, premature birth, æ. 0-0-2, b. Ded., of Bernard A. & Annie M. L., Boston, do.

16 Michael, 3: 4: 64, delirium tremens, æ. 37-0-0, b. Ire., of Wm. & Ann. [soldier.]

ROSWELLER.

47 Peter, 8: 18: 55, dysentery, æ. 0-11-20, b. Ded., of Peter & Eliza.

91 Peter, 7: 4: 61, consumption, æ. 40-6-0, b. Germ., of Jacob & Eliz'h, Germ., do.

ROURKE.

28 Ellen, 4: 8: 85, consumption, æ. 70-0-0, b. Ire., of John & Katharine, Ire., do.

ROWE.

92 Emma, 9: 22: 82, gastritis, æ. 0-0-10, b. Ded., of Andrew J. & Sarah, Manchester N. H., Eng.

ROYAL.

70 Amos, 12: 9: 61, typhus fever, æ. 21-8-22, b. Pownal Me., of Cyrus & Betsy.

RUMRILL.

113 Wilfred, 10: 1: 48, scrofula, æ. 0-1-0, b. Ded., of Wm. & Jane.

RUNDY.

14 Eliz. C., 6:22:47, consumption, æ, ——.

RUNGE.

15 Chas. G., 3:4:79, heart dis., æ. 73-10-21, b. Germ.

65 Wilhelmine (Herger), 4:14:62, consumption, æ. 44-6-0, b. Prussia, of - - & ——, Prussia, do.

RUSSELL.

35 Cara L., 4:18:80, typhoid fever, æ. 4-9-7, b. Ded., of Fred'c L. & Helen L., Ded., Newton.

19 Louisa (French), w. of Ira, 2:11:89, heart dis., æ. 75-2-0, b. W. Cambridge, of Moses & Hannah (Wheeler), Ded., Concord.

9 Nathan, 2:12:51, consumption, æ. 29-0-13, b. Shrewsbury Vt., of Nathan & Betsy.

25 Sarah R. (French), w. of John R., 4:10:55, childbirth, æ. 27-5-25, b. Boston, of Jefferson & Eliz'h.

70 Sarah W. (Bush), w. of John I., 7:8:90, old age, æ. 91-8-0, b. Portland Ct., of Elisha & Esther, Ct., R. I.

RUTZLER.

25 Geo. J., 3:27:87, hydrocephalus, æ. 0-4-14, b. Ded., of Theobald & Mary E., France, Ire.

37 Jas., 5:6:85, inanition, æ. 0-0-28, b. Ded., of Jos. T. & Mary E., France, Ire.

42 Mary E., 5:23:87, hydrocephalus, æ. 0-6-10, b. Ded., of Theobald & Mary E., France, Ire.

38 Theobold, 5:7:85, inanition, æ. 0-0-29, b. Ded., of Jos. T. & Mary E., France, Ire.

RYAN.

45 James, 6:23:86, spinal caries, æ. 12-4-5, b. Ded., of Thos. & Mary, Ire., do.

1 Joanna, 3:11:66, membranous croup, æ. 2-0-1, b. Blackstone, of Timothy & Julia.

52 John, 9:22:53, falling from cars, æ. 16-11-0, b. Ire., of Phillip & Julia.

30 Julia (McDonald), 3:26:83, chronic bronchitis, æ. 75-5-0, b. Ire., of Martin & Margaret, Ire., do.

92 Mary E., 10:30:80, convulsions, æ. 0-4-0, b. Ded., of Daniel H. & Susan, Boston, Ire.

10 Michael, 4:11:63, lung fever, æ. 3-11-0, b. Ded., of Patrick & Mary, Ire., do.

84 Patrick, 11:23:60, typhoid fever, æ. 50-0-0.

98 Philip, 9:20:83, old age, æ. 83-4-0, b. Ire., of John & Margaret, Ire., do.

107 Susan (Ryan), 12:31:80, acute alcoholism, æ. 34-0-0, b. Ire., of Michael & Spellecy, Ire., do.

SABIN.

111 Benazah, 10:23:65, heart disease, æ. 72-5-0, b. ——, of John & Temperance.

50 Betsy W. (Wood), 6:16:75, pneumonia, æ. 82-4-0, b. Washington N. H., of Ebenezer & Phebe B.

SACK.

61 Chas., 11:21:58, stoppage, æ. 32-0-0, b. Germ., of Chas. & Sarah.

SADLER.

27 Betsy, 9: 24: 47, fever, æ. 84-0-0.

ST. DENNIS.

1 Josephine (Rann), 1: 28: 73, confinement, æ. 19-0-0, b. Canada, of Andrew & Barzlis, Canada, do.

3 Mary (——), w. of ——, 3: 28: 74, consumption, æ. 24-0-0, b. Quincy, of Edw. & Bridget, Montreal, Ire.

4 Rosanna, 9: 5: 73, teething, æ. 0-8-0, b. Dedham, of David & Mary, Canada, do.

ST. GODERD.

74 Melvina, 9: 19: 77, cholera infantum, æ. 0-10-26, b. Vermont, of Jules & Melvina, Canada, do.

SAMPSON.

45 Cynthia, 6: 17: 77, erysipelas, æ. 87-2-14, b. Middleboro, of Lemuel & Mary, Plymouth, do.

31 Ezra W., 1: 15: 67, chronic pleurisy, æ. 69-1-15, b. Duxbury, of Sylvanus & Sylvia C., Duxbury, do.

17 Mary (Sampson), 2: 15: 57, lung fever, æ. 92-8-15, b. Middlebury, of Nehemiah & Lucy.

67 Selina W. (Wadsworth), 7: 25: 60, cancer, æ. 59-2-0, b. Duxbury, of Ahira & Deborah, Duxbury, do.

SANBORN.

51 Josiah E., 7: 5: 66, found dead, æ. 48-0-0.

62 Nellie R. (Sanborn), 6: 24: 71, inflam. of bowels, æ. 23-2-0, b. Scotland, of Wm. & Eliz'h, Glasgow, do.

SANDERS.

81 Mary A., 10: 9: 57, ——, æ. 1-0-0, b. Ded., of Austin & Lucy.

SANDERSON.

24 Joseph, 3: 11: 75, old age, æ. 85-3-0, b. Waterford Me., of Stephen & Polly, Littleton, Harvard.

46 Polly (Bryant), 8: 31: 74, old age, æ. 81-7-0, b. Waterford Me., of Richard & Mary, Harvard, Waterford.

SAWIN.

48 ——, 4: 9: 46, fever, æ. 0-8-0, b. Ded., s. of —— & ——.

206 (D. at Walpole) Freddie M., 12: 21: 64, diphtheria, æ. 4-10-21, b. Norwich Ct., of Lorenzo & Caroline E., Medfield, Ded.

68 Levi, 2: 9: 56, old age, æ. 96-0-0, b. Natick.

SAWYER.

16 Samuel C., 9: 26: 46, wheel run over him, æ. 50-0-0.

SCANNELL.

28 Augustin, 6: 19: 58, croup, æ. 4-9-0, b. Canton, of Dennis & Hannah.

32 John B., 7: 11: 58, croup, æ. 1-9-5, b. Medfield, of Dennis & Hannah.

30 Margaret, 6: 23: 58, measles, æ. 3-4-0, b. Taunton, of Dennis & Hannah.

105 Margaret (Kelly), 12: 31: 71, consumption, æ. 38-2-0, b. Ire., of Patrick & Margaret, Ire., do.

SCHERMERHORN.

2 John I., 1: 16: 76, rheumatism of heart, æ. 52-0-0, b. N. Y. State, of John & Catharine Y., N. Y. State, do.

SCHEUSTEN.

24 Margaret, 9: 16: 47, dysentery, æ. 38-0-0.

SCHLUSEMEYER.

8 Charles H., 1: 24: 85, tumor, æ. 15-7-27, b. Medway, of John H. & Marietta T., Boston, Medway.

59 Irving C., 6: 29: 82, spinal meningitis, æ. 2-4-13, b. Medway, of William & Adelaide L. (Daniels), Boston, Franklin.

62 John E., 7: 11: 82, progressive paralysis, æ. 74-7-22, b. Germany, of Girard & Elizabeth, Germ., do.

93 Sarah J., 3: 20: 73, consumption, æ. ——, b. Medfield, of John E. & Anna M. (Gauman), Germ., do.

SCHMETS.

61 Wm., 6: 4: 71, heart dis., æ. 46-0-0, b. Germ., of Daniel & Mary, Germ., do.

SCHMIDT.

78 Theodore, 11: 8: 86, phthisis, æ. 33-9-17, b. Germ., of Louis G. & Sophia, Germ., do.

SCHNEIDER, SNYDER.

81 Aurelia, 8: 19: 89, convulsions, æ. 0-0-8, b. Ded., of John B. & Bertha (Eis), Germ., Ded.

97 Chas., 12: 1: 67, croup, æ. 6-10-0, b. Ded., of Conrad & Mary A., Germ., do.

31 Conrad, 3: 3: 88, cancer, æ. 65-0-0, b. Germ.

13 John, 7: 5: 65, typhoid fever, æ. 38-7-16, b. Switz., of Casper & Eliz'h.

79 Mary A. (Sulkoski), 11: 15: 68, inflam. of lungs, æ. 38-0-0, b. Rox, of John & Julia M., Poland, Ire.

SCHOPF.

4 Barbara (Seuss), 1: 11: 78, heart dis., æ. 51-1-0, b. Germ., of —— & ——, Germ., do.

SCHULER.

91 Wm., 12: 9: 75, marasmus, æ. 0-3-8, b. Ded., of Samuel & Abberleine, Switz., Germ.

SCOTT.

43 Geo. J., 8: 27: 58, cholera infantum, æ. 0-10-13, b. Ded., of James & Eliz'h.

22 Joel, 5: 6: 58, congestion of lungs, æ. 46-0-0, b. Newport N. H., of Joel & Mary.

70 Mary J. (Crocker), 9: 13: 77, uterine tumor, æ. 41-6-9, b. Va., of —— & Jane, ——, Va.

SCULLY, SCULLEY.

57 Ellen, 6: 9: 81, old age, æ. 87-0-0, b. Ire., of John & Mary, Ire., do.

18 Patrick, 4: 13: 62, colic, æ. 1-8-0, b. Ded., of Patrick & Mary.

78 Patrick, 10: 1: 77, Bright's dis., æ. 45-0-0, b. Ire., of Patrick & Bridget, Ire., do.

SEABURY.

71 Catherine (Bartlett), w. of Jos., 5: 25: 88, catarrhal pneumonia, æ. 72-3-13, b. S. Plymouth, of Ivory H. & Betsey (Clark), S. Plymouth do.

SEAVER.

18 Dolly A. (Austin), 2: 8: 80, old age, æ. 85-0-6, b. Stoughton, of Wm. & Anne C., Taunton, Attleboro.

2i Lewis, 9: 4: 47, consumption, æ. ——.

49 M. Cutler, 4: 28: 65, typhus fever, æ. 18-0-0, b. Worcester, of Jas. M. & ——. [soldier.]

SEAVEY.

114 Edw. A., 12: 18: 84, scarlet fever, æ. 11-2-18, b. Ded., of Henry & Mary E., Charlestown, Ded.

SEERY, SERE.

134 Kate (McManus), w. of Morris. 12: 11: 88, hypertrophy of heart, æ. 60-0-0, b. Ire., of Barney & Rosa, Ire., do.

92 Michael, 12: 28: 75, consumption, æ. 40-0-0, b. Ire., of —— & ——, Ire., do.

SENNOTT.

82 Mary J. (Hurley), w. of Patrick F., 6: 15: 88, heart dis., æ. 36-3-20, b. Ire., of David & Joanna, Ire., do.

SEYMOUR.

30 Delia, 4: 27: 75, typhoid fever, æ. 20-0-0, b. Canada, of Francis & Prospere K., Canada, do.

SHALER.

44 Rebecca, 9: 18: 59, dis. of heart, æ. 46-0-0.

SHAPLEIGH.

24 Augustus, 4: 26: 53, croup, æ. 4-5-9, b. Ded., of Jona. & Rebekah G.

89 Livia (Remick), 3: 22: 71, phthisis, æ. 64-2-15, b. Eliot Me., of Thos. & Livia, Eliot Me., do.

56 Lydia A., 8: 21: 61, consumption, æ. 11-9-0, b. Eliot Me., of Jas. & Levia, Eliot Me., do.

12 Marilla M., 3: 13: 61, consumption, æ. 24-6-9, b. Eliot Me., of James & Levia (Remick).

134 Nathan E., 5: 3: 65, consumption, æ. 21-2-23, b. Eliot Me., of Jas. & Livia.

SHATTUCK.

97 Achsah F. (Sherwin), 10: 29: 73, congestion of lungs, æ. 81-6-19, b. Townsend, of John & ——.

44 Chas. A., 4: 12: 50, consumption, æ. 28-0-0, b. Ded., of Ebenezer & ——.

125 Chas. H., 12: 27: 62, typhoid fever, æ. 2-5-20, b. Ded., of Henry F. & Hannah J., Ded., Dracut.

37 Christiana (Smith), 6: 28: 74, old age, æ. 74-0-0, b. Germ., of Adam & Fredericka, Germ., do.

56 Eben, 5: 23: 51, consumption, æ. 64-0-0, b. Pepperell, of Eben & ——.

114 Emma J., 7: 4: 61, cyanosis, æ. 0-0-1, b, Ded., of Henry F. & Hannah J.

185 Geo. F., 3: 29: 64, ——, æ. 0-2-19, b. Ded., of Henry F. & Hannah J., Ded., Lowell.

150 Jennie E., 11: 7: 65, dropsy, æ. 0-2-9, b. Ded., of Henry F. & Hannah J.

97 Marietta, 8: 4: 55, consumption, æ. 31-0-0, b. Ded., of Eben'r & Achsah.
27 Martha M., 4: 21: 55, consumption, æ. 15-6-1, b. Ded., of Willard & Eliz'h.
15 Sarah E., 5: 5: 52, consumption, æ. 16-0-0, b. Ded., of Wm. & Eliz'h.

SHAW.
84 Catharine P. (Pollock), 12: 10: 73, heart dis., æ. 69-5-6, b. Poestenkill N.Y., of John & Anna, Poestenkill N. Y., do.
56 Chas. B., 11: 30: 69, paralysis, æ. 72-0-22, b. Boston, of Noah & Sally, Abington, Wrentham.
76 Chas. W., 9: 12: 78, debility, æ. 0-0-5, b. Ded., of Chas. M. & Frances M., Blackstone, Deerfield N. H.
96 Mary (Patterson), 9: 15: 83, congestion of brain, æ. 81-6-1, b. Boston, of Enoch & Mary Adams, Northboro, Newton.
40 Noah, 12: 17: 50, apoplexy, æ. 82-6-24, b. Abington, of Daniel & Rebecca.

SHEDD.
16 Mary P., 1: 14: 45, consumption, æ. 27-0-0.
59 Wm., 7: 2: 85, inanition, æ. 0-0-1, b. Ded., of Wm. & Mary, Boston, Ire.

SHEEHAN, SHEHAN.
80 Cornelius, 11: 20: 68, lung fever, æ. 57-0-0, b. Ire., of —— & ——, Ire., do.
90 Hannah, 9: 18: 67, consumption, æ. 21-0-0, b. Ire., of Perry & Ellen, Ire., do.
103 Jeremiah, 12: 15: 76, teething, æ. 0-8-0, b. Ded., of Timothy & Maggie, Ire., Boston.
81 Jeremiah, 9: 1: 82, dysentery, æ. 68-0 0, b. Ire., of Timothy & Catherine, Ire., do.
103 Jerry, 12: 26: 67, lung fever, æ. 3-0-0, b. Ire., of Jerry & Ellen, Ire., do.
90 John, 11: 23: 75, consumption, æ. 19-0-0, b. Ded., of Edw. & Hannah, Ire., do.
21 Lena, 2: 27: 74, whooping cough, æ. 0-10-17, b. Bridgewater, of —— & Mary, ——, Ire.
32 Maggie J. (Cunningham), 5: 5: 77, consumption, æ. 18-10-0, b. Boston, of Barney & Mary, Ire., do.
16 Michael, 3: 23: 62, whooping cough, æ. 0-0-10, b. Ded., of Patrick & Margaret.
24 Morris, 3: 13: 84, meningitis, æ. 1-2-17, b. Ire., of Dennis & Mary, Ire., do.
61 Richard, 8: 6: 78, consumption, æ. 24-1-0, b. Boston, of Edw. & Honora, Ire., do.
75 Thos., 10: 20: 68, dropsy, æ. 10-0-0, b. Ded., of Edw. & Honora.

SHEPARD, SHEPHERD.
28 Eliz'h A. (Brown), 4: 19: 77, erysipelas, æ. 73-10-28, b. Boston, of Elisha & Nancy, Brighton, Charlestown.
43 (D. at Boston) Geo. H., 3: 30: 88, broken neck, æ. 50-0 0.
53 Geo. O., 9: 23: 53, consumption, æ. 0-9-20, b. Ded., of Nath'l & Sarah E.
13 Jesse M., 9: 27: 74, cholera infantum, æ. 0-4-0, b. Charlestown, of John L. & Celia M., Plainfield Ct., Ded.
38 Sarah (Lothrop), w. of Nath'l, 6: 30: 55, ——, æ. 35-0-0, b. Sharon, of Darius & Nancy.
49 Sarah E. (Guild), w. of Nathaniel, 12: 21: 52, childbed fever, æ. 27-5-27, b. Belfast Me., of Heman & Hannah.

SHERIDAN.

61 ——, 6: 1: 67, stillborn, b. Ded., s. of William H. & Mary D., Providence R. I., Mendon.

64 James, 12: 14: 58, consumption, æ. 36-9-0, b. Germ., of Cornelius & Ann.

88 John, 9: 8: 49, dysentery, æ. 21-0-0, b. Ire.

75 John, 8: 28: 75, old age, æ. 78-0-0, b. Ire., of Jas. & Julia, Ire., do.

63 Mary, 12: 6: 58, imperfection of throat, æ. 0-3-15, b. Ded., of James & Elizabeth.

27 Thos., 3: 28: 57, scarlatina, æ. 2-10-0, b. Ded., of John & Mary.

SHERMAN.

53 Caspar C., 9: 5: 55, disease of brain, æ. 4-2-17, b. Ded., of Charles B. & Sarah C.

69 Roger M., 12: 1: 53, cholera infantum, æ. 1-3-9, b. Ded., of Charles B. & Sarah C.

SHERRIFF.

44 Ellen (Fellows), 5: 22: 75, pneumonia, æ. 66-5-6, b. Boston, of John & Joanna, Ipswich, do.

73 John L., 8: 26: 80, Bright's dis., æ. 72-0-10, b. Exeter N. H., of Benj. P. & Martha (Gilmore), Exeter N. H., Portsmouth N. H.

SHERWIN.

23 Anna, 3: 9: 76, heart dis., æ. 72-4-4, b. N. Ipswich N. H., of David & Hannah P., Boxford, N. Ipswich N. H.

90 Mary K. (Gibbens), 10: 27: 76, paralysis, æ. 65-10-6, b. Boston, of Daniel L. & Mary K., Boston, N. S.

46 Thomas, 7: 23: 69, heart disease, æ. 70-3-27, b. Westmoreland, of David & Hannah, Boxford, do.

SHEVER.

59 Mary E., 3: 26: 71, rheumatic fever, æ. 5-6-0, b. Newark N. J., of Henry & Honora, Germ., Ire.

SHINE.

12 ——, 1: 19: 89, stillborn, b. Ded., s. of Thos. P. & Delia (Dowling), Ded., Ire.

SHMETT.

75 ——, 8: 18: 81, stillborn, b. Ded., of Theodore & Louisa, France, do.

76 Louisa (Studer), 8: 18: 81, hemorrhage, æ. 22-9-0, b. France, of Joseph & Euphringer, France, do.

SHOREY.

59 Frank H., 1: 24: 62, consumption, æ. 24-2-22, b. Boston, of John & Cornelia G., S. Berwick Me., Ded.

84 John, 9: 4: 49, liver comp., æ. 45-0-19, b. South Berwick Me., of John & Sarah.

5 (D. at Minneapolis, Minn.) John C., 12: 2: 62, hemorrhage of lungs, æ. 26-6-0, b. Boston, of John & Cornelia G.

1 Sarah (Falls), 1: 8: 52, old age, æ. 84-6-0, b. Berwick Me., of Stephen & Martha.

33 Theodore, 6: 18: 53, drowned, æ. 12-0-0, b. Ded., of John & Cornelia.

SHORTMAN.

115 ——, 10: 19: 88, premature birth, æ. 0-0-5, b. Ded., d. of Wm. F. & Annie (Ludelwick), Germany, do.

SHUBART.

36 Nicholas, 1: 27: 63, lung fever, æ. 19-0-0, b. Italy. [soldier.]

SHUMAN.

32 Henry, 3: 31: 83, heart dis , æ. 80-4-0, b. Germany.

SHUMWAY.

18 Erastus, 6: 8: 51, tumor, æ. 40-0-12, b. Jamaica Vt., of Lewis & Lucy.

8 Erastus D., 2: 11: 55, dis. of brain, æ. 3-7-2, b. Ded., of Erastus & Harriet N.

132 Geo. E., 6: 29: 63, congestion of lungs, æ. 0-1-17, b. Ded., of Elbridge E. & Amanda F., Dover, Woonsocket R. I.

SHUTTLEWORTH.

17 Hannah, 2: 22: 86, paralysis, æ. 86-0-6, b. Ded., of Jere'h & Sukey Richards). Ded., do.

50 Jeremiah, 6: 13: 72, typhoid fever, æ. 70-0-26, b. Ded., of Jere'h & Sukey, Ded., do.

84 Samuel, 4: 8: 64, paralysis of brain, æ. 56-4-6, b. Ded , of Jeremiah & Sukey, Ded., do.

SIBLECH.

85 Tekla, 12: 25: 57, brain fever, æ. 2-6-0, b. Ded., of Henry & Christopha.

SIMMONS.

52 Fred'k, 9: 19: 74, consumption, æ. 28-1-19, b. Ded., of Jos. & Ann M., Bristol R. I., do.

51 Joseph, 7: 10: 86, pneumonia, æ. 73-9-10, b. Bristol R. I., of —— & Eliz'h (Wilson), Vt., Bristol R. I.

75 Lillian M., 11: 8: 73, ——, æ. 1-9-29, b. Ded., of Jos. & Lillie A., Fairhaven, Craftsbury Vt.

SIMONDS.

62 Sarah R., 6: 8: 83, old age, æ. 82-2-14, b. Beverly, of —— & ——, Beverly, do.

SIMPSON.

45 Annie L., 4: 4: 88, meningitis, æ. 0-8-27, b. Ded., of Thos. H. & Margaret E., N. S., do.

44 Eliz'h F. (Thompson), 6: 17: 86, typhoid fever, æ. 38-9-0, b. Framingham, of Monroe & Annie E., Framingham, do.

111 Gertrude, 10: 31: 89, averted development, æ. 0-3 11, b. Ded., of Robert P. & Susan M. (Murray), Portland Me., Ded.

76 John, 9: 22: 77, drowned, æ. 40-0-0.

47 John J., 6: 15: 84, interceptine of intestines, æ. 0-2-26, b. Ded., of Robert P. & Susan M. A., Portland Me., Ded.

SINCLAIR.

35 ——, 4: 6: 89, premature birth, æ. 0 0-1, b. Ded., s. of —— & Maggie, ——. N.B.

SKARRATT.

2 Edward, 3: 17: 66, consumption, æ. 50-0-0, b. Ire.

SKENNEN.
79 John, 10: 25: 60, dropsy, æ. 0-6-11, b. Rox., of John & Margaret, Ire., do.

SKILLINGS, SKILLIN.
22 Eliz'h, 3: 27: 77, paralysis, æ. 77-8-0, b. Boston, of John & Mary F.
32 Mary, 4: 11: 49, old age, æ. 80-0-0.
86 Walter E., 3: 12: 58, ——, æ. ——, b. Ded., of Daniel D. & Mary A.

SKINNER.
8 Alice F. (Gilbert), 1: 26: 81, consumption, æ. 35-0-0, b. Oldtown Me., of L. G. & E. W., Parkman Me., Oldtown Me.
29 George, 2: 4: 64, lung fever, æ. ——. [soldier.]

SLADE.
5 ——, 8: 9: 46, throat distemper, æ. 3-0-0.

SLATTERY.
102 Catharine (Doggett), 10: 23: 49, cancer, æ. 35-0-0, b. Ire., of Chas. & Catharine.
97 Ellen, 2: 7: 70, consumption, æ. 18-10-0, b. Ire., of Patrick & Ellen, Ire., do.
104 Ellen, 6: 16: 72, old age, æ. 67-0-0, b. Ire.
3 James, 2: 27: 70, tumor in throat, æ. 1-0-0, b. Ded., of Patrick & Ellen, Ire., do.
42 John, 8: 13: 53, fit, æ. 20-0-0, b. Ire., of Patrick & Catharine.
64 John, 7: 8: 71, ——, æ. 0-1-12, b. Ded., of Daniel & Mary, Ire., N. H.
16 Patrick, 3: 31. 58, intemperance, æ. 25-0-0, b. Ire., of Patrick & Catharine.
10 Patrick, 7: 12: 67, accidental, æ. 63-0-0, b. Ireland, of Patrick & Catharine, Ireland, do.
99 Patrick, 12: 14: 73, consumption, æ. 32-5-0, b. Ireland, of Patrick & Ellen, Ireland, do.

SLOAN.
14 Herbert E., 7: 22: 72, cholera infantum, æ. 0-9-9, b. Boston, of George W. & Sarah L.

SLOMAN.
81 Elizabeth (Clarenbom), 9: 6: 74, cholera morbus, æ. 82-0-0, b. Southport Me., of —— & Kitty.

SMALL.
114 Chas. H., 12: 30: 79, paralysis of brain, æ. 30-6-0, b. Ded., of Jonathan & Jane L., Harwich, Charlestown.
91 Hannah (Wheat), 10: 26: 78, suffocation, æ. 90-2-0, b. Hollis N. H., of Joseph & Mary, Lincoln, do.
65 Jane S., 6: 14: 83, cancer, æ. 47-7-8, b. Ded., of Jonathan & Jane L., Harwich, Charlestown.
13 Jonathan, 2: 24: 79, paralysis, æ. 76-6-11, b. Harwich, of Thomas & Betsey, Harwich, Orleans.
22 Thos., 5: 24: 54, dropsy, æ. 80-1-0, b. Harwich, of Jonathan & Bethiah.

SMALLWOOD.
61 Harriet (Guild), 8: 22: 56, apoplectic fits, æ. 24-0-0, b. Walpole, of Leonard & Hannah.

SMITH.

6 ——, 8: 19: 44, ——, æ. 0-4-4, b. Ded., s. of Henry & Mary A.

21 ——, 5: 16: 54, infantile dis., æ. 0-0-3, b. Ded., d. of Franklin & Bidelia.

12 ——, 2: 12: 85, stillborn, b. Ded., d. of Theodore & Delphene, France, do.

52 Abner, 3: 29: 71, old age, æ. 84-6-10, b. Beverly, of Jonathan & Lucy, Middleton, Hingham.

69 Agnes, 7: 21: 87, diphtheritic croup, æ. 2-4-0, b. Ded., of Michael & Bridget, Ireland, do.

27 Amanda F. (Smith), w. of Metcalf D., 2: 14: 90, heart disease, æ. 54-3-6, b. Laconia N. H., of Isaiah & Fanny H. (Gould), New Hampton N. H., Holderness N. H.

53 Angelie, 7: 20: 86, exhaustion, æ. 0-5-1, b. Maynard, of Theodore & Delphene, France, do.

9 Anna, 3: 22: 63, scarlet fever, æ. 3-10-8, b. Ded., of Thomas & Bridget, Ireland, do.

95 Anna (Rhoades), 5: 24: 68, old age, æ. 78-11-10, b. Ded., of Eliph't & Mercy, Dedham, Sharon.

86 Anna R., 12: 21: 73, consumption, æ. 18-8-14, b. Ded., of Franklin & Bidelia, Dedham, Ireland.

1 Arthur H., 1: 6: 81, gastro enteritis, æ. 0-4-7, b. Ded., of John W. & Sarah R., Eng., Canton.

44 Asahel, 2: 20: 46, consumption, æ. 65-0-0, b. Ded., of Henry & ——.

34 Asahel H., 5: 10: 78, consumption, æ. 20-6-0, b. Ded., of Franklin & Bidelia, Dedham, Ireland.

64 Benjamin, 8: 29: 77, liver complaint, æ. 63-5-0, b. Ded., of Asahel & Rebecca, Roxbury, Stoddard N. H.

2 [Bidelia] (Mullen), 1: 15: 83, pericarditis, æ. 59-8-0, b. Ire., of John & Eliz'h, Ireland, do.

80 Caroline (Jesse), 4: 13: 64, consumption, æ. 31-0-0, b. France, of Francis A. & Maylener, France, do.

55 Carrie D., 4: 19: 67, spinal complaint, æ. 37-8-17, b. Walpole, of Leonard & Alona, Walpole, Medfield.

37 Catharine, 9: 7: 54, typhoid fever, æ. 15-4-15, b. Eng., of John & Ann.

65 Catharine (Fales), 10: 5: 66, cancer, æ. 76-5-17, b. Walpole, of Moses & Rebecca.

2 Catharine, 1: *21: 67, convulsion fit, æ. 0-0-21, b. Ded., of Thos. & Bridget, Ire., do.

34 Chas. A., 9: 23: 51, infantile, æ. 0-0-22, b. Ded., of Chas. & Ann.

27 Chas. W., 4: 11: 78, consumption, æ. 27-0-0, b. Ire., of Chas. & Rebecca, Ire., do.

50 Clara E., 7: 11: 68, inflam. of brain, æ. 0-8-0, b. Ded., of Timothy & Emily, Stoughton, Scituate.

37 Edgar C., 10: 17: 50, whooping cough, æ. 0-5-0, b. Gardiner Me., of Edwin A. & Hannah M.

108 Eliz'h, 11: 30: 81, diphtheria, æ. 11-8-0, b. Ded., of Thos. & Bridget, Ire., do.

36 Ellen F. (Flinn), 4: 21: 80, consumption, æ. 33-0-0, b. Ire., of John & Stracia, Ire., do.

46 Eltheir S. (Phinney), 5: 31: 85, phthisis pulmonalis, æ. 46-10-23, b. Eastport Me., of Nathaniel M. & Mary M. (Harrington), Machiasport Me., Eastport Me.

6 Emerson W., 1: 17: 86, empyema, æ. 43-10-11, b. Stoughton, of Judson & Eliz'h, Randolph, do.

48 Emma F., 4: 22: 65, dis. of throat, æ. 0-0-14, b. Ded., of John A. & Georgia.

17 Fanny (Howe), 1: 31: 74, consumption, æ. 80-5-0, b. Baldwin Me., of Jacob & Betsy, Ipswich, Boxford.

105 Fannie A. (Greely), w. of Elmer E., 10: 24: 90, typhoid fever, æ. 24-6-24, b. Ded., of Jas. & Abbie (Smith), St. Johnsbury Vt., Ded.

74 Florence, 8: 1: 87, marasmus, æ. 24-10-29, b. Foxboro, of Eliph't & Mary A., Ded., Walpole.

23 Frances A. (Pitts), 4: 13: 79, consumption, æ. 30-4-15, b. Canton, of James & Lavinia, Readfield Me., Newbury N. H.

53 Frank T., 6: 13: 87, morbilli, æ. 0-8-17, b. Boston, of Henry C. T. & Hilda J., Germ., Sweden.

10 Frederick H., 3: 6: 53, lung fever, æ. 1-6-3, b. Dedham, of Henry & Charlotte.

48 Georgianna E., 10: 29: 62, typhoid fever, æ. 17-5-10, b. Franklin, of Timothy & Emily, Stoughton, Scituate.

79 (D. at Walpole) Hannah (Whiting), 11: 20: 61, apoplectic fits, æ. 80-6-0, b. Ded., of Nath. & Eliz'h, Ded., ——.

73 Harry T., 7: 21: 65, drowned, æ. 15-8-22, b. Ded., of Chas. & Wealthy W. K.

94 Harvey, 9: 2: 65, scrofula, æ. 42-7-8, b. Rehoboth, of Zebina & Lydia.

76 Henry, 11: 26: 66, insanity, æ. 50-2-8, b. Medfield, of Jos. & Catherine.

28 Herbert, 3: 9: 81, convulsions, æ. 1-2-0.

57 Irving, 5: 11: 67, croup, æ. 7-10-10, b. Ded., of Henry & Charlotte, Ded., do.

63 (D. at Roxbury), Isaacus, 2: 19: 54, purple fever, æ. 36-0-0, b. Ded., of Timothy & [Nabby.]

96 Jacob, 4: 25: 64, dysentery, æ. ——. [soldier]

45 James, 6: 11: 84, typho pneumonia, æ. 60-11-0, b. Ireland, of John & Mary, Ireland, do.

175 John, 2: 25: 64, softening of brain, æ. 79-2-22, b. Ded., of John & Abigail.

1 John, 1: 15: 67, convulsion fit, æ. 0-0-17, b. Dedham, of Thomas & Bridget, Ireland, do.

85 John W., 12: 5: 77, cerebral meningitis, æ. 54-0 0, b. England, of Elias & Elizabeth, Eng., do.

61 Josephine, 9: 19: 44, fever, æ. 0-11-0, b. Ded.

32 Josiah, 2: 12: 45, consumption, æ. 65-0-0, b. Ded.

23 (D. at Walpole) Leonard, 4: 3: 65, disease of kidneys, æ. 77-0-0, b. Walpole, of Isaac & Mary.

55 Lephy D., 11: 15: 54, consumption, æ. 20-1-15, b. Rehoboth, of Zebina & Lydia.

111 Lucy, 12: 4: 81, diphtheria, æ. 3-10-9, b. Dedham, of Thomas & Bridget, Ireland, do.

90 Lydia (Harvey), 10: 8: 63, cancer, æ. 69-8-21, b. Taunton, of Joel & Abigail, Taunton, do.

13 Lydia A., 1: 2: 60, consumption, æ. 36-0-12, b. Rehoboth, of Sabina & Lydia.

78 (D. at Foxboro) Malinda A., 8: 19: 58, liver complaint, æ. 0-4 20, b. Ded., of Charles & Hannah.

102 Margaret, 12: 24: 67, canker, æ. 1-0-14, b. Dedham, of James & Hannah, Ireland, do.

56 Margaret, 6: 27: 75, scrofulosis, æ. 17-0-0, b. Boston, of —— & Margaret F., Ireland, do.

65 Margaret V., 7: 9: 82, convulsions, æ. 0-3-19, b. Ded., of Michael & Bridget, Ireland, do.

24 Mary A. (McIntosh), w. of Henry, 7: 20: 44, consumption of blood, æ. 20-0-0, b. Newton.

69 Mary E., 8: 13: 84, consumption, æ. 20-10-23, b. Ded., of Thomas & Bridget, Ireland, do.

40 Mary J., 8: 15: 58, croup, æ. 5-11-23, b. Ded., of Francis & Caroline.

8 Melinda E., 10: 6: 45, ——, æ. 36-0-0, b. Ded.

133 Milly (Lewis), 2: 1: 62, dropsy, æ. 63-0-0, b. Ded., of Andrew & Mary.

114 Nabby (Colburn), w. of Timothy, 10: 18: 88, old age, æ. 97-7-24, b. Ded., of Isaac & Eliz'h (Dexter), Ded., Marlboro.

106 Nathaniel, 10: 1: 61, disease of heart, æ. 73-9-9, b. Ded., of Nath'l & Nancy, Dedham, ——.

1 Olive, w. of Abner, 5: 26: 44, old age, æ. 82-0-0, b. Ded.

68 Rebecca (Edes), 8: 10: 79, paralysis, æ. 91-10-24, b. Stoddard N. H., of Samuel & ——, Needham, Ded.

59 Sarah (Lewis), 5: 20: 71, old age, æ. 92-0-0, b. Rox., of Samuel & ——.

9 Sarah R. (Hamilton), 1: 27: 81, compsion of lungs, æ. 25-0-0, b. Canton, of Wm. M. & Jane, Scituate, Me.

120 Susan I., 8: 24: 64, cholera infantum, æ. 0-6-24, b. Ded., of David C. & Dorothy, Eng., do.

30 Thos., 2: 4: 64, lung fever, æ. 22-0-0. [soldier].

20 Thos., 2: 4: 66, consumption, æ. 22-0-0, b. Rox.

113 Thomas, 12: 9: 81, diphtheria, æ. 11-8-0, b. Ded., of Thomas & Bridget, Ireland, do.

101 Thomas, 8: 20: 88, old age, æ. 79-0-9, b. Ded., of Josiah & Hannah Lewis, Ded., W. Roxbury.

135 Timothy, 12: 6: 61, lung fever, æ. 68-9-0, b. Needham, of Timothy & Mehitable.

9 Warren G., 1: 30: 76, canker, æ. 0-2-20, b. Ded., of Charles & Edith B., Boston, Wisconsin.

77 (D. at Hyde Park) William, 12: 10: 64, consumption, æ. 63-0 0, b. England, of Joseph & Mary.

95 William O., 9: 26: 49, cholera infantum, æ. 1-7-20, b. Ded., of William P. & Anna.

59 Zebina, 6: 13: 65, accidental, æ. 43-10-0, b. Taunton, of Zebina & Lydia.

SNELL.

50 ——, 4: 18: 46, fever, æ. 6-0-0, b. Ded., of John D. & —— —.

40 John D., 7: 9: 57, diabetes, æ. 45-0-0, b. Halifax, of Wm. & Nancy.

8 Martha M., 3: 3: 53, consumption, æ. 20-10-27, b. Dedham, of George & Mary.

8 Mary (Lyon), 1: 27: 78, cancer, æ. 75-0-0, b. W. Rox.

SNELLING.

142 Angeline H. (Tufts), w. of Nath'l P., 12: 25: 88, paralysis, æ. 80-10-19, b. Portland Me., of Andrew & Ann (Bradley), Medford, Eng.

SNOW.

101 Amanda, 3: 31: 86, degeneration of stomach, æ. 57-9-5, b. Orleans, of Thatcher & Mercy, Orleans, do.

33 Bridget, 12: 31: 63, consumption, æ. 19-0-0, b. Ire., of Dennis & Ann.

98 Ciasimay, 8: 13: 61, cholera infantum, æ. 0-11-13, b. Ded., of Enos S. & Amelia, Chatham, Me.

17 Denis, 10: 28: 71, old age, æ. 83-0-0, b. Ire., of —— & ——, Ire., do.

17 Edward, 2: 26: 61, ——, æ. 46-0-0, b. Dublin N. H., of Ezra & Mary.

34 Hattie A. (Hill), w. of Enos S., 3: 11: 90, anasarca, æ. 49-3-1, b. South Berwick Me., of Jonathan & Sarah W. (Brown), Billerica, South Brunswick Me.

98 Joseph, 6: 21: 66, rheumatism, æ. 70-6-19, b. Danvers, of Joseph & Martha.

69 Mary, 11: 7: 66, consumption, æ. 19-8-0, b. Ire., of Dennis & Ann.

14 Patrick, 5: 3: 63, consumption, æ. 30-0-0, b. Ireland, of Dennis & Ann, Ireland, do.

SNYDER. (*See Schneider.*)

SONNENBERG.

8 Wilhelmine L., 2: 27: 61, consumption, æ. 18-6-0, b. Germ., of Henry F. G. T. & *Wilhelmine.

SOULE.

31 Antonette G., 8: 25: 71, dysentery, æ. 0-6-29, b. Ded., of Henry C. & Jennie, Dedham, do.

4 Herbert M., 1: 8: 89, pleuro pneumonia, æ. 13-2-6, b. Ded., of Fred S. & Hattie N. (Draper), Ded., do.

56 Juliette (Follansbee), w. of Greenwood E., 5: 23: 90, chronic heart disease, æ. 43-11-24, b. Pittston Me., of Alonzo & Nancy S. (Mackintosh), Pittston Me., Canton.

88 Maria A. (Colburn), 10: 10: 79, cancer, æ. 59-0-0, b. Dedham, of Abijah & Susanna C., Ded., Medfield.

104 Sally (Colburn), 12: 13: 80, old age, æ. 94-1-13, b. Ded., of Lewis & —— (Smith), Dedham, do.

SOUTHGATE.

5 Samuel, 1: 5: 77, paralysis, æ. 70-6-14, b. Leicester, of Samuel & Hannah W., Leicester, do.

SOUTHWICK.

87 Eliza (McGanague), 10: 14: 79, heart disease, æ. 56-0-0, b. Ireland, of —— & ——, Ireland, ——.

SPARROW.

37 ——, 4: 21: 80, stillborn, b. Ded., of Thos. & Mary A., N. C., Va.

32 Mary E., 3 : 31 : 84, gastro enteritis, æ. 0-1-22, b. Dedham, of Thomas & Mary A., N. C., Va.

SPAULDING, SPALDING.

30 (D. at Boston) Erastus G., 1 : 3 : 67, cancer, æ. 52-7-0, b. Newbury N. H., of Warren & Sarah, Warwick R. I., Washington N. H.

82 Harriet F. (Fisher), 11 : 9 : 60, pleurisy, æ. 44-6-12, b. Prov. R. I., of —— & Abigail G., ——, Warwick R. I.

47 Henrietta, 10 : 17 : 62, consumption, æ. 22-1-26, b. Warwick R. I., of Erastus G. & Harriet F., Bradford N. H., Prov. R. I.

38 Herman F., 11 : 24 : 50, typhus fever, æ. 5-2-1, b. Warwick R. I., of Erastus G. & Harriet F.

60 Hope A., 6 : 21 : 60, scarlatina, æ. 6-5-17, b. Ded., of Erastus G. & Harriet F., Bradford N. H., Prov. R. I.

57 Sally (Harrington), 6 : 22 : 82, hydrothorax, æ. 95-0-0, b. Chelmsford, of Timothy & Sarah, Lancaster, do.

SPEAR.

41 Caroline J. W. (Seymore), 6 : 2 : 86, blood poisoning, æ. 59-1-0, b. Easton, of Benj. & Mary, Plymouth, do.

88 Chas. H., 9 : 7 : 53, dis. of throat, æ. 7-0-0, b. Ded., of Joshua & Mary.

102 Joshua H., 2 : 1 : 72, liver comp., æ. 56-0-4, b. Boston, of Peter & ——.

36 Maria B. (Bullard), 3 : 18 : 66, paralysis, æ. 62-10-14, b. Ded., of John & Lucy.

46 Peter P., 5 : 5 : 50, fit, æ. 62-0-0.

SPENCER.

37 Thos., 2 : 15 : 64, small pox, æ. 22-0-0, b. Delaware. [soldier.]

SPILLANE.

110 Jas., 12 : 3 : 84, cirrhosis of liver, æ. 60-0-0, b. Ire., of Wm. & Mary, Ire., do.

SPRAGUE.

4 Chas. A., 2 : 11 : 50, bowel comp., æ. 0-4-0, b. Ded., of Stephen & Anna.

89 Edgar F., 9 : 10 : 49, cancer, æ. 0-13-0, b. Ded., of Stephen & Ann E.

28 Margaret L., 9 : 10 : 50, whooping cough, æ. 2-2-0, b. Ded., of Samuel & Mary.

32 Mary (Kingsbury), 6 : 18 : 53, typhoid fever, æ. 41-8-0, b. Canton, of Jona & Angelette.

STACKPOLE.

69 Edw. W., 6 : 20 : 83, R. R. accident, æ. 21-0-0, b. Newmarket N.H., of Wm.W. & Eliz'h, Kennebunk Me., Northwood N. H.

STALL.

54 Eliz'h (McGuirren), 11 : 20 : 59, consumption, æ. 25-0-0, b. Ire., of Andon & Emily.

STANLEY.

73 Wilford, 8 : 12 : 81, convulsions, æ. 0-10-5, b. Sherborn, of Wilford & Maud, Winchenden, Fitchburg.

STAPLES.

123 Charles G., 12 : 3 : 87, cyanosis, æ. 0-1-24, b. Ded., of George T. & Sarah L., Boston, do.

91 Emily L., 7: 20: 88, consumption. æ. 28–11–4, b. Newmarket N. H., of Samuel & Lucy J., York Me., Newmarket N. H.

22 Jedida S., 3: 15: 85, consumption, æ. 86–10–0, b. Brookfield, of Elias & Jedida, Brookfield, Edgartown.

STARE.

134 James W., 10: 3: 64, dropsy, æ. 45–0–0, b. Eng., of Dennis & Barbara, Eng., do. [soldier.]

STARRETT.

53 Sally C. (Cole), 5: 18: 65, old age, æ. 72–6–0, b. Waldoboro Me., of —— & Schenk.

STEARNS.

13 Edward M., 2: 12: 82, acute catarrh, æ. 0–5–22, b. Ded., of George C. Jr. & Mary N., N. Y. City, Ded.

60 Mary, 12: 18: 54, consumption. æ. 63–0–0, b. Lancaster, of Eli & Mary.

78 Mary, 6: 6: 88, dis. of kidney and liver, æ. 1–0–4, b. Ded., of Albert B. & Sarah J., Rowe, Brooklyn N. Y.

STEFAN.

66 (D. at Boston) Anna V. (Pasek), wife of Adelbert, 6: 26: 90, intestinal ulceration, æ. 52–4–22, b. Bohemia, of Matthias & Marie, Bohemia, do.

STEINER.

107 Eliza (Hoffman), w. of Ferdinand, 10: 7: 87, dis. of brain, æ. 74–0–0, b. Germ., of Daniel & Corde, Germ., do.

STETEFIELD.

63 Charles W., 7: 5: 71, old age, æ. 84–0–0, b. Germ.

STETSON.

40 Betsy F., 8: 4: 53, dysentery, æ. 3–8–12, b. Halifax, of Jos. & Cordelia.

35 Cordelia (Allen), 4: 28: 85, consumption, æ. 64–11–13, b. Halifax, of Seth & Lucy, E. Bridgewater, Halifax.

58 Fletcher L., 5: 17: 67, inflam. of bowels, æ. 9–28–0, b. Halifax, of Joseph & Cordelia, Me., Halifax.

STEVENS.

80 Clarissa H., 9: 29: 76, dysentery, æ. 87–1–25, b. Athol.

11 Nancy (Gyer), 2: 7: 81, apoplexy, æ. 74–2–8, b. Friendship Me., of —— & ——, Maine, do.

97 (D. in Va.) Nelson R., 3: 1: 62, typhoid fever, æ. 19–0–24, b. Rumney N. H., of J. N. & E. C. C., Haverhill N. H., Meredith N. H.

112 Roberta P., 11: 19: 90, congestion of lungs, æ. 38–11–5, b. N. B., of Edw. & Sarah A. (Kane), N. B., Eastport Me.

STEWART.

84 Florence M. V., 11: 14: 86, convulsions, æ. 0–0–8, b. Ded., of Isaac & Florence M. A., Ire., Spain.

178 Jane (Deveman), 3: 1: 64, heart disease, æ. 27–10–25, b. Scotland, of Peter & Mary, Scot., do.

63 Joseph, 7: 30: 84, heart disease, æ. 79–0–21, b. Nova Scotia, of James & Ann, England, do.

67 William, 6: 18: 83, heart disease, æ. 75-0-0, b. N. B., of James & ——, N. S., England.

STILL.

27 (D. at Westboro) Frank E., 2: 20: 88. membraneous croup, æ. 10 3-14, b. Ded., of J. Edwin & Emma A., Ded., N. H.

36 Martha A. (Childs), 5: 13: 78. disease of liver, æ. 68-4-0, b. Hallowell Me.

STIMSON.

24 Charlotte G. (Lealand), 3: 26: 78, cancer, æ. 44-9-19, b. Phila., of Charles & Charlotte F., Needham, Milford.

44 Edward, 6: 12: 78, effusion of water on brain, æ. 54-7-14. b. Ded., of Jeremy & Hopestill G., Hopkinton, Milford.

138 (D. at N. Y. City) Eliz'h B., 1: 5: 87, entonitis, æ. 1-2-16, b. Ded., of Fred J. & Eliz'h B. (Abbott), Ded., Boston.

27 Hopestill (Godfrey), 9: 12: 56, apoplexy. æ. 66-9-0, b. Milford, of Benjamin & ——.

48 Jeremy, 8:12: 69, old age, æ. 86-0-0, b. Hopkinton.

8 Mary P. (Parker), 1: 5: 75, old age, æ. 87-5-10, b. Norton, of Daniel & Abby, Norton, do.

STOCKBRIDGE.

202 Emma F., 10: 23: 64, ——, æ. 14-1-2, b. Ded., of A. P. & Maria.

STOCKWELL.

51 Mary E., 5: 25: 81, diphtheria, æ. 7-1-16, b. Spencer, of Geo. H. & Ruth P., Sutton, Grafton.

STOLLS.

26 Chas., 4: 22: 83, tubercular meningitis, æ. 2-1-16, b. Dedham, of Robert & Bertha, Germ , do.

STONE.

25 ——, 11: 9: 46, consumption, æ. 25-0-0.

88 ——, 12: 26: 73, stillborn, b. Dedham, of Joseph & Lillies B., Charlestown, Waterford Pa.

13 Eliph't, 2: 5: 86, dropsy, æ. 72-8-26, b. Hubbardston, of Samuel & Hannah (Davenport), Hubbardston. Dorch.

95 Geo. W., 8: 11: 57, hydrophobia, æ. 59-0-0.

87 Lillies B. (Blakie), 12: 26: 73, convulsions, æ. 28-9-0, b. York N. Y., of Alex'r & Nancy K., N. S., ——.

205 Mary S. (Staples), 12: 10: 64, consumption, æ. 64-0 13, b. S. Brookfield, of Elias & Jedida K., Mendon, Edgartown.

STOOMES.

87 (D. at Boston) Henry, 9: 5: 89, typhoid fever, æ. 40-0-0. b. England, of & ——, England, do.

STORM.

81 Antony, 9: 23: 69, cholera infantum, æ. 0-5-11, b. Dedham, of Nicholas & Emma, Germ., Eng.

STORRS.

93 Chas. O., 12: 23: 86, cerebellar hemorrhage, æ. 45-0-16, b. Willington Ct., of Royal O. & Lora Lee, Mansfield Ct., Vernon Ct.

49 Frances L., 5: 4: 89, diphtheria, æ. 2-5-14, b. Dudley, of Fred'k R. & Amelia C. (Videto), Webster, N. S.

15 Lora, 2: 15: 83, difficult birth, æ. 0-0-1, b. Ded., of Fred R. & Amelia C., Webster, N. S.

8 Lucy (Ingalls), 1: 22: 87, paralysis, æ. 79-9-11, b. Pomfret Ct., of Ephraim & Lucy, Pomfret, do.

41 Mary L., 4: 19: 89, diphtheria, æ. 4-9-29, b. Worcester, of Fred'k R. & Amelia C. (Videto), Webster, N. S.

72 Royal O., 5: 25: 88, heart dis., æ. 72-8-19, b. Mansfield Ct., of Royal & Eunice Freeman, Mansfield Ct., do.

STOWE.

50 Chas., 7: 5: 86, cystitis chronic, æ. 83-1-22, b. Ded., of Timothy & Prudence, Ded., do.

23 John, 2: 19: 73, paralysis, æ. 75-0-0, b. Mass., of —— & ——, Mass., U. S.

102 Mary (McGrath), 11: 30: 85, hypertrophy of heart, æ. 74-0-0, b. Ire., of Henry & ——, Ire., ——.

12 (D. at Newton), Sally, 1: 1: 60, dropsy, æ. 75-8-0.

26 William, 4: 11: 55, dis. of liver, æ. 51-5-0, b. Natick, of —— & Hepzibah.

STOWELL.

123 Abby C. (Dean), 5: 21: 67, lung fever, æ. 49-11-14, b. Fitchburg, of Francis & Hannah, Ded., Canton.

STRONG.

2 ——, 7: 3: 46, throat distemper, æ. 3-0-0, b. Ded., of John & ——.

32 Oberan, 9: 17: 50, whooping cough, æ. 2-1-0, b. Ded., of Wm. & Ellen.

STUFFENBURG.

16 Willie M., 3: 13: 55, consumption, æ. 48-2-21, b. Germ.

STURTEVANT.

34 George W., 1: 11: 63, croup, æ. 18-0-0. [soldier.]

SULDUSKI.

104 Eliza (Gilman), 11: 19: 84, heart dis., æ. 55-0-0, b. Ire., of Richard & Kate, Ire., do.

SULKOSKI.

166 John, 1: 3: 64, lung fever, æ. 70-0-0, b. Poland, of —— & ——, Poland, do.

78 Julia (Welch), 10: 31: 68, inflam. of lungs, æ. 63-0-0, b. Ire., of John & Julia, Ire., do.

SULLIVAN. (See also O'Sullivan.)

90 ——, 2: 25: 68, stillborn, b. Ded., of Daniel & Julia, Ire., do.

25 ——, 6: 7: 70, stillborn, b. Ded., d. of Daniel & Julia, Ire., do.

90 ——, 4: 1: 71, stillborn, b. Ded., s. of Daniel & Julia, Ire., do.

26 Bridget (Williams), 3: 25: 82, homicide, æ. 50-0-0, b. Ireland, of John & Ann, Ire., do.

19 Catharine, 6: 17: 50, colic, æ. 3-5-20, b. Ded., of John & Cath. S.

18 Catharine (Shields), 2: 17: 57, consumption, æ. 39-0-0, b. Ire., of Marcus & Catharine.

32 Catherine (Nolan), 12: 30: 63, childbirth, æ. 32-0-0, b. Ire., of Wm. & Catharine, ——, Ire.

8 Catharine (Sullivan), 5:17:66, childbirth, æ. 37-0-0, b. Ire., of John & Bridget.
4 Dan, 2:26:67, liver comp., æ. 0-0-25, b. Ded., of Cornel's & Hannah, Ire.,do.
18 Daniel F., 2:10:89, progressive paralysis, æ. 58-6-26, b. Canada, of Daniel F. & Margaret (Ferguson), Canada, do.
12 Ellen (Moriarty), 10:28:70, heart dis., æ. 80-0-0, b. Ire., of —— & ——. Ire., do.
18 Ellen (Church), 3:4:87, bronchial pneumonia, æ. 78-0-0, b. Ire., of Thos. & Mary, Ire., do.
41 Harriet, 5:22:87, heart dis., æ. 68-0-0, b. Scot.
20 James, 1:21:60, heart dis., æ. 14-6-0, b. Ded., of John & Cath., Ire., do.
96 Jeremiah, 3:23:66, infantile debility, æ. 0-0-1, b. Ded., of Cornelius & Julia.
14 Johanna, 2:18:85, old age, æ. 70-0-0, b. Ire., of Timothy & Ellen, Ire., do.
19 John, 3:1:57, consumption, æ. 36-0-0, b. Ire, of James & Catherine.
41 John, 6:17:61, ——, æ. 8-2-29, b. Ded., of David & Ellen, Ire., do.
16 John, 1:16:69, scarlet fever, æ. 1-0-0, b. Ded., of David & Ellen, Ire., do.
77 John, 7:30:69, inflam. of bowels, æ. 50-1-13, b. Ded., of John & Ellen, Ire.,do.
30 John 2d, 4:1:82, suicide, æ. 40-0-0, b. Ire., of David & Julia. Ire., do.
105 Kate (Post), w. of Michael, 10:11:89, fractured femur, æ. 82-0-0, b. Ire., of George & Ann (Chambers), Ire., do.
42 Mary A., 6:19:61, ——, æ. 5-10-17, b. Ded., of David & Ellen, Ire., do.
45 Mary E., 5:28:70, membraneous laryngitis, æ. 8-8-27, b. Ded., of John & Mary, Ire., do.
108 Michael H., 5:23:64, fall from cars, æ. 29-0-17, b. Ire., of Michael & Ellen.
22 Timothy, 3:28:55, old age, æ. 95-0-0, b. Ire.
39 Timothy F., 5:19:70, diphtheria, æ. 9-0-0, b. Ded., of Jerry & Margaret. Ire., do.

SULLY.
64 (D. at Quincy) Horace H., 7:23:68, drowned, æ. 16-0-0, b. ——, of John &——.

SUMNER.
8 Alice (Pollard), 1:24:57, consumption, æ. 74-2-7, b. Hubbardston, of Joel & Mary.
90 Anna A. (Chickering) 8:28:65, paralysis, æ. 53-7-3, b. Ded., of Jabez & Deborah T. F.
104 Chas., 10:10:89, heart dis., æ. 66-7-9, b. Ded., of Seth & Alice (Pollard), Stoughton, Hubbardston.
85 Edgar N., 9:27:55, cholera infantum, æ. 1-5-13, b. Ded., of Nathaniel N. & Mary E.
32 Edward, 4:18:85, suicide, æ. 74-8-15, b. Rox., of Edw. & Johanna, Roxbury, Shrewsbury.
112 Edwin S. P., 10:14:62, slow fever, æ. 2-9-5, b. Ded., of N. N. & Mary E., Ded., Sharon.
41 Francis W., 9:9:59, consumption, æ. 33-28-0, b. Ded., of Seth & Alice.
78 George, 6:17:54, consumption, æ. 30-2-24, b. Ded., of Jabez & Rebecca.
119 Harold A., 10:28:88, meningitis, æ. 2-1-25.
94 Jos. 2d, 3:8:59, consumption, æ. 28-5-4, b. Ded., of Nath'l & Betsy.
22 Mirick P., 2:19:89, paralysis, æ. 81-0-24, b. Ded., of Seth & Alice (Pollard), Stoughton, Hubbardston.

120 Moses, 12 : 6 : 62, congestion of brain, æ. 62-4-13, b. Ded., of Nath'l & Eliz'h,
     Ded., do.
49 Philenia A. (Tucker), 6 : 5 : 82, apoplexy, æ. 62-1-3, b. Raymond N. H., of
     Bernard & Sally, Raymond N. H., do.
68 Rebecca (Ellis), 11 : 9 : 61, erysipelas, æ. 67-5-0, b. Ded., of John & Rebecca.
85 Susan A. (Weatherbee), 3 : 10 : 58, consumption, æ. 51-0-0, b. Ded., of David
     & Lucy.
55 Thomas, 1 : 19 : 56, old age, æ. 76-0-0, b. Ded., of George & Margaret.
138 Wm., 12 : 31 : 67, consumption, æ. 71-6-0, b. Ded., of Wm. & Mary, Ded., do.
74 Wm. R., 9 : 1 : 60, typhus fever, æ. 59-10-22, b. Boston, of Sam'l & Martha S.,
     Boston, do.

SUTHERLAND.
102 Frank, 5 : 13 : 64, small pox, æ. ——. [soldier.]

SUTTON.
76 Enoch, 12 : 25 : 53, dis. of lungs, æ. 47-5-0, b. Cohasset, of John & Alice.
150 Fred'k, 12 : 10 : 64, chronic diarrhoea, æ. 19-0-0, b. Eng. [soldier.]
78 Wm., 9 : 17 : 78, consumption, æ. 32-0-0.

SWALLOW.
115 Eliz'h (Noonan), w. of Thos., 11-5-89, R. R. accident, æ. 38-0-0, b. Ire., of
     Michael & Mary, Ire., do.

SWANMAN.
27 Cort, 6 : 14 : 58, intemperance, æ. 48-0-0, b. Germany.

SWARTZ.
59 Chas. F., 7 : 26 : 84, hepatitis, æ. 22-2-29, b. Ded., of Chas. & Jane Barnes,
     Holland, do.

SWEENEY.
44 Catharine (Martin), 5 : 26 : 85, heart dis., æ. 35-0-0, b. Ire., of Dennis &
     Ellen, Ire., do.
25 Daniel, 5 : 8 : 62, lung fever, æ. 1-2-8, b. Ded., of Jere'h & Julia C.
97 Edw., 10 : 6 : 82, enteritis, æ. 1-1-2, b. Hyde Park, of Jere'h & Julia, Ire., do.
79 John R., 8 : 6 : 90, whooping cough, æ. 0-5-22, b. Ded., of Jere'h & Katie V.
     (Hartnett), Ire., Ded.
88 Julia, 11 : 12 : 72, teething, æ. 1-0-9, b. Ded., of Jerry & Julia, Ire., do.
89 Julia Morrissey), w. of Edw., 9 : 3 : 87, inflam. of bowels, æ. 60-0-0, b. Ire., of
     Jere'h & Kate, Ire., do.
62 Kate, 8 : 5 : 79, teething, æ. 0-6-0, b. Ded., of Jere'h & Julia, Ire., do.
69 Nellie, 8 : 19 : 80, dis. of heart, æ. 7-5-0, b. Ded., of Jerry & Julia, Ire., do.
28 Richard, 1 : 16 : 68, burned, æ. 1-0-26, b. Ded., of Jere'h & Julia.
65 Richard, 9 : 6 : 73, drowned, æ. 5-4-0, b. Ded., of Jere'h & Julia, Ire., do.

SWETT.
72 (D. at Braintree) Abigail (Mason), w. of Edw. S., 6 : 29 : 89, brain exhaustion,
     æ. 91-2-12, b. Ded., of Thaddeus & Anna (Smith), Ded., do.
78 John S., 10 : 6 : 72, consumption, æ. 61-5-26, b. Boston, of Samuel & Eliz'h D.,
     Boston, do.
61 Laura P., 10 : 6 : 55, dysentery, æ. 2-3-0, b. Ded., of John & Nancy N.

11 Polly (Wood), 3: 12: 56, cancer, æ. 78-0-0, b. Rutland, of Jos. & Dolly.
75 Samuel, 12: 25: 53, liver comp., æ. 79-4-11, b. Boston, of —— & Eliz'h.

SYLVESTER.
29 Sarah H. (Loring), 7: 29: 54, consumption, æ. 44-0-2, b. North Yarmouth, of Jacob & Olive.

TAFT.
100 Adelaide S., 12: 10: 67, consumption of bowels, æ. 2-10-19, b. Ded., of Josephus G. & Ann E., Ded., Sandlake N. Y.
126 (D. at Hull Gut) Arthur G., 9: 22: 89, drowning, æ. 20-2-11, b. Ded., of Josephus G. & Anne E. (Shaw), Ded., [Sandlake] N. Y.
83 Eliza H. (Flagg), 8: 10: 63, hip comp., æ. 65-0-0.
10 Ezra W., 2: 8: 85, carcinoma of liver and stomach, æ. 84-5-13, b. Uxbridge, of Fred'k & Abigail (Wood), Uxbridge, Upton.
110 Fred A., 6: 19: 64, congestion of brain, æ. 0-7-0, b. Ded., of Fred. A. & Cornelia S., Ded., do.
76 Harris A., 9: 14: 84, typhoid dysentery, æ. 8-2-16, b. Ded., of Cornelius A. & Maria L., Ded., do.
9 Mary A., 2: 7: 56, heart dis., æ. 52-5-0, b. Uxbridge, of Fred'k & Abigail.

TALBOT.
180 Abby B. (Dean), 3: 11: 64, consumption, æ. 20-11-28, b. Ded., of Ebenezer & Mary, Ded., do.
132 Albert M., 4: 12: 65, dis. of brain, æ. 2-9-5, b. Ded., of Geo. & Caroline A.
104 Alvin, 9: 18: 66, phthisis, æ. 43-10-21, b. Medfield, of Joel & Hannah.
203 Caroline A. (Robbertson), 12: 5: 64, consumption, æ. 32-1-15, b. Bromfield Me., of James & Betsey, Eaton N. H., *Buxton Me.
74 Catharine, 6: 29: 69, dropsy, æ. 68-1-8, b. Ded., of Enoch & Catharine, Stoughton, Newport R. I.
54 Eliz., 1: 18: 50, consumption, æ. 33-0-0, b. Ded., of Joel & ——.
46 John, 8: 5: 60, congenital, æ. 0-0-1, b. Ded., of John C. & Frances G., Ded., Sharon.
126 John C., 10: 12: 61, slow fever, æ. 33-6-2, b. Ded., of Enoch & Mary S., Ded., Greenfield N. H.
10 Josiah, 5: 5: 47, dis. of heart, æ. ——.
47 Sarah A., 2: 2: 56, croup, æ. 1-6-25, b. Ded., of Ebenezer F. & Eliz'h.
36 Sylvester W., 4: 20: 47, consumption, æ. 49-0-0, b. Dighton.
81 Sylvester W., 8: 30: 49, dysentery, æ. 3-0-0, b. Ded., of Sylvester W. & Margaret G.

TALPEY.
50 Octavius, 1: 26: 52, consumption, æ. 33-0-0.

TAMTAS.
65 (D. at Boston) Daniel A., 4: 4: 54, ——, æ. 42-9-0.

TAPLEY.
44 ——, 8: 17: 53, cholera infantum, æ. 0-0-10, b. Ded., s. of Wm. T. & Martha M.
52 Edgar A., 6: 20: 79, typhoid fever, æ. 28-4-20, b. Ded., of Wm. T. & Martha A., Surrey Me., Monmouth Me.

82 Martha A. (Hale), 9:9:85, dis. of brain, æ. 64-8-10, b. Monmouth Me., of Tappan & Eliz'h, N. H., Me.

TARBELL.
112 Rachel T., 11: 1: 89, diphtheria, æ. 3-1-0, b. Ded., of John F. & Annie (Tower), Pepperell, Boston.

TARNEY.
18 Bridget, 3: 23: 55, consumption, æ. 21-0-0, b. Ire., of Thos. & Rafferty.

TAY.
64 Patrick, 8: 16: 72, marasmus, æ. 1-0-25, b. Bridgewater, of Patrick H. & Sabina, Ire., do.

TAYLOR.
11 Chas. E., 2:20:55, dis. of brain, æ. 1-4-17, b. Randolph,of Chas. A. & Fanny S.

84 Edw., 8: 17: 90, premature birth, b. Ded., of Wm. A. & Theresa (Mulkern), Eng., W. Rox.

78 Emma J., 10: 13: 60, consumption, æ. 0-4-27, b. Waltham, of Abram & Betty, Eng., do.

85 Jas., 8: 29: 89, exhaustion, æ. 0-0-2, b. Ded., of Geo. & Josephine, Framingham, Boston.

59 Mary, 8: 16: 86, convulsions, æ. 0-1-4, b. Ded., of Wm. A. & Theresa, Eng., W. Rox.

41 Sadie J., 4: 24: 83, hereditary syphilis, æ. 1-10-0, b. Ded., of Chas. H. & Cora, Framingham, Boston.

TEBBETTS. (See also Tibbetts.)
91 Sarah A., 12:22:60, fits, æ. 0-4-0, b. Ded., of Wm. R. & Eliza, Rome Me., Ireland.

TEMPERLY, TIMPELLY.
53 Catherine F., 7:17:66, cholera infantum, æ. 0-3-11, b. Ded., of Temperly & Catherine.

34 Ellen, 3: 9: 88, erysipelas, æ. 20-0-0, b. Ire., of Patrick & Bridget (Quigley), Ire., do.

66 Thos., 8: 19: 64, cholera infantum, æ. 1-6-0, b. Ded., of Thos. & Catharine.

TEMPLE.
68 John P., 8: 27: 64, cholera infantum, æ. 0-4-17, b. Ded., of Thos. & Catharine, Ire., do.

THAYER.
99 Addie C., 4: 9: 62, scarlet fever, æ. 2-3-1, b. Ded., of Tyler & Lucy E., Mendon, Vt.

27 Clara, 1: 30: 64, infantile dis., æ. 0-0-18, b. Ded., of John H. B. & Mary S. W., Ded., do.

95 Elisha S., 8: 18: 60, cholera infantum, æ. 0-2-0, b. Ded., of John H. B. & Mary S. W., Ded., do.

10 Hannah E. (Stearns), 4: 10: 50, inflam. of bowels, æ. 22-3-0, b. Boston, of Levi & Naomi.

8 Horace, 2: 2: 64, brain fever, æ. 19-0-0. [soldier.]

79 Jennie A., 2: 5: 59, dis. of head, æ. 1-5-0, b. Ded., of Tyler & Lucy E.

38 John H. B., 4:27:73, consumption, æ. 42-10-18, b. Ded., of Elisha & Nancy, Braintree, Canton.

57 Nancy, 5:30:51, consumption. æ. 25-0-0, b. Ded.

4 Nancy (Billings), 2:5:54, lung fever, æ. 59-3-24, b. Canton, of Peter & Rebecca.

198 Norris A., 8:31:64, congestion of lungs, æ. 2-3-10, b. Ded., of Tyler & Lucy, Mendon, Andover Vt.

THISSELL.

7 Wm. H., 3:9:50, lung fever, æ. 2-7-19, b. Ded., of Wm. & Pamelia.

THOMAS.

10 Charlotte E., 1:8:75, consumption, æ. 27-4-15, b. Weymouth, of John W. & Sarah B., Weymouth, do.

23 Edmund, 3:2:74, found dead, æ. 63-8-9, b. Weymouth, of Andrew & ——.

26 Edmund S., 3:22:76, empyema, æ. 6-1-18, b. Ded., of Edmund & Mary E., Weymouth, Ded.

42 Erasmus, 3:14:65, chronic diarrhoea, æ. 27-0-0, b. Wales. [soldier.]

14 Evan, 2:7:79, pneumonia, æ. 46-0-0, b. Tremont Me.

92 John W., 7:20:88, progressive paralysis, æ. 73-3-19, b. Weymouth, of Andrew & Polly, Weymouth, do.

30 John W., 3:4:90, hemorrhage, æ. 40-3-20, b. Weymouth, of John W. & Sarah (Blanchard), Weymouth, do.

THOMPSON.

32 ——, 9:29:47, fever, æ. 25-0-0, b. ——, s. of —— & ——.

32 Caroline (Phillips), 1:16:67, diphtheria, æ. 23-0-0, b. Ded., of Geo. & Mary, Germ., do.

41 Chas., 6:1:78, valv. dis. of heart, æ. 60-0-0, b. W. Rox., of Harry & Eliza.

14 Eliza, 5:4:51, apoplexy, æ. 73-0-0, b. Needham.

127 Harriet, 11:17:88, apoplexy, æ. 85-1-0, b. Ded., of Charles H. & Eliza, U. S., do.

3 Jacob, 6:27:48, fever sore, æ. 38-0-0.

63 Jacob N., 8:15:72, cholera infantum, æ. 0-9-6, b. Cambridge, of Jacob & Kate S., Germ., do.

48 John, 3:12:64, pneumonia, æ. 32-0-0, b. Hatfield, of Stephen & Margaret, ——, Albany N. Y. [soldier.]

32 John, 3:3:88, pneumonia, æ. 76-0-0, b. Scot., of Jas. & Elwood, Scot., do.

2 Lucy A., 1:26:48, consumption, æ. 20-0-0.

30 Lydia J. (Lewis), 6:4:60, anaemia, æ. 17-7-17, b. Brunswick Me., of Levi & Margaret, Brunswick Me., do.

49 Mary (Sideself), 6:7:75, paralysis, æ. 61-0-0, b. Scotland, of Adam & ——, Scot., do.

96 Mary J., 6:22:55, consumption, æ. 23-0-0, b. Ded., of Joshua P. & Caroline.

43 Oliver T., 4:20:80, cancer, æ. 66-3-26, b. W. Rox., of Chas. H. & Eliza, U.S., do.

85 Robert, 8:2:54, dis. of kidneys, æ. 67-0-0.

123 Roxa M., w. of Edwin, 12:31:48, consumption, æ. 35-0-0, b. Dedham.

63 Sally (Rhoades), 10:15:56, apoplectic fits, æ. 65-0-0, b. Dedham, of Eliph't & Mercy.

89 Samuel, 11:20:60, congestion of brain, æ. 70-0-0, b. S. Berwick Me.

38 Sumner, 2:15:65, small pox, æ. 31-0-0. [soldier.]

67 Wm. C., 7:10:65, cholera infantum, æ. 0-7-10, b. Ded., of John K. & Eliz'h.

THORNTON.

9 Caroline A., 3:17:54, lung fever, æ. 1-2-18, b. Ded., of Thos. A. & Ann.

68 Eliza J., 8:2:81, cholera infantum, æ. 0-5-0, b. Boston, of Henry H. & Philippa C., Ireland, England.

50 Jane (Apthorp), 9:12:58, chronic diarrhoea, æ. 59-11-42, b. Chatham, of William & Elizabeth.

109 Joseph, 12:29:70, old age, æ. 77-0-0, b. Prov. R. I., of Jos. & Jane, Prov. R. I., Cape Cod.

68 Joseph A., 9:15:86, Bright's dis., æ. 48-7-19, b. Ded., of Joseph A. & Jane, Cranston R. I., Chatham.

52 Jos. S., 3:10:70, brain dis., æ. 3-8-10, b. Ded., of Jos. & Margaret, Ded., Boston.

70 Josephine, 9:10:72, cholera infantum, æ. 0-7-5, b. Ded., of Jos. & Margaret, Ded., Boston.

65 Lizzie, 8:29:77, cholera infantum, æ. 1-1-0, b. Ded., of Jos. & Margaret, Ded., Boston.

THORP.

80 Albert G., 10:9:77, typhoid fever, æ. 17-11-9, b. N. Y. City, of Albert G. & Mary L., Rahway N. J., Phila. Pa.

4 Sarah A. (Morse), 1:6:87, Bright's dis., æ. 74-4-21, b. Fairfax Me., of Elisha & Eliz'h.

THURSTON.

86 Chas. O., 11:16:69, congestion of bowels, æ. 6-0 29, b. Boscawen N. Y., of Nath'l & Hannah C., Boscawen N. Y., do.

TIBBETTS. (*See also Tibbetts.*)

62 ——, 3:13:62, infantile dis., æ. 0-0-1, b. Ded., d. of Jos. N. & Mary C., Lee N. H., Boston.

62 ——, 3:13:62, infantile dis., æ. 0-0-1, b. Ded., d. of Jos. N. & Mary C., Lee N. H., Boston.

59 Eliza A. H. (Gilmor), 4:8:56, lung fever, æ. 33-0-0, b. Wrentham, of Marcus & Eliza.

TILDEN.

83 Atherton, 8:18:87, pneumonitis, æ. 86-0-16, b. Marshfield, of Atherton & Mary W. (Magoun), Marshfield, Pembroke.

44 Mary, 10:15:44, fever, æ. 28-0-0.

133 (D. at Boston) Myron, 3:14:87, Bussey Bridge accident, æ. 29-11-14, b. Bridgewater, of Lucius & Margaret, Barnstable, Mansfield.

TILLSON.

22 Lucinda (Whiton), 4:20:53, consumption, æ. 83-0-0, b. Halifax, of Samuel & Susanna.

TIMMINS.

2 Martin, 6:9:57, consumption, æ. 62-0-0, b. Ireland.

TIMPER.

45 (D. at Taunton) Isabella, w. of Louis J., 4:21:89. phthisis, æ. 38-2-18, b. Eng., of —— & ——, Germ., Scot.

113 Louis J., 10: 28: 87, consumption, æ. 43-6-0, b. Germ., of Christian J. & Willhelm, Germ., do.

130 Louisa, 12: 16: 87, inanition, æ. 0-4-9, b. Ded., of Louis J. & Isabel, Germ., England.

TISDALE.

89 ——, 8: 18: 55, canker, æ. ——, b. Ded., — of Josiah & Susan P.

58 Ellen, 6: 17: 52, brain fever, æ. 0-2-0, b. Ded., of Aurelius & ——.

10 (D. at Taunton) Jas. W., 1: 11: 90, phthisis, æ. 63-5-22, b. Walpole, of Peter & Sally (Swan), Walpole, Ded.

17 Nancy (Cole), 4: 13: 62, dropsy of heart, æ. 44-6-28, b. Rehoboth, of Otis & ——.

TITCOMB.

38 Ann M. (Delesdernier), 12: 5: 56, typhoid fever, æ. 79-0-8, b. N. S., of Peter F. & Eliz'h.

24 Edward E., 7: 21: 52, congestion of brain, æ. 49-1-14, b. Portland Me., of Pearson & Ann M.

72 Pearson, 12 : 11 : 55, paralysis, æ. 78-4-9, b. Newburyport. of John & Elizabeth.

1 Sarah A. (Montague), w. of Edw., 1: 24: 50, consumption, æ. 43-8-14.b. Ded., of Wm. & Jane.

TITUS, TYTUS.

14 Virgil, 1: 9: 69, paralysis, æ. 69-3-0, b. Attleboro, of Peter & Mary, Paw-tucket R. I., do.

72 William R., 7: 9: 63. dropsy, æ. 27-0-0, b. Penn. [soldier.]

TOBIN.

89 Abbie, 2: 54: 68, scarlatina, æ. 2-7-0, b. Dedham, of John & Catharine, Ireland, do.

122 Catharine, 5: 14: 67, infantile disease, æ. 0-0-2, b. Ded., of John & Catharine, Ireland, do.

74 Ellen, 7: 4: 64, small pox, æ. 2-0-0, b. Ire., of Thos. & Ellen.

71 Margaret, 5: 19: 69, congestion of brain, æ. 0-11-0, b. Ded., of William & Nancy, Ire., do.

149 William, 10: 22: 65, dysentery, æ. 0-9-15, b. Ded., of William & Nancy.

TOLTON.

50 Lucy (Read), 8: 10: 77, congestion of brain, æ. 55-0-0, b. Md., of Daniel & Katie, Va., do.

TOMPKINS.

55 Alexander A., 6: 7: 81, phthisis pulmonalis, æ. 28-0-0, b. Georgia, of Alex'r & Amy, Ga., do.

TOOMEY, TWOMEY.

103 Catherine (Hines), 12: 18: 78, heart disease, æ. 66-0-0, b. Ire., of John & Ireland, do.

54 Fred. P., 6: 24: 75, scarlet fever, æ. 0-11-0, b. Ded., of Patrick & Ellen, Ireland, do.

78 Joseph, 11: 29: 71, slow fever, æ. 4-1-9, b. Dedham, of Patrick & Ellen, Ireland, do.

13 Timothy, 2: 13: 64, scarlet fever, æ. 2-0-0, b. Ded., of Patrick & Ellen.

69 William, 8: 18: 76, consumption, æ. 75-0-0, b. Ireland, of John & Margaret, Ireland, do.

TOWER.

70 Francis, 9: 1: 78, dysentery, æ. 4-0-3, b. Ded., of Charles E. & Margaret M., Ded., N. S.

40 Hollis, 10: 9: 52, congestion of brain, æ. 1-7-23, b. Ded., of Luther W. & Fanny E.

117 Mary (Ware), 11: 20: 65, inflammation of stomach, æ. 67-0-0, b. Needham, of Nath'l & Mary.

29 William F., 3: 22: 69, water on brain, æ. 0-2-4, b. Ded., of Charles E. & Margaret M., Ded., N. S.

TOWLE.

6 Mary (Jones), 4: 19: 66, bronchitis, æ. 70-0-0, b. Ire.

TOWNE.

57 Ann R. (Newell), 6: 4: 65, childbed fever, æ. 32-2-4, b. Dover, of Jesse & Permelia.

45 John H., 8: 3: 49, dysentery, æ. 2-0-0, b. Ded., of John & ——.

TRACY.

116 Alice F., 11: 12: 87, broncho pneumonia, æ. 1-0-14, b. Ded., of Andrew & Theresa, Ire., N. B.

17 Andrew, 2: 28: 60, croup, æ. 3-8-9, b. Ded., of Jas. & Mary.

102 Catherine (Rogers), 12: 12: 76, old age, æ. 75-0-0, b. Ire., of Andrew & Grace, Ire., do.

49 Mary, 9: 12: 58, consumption, æ. 46-0-0, b. Ireland.

23 Mary A., 9: 11: 67, cholera infantum, æ. 0-5-26, b. Ded., of Patrick & Catharine, Ire., do.

76 Patrick, 8: 28: 79, dysentery, æ. 78-8-0, b. Ire., of Owen & ——.

97 Thos., 8: 1: 61, drowning, æ. 33-0-0, b. Ire., of Peter & Rose, Ire.,do. [soldier.]

TRAMPLEASURE, TROMPLEASURE.

79 ——, 8: 5: 67, ——, æ. 0-0-1, b. Ded., s. of Thos. & *Helen, *Glenham N. Y., Woonsocket R. I.

97 Eliz'h,11: 18: 85, angina pectoris, æ. 81-1-17, b. Eng., of —— & ——, Eng.,do.

TREEN.

10 Joseph, 8: 22: 70, cholera morbus, æ. 65-4-26, b. N. S., of Henry & Lillace, Dover N. Y., do.

TREFREY.

92 Adda L., 10: 18: 63, inflam. of bowels, æ. 11-9-9, b. Ded., of James & Mary S., Marblehead, Canton.

16 James, 10: 7: 48, old age, æ. 79-0-0.

42 Mary S. (Shepard), 2: 8: 71, consumption, æ. 46-6-21, b. Canton, of Nathaniel & ——.

TRESCOTT.
50 Elijah, 12: 18: 59, paralysis, æ. 76-9-0, b. Dorch., of Ebenezer & Deborah.

TRIPP.
26 Phebe S., 3: 13: 49, croup, æ. 8-9-0.

TROWBRIDGE.
81 Agnes, 9: 5: 81, dysentery, æ. 2-5-21, b. Hudson, of Augustus S. & Ada, Canada, Ledyard Ct.

TUBBS.
69 Benj. II.. 6: 29: 54, cholera, æ. 49-0-0, b. Hanson.
61 Elvira, 9: 17: 51, dropsy, æ. 17-0-0, b. Ded., of Benj. II. & ——.
68 Shepard, 3: 4: 58, consumption, æ. 21-0-0, b. Ded., of Benj. & U. A. L.

TUCKER.
9 ——, 8: 26: 46, dysentery, æ. 2-0-0, b. ——, of Geo. & ——.
82 ——, 10: 1: 78, stillborn, b. Ded., s. of Thos. & Eliza, Eng., Vt.
30 Eliz. (Mann), w. of Geo. W., 11: 21: 44, puerperal fever, æ. 21-0-0, b. Ded., of Herman & ——.
118 Geo. E., 10: 24: 88, heart dis., æ. 68-7-25, b. Canton, of Nathan & Hannah, Canton, Randolph.
170 (D. at Chicago, Ill.) J. J., 1: 13: 64, consumption, æ. 36-3-7, b. Halifax Vt., s. of Amos & Amanda, Halifax Vt., do.
148 Mary (Orne), 10: 19: 65, apoplexy, æ. 71-0-4, b. Corinth Vt., of Jos. & Jane.
27 Rebecca, 9: 9: 50, liver comp., æ. 70-5-9, b. Milton, of Jeremiah & Rebecca.
31 Susanna (Ford), 4: 24: 57, old age, æ. 90-1-21, b. Milton, of Nathan & Waitstill.

TULLY.
4 Eliza (Kernan), 1: 8: 85, pneumonia, æ. 75-0-0, b. Ire., of Matthew & Eliza (Lynch), Ire., do.
51 Martin, 9: 20: 53, dis. of brain, æ. 0-10-0, b. Ded., of Martin & Mary.
5 Michael, 1: 21: 84, old age, æ. 98-0-0, b. Ire., of John & Sibbel, Ire., do.

TUPPER.
85 Ellen (Carey), 11: 19: 86, phthisis, æ. 25-0-0, b. N. S., of Geo. & Eliza, N. S., do.
56 Ellen, 6: 18: 87, bronchial pneumonia, æ. 0-8-0, b. Ded., of William F. & Ellen, N. S., do.
44 Eva G., 5: 23: 87, measles, æ. 1-10-0, b. Ded., of Wm F. & Ellen, N. S., do.

TURLEY.
33 John, 3: 10: 66, consumption, æ. 42-0-0, b. Ire.

TURNER.
36 Amelia L., 8: 26: 59, cholera infantum, æ. 0-10-0, b. Ded., of Francis & Amelia B.
24 Betsey, 5: 8: 65, old age, æ. 75-0-0, b. Ded., of Hezekiah & Betsy.
155 Chas. W., 4: 11: 64, consumption, æ. 42-6-0, b. Ded., of Hezekiah & Sally P., Dedham, Boston.
64 Edward, 7: 20: 75, tuberculosis, æ. 29-6-0, b. Boston, of Otis & H. Cordelia, Boston, do.
68 Eliza, 8: 28: 68, ——, æ. 40-0-0, b. Ire.
68 Francis E., 11: 5: 55, scarlet rash, æ. 0-3-13, b. Ded., of Francis & Amelia B.

161 Henrietta E., 6: 26: 64, congestion, æ. 7-2-0, b. Boston, of Charles & Henrietta G.

  4 Hezekiah, 1: 3: 64, heart dis., æ. 72-0-0, b. Ded., of Hezek'h & ——, Ded., ——.

— (D. at Canton) Jemima (Draper), w. of James, 9: 14: 56, ——, æ. 99-10-7, b. Ded., of Eben'r & Sybil.

34 Lavina R. (Richards), w. of Francis, 9: 7: 52, consumption, æ. 23-4-15, b. Newport N. H., of Leonard & Phebe.

60 Martha R., 9: 10: 51, fever, æ. 13-0-0, b. Ded., of Sabin & ——.

  5 Mary A. (Taubert), 1: 15: 82, carcinoma of stomach, æ, 60-10-0, b. N. Y. City, of —— & Mary A. (Fairlee), Germ., N. Y. City.

64 Sabin, 10: 24: 51, fever, æ. 55-0-0, b. Ded.

66 Sally (Pratt), 4: 25: 54, consumption, æ. 54-0-0, b. Rox., of Wm. & Ruth.

57 Silence, 2: 12: 47, ——, æ. 78-0-0.

TUTTLE.

38 ——, 2: 11: 75, stillborn, b. Ded., of Levi F. & Rosa B., Dedham, W. Thomaston Maine.

106 Clara T., 11: 26: 81, consumption, æ. 18-8-0, b. Manlius N. Y., of Martin W. & Lucy M., Bennington Vt., Geddes N. Y.

114 Clarissa A., 11: 10: 87, premature birth, æ. 0-0-1, b. Ded., of Julius H. & Jennie C., Littleton, Ded.

33 Eleanor M., 3: 22: 89, pneumonia, æ. 0-11-25, b. Boston, of Geo. S. & Mary Stillman, Hamden Ct., Wethersfield Ct.

167 Lizzie F., 1: 6: 64, consumption, æ. 1-4-0, b. Roxbury, of John & Eliza J., Madbury N. H., Canton.

  7 Malvina W. (Twaing), 1: 29: 58, consumption, 25-4-0, b. Orleans, of Eben'r & Mary.

77 Martin W., 9: 17: 76, peritonitis, æ. 44-0-2, b. Little Falls N. Y., of Chauncey & Dolly W., North Haven Ct., Deerfield.

87 Mary E., 2: 5: 57, consumption, æ. 0-10-28, b. Ded., of Levi & Louisa.

39 Rosa B. (Achorn), 2: 14: 75, uræmia, æ. 24-11-2, b. Rockland Me., of Henry & Harriot A., Waldoboro Me., ——.

TWITCHELL.

79 Chas. W., 11: 9: 86, empyema, æ. 17-3-12, b. Ashland, of Edw. P. & Emma F., Sherborn, Attica N. Y.

TWOMEY. (*See also Toomey.*)

TYLER.

21 Clara B. A., 3: 27: 61, meningitis, æ. 9-11-8, b. Dedham, of David & Clarissa B.

39 David, 2: 1: 67, dropsy on brain, æ. 52-0-7, b. Richmond N. H., of Moses & Abigail, Richmond N. H., Royalston.

TYNAN.

94 Margaret, 10: 20: 79, diphtheria, æ. 6-0-0, b. Ded., of John & Hanora, Ire., do.

TYRRELL.

65 Catharine M., 8: 10: 64, dysentery, æ. 2-2-4, b. Manchester N. H., of Eugene & Margaret.

UPHAM.
65 Eliza (Pratt), 11:9:74, old age, æ. 71 1-25, b. Ludlow Vt., of Abel & Betsy.
26 Enos, 6:13:45, fever, æ. 61-0-0, b. Canton.

UPTON.
31 Theodore J., 9:26:47, erysipelas, æ. 35-0-0.

VAN BRUNT.
28 Gershom G., 12:17:63, pleurisy, æ. 63-0-0, b. N. J., of Nicholas & Eliz'h (Jaques).

VAN HOEVENBURG.
112 Clara A. (Hill), 12:12:82, pulmonary consumption, æ. 28-4-12, b. Ded., of Geo. W. & Martha A., R. I., Me.

VAN WAGENEN.
91 Willis, 8:5:83, peritonitis, æ. 44-5-16, b. Sharon N. Y., of Rynier & Emily Goodyear, Sharon N. Y., Lawyersville N. Y.

VARNEY.
23 ——, 10:28:46, bowel comp., æ. 3-0-0, b. Ded., of Gideon & ——.
27 Mahala, w. of Gideon, 11:26:46, fever, æ. 26-0-0.
17 Mahala, 11:2:48, fever, æ. 28-0-0.

VAUGHN.
8 Edward, 2:14:58, dropsy, æ. 47-0-0.

VENNER.
88 Margaret E., 10:13:84, marasmus, æ. 0-3-0, b. Ded., of Walter & Eliz'h H., Richmond Me., Lowell.

VINCENT.
65 ——, 5:6:88, stillborn, b. Ded., s. of Chas. & Mary J., Eng., Ire.

VOGEL.
72 Henry W., 6:13:62, teething, æ. 1-6-24, b. Ded., of Albert & Martha, Germ., do.
23 Wm., 5:10:58, lung fever, æ. 3-11-0, b. Ded., of Jos. & Flora.

VOLK.
91 Adeline S., 10:14:84, cholera infantum, æ. 0-10-15, b. Ded., of Leo & Celia, Boston, do.
30 Rosa L., 3:19:81, drowning, æ. 2-7-13, b. Boston, of Leo & Celia, Boston, do.

VOLLERT.
20 Amelia B., 2:24:84, eclampsia infantum, æ. 0-4-9, b. Ded., of Wm. E. & Susannah (Selcer), Germ., do.
56 Eva (Bayer), 7:29:77, consumption, æ. 29-3-0, b. Germ., of Kasper & Mary, Germ., do.

VOSE.
50 Abby H., 8:26:55, dropsy, æ. 32-0-0, b. Boston, of Thos. & Abigail G.
72 Abigail G. (Howe), 10:17:73, congestion of lungs, æ. 83-6-28, b. Dorch., of Geo. & Mary A., Dorch., do.
101 Henry M., 12:2:80, suicide, æ. 50-0-0, b. Boston, of Thos. & Abigail, Dorch., do.

WADE.

38 Edw., 4: 17: 89, pneumonia, æ. 55-0-0, b. Ire., of —— & ——, Ire., do.

36 Mary (Coughlin), 4: 22: 76, paralysis, æ. 54-0-0, b. Ire., of Daniel & Catherine, Ire., do.

96 Wm., 8: 7: 88, consumption, æ. 78-0-0, b. Ire., of John & Margaret, Ire., do.

WAGNER.

84 Frank, 10: 5: 69, croup, æ. 4-1-23, b. Ded., of John P. & Josephine, France, Germ.

125 (D. at Boston) Jacob I., 4: 16: 89, diphtheria, æ. 5-3-8, b. Boston, of Jacob & Amelia, Germ., Boston.

85 Josephine, 10: 11: 69, cholera infantum, æ. 0-2-0, b. Ded., of John P. & Josephine, France, Germ.

105 Peter, 8: 17: 62, drowning, æ. 33-0- 0, b. Luxemburgh, of Tean & Maria.

WAITE.

74 Chas., 10: 31: 71, marasmus, æ. 0-5-11, b. Bridgewater, of James II. L. & Lucinda, Deerfield, Bernardston.

68 Mary E. (Adams), 7: 12: 65, consumption, æ. 27-2-4, b. Attleboro, of Charles & Mary J.

WAKEFIELD.

13 Jane (Perry), [w. of Thomas L.], 3: 25: 53, [heart disease], æ. 32-[10]-3, b. Brookline Vt., of Wm. & Lura.

85 Thos. L., 6: 21: 88, disease of spinal cord and brain, æ. 71-0-6, b. Londonderry Vt., of Thos. B. & Submit (Ross), Londonderry Vt., Ashby.

WALDRON.

131 Alfred, 12: 2: 88, convulsions, æ. 0-0-1, b. Ded., of James G. & Hannah J. (Guiney), Warrensburg N. Y., Cambridge.

WALES.

93 Alfred D. S., 10: 11: 79, diphtheria, æ. 3-1-7, b. Ded., of Samuel M. & Abbie S., Roxbury Vt., Williamstown Vt.

67 Martha A. (Sigourney), 7: 30: 75, dis. of bowels, æ. 63-9-15, b. Boston, of Daniel & Martha W.

95 Mary (Eastman), w. of Asa B., 9: 29: 89, brain disease, æ. 84-11-3, b. Dresden Me., of Hubbard & Mary, Dresden Me., do.

71 Nason G., 8: 11: 85, gastro-enteritis, æ. 2-9-17, b. Ded., of Samuel M. & Abbie S., Roxbury Vt., Williamstown Vt.

35 Samuel, 6: 19: 60, consumption, æ. 56-8-25, b. Stoughton, of Samuel & Mary C., Braintree, Milton.

WALKER.

93 John P., 8: 1: 88, meningitis, æ. 0-0-24, b. Ded., of John & Nettie H., N. Y. City, Quincy.

WALL, WALLS.

55 Catharine (Quinn), 11: 23: 69, old age, æ. 79-5-0, b. Ireland, of —— & Ellen, Ireland, do.

50 Wm., 11: 7: 59, inflam. of lung, æ. 65-0-0, b. Ire.

64 William, 7: 24: 85, tetanus infantum, æ. 0-0-3, b. Ded., of William & Mary, Nova Scotia, Dedham.

WALLACE.
48 Stephen B., 6: 26: 84, phthisis, æ. 26-8 12, b. Petersburg Va., of Dennis & Emily J., Petersburg Va., Raleigh Va.

WALLEY, WOLLEY.
68 Edward J., 7: 7: 90, consumption, æ. 30-5-8, b. Ded., of James & Julia (Brogan), Canada, Ire.
58 Edwin A., 7: 10: 79, softening of brain, æ. 57-8-0, b. Sterling, of Jos. & ——.
97 Eliz'h J., 12: 25: 72, lung fever, æ. 62-2-25, b. Ire., of —— & ——, Ire., do.
85 James H., 9: 4: 49, whooping cough, æ. 0-10-1, b. Ded., of Jas. & ——.
47 Jos. H., 5: 14: 81, cerebro spinal meningitis, æ. 5-11-0, b. Ded., of Howell M. & Mary A., Boston, Ire.
45 Sarah J., 5: 4: 81, consumption, æ. 30-10-14, b. Dedham, of James & Ellen, Canada, Ire.

WALSH (*See Welch*).

WALTON.
134 (D. at Boston) Eliz'h A., 3: 14: 87, Bussey Bridge accident, æ. 16-3-14, b. Needham, of Jacob & Kate, Andover, Boston.
14 Frank L., 1: 27: 89, heart disease, æ. 10-0-7, b. Taunton, of Jacob & Kate E. (McLaughlin), S. Andover, Boston.
56 Horace C., 5: 29: 83, convulsions, æ. 1-1-1, b. Ded., of Horace M. & Lydia E. Salem, Gloucester.

WARD.
39 Abigail (Mixer), 6: 1: 86, consumption, æ. 69-7-19, b. Boston, of Charles & Mehitable (Smith), N. H., Ded.
83 Caleb B., 11: 13: 86, consumption, æ. 73-6-9, b. Ashburnham, of Jacob & Sarah W., Ashburnham, do.
86 Edw. L., 9: 30: 85, oedem of lungs, æ. 62-2-0, b. Wilton Me., of William & Sarah, Framingham Me., Newburyport.
72 Nellie M., 9: 6: 78, enteritis, æ. 0-6-20, b. Ded., of Frank H. & Emma J., Ded., Newport N. H.

WARDLE.
70 George H., 8: 10: 71, ——, æ. 1-6-1, b. Ded., of Robert L. & Mary C., Woodstock N. Y., Boston.
37 Mabel, 2: 9: 68, inflam. of bowels, æ. 0-0-7, b. Ded., of Robert L. & Mary C., N. Y., Boston.
23 Mary S. (Van Buren), 3: 15: 82, acute Bright's dis., æ. 80-2-15, b. Phila. Pa., of Abraham & Mary S.

WARE.
68 Huldah G. (Hale), 8: 14: 76, hepatitis, æ. 68-0-0.

WARNOCK.
83 Mary F., 8: 4: 65, dysentery, æ. 4-0-0, b. Ded., of Samuel L. & Sarah J.
77 Samuel L., 7: 25: 65, dysentery, æ. 37-0-0, b. Ire., of Richard & Ann.

WARREN.
21 Eliz'h, 2: 8: 73, disease of brain, æ. 72-5-18, b. Leominster, of Oliver & Mary, Littleton, Boston.

69 Erank, 9: 7: 68, cholera infantum, æ. 0-1-0, b. Ded., of Frank & Delia, Salem, Rox.

44 Mary (Walker), 7: 5: 61, old age, æ. 91-10-23, b. Boston, of Wm. & Mary, Boston, do.

WASHBURN.

49 Lydia (Shaw), 4: 28: 68, consumption, æ. 72-8-23, b. Raynham, of Jona. & Lydia G.

WASHINGTON.

53 Geo., 3: 25: 64, erysipelas, æ. ——. [soldier.]

WATERS.

74 Hannah L. (Leland), 10: 24: 73, paralysis, æ. 59-10-26, b. Ded., of Richard & Hannah, Ded., do.

WEATHERBEE.

36 Alfred F., 4: 9: 75, brain fever, æ. 36-3-0, b. Ded., of Comfort & Unity F., Ded., Walpole.

35 Comfort, 3: 31: 75, lung fever, æ. 62-4-11, b. Ded., of Comfort & Reney, Ded., do.

40 David, 10: 9: 46, old age, æ. 83-0-0, b. Ded.

8 Edw., 1: 29: 80, diphtheria, æ. 37-10-29, b. Ded., of Jesse & Louisa, Ded., do.

19 Fred'k, 2: 6: 80, diphtheria, æ. 34-11-6, b. Ded., of Jesse & Louisa, Ded., do.

30 James, 5: 8: 55, ——, æ. 70-0-0.

62 Jesse, 7: 13: 75, obstruction of bowels, æ. 59-5-0, b. Ded., of Jabez & Sally, Ded., do.

26 John E., 3: 20: 84, chronic hepatitis, æ. 65-10-11, b. Ded., of Jabez & Sally, Ded., do.

37 John H., 4: 26: 73, scarlet fever, æ. 7-11-9, b. Ded., of John E. & Harriet A., Ded., do.

121 Louis F., 4: 27: 63, croup, æ. 3-1-24, b. Ded., of Franklin D. & Maria S., Ded., do.

13 Lucy (Morse), 3: 22: 54, old age, æ. 88-9-20, b. Ded., of Ezra & Mary.

51 Lucy M. (Gay), 10: 17: 54, paralysis, æ. 29-6-17, b. Walpole, of Benj. N. & Nancy.

52 Millicent, 10: 20: 50, old age, æ. 93-0-0.

97 Milly C. (Richards), 11: 18: 78, asthma, æ. 70-11-18, b. Ded., of Moses & Hannah, Ded., do.

119 Moses, 11: 21: 65, lung fever, æ. 64-3-10, b. Ded., of Comfort & Reney.

—— (D. at Boston) Reuben, 1: 27: 52, palsy, æ. 52-0-0, b. Ded., of Comfort & Irene.

8 Sally (Endicott), w. of Jabez, 3: 31: 52, lung fever, æ. 59-11-12, b. Ded., of John & Mary.

127 Susannah, 10: 14: 61, old age, æ. 92-10-15, b. Ded., of Benj. & Susanna, Ded., Westmoreland.

35 Unity, w. of Comfort, 3: 31: 47, fever, æ. 25-0-0, b. Walpole.

WEATHERS.

7 Jennie E., 1: 19: 82, diphtheria, æ. 4-0-3, b. Ded., of Isaac W. & Martha M., N. S., Ded.

WEBB.

54 Betsey J. (Barnard), 9:5:55, typhoid fever, æ. 28-0-0, b. Charlemont, of John & Almira.

56 Edna J., 9:8:55, consumption, æ. 0-0-13, b. Ded., of John & Betsy J.

55 Edw. A., 9:6:55, consumption, æ. 0-0-11, b. Ded., of John & Betsy J.

48 Harriet A., 2:25:56, typhoid fever, æ. 19-11-0, b. Ded., of Moses E. & Rebecca.

19 Richard, 8:1:47, fits, æ. 76-0-0.

90 Willard, 10:14:85, paralysis, æ. 75-0-0, b. Ded., of Ebenezer & Lucy, Ded, Shirley.

WEBBER, WEBER.

37 Abba S. C. (Smith), 4:28:82, old age, æ. 81-8-0, b. Sharon, of Israel & Zipora, Sharon, do.

89 Alfred, 9:18:67, cholera morbus, æ. 4-0-7, b. Ded., of Anthony & Johanna, Germ., do.

34 Arnold R., 5:11:87, heart dis., æ. 0-6-7, b. Ded., of Rudolph & Bertha S., Switz., Ded.

100 Chas., 12:6:78, inflam. of bowels, æ. 13-8-0, b. Ded., of Antonio & Johanna, Germ., do.

29 Everett E., 4:20:74, lung fever, æ. 1-2-20, b. Ded., of Emerson B. & Christy, Ware N. H., P. E. I.

76 Jason L., 8:30:75, consumption, æ. 62-0-16, b. Kennebunk Me.

108 Johanna (Runge), w. of Anton, 10:10:87, paralysis, æ. 49-7-21, b. Germ., of Chas. & Johanna, Germ., do.

WEBSTER.

32 Benj. M. E., 2:5:64, scarlatina, æ. 5-7-0, b. Buffalo N. Y., of John E. & Phebe A., N. Y. City, Camden Me.

34 John E., 2:11:64, croup, æ. 1-8-0, b. Ded., of John E. & Phebe, N. Y. City, Camden Me.

36 Lula B., 2:12:64, scarlet fever, æ. 3-7-18, b. Charlestown, of John E. & Phebe H., N. Y. City, Camden Me.

82 Wm. G., 7:29:83, drowning, æ. 48-0-0, b. N. S., of Geo. & Katharine.

WEED.

36 Chas., 2:12:65, siphilis, æ. 23-0-0, b. New Canaan Ct. [soldier.]

88 T. Clement, 10:22:78, heart dis., æ. 28-2-0, b. Malden, of Otis H. & Susan, N. Brookfield, Boston.

WEEKS.

11 Edw. F., 2:2:57, lung fever, æ. 0-0-7, b. Ded., of Luther C. & Martha.

60 Emma F., 10:4:55, lung fever, æ. 1-8-14, b. Ded., of Luther C. & Martha.

6 Frances E. (Fish), w. of Henry W., 1:4:88, dis. of liver, æ. 41-8-23, b. Ded., of Jas. F. & Frances M., Salem, Ded.

10 Geo. L., 2:13:51, lung fever, æ. 4-10-4, b. Stoneham, of Luther C. & Martha.

30 Henrietta, 7:30:54, cholera infantum, æ. 0-6-10, b. Ded., of Luther C. & Martha.

61 Luther C., 7:26:84, softening of brain, æ. 65-9-8, b. Danville Vt., of Peaslee & Sally, ——, Canterbury Vt.

11 Nathan E., 2: 17: 51, lung fever, æ. 2-0-7, b. Stoneham, of Luther C. & Martha.

13 Nathan O., 1: 10: 73, consumption, æ. 30-2-2, b. Ded., of Luther C. & Martha, Danville Vt., Andover.

WELCH, WALSH, WELSH.

46 Catharine (Kilroy), 9: 30: 59, cholera morbus, æ. 42-1-0, b. Ire., of Thomas & Elizabeth.

4 Ellen C., 1: 23: 83, scarlatina, æ. 6-1-24, b. Ded., of William B. & Fanny L., N. B., Boston.

129 Frank, 11: 7: 67, consumption, æ. 24-3-0, b. Ire., of Patrick & Mary, Ire, do.

19 Henry, 1: 6: 64, apoplexy, æ. 40-0-0, b. Ireland. [soldier.]

8 John, 7: 7: 70, stoppage, æ. 0-2-19, b. Ded., of Stephen & Johanna, Ire., do.

12 John, 7: 26: 71, old age, æ. 81-3-0, b. Ire., of Thos. & Mary, Ire., do.

16 Lulu F., 2: 19: 83, nephritis, æ. 3-10-17, b. Ded., of Wm. B. & Fanny L., N. B., Boston.

72 Maggie, 8: 20: 85, marasmus, æ. 0-5-29, b. Dedham, of Thomas F. & Mary A., West Roxbury, Ireland.

80 Mary, 9: 19: 80, marasmus, æ. 0-1-21, b. Boston, of Wm. & Mary, Ire., do.

30 Mary A. (Welch), 4: 11: 85, pneumonia, æ. 29-1-7, b. Ire., of Jas. & Mary, Ireland, do.

91 (D. at Maynard) Mary E. (Wilton), 9: 10: 89, ——, æ. 38-4-0, b. Ireland, of Patrick & ——, Ireland, do.

104 Patrick, 10: 31: 68, dis. of lungs, æ. 28-11-15, b. Ireland, of Patrick & Mary W., Ireland, do.

82 Sarah (Anderson), 9: 18: 79, paralysis, æ. 75-3-7, b. Ireland, of Archibald & Sarah, Ireland, do.

76 Stephen, 12: 10: 64, convulsions, æ. 0-0-16, b. Ded., of Stephen & Hannah.

183 Thos., 3: 25: 64, consumption, æ. 33-0-0, b. Ire., of Patrick & Charlotte, Ireland, do.

20 Wm., 2: 9: 80, accident, æ. 29-3-0, b. Ireland, of Jas. & Mary, Ire., do.

WELD.

75 (D. at Wareham) Lathrop M., 8: 18: 82, drowning, æ. 8-0-23, b. Ded., of Stephen M. & Eloise R., West Roxbury, Milton.

89 Maria L. (Davis), w. of Jos. R., 8: 28: 90, anæmia, æ. 70-3-28, b. W. Rox., of Joel & Sophia R. (Mayo), Roxbury, do.

100 Stephen M., 9: 17: 87, heart dis., æ. 17-0-15, b. Ded., of Stephen M. & Eloise R., West Roxbury, Milton.

WELLER.

68 Florentine (Schwedler), 8: 5: 70, dysentery, æ. 23-3-3, b. Germ., of Charles A. & Caroline, Germany, do.

WENNER.

20 Millie C., 10: 30: 68, scarlet fever, æ. 7-6-0, b. Dedham.

WENTWORTH.

46 Alonzo B., 4: 21: 80, meningitis, æ. 1-7-27, b. Ded., of Alonzo B. & Isabella S. (Goodwin), Somersworth N. H., Sanford Me.

10 Charles H., 6: 21: 44, drowned, æ. 5-0-0.

87 Chas. M., 11: 27: 86, R. R. accident, æ. 34-9-27, b. Berwick Me., of Chas. H.
& Sarah H., Rochester N. H., Somersworth N. H.

83 (D. at Anchorage, Ky.) Eben C., 9: 8: 84, killed on railroad, æ. 39-10-0, b.
Sanford Me., of Amasa & Susan W., Me., do.

77 Katherine, 8: 30: 79, teething, æ. 0-6-9, b. Ded., of Alonzo B. & Isabel,
Somersworth N. H., Sanford Me.

98 Susan W. (Norrell), 3: 27: 86, heart dis., æ. 73-9-26, b. Sanford Me., of Eben'r
& Mary (Hill), York Me., Sanford Me.

WESLEY.

44 Hattie, 3: 31: 88, dis. of brain, æ. 40-0-0, b. Southern State.

WEST.

65 Wm., 7: 20: 81, consumption, æ. 35-1-8, b. N. S., of Wm. & Margaret
(McDorman), N. S., do.

WETMORE.

75 Eunice M., 10: 27: 86, diphtheria, æ. 2-7-7, b. Ded., of Jas. H. & Eliz'h A.,
N. B., Boston.

27 Marion L., 5: 4: 83, premature birth, æ. 0-0-8, b. Ded., of Howard F. &
Lucy H., Boston, Cambridge.

WETZEL.

62 Aloysius, 10: 26: 74, typhoid fever, æ. 15-3-6, b. France, of Jos. & H. Mary,
France, do.

55 Joseph, 6: 19: 80, consumption, æ. 55-4-0, b. Germ, of Joseph & Ruttler,
Germ., do.

73 Mary A. (Studer), w. of Jos., 5: 26: 88, dyspepsia, æ. 68-8-7, b. Germ., of
Diveer & Hase (Derventz), Germ., do.

57 Mary T., 10: 8: 74, typhoid fever, æ. 21-0-8, b. France, of Joseph & H Mary,
France, do.

WEYSSER.

89 Charles, 12: 8: 62, pleurisy, æ. 23-9-9. [soldier]

WHEATON.

41 Jesse, 11: 5: 47, old age, æ. 84-0-0, b. Dighton.

89 Mary (McKenna), 11: 14: 72, abscess, æ 22-6-23, b. on the sea, of Mic'rel &
Sarah, Ire., do.

WHEELER.

43 Chas. C., 5: 10: 80, premature birth, æ. 0-0-20, b. Ded., of Andrew A. &
Sarah, ——, N. B.

WHEELOCK.

48 Mary A., 6: 17: 50, consumption, æ. 34-0-0, b. Wrentham, of Elijah & ——.

110 Mary E , 10: 10: 62, diphtheria, æ. 11-5-18, b. Ded., of Elijah & Mary C.

WHINPEY.

39 John, 4: 28: 73, accidental, æ. 40-5-12, b. Eng., of Edw. & Eliz'h, Eng., do.

WHITCOMB.

75 Levi, 11: 21: 59, varioloid, æ. 62 0-0.

92 Walter H., 4: 18: 68, consumption, æ. 19-4-0, b. Boston, of Samuel P. &
Mary E., Dresden Me., Boston.

WHITE.

45 ——, 3: 9: 46, consumption, æ. 23-0-0, b. Ded., d. of Jason & ——.

45 ——. 12: 23: 47, consumption, æ. 1-0-0, b. ——, d. of —— & ——.

16 Alexander, 5: 22: 75, typhoid fever, æ. 16-2-5, b. Canada, of Alex'r & Philemopoton, Canada, do.

39 Asa, 7: 1: 49, consumption, æ. 45-0-0.

83 Frank E., 9: 17: 55, cholera infantum, æ. 0-8-11, b. Ded., of Nelson & Eliza M.

43 Georgiana, 7: 23: 57, inflam. of bowels, æ. 11-0-21, b. Boston, of John II. & Emeline.

91 Grace E., 9: 20: 82, teething, æ. 1-0-1, b. Ded., of John W. & Annie E., Ded., Boston.

17 Grace E., 1: 23: 90, phthisis pulmonalis, æ. 28-2-0, b. Sharon, of David L. & Martha A. (Ingraham), Foxboro, Franconia N. H.

20 Harry N., 2: 10: 88, whooping cough, æ. 0-5-21. b. Boston, of Henry C. & Ellen M., Fitzwilliam N. H., Boston.

73 Henry W., 7: 30: 87, cholera infantum, æ. 0-10-6, b. Ded., of J. Warren & Annie E., Ded., Boston.

117 Henry W., 10: 22: 88, marasmus, æ. 1-0-1, b. Ded., of John W. & Annie Eliz'h, Ded., Boston.

36 James, 4: 9: 73, old age, æ. 67-0-0, b. Ire., of —— & ——, Ire., do.

51 John, 2: 1: 52, lung fever, æ. 64-0-0, b. Concord, of John & Sally.

17 John, 3: 16: 79, heart dis., æ. 72-5-15, b. Ire., of —— & Eliz'h, Ire., do.

30 John II., 3: 26: 69, consumption, æ. 56-1-19, b. Boston, of Henry & Sally, Boston, do.

90 Lilly R., 10: 1: 79, cholera morbus, æ. 7-1-17, b. Ded., of John II. & Ruth, Eng., do.

43 Lois, 3: 23: 50, old age, æ. 76-0-9, b. Ded.

68 Lucy (Stowell), 11: 30: 53, old age, æ. 80-0-0, b. Ded., of Isaac & Mary.

77 Martha A. R., 6: 25: 54, dysentery, æ. 6-7-14, b. Walpole, of Reuben & Catharine A.

28 Mary (Conlon), 4: 21: 78, cancer, æ. 48-0-0, b. Ire., of Robert & Margaret, Ireland, do.

47 Mary II. (Holmes), 6: 8: 73, paralysis, æ. 72-8-16, b. Dorch., of Issachar & Mary C., Canton, Rox.

101 Michael G., 12: 18: 63, lung fever, æ. 58-0-0, b. Ireland, of Thomas & Mary, Ireland, do.

54 Prudence, 8: —: 47, ——, æ. 75-0-0.

70 Ralph D., 10: 9: 86, consumption, æ. 0-1-21. b. Boston. of Erwin C. & Isabella, Sharon, Canada.

50 Roxana, 2: 16: 51, fit, æ. 61-0-0, b. York.

84 Susan R., 8: 21: 63, scarlet fever, æ. 4-1-0, b. New York, of John & Eliz'h, Ireland, do.

53 Walter, 8: 25: 57, disease of heart, æ. 66-0-26, b. Mansfield, of Isaac & Mehitable.

76 Warren A., 10: 24: 68, lung fever, æ. 2-2-3, b. Ded., of Walter E. & Fidelia, Ded., Colerain.

87 Wilfred E., 9: 30: 85, cyanosis, æ. 1-3-22, b. Ded., of J. Warren & Annie E., Dedham, Boston.
34 William H., 4: 19: 76, pneumonia, æ. 0-6-24, b. Bridgewater, of —— & Lydia, ——, N. S.

WHITELAW.
130 Agnes S., 12: 1: 88, exhaustion, æ. 50-5-16, b. Bangor Me., of William S. & Abby S., Scotland, Hallowell Me.

WHITING.
93 Abigail, 10: 7: 67, paralysis, æ. 73-0-0, b. Ded., of Nathaniel & Elizabeth, Dedham, do.
70 Avery, 9: 30: 75, malignant dis. of liver, æ. 65-3-0, b. Francestown N. H., of Nath'l & Betsey R., Francestown N. H., Ded.
15 Chas., 5: 27: 50, heart comp., æ. 40-8-20, b. Ded., of Hezekiah & Mary.
73 Chas. F., 6: 25: 62, disease of brain, æ. 30-10-9, b. Ded., of William & Margaret H., Ded., Pelham N. H.
153 Eaton, 12: 6: 63, old age, æ. 81-0-28, b. Ded., of Nath'l & [Eliz'h]. Ded., do.
15 Edward, 10: —: 44, lung fever, æ. 79-0-0, b. Ded.
27 Edwin, 4: 7: 85, disease of kidneys, æ. 79-2-11, b. Ded., of Abner & Locada, Dedham. do.
22 Eliz'h (Fuller), 6: 17: 44, consumption, æ. 78-0-0, b. Ded.
56 Eliz'h (Crehore), 1: 3: 62, consumption, æ. 58-6-26, b. Milton, of John S. & Hannah, Milton, Sterling.
19 Eliz'h P., 6: 18: 52, rheumatism, æ. 56-0-0, b. Ded., of Joshua & Mary.
104 Elizabeth T., 11: 10: 79, dropsy, æ. 68 7-43, b. Ded., of Isaac & Thankful. Dedham, Barre.
113 Emma J., 12: 26: 82, pulmonary consumption, æ. 19-11-19, b. Ded., of Moses & Ann J., Ded., Milton.
116 Eunity (Fales), 12: 9: 83, paralysis, æ. 87-4-0, b. Ded., of Aaron C. & Hephzibah (Everett), Walpole, Ded.
18 George, 2: 20: 61, lung fever, æ. 69-6-5, b. Ded., of Moses & Sarah.
21 Harriet R. (Crehore), 3: 19: 77, paralysis, æ. 71-0-3, b. Milton, of John S. & Hannah L., Dorch., Canton.
78 Hattie E., 6: 28: 74, rheumatic fever, æ. 24-5-0, b. Wrentham, of Otis & Levina, Wrentham, do.
52 Hezekiah, 5: 31: 76, Bright's disease, æ. 71-6-0, b. Ded., of Hezekiah & Mary G., Dedham, Walpole.
46 Horace, 5: 12: 81, pneumonia, æ. 63-3-0, b. Ded., of Peltiah & Polly, Bellingham, Francestown N. H.
84 Ira, 5: —: 53, mortification, æ. ——, b. Ded.
59 Isaac, 8: 17: 66, old age, æ. 89-11-7, b. Ded., of Moses & Sarah.
26 Isaac, 1: 18: 72, heart dis., æ. 52-11-10, b. Ded., of Isaac & Thankful G. W., Ded., Barre.
88 Joseph, 6: 8: 64, dis. of heart, æ. 59-5-8, b. Ded., of Hezekiah & Mary, Ded., Walpole.
39 Lemuel, 11: 13: 51, cancer, æ. 78-8-17, b. Ded., of Moses & Sarah.
30 Loacada (Whiting), w. of Abner, 8: 28: 52, cancer, æ. 85-10 1, b. Ded., of Joshua & Eliz'h.

70 Lucinda F. (French), 10: 6: 62, lung fever, æ. 73-9-21, b. Billerica, of Samuel
& Eunice.

35 Mary (Guild), 3: 17: 66, old age, æ. 93-8-27, b. Walpole, of Jos. & Olive.

61 Mattie E., 6: 21: 81, consumption, æ. 25-0-6, b. Ded., of Moses & Ann J.
Ded., Milton.

5 Molly (Gay), 2: 15: 53, consumption, æ. 72-3-0, b. Ded., of Ebenezer & Martha.

36 Moses, 5: 13: 87, apoplexy, æ. 67-1-25, b. Ded., of Peletia & Polly, Franklin,
Francestown.

47 Olive (Smith), 4: 29: 79, old age, æ. 73-0-0, b. Fitzwilliam N. H., of Eben'r &
Olive C.

94 Otis B., 5: 1: 55, consumption, æ. 31-0-0, b. Franklin.

137 Pelatiah, 10: 6: 64, old age, æ. 86-10-24, b. Franklin, of Pelatiah & Hannah,
Ded., Franklin.

53 Polly, 9: 22: 74, old age, æ. 85-3-0, b. Francestown N. H.

14 Rebecca F. (Dean), 2: 12: 82, paralysis, æ. 70-2-24, b. Ded., of Jos. & Hannah,
Ded., do.

28 Sally, 12: 29: 46, fever, æ. 52-0-0, of Moses & ——.

37 Samuel, 4: 5: 45, chronic bowel complaint, æ. 33-0-0, b. Ded., of Hezekiah &
[Mary.]

71 Samuel G., 7: 25: 87, old age, æ. 84-10-18, b. Ded., of Calvin & Eliz'h, Ded., do.

24 Thankful G. W. (Wilson), w. of Isaac, 4: 9: 55, inflam. of liver, æ. 73-0-3, b,
Barre, of Wm. & Alice.

123 Walter H., 11: 2: 88, consumption, æ. 27-3-4, b. Ded., of Moses & Ann J.
(Beal), Ded., Milton.

3 Wm. B., 1: 15: 83, pneumonia, æ. 23-5-26, b. Ded., of Moses & Ann J., Ded.,
Milton.

WHITMARSH.

40 Geo. S., 2: 24: 65, scarlatina, æ. 18-0-0, b. Dighton. [soldier.]

WHITNEY.

45 Emily A., 10: 11: 44, fever, æ. 24-0-0, b. Natick.

49 Mary M., 4: 24: 90, enlargement of liver, æ. 92-0-20, b. Athol, of Jabez &
Eliz'h (Mayo), Rox., Warwick.

58 Sarah W., 9: 23: 55, dis. of brain, æ. 1-4-0, b. Ded., of Samuel S. & Sarah.

41 Samuel S., 7: 15: 44, cholera infantum, æ. 0-10-0.

37 Samuel S., 6: 39: 55, paralysis, æ. 40-5-25, b. Natick, of Geo. & Esther.

WHITTEMORE.

34 Nath R., 10: 5: 47, consumption, æ. 35-0-0.

WHITTEN.

23 Anna C., 4: 13: 86, consumption, æ. 19-1-23, b. Boston, of Abram & Ruth
(Warren), Plymouth, do.

24 Ewing B., 2: 24: 89, consumption, æ. 28-0-29, b. Plymouth, of Abel & Ruth
W. (Sears), Plymouth, do.

WHITTIER.

20 Harriet E. (Rice), 11: 14: 65 ——, æ. 47-0-0, b. Andover, of Daniel &
Maria G.

WIDEMAN.

2 Metus, 1: 20: 62, consumption, æ. 32-0-0, b. Germ.

WIGGIN.

109 Catharine L., 10: 24: 61, consumption, æ. 85-9-14, b. Dedham, of Rufus & Hannah, Dedham, do.

9 Herbert A., 2: 22: 58, cholera infantum. æ. 0-11-16, b. Dedham, of Andrew & Catharine L.

87 Russell B., 4: 11: 64, croup, æ. 1-10-0, b. Dedham, of Thomas & Charlotte S., Dedham, do.

35 Thomas, 8: 5: 58, disease of brain, æ. 60-4-0, b. Stratton N. H., of Aaron & Rachel C.

2 Thos., 1: 3: 79, anaemia, æ. 49-0-0, b. Harmony Me., of Thos. & Eliza W., Stratham N. H., Washington D. C.

WIGHT.

57 Abigail R. (Richardson), w. of Aaron W., 6: 23: 87, old age, æ. 96-6-19, b. Holliston, of Ezra & Jemima Lovell, Medway, do.

5 Charles S., 1: 7: 87, consumption, æ. 52-9-10, b. Ded., of Joel & Rebecca M., Dedham, do.

34 Danforth P., 6: 8: 74, paralysis, æ. 82-4-0, b. Ded., of Ebenezer & Catharine, Ded., do.

72 Danforth P., 7: 12: 90, septicaemia, æ. 50-1-9, b. N. Y. City, of Edw. & Caroline (Stimson), Dedham, do.

43 Ebenezer, 2: 14: 71, apoplexy, æ. 67-4-6, b. Ded., of Ebenezer & Catharine, Dedham, do.

68 Eliza W. (Fuller), w. of Eleazer, 5: 13: 88, pneumonia, æ. 80-2-23, b. Walpole, of Joel & Susan (Billings), ——, Canton.

32 Hannah (Fisher), w. of Jason, 9: 4: 51, dropsy, æ. 62-1-25, b. Sharon, of Jacob & Sarah.

60 Joel, 8: 20: 86, ossification of valves of heart, æ. 80-0-11, b. Ded., of Joel & Lois (Holmes), Ded., do.

7 (D. at Walpole) John K., 1: 6: 88, shock, æ. 69-5-16, b. Medway, of Aaron W. & Abigail R., Medway, Holliston.

19 Joseph, 1: 30: 73, consumption, æ. 65-6-5, b. Ded., of Andrew & Margaret, Dedham, Canton.

49 Margaret (Cobbett), w. of Andrew, 8: 24: 55, consumption, æ. 72-6-10, b. Ded., of Philip & Mary.

70 Nath'l, 9: 3: 48, consumption, æ. 38-0-0.

38 Rebecca (Gay), 4: 26: 80, pleuro pneumonia, æ. 69-7-17, b. Ded., of Joel & Polly, N. H., Ded.

94 Samuel, 7: 23: 57, consumption, æ. 71-0-0, b. Ded., of Jos. & — —.

165 Samuel, 11: 8: 64, palsy, æ. 87-0-0, b. Ded., of Joseph & Miriam L., Dedham, Stoughton.

54 Sophia D. (Churchill), 7: 5: 72, heart disease, æ. 34-11-27, b. Fairlee Vt., of Wm. L. & Minerva, Fairlee Vt., do.

86 Susan E., 9: 4: 89, consumption, æ. 22-11-22, b. Windsor Vt., of Chas. S. & Sophia D. (Churchill), Ded., Post Mills Vt.

86 Wm. C., 9: 5: 82, constriction of bowel, æ. 19-0-2. b. Meriden Ct, of Charles S. & Sophia D., Ded., W. Fairlee Vt.

WILBUR.
5 Lucy M. (Gay), w. of Augustus, 1: 8: 89, typhoid pneumonia, æ. 44-5-21, b. Boston, of Albert & Calista B. (Knight), Ded., Coventry Vt.

WILD.
38 ——, 10: 12: 47, ——, æ. ——.
21 Minna (Fischer), w. of Emil, 6: 29: 52, consumption, æ. 25-6-0, b. Germany, of Bernard & Maria.
25 Minna, 8: 8: 52, bowel comp., æ. 0-3-10, b. Ded., of Emil & Minna.

WILKINSON.
12 Ezra, 2: 6: 82, paralysis, æ. 80-11-23, b. Wrentham, of Noah & Hannah (Cheever), Wrentham, do.
14 Ware, 9: 1: 71, mortification of foot, æ. 70-4-2, b. Townsend Vt., of Elijah & ——, Weston, Townsend.

WILLARD.
58 Sally. 7: 27: 48, old age, æ. 74-0-0.
35 William, 11: 19: 71, old age, æ. 79-0-0, b. Eng.

WILLCUTT.
17 Elbridge G., 2: 15: 85, endocarditis, æ. 4-1-8, b. Ded., of Lyman D. & Merriel L., Cohasset, do.

WILLIAMS.
57 ——, 12: 31: 47, consumption, æ. 35-0-0.
10 Charles, 2: 21: 76, pneumonia, æ. 39-0-0, b. Fayville.
136 Sally, 12: 18: 67, dropsy, æ. 61-0-0, b. Easton.

WILLIAMSON.
7 Martin W., 1: 30: 83, erysipelas, æ. 59-7-0, b. Eng., of —— & ——, Eng., do.

WILLIE.
82 Louis, 9: 2: 82, heart dis., æ. 45-10-0, b. France, of John & Agatha, Switz., France.

WILLIS.
28 Lyman, 2: 28: 88, bronchitis, æ. 89-6-20, b. Bridgewater, of Jonah & Abigail, Bridgewater, do.

WILSON, WILLSON.
39 Alexander, 2: 18: 64, delirium tremens, æ. ——. [soldier.]
29 Frank S., 8: 19: 51, dysentery, æ. 1-0-8, b. Clinton, of Jacob & Betsy.
51 (D. at Charlestown) George, 9: 13: 56, canker rash, æ. 0-5-3, b. Ded., of Jos. & Eliza.
25 Geo., 4: 3: 77, suicide, æ. 43-0-0.
36 John F., 7: 9: 53, erysipelas, æ. 62-0-25, b. Need., of John & Abigail.
59 Lucia N. (Mann), 10: 12: 74, humor, æ. 66-10-25, b. Ded., of Herman & Sarah H., Ded., Boston.
181 (D. at Walpole) Lucy (Capen), 3: 18: 64, dis. of lungs, æ. 68-11-), b. Ded., of Nathaniel & [Submit.]
41 Maria O., 10: 15: 52, consumption, æ. 32-7-8, b. Ded., of John F. & Polly.

47 Molly (Ingalls), 10: 14: 59, old age, æ. 93-8-17, b. Abington, of Ephraim & Mary.

16 Polly S. (Osgood),1 : 18: 74, paralysis, æ. 78-6-0, b. Woodstock Vt., of —— & Molly.

67 Reuben S., 11: 20: 74, consumption, æ. 68-11-24, b. Pelham, of Wm. & ——.

18 (D. at Boston) Samuel S., 1: 25: 90, Bright's dis., æ. 70-0-0, b. Charlestown, of John & ——, Charlestown, ——.

50 Wm. H., 8: 20: 49, dysentery, æ. 3-8-0, b. Ded., of Reuben S. & Lucia.

WINCHENBACH.

72 Oscar W., 8: 26: 84, convulsions, æ. 2-4-29, b. Boston, of Daniel & Sarah L., Friendship Me., Waldoboro Me.

WINCHESTER.

29 Stephen S., 4: 27: 80, alcoholism, æ. 45-0-0, b. Boston, of Stephen & Lucinda, Boston, Me.

WINDER.

14 George, 4: 20: 68, consumption, æ. 20-0-0, b. N. S., of Spencer & Lucy.

WING.

87 Mary A., 3: 21: 55, dis. of heart, æ. 0-2-14, b. Ded., of Josiah D. & Clara D.

39 Wm. B., 5: 4: 84, pleuro pneumonia, æ. 35-9-9, b. Nantucket, of Geo. W. & Phronissa, Fayette, Lewiston Me.

WINSHIP.

74 Julia P. (Pettee), 12: 5: 48, consumption, æ. 64-0-0, b. Ded., of Abial & ——.

WINSHMAN.

12 Albert, 1: 19: 90, occlusion of bowels, æ. 0-0-4, b. Ded., of Chas. H. & Augusta W. (Stein), Germ., do.

98 Carl, 10: 10: 82, cholera infantum, æ. 0-0-12, b. Ded., of Chas. & Augusta, Germ., ——.

WINSLOW.

146 Eddie L., 9: 23: 65, dysentery, æ. 2-6-0, b. Ded., of Geo. S. & Sarah A.

14 Herbert, 1: 2: 70, loss of blood, æ. 0 0-3, b. Ded., of Martin & Martha W., Ded., Walpole.

25 Olive C. (Smith), 9: 17: 67, ——, æ. 60-2-23, b. Ded., of John & Anna, Ded., do.

113 Susie F., 12: 24: 66, teething, æ. 1-2 28, b. Ded., of Elisha F. & Olive S.

WINTERHALTER.

54 Aloysius, 4: 14: 67, old age, æ. 87-1-8, b. Germ., of John G. & Frances, Germ., do.

WIRK.

44 Louisa, 8: 28: 58, cholera infantum, æ. 0 6-0, b. Lawrence, of Wm. & Joanna.

WIRTH. (*See also Worth.*)

63 ——, 9: 3: 73, stillborn, b. Ded., of Debold & Anna, Germ., do.

WISE.

4 Florence A., 2: 26: 71, inanition, æ. 0-0-21, b. Ded., of Chas. H. & Frances (Slade), Boston, do.

WITHINGTON.

57 ——, 5: 26: 83, premature birth, b. Ded., s. of Waldo P. & Ada E. Sullivan, Ded., Richmond Vt.

41 ——, 5: 10: 85, stillborn, b. Ded., s. of Waldo P. & Ada E. (Sullivan), Ded., Richmond Vt.

117 Annie I. (White), w. of Otis W., 11: 12: 87, tuberculosis, æ. 39-1-19, b. Argyle N. Y., of John & Eliz'h. Ire., do.

72 Roy C., 7: 30: 87, cholera infantum, æ. 1-3-23, b. Ded., of Waldo P. & Ada E., Ded., Richmond Vt.

WITZKIE.

56 ——, 6: 3: 65, ——, æ. 0-0-5, b. Ded., s. of Amand & Matilda.

WODE.

57 Caroline C., 9: 17: 60, cholera infantum, æ. 0-9-3, b. Ded., of Fred'c & Caroline E., Germ., Andover.

WOKECK.

26 Geo. H., 1: 29: 64, teething, æ. 0-8-0, b. Ded., of Fred H. & Louisa.

WOLCOTT.

87 Caroline M., 9: 15: 81, consumption, æ. 55-0-0, b. Portland Me., of Timothy & Jane W., Great Barrington, Minot Me.

48 John W., 6: 4: 85, pneumonia, æ. 65-10-3, b. Portland Me., of Timothy & Jane Welcome, ——, Minot Me.

WOLKINS.

87 John F., 11: 2: 75, heart dis., æ. 70-0-0, b. Germ.

WOLLEY. (*See Walley*)

WOOD. WOODS.

31 Amos, 8: 7: 54, apoplexy, æ. 58-8-12, b. Concord, of Amos & ——.

71 Belcher S., 6: 29: 89, pleurisy, æ. 75-11-15, b. Camden Me., of Sylvester & Laura (Thorndike), Me., do.

94 Caroline (Witherell), 12: 31: 86, cancer, æ. 80-9-2, b. Norton, of —— & Lydia.

71 Caroline A. (Goodwin), 6: 7: 62, congestion of lungs, æ. 45-9-0, b. Vassalboro Me., of Geo. & Relief, Plymouth, Vassalboro.

9 Carrie G., 8: 1: 70, cholera infantum, æ. 0-3-22, b. Ded., of Geo. & ——.

10 Chas., 2: 5: 64, lung fever, æ. ——. [soldier.]

52 Francis W., 8: 25: 57, cholera infantum, æ. 0-7-23, b. Ded., of Chas. S. & Mary A.

14 Geo. A., 3: 23: 58, ——, æ. 10-4-0, b. Ded., of Belcher S. & Hannah.

63 Geo. B., 10: 15: 55, cholera infantum, æ. 2-3-3, b. Ded., of Oliver P. & Beulah.

18 Hannah (Whiting), 2: 12: 74, paralysis, æ. 58-9-0, b. Dedham, of Peletiah & Polly.

49 John J., 11: 1: 62, delirium tremens, æ. 28-9-0, b. Ireland. [soldier.]

86 (D. at Walpole) Lucy (Sumner), 5: 22: 59, old age, æ. 82-0-0, b. Ded., of Geo. & Margaret.

23 Mary A. (Johnson), w. of Wm. G., 7: 20: 52, heart comp., æ. 48-2-20, b. Scot., of James & Mary.

14 Mary A. (Coburn), w. of Chas. S., 1: 22: 88, Bright's dis., æ. 53-5-6, b. Ded., of Chas. & Hannah, Talarmo Me., Halifax.

63 Nathaniel, 8: 5: 47, old age, æ. 77-0-0, b. N. H.

108 (D. at Medfield), Rebecca (Draper), 12: 26: 70, old age, æ. 85-0-0, b. Medfield, of Jos. & ——, Ded., do.

67 Rufus C., 7: 29: 85, paralysis, æ. 67-1-29, b. Palmer, of Hollis & Abigail.
13 Susan F. (Pratt), 3: 15: 61, ——, æ. 23-2-8, b. Medway, of Philip & Naomi G.
88 Wm. G., 10: 3: 63, consumption, æ. 47-0-0, b. Jamaica W. I., of Wm. W. &
    Rachel, Eng., do.

WORKMAN.

52 John B., 5: 7: 90, consumption, æ. 32-0-0, b. Ire., of Thomas & Jane Blair,
    Ire., do.

WORTH. *(See also Wirth.)*

38 ——, 1: 24: 71, stillborn, b. Ded., d. of Diebold & Mary U., Germ., do.
30 Hannah K. (Mayhew), 5: 8: 78, cancer, æ. 79-3-13, b. Edgartown, of Wm. M.
    & Jane K., Edgartown, do.

WORTHINGTON.

106 Isaiah, 5: 18: 64, small pox, æ. ——. [soldier.]
21 Sally E. (Ellis), 6: 29: 56, consumption, æ. 65-1-20, b. Ded., of Abner &
    Martha M.

WRIGHT.

68 (D. at Roxbury) Catharine (Colburn), 6: 7: 54, consumption, æ. 52-0-0, b. Ded.,
    of Danford & ——.
82 Clara A., 9: 5: 81, mal-nutrition, æ. 0-0-17, b. Ded., of H. Estes & Clara A.,
    Belchertown, Lowell.
36 Edson L., 5: 26: 86, typhoid fever, æ. 16-4-4, b. N. S., of William & Susan,
    N. S., ——.
99 Lillia (Ewer), 12: 11: 76, dropsy, æ. 24-8-27, b. Ded., of Charles B. & Char-
    lotte B., ——, Ded.

YAEGER.

20 Chas., 2: 19: 74, croup, æ. 0-5-0, b. Ded., of Chas. & Leanor, Germ., do.

YOUNG.

10 ——, 1: 7: 84, stillborn, b. Ded., d. of Chas. R. & Mary O., Milton, Dover.
65 Alice S., 11: 13: 53, consumption, æ. 10-0-16, b. N. S., of Henry & Mary.
111 Elisha, 11: 20: 49, heart comp., æ. 72-6-20, b. Chatham.
51 Ellen R., 9: 12: 58, dysentery, æ. 2-0-2, b. Ded., of Joshua & Tamsin.
62 Elvira R., 11: 7: 53, consumption, æ. 12-3-0, b. N. S., of Henry & Mary.
83 Esther (Snow), 5: 18: 61, paralysis, æ. 68-9-25, b. Chatham, of Aaron & Abi-
    gail, Chatham, do.
15 James E., 3: 30: 54, consumption, æ. 20-11-5, b. N. S., of Henry & Mary L.
41 John, 2: 23: 63, consumption, æ. 35-0-0, b. Suffield Ct. [soldier.]
99 Joshua E., 10: 6: 49, dysentery, æ. 1-6-0, b. Ded., of Joshua & Mary E.
51 Mary E., 8: 23: 49, typhus fever, æ. 20-0-0, b. Mass.
37 Mary E., 7: 4: 53, consumption, æ. 18-3-25, b. Nova Scotia, of Henry &
    Mary.
92 Philander S., 10: 19: 84, paralysis, æ. 57-10-23, b. Chatham, of Elisha &
    Esther Snow, Chatham, do.
95 Thos., 4: 22: 64, pneumonia, æ. ——. [soldier.]

ZIERSCH.

62 Chas. A. Theo., 6: 12: 90, Bright's disease, æ. 55-11-20, b. Germ., of Ferdi-
    nand & Julia (Breslau), Germ., do.

SOLDIERS.

The following is a list of the men who are recorded as soldiers, some of whom are Dedham men, others are men who died in camp at Readville. This list includes also a few names of men known to have died while in service, though not recorded as soldiers.

Adams, Amos,	1	Green, John,	81	Park, Henry M.,	144
Alexander, John,	3	Joseph,	81	Peterson, Chas. F.,	147
Perry C.,	3	Gross, Nathaniel,	82	Pratt, Albert E.,	151
Allen, Chas. A.,	3	Guild, Oscar S.,	83	Price, Abraham,	152
James,	3				
Alston, Wm.,	4	Haley, John,	85	Reader, George J.,	154
Anderson, Robert,	4	Hase, Benj.,	89	Reim, Otto,	155
Andrews, Newell,	4	Hatton, Edw. E.,	90	Rhoades, Willard F.,	156
Atchkinson, John,	5	Hawkins, James J.,	91	Roberson, Silas,	159
		Hayden, Thornton,	91	Wm.,	159
Bartholomew, Stephen,	9	Heath, Wm.,	92	Ross, Michael,	160
Bigelow, John,	12	Herring, Edwin J.,	94		
Blake, John,	13	Hinkley, Ambrose,	96	Seaver, M. Cutler,	164
Boyd, Milton T.,	15	Homer, Elnathan L.,	98	Shubart, Nicholas,	167
Brandon, John R.,	16	Howard, Oramel,	99	Skinner, George,	168
Bryson, Henry L.,	20			Smith, Jacob,	170
		Jefferson, Austin,	103	Thomas,	171
Carroll, Chas. W.,	24	Jewett, Franklin M.,	103	Spencer, Thomas,	173
Chapman, Geo. A.,	27	Johnson, E. A.,	103	Stare, James W.,	174
Cole, Peter,	35	George,	103	Stevens, Nelson R.,	174
Cooper, Henry,	38	George R.,	103	Sturtevant, Geo. W.,	176
Cox, Edward G.,	39			Sutherland, Frank,	178
Crittenden, J. R.,	40	Kane, Paul,	105	Sutton, Frederick,	178
Crowell, Geo. W.,	41	Kenelly, James,	107		
Cruse, Thomas,	41			Thayer, Horace,	180
Cunningham, John,	42	Lathrop, Julius M.,	113	Thomas, Erasmus,	181
		Lee, Alfred,	114	Thompson, John,	181
Daley, Michael D.,	43	John,	114	Sumner,	182
Diggs, John,	49	Samuel,	114	Tytus, William R.,	183
Disbrow, Theodore,	49	Locklie, E.,	116	Tracy, Thomas,	184
Donley, John,	51				
Donovan, John,	51	McCarty, Jeremiah,	120	Washington, George,	190
Doughty, John,	51	McGowan, Wm.,	123	Welsh, Henry,	192
		Malby, Martin,	126	Weysser, Charles,	193
Eddy, Seth W.,	57	Marshall, Levi,	128	Whitmarsh, Geo. S.,	196
Everett, Henry C.,	61	Mason, Edward B.,	129	Wilson, Alexander,	198
		Mignault, D. R.,	131	Wood, Charles,	200
Finn, John,	67	Mulrooney, Wm.,	136	Woods, John J.,	200
Francis, Benj. D.,	72	Murphy, John,	137	Worthington, Isaiah,	201
Franklin, Chester,	72				
		Nevin, John,	138	Young, John,	201
Gibson, Robert,	78			Thomas,	201
Gifford, Henry A.,	78	Owens, John,	144		

PLACE INDEX.

[CITIES AND TOWNS IN THE UNITED STATES.]

INDEX OF MAIDEN NAMES.